French Politics and Society

French Politics and Society

Second edition

ALISTAIR COLE
School of European Studies, Cardiff University

PEARSON
Longman

Harlow, England • London • New York • Boston • San Francisco • Toronto • Sydney • Singapore • Hong Kong
Tokyo • Seoul • Taipei • New Delhi • Cape Town • Madrid • Mexico City • Amsterdam • Munich • Paris • Milan

Pearson Education Limited
Edinburgh Gate
Harlow
Essex CM20 2JE
England

and Associated Companies throughout the world

Visit us on the World Wide Web at:
www.pearsoned.co.uk

First published 1998 by
Prentice Hall Europe
Second edition published 2005

ISBN 0 582 47367 5

British Library Cataloguing-in-Publication Data
A catalogue record for this book is available from the British Library

Library of Congress Cataloging-in-Publication Data
Cole, Alistair, 1959–
    French politics and society / Alistair Cole. — 2nd ed.
        p. cm.
    Includes bibliographical references (p.   ) and index.
    ISBN 0-582-47367-5 (pbk. : alk. paper)
    1. France—Politics and government—1945– 2. France—Social conditions—1945–1995.
3. France—Social conditions—1995– I. Title.
JN2594.2.C63 2005
306.2′0944—dc22

                                                                    2004050653

10 9 8 7 6 5 4 3 2 1
08 07 06 05 04

Typeset in 9.5/12.5pt Stone serif by 35
Printed and bound in Malaysia

The publisher's policy is to use paper manufactured from sustainable forests.

Contents

Part 2 Institutions and power

Part 3 Political forces and representation

List of illustrations

List of tables

Preface

In the preface to the first edition, *French Politics and Society* aspired to be a student text 'with a difference'. I hope the book has fulfilled this ambition. The second edition is best described as revised and updated. It is updated because it takes account of developments up to the end of 2003, in particular the experience of the third 'cohabitation' (1997–2002), the 2002 presidential and parliamentary elections, and the first eighteen months or so of the Raffarin government. Above all, the book is revised, insofar as my own thinking on France has evolved over time. The new edition of the book also incorporates many comments from students (especially) and colleagues, who have pointed out inconsistencies or suggested improvements. The result is a book that is rather different from the first edition. Part 1 (The making of modern France) is more or less unchanged, though the historical section has been slimmed down and the chapter on political culture extended. Part 2 (Institutions and power) now looks different from that in the first edition. The three chapters on the constitution, Presidents and Prime Ministers and parliament have been re-organised into two chapters, the second of which now includes more extensive commentary on the judicialisation of French politics. Chapter 6 ('The immobile state?') builds on the older Chapter 7 (An administrative state?), but includes much fuller commentary on efforts to reform the state since the late 1980s. I am indebted to Glyn Jones of Southampton Institute for much of the information therein. Chapter 7 (Local and regional government) is recognisable as an update of the original Chapter 8 ('Local and regional governance').

Turning to Part 3 (Representative forces) I have trimmed the three chapters on political parties to two. I hope that nothing has been lost in the exercise. There is also a revised and extended chapter on pressure politics. The most significant changes have occurred in Part 4 (Reshaping modern France). The old Chapter 13 ('French society and economy') no longer exists in a recognisable form. In its place are two new chapters. The first of these (Chapter 12) is on society, citizenship and identity, much of the reflection for which took place in the course of an Economic and Social Research Council sponsored project on regional governance in France and the United Kingdom. I thank the Council for its support. I repeat my thanks for the contribution of Tim Stenhouse to the section on immigration in this chapter. The second new chapter in Part 4 (The economy and economic governance) acknowledges the centrality of processes of economic governance in understanding the nature of and challenges to the

Map 1 French regions and departments

French model of politics and policy-making. The new Chapter 13 deals with Europe and Europeanisation in a more forthright manner than in the first edition. The final chapter draws together the main threads of the book.

French Politics and Society remains primarily aimed at undergraduates studying French politics in a wide range of possible courses and degree schemes in further and higher education. It also endeavours to attract postgraduate students and professional researchers into French and European politics working in several disciplines, notably political science, European studies, history and sociology. The book is dedicated above all to those undergraduate students on French politics courses and those involved in postgraduate study whose interest ensures that the study of modern and contemporary France remains a thriving and important field.

Alistair Cole
January 2004

Acknowledgements

We are grateful to the following for permission to reproduce copyright material:

Illustration 5: President Jacques Chirac, 11 March 2004, delivers a speech at the Sorbonne University in Paris; REUTERS/POOL/Patrick Kovarik, JNA/FRANCE, PARIS, photo by POOL – STF. Illustration 6: Prime Minister Jean Raffarin, 10 February 2004, in the National Assembly when members voted to ban religious clothing and symbols from French state schools; REUTERS/Victor Tonelli, MAL/ FRANCE, PARIS, photo by STRINGER/FRANCE. 10/02/2004 [X012820020040210e02a0005l, x01282]

Chapter 8: an earlier version of this chapter was published with the title, 'Stress, strain and stability in the French party system.' In J. Evans (Ed.) (2002) *The French Party System*. Manchester: Manchester University Press, pp. 11–26. Alistair Cole is grateful to MUP and to Jocelyn Evans for allowing a modified version of this chapter to be reprinted here.

List of abbreviations

CAP	Common Agricultural Policy
CDF	Charbonnages de France
CDS	Centre des Démocrates Sociaux
CERES	Centre de Recherches et d'Études Socialistes
CES	Comité Économique et Social
CESR	Comité Économique et Social Régional
CFDT	Confédération Française Démocratique du Travail
CGPME	Confédération Générale des Petites et Moyennes Entreprises
CGT	Confédération Générale du Travail
CMP	Commission Mixte Paritaire
CNPF	Conseil National du Patronat Français
CPNT	Chasse Pêche Nature Tradition
CSA	Conseil Supérieur de l'Audiovisuel
DATAR	Délégation à l'Aménagement du Territoire et à l'Action Régionale
DDE	Direction Départmentale d'Équipement
DGD	Dotation Générale de Décentralisation
DGE	Dotation Générale d'Équipement
DIV	Délégation Interministérielle à la Ville
EC	European Community
ECSC	European Coal and Steel Community
EDF	Electricité de France
EEC	European Economic Community
EMS	European Monetary System
EMU	Economic and Monetary Union
ENA	École Nationale d'Administration
EU	European Union
EURATOM	European Atomic Energy Agency
FD	Force Démocrate
FEN	Fédération de l'Éducation Nationale
FN	Front National
FNLC	Front National pour la Libération de la Corse
FNSEA	Fédération Nationale des Syndicats des Exploitants Agricoles
FO	Force Ouvrière
FSU	Fédération Syndicale Unitaire
GATT	General Agreement on Tariffs and Trade

GDF	Gaz de France
GDP	Gross Domestic Product
LO	Lutte Ouvrière
MDC	Mouvement des Citoyens
MEDEF	Mouvement des Enterprises de France
MPF	Mouvement pour la France
MRG	Mouvement des Radicaux de Gauche
MRP	Mouvement Républicain Populaire
MSI	Movimento Sociale Italiano
NATO	North Atlantic Treaty Organisation
ONI	Office National d'Immigration
PCF	Parti Communiste Français
PR	Parti Républicain
PS	Parti Socialiste
PSU	Parti Socialiste Unifié
RI	Républicains Indépendents
RPF	Rassemblement pour la France
RPR	Rassemblement pour la République
SFIO	Section Française de l'Internationale Ouvrière
SGCI	Secrétariat Général du Comité Interministeriel
SNES	Syndicat National de l'Enseignement Secondaire
SOFRES	Société Française des Enquêtes par Sondage
SPD	Sozialedemokratische Partei Deutschlands
TGV	Train à Grande Vitesse
TPG	Trésorier-Payeur Général
UDF	Union pour la Démocratie Française
UDR	Union des Démocrates pour la République
UK	United Kingdom
UMP	Union pour une Majorité Populaire
UNR	Union pour la Nouvelle République
UPA	Union Patronal des Artisans
US	United States
USSR	Union of Soviet and Socialist Republics
WEU	West European Union

A glossary of difficult expressions

Atlanticism   This refers to the belief in and practice of the Atlantic Alliance, the military alliance of the USA and western Europe. France has always had a peculiar status within the alliance, particularly since 1965, when General de Gaulle withdrew France from the military command structure of NATO. France has once again participated in NATO meetings since 1995.

Autogestion/Parti autogestionaire   *Autogestion* can be translated literally as self-management, but loses something in the translation. It refers to a belief in decentralised management and workers' control, as voiced by students and workers in the May 1968 events. The Socialist Party officially declared itself an 'autogestionnaire' party in the 1970s, but even then the notion appeared highly ambiguous. It was forgotten once the Socialists were in government after 1981.

Dirigiste   This refers to the process whereby the French State adopted an interventionist and directive approach to the management of the economy and industry in the post-1945 period.

Dreyfus Affair   The Dreyfus Affair polarised French society during the 1890s and early 1900s. *L'Affaire* involved a Jewish lieutenant, wrongly accused by the army High Command of selling military secrets to the Germans and exiled to Devils' Island, before finally being recognised as innocent. In the course of the Dreyfus Affair, republicans launched a bitter attack against the army and the Church, accused of espousing anti-Semitism in order to sabotage the Republic. For their part, opponents of Dreyfus taxed the republicans with treachery to the nation because their attacks called into question the integrity of the Church and the army, the two pillars of French national identity.

Deputy-mayor   This refers to the practice whereby deputies (members of the National Assembly) are often mayors as well.

Enarchie   This refers to the influence exercised by graduates of the National Administration School (École Nationale d'Administration), who form a powerful elite in the spheres of politics, the civil service and the economy.

High-tech Colbertism   This phrase was coined by Elie Cohen. Colbertism refers to the tradition of central state interventionism in economic and industrial management, after Louis XIV's minister Colbert in the seventeenth century. High-tech Colbertism thus refers to state interventionism in the contemporary context.

Incivisme   Literally translated as uncivic behaviour, *incivisme* implies rather more than this in the French, carrying connotations of a tendency in French political culture to challenge those in authority, and to rebel against rules dictated from on high.

Léon Blum   Socialist leader of the Popular Front government elected in 1936, the first Socialist-led government in French history. The Popular Front was an alliance between Socialists and the Radicals, supported by the Communists who did not however participate in the government. The Popular Front government pushed through many symbolic social reforms, such as the 40-hour week, and paid holidays, but became destablised by problems of economic management, as well as by the impact of the Spanish Civil War, and the ascension of fascism in Europe.

Neo-corporatist   The term neo-corporatist can be defined as a pattern of group-state relations, where the state engages in very close cooperation with representatives of labour and capital in making economic policy. This is typified notably by: collective wage agreements negotiated between the state, employers and the trade unions; the representation of capital and labour on key policy-making committees; the existence of one single trade union and one employers' federation.

Présidentiable   This phrase refers to an individual who is (or who aspires to be) a credible candidate for the post of President of the Republic.

Poujadist   This refers to a populist right-wing movement named after Pierre Poujade, elected deputy in 1956 at the head of a movement of small-businessmen and shopkeepers. Poujadist became synonomous with reactionary resistance to cosmopolitanism, and social and economic modernisation.

Taylorian   Describes a method of organisation of the workplace based on the rigid application of routines, timekeeping and hierarchy.

A guide to further reading

In the first edition of *French Politics and Society*, we concluded each chapter with an indicative bibliography. In response to suggestions from several readers, we have decided in this second edition to organise things rather differently. A very extensive bibliography is included at the end of the book, providing full reference to the sources used in the preparation of this second edition. This brief guide is intended to indicate the four or five sources likely to be the most useful for students interested in finding out more about the topic of each chapter. I do not even attempt to be exhaustive, and the sources mentioned are not necessarily those that are most widely cited. The selection is subjective. They are sources that I have found useful, stimulating, even occasionally irritating. Most sources are in English in this English-language edition. Those students interested in pursuing French language inquiry will find many more sources cited in the French language in the bibliography.

There are a number of good textbooks in English. Knapp and Wright (2001) is very thorough and contains detailed information on institutions. Stevens (2003) and Elgie (2003) are both institutionally focused books, with reliable descriptions of the main institutions. Howarth and Varouxakis (2003) and Bell (2002) provide useful entry-level texts. Elgie and Griggs (2000) present a thorough literature review. Guoyomarch, Hall, Hayward and Machin (2001) is uneven, but contains some useful commentary. In French, Lagroye, François and Sawicki (2002) offer extensive, theoretically informed analysis.

The literature on the historical period covered by the chapters in Part 1 is vast. No attempt can do justice to the body of scholarship. What follows is a personal preference amongst the English language sources relevant to **Chapter 1** (the French literature being so vast as to defy classification). Hazareesingh (1994) is a thought-provoking study emphasising underlying continuities in modern France. Gildea (1996) presents an interesting, if slightly erratic and anecdotal account of post-war France. Jackson (2001) has recently published the best study by far of the Vichy period. Williams (1964) remains a classic, an epic work that has stood the test of time well.

In **Chapter 2**, we observed the Fifth Republic mainly through the experience of successive presidents. The Gaullist period has produced a vast literature, much of it referred to in the bibliography. Lacouture's 1965 biography of De Gaulle is a classic. A more recent introduction, which is also accessible and well-written, is Shennan (1993). Williams and Harrison (1965) remains valuable, not least for appreciating the empiricist manner in which French politics was studied in the 1960s. There are a number of good studies of de Gaulle and various aspects of Gaullism (Charlot, 1970; Dreyfus, 1982; Knapp, 1994). In contrast with de Gaulle, Pompidou appears as the largely forgotten President, with only two works of note (Muron, 1994; especially Roussel, 1984). The somewhat tarnished reputation of the Giscard d'Estaing presidency owes something to its representation in the French (Duhamel, 1980 and Duverger, 1977) and English language works consecrated to it. The main English language text is still that of Frears (1981). In French, Berstein, Rémond and Sirinelli (2003) have recently sought to rehabilitate the reputation of Giscard d'Estaing, as a modernising, centrist, pro-European president. Mitterrand's fourteen-year term produced more works than any other. Many of the most important French works are mentioned in the bibliography. My favourite is the incisive journalistic account of Favier and Roland (1990, 1991). In English there are a number of studies, either focussing on Mitterrand himself (Cole, 1994; Friend, 1998), or on the policy record of the Mitterrand presidency (Daley, 1996; McClean, 1997). In contrast, Chirac has attracted remarkably little attention, with no really serious biographical study (though Colombani is worth a read). The Jospin government is the subject of a special issue of *Modern and Contemporary France* (August 2002).

The classic works on French political culture are those mentioned in **Chapter 3**. Crozier (1963, 1970) and Hoffmann (1965) are still worth reading. In English, the two major works are Gaffney and Kolinsky (1991), my favourite, and Eatwell (1996). There are two recent additions to this list. Berstein (1999) is a very valuable book, tracing the main political and philosophical traditions that come together to form French political culture. Brechon, Laurent and Perrineau (2000) provide useful empirical evidence to test prevailing assumptions of French political culture.

Much has been written about the core executive in France, the subject of **Chapter 4**. All the leading texts have good accounts. The reader interested in understanding the nuts and bolts of the operation of the governmental machine will find much information in Knapp and Wright (2001) Stevens (2003) and Elgie (2003). Hayward and Wright (2002) is the major institutional study for those interested in exploring in more depth. In French, the classic works are those of Duverger (1986), Massot (1987, 1997) and Fournier (1987). Specifically on the presidency, Hayward (1993) remains very valuable, while Elgie (1993) contains a lot of information on the French Prime Minister. Readers interested in developing further the institutions studied in **Chapter 5** are invited to consult Stone (1992) on the Constitutional Council, Huber (1996) or Frears (1991) on the French Parliament and Knapp and Wright (2001) on the Council of State. One of the finest articles ever written on French politics was that of Vincent Wright (2000), the much missed and incomparable mentor of a generation of students. Feuillée-Kendal (1998) presents a succinct and very useful presentation of the debate on the role of the judiciary in France.

Of the various themes studied in **Chapter 6**, Stevens (2003) and Bézès are very good on the French civil service and Howarth and Varouxakis (2003) are good on French elites. The French organisational sociologists are definitely worth reading: Crozier and Friedberg (1977) and Friedberg (1974) in particular. Clark (2000) provides a very useful comparative overview of public service reform in France. Howarth (2001) has edited an excellent special issue of the journal *Public Policy and Administration*, dedicated to comparing public administration in France and the United Kingdom. The article by Smith (2001) in particular gives a nice summary of the debate in France. Le Galès and Thatcher (1995) is a good edited collection on policy networks and the reshaping of the French state. The reader interested in developing further the themes raised in **Chapter 7** will find a full account in Cole and John (2001), Loughlin and Mazey (1995) and Schmidt (1990). The classic French works are those of Crozier and Thoenig (1975), Le Galès (1993, 1995, 2002) and Mabileau (1997). Michel (1998) is worth a read, as is Gaudin (1999).

The literature on French political parties, dealt with in **Chapters 8** and **9**, is vast. A very good and up to date summary is that of Evans (2003), which covers all the main parties up to and beyond the 2002 elections. Hanley (2002) provides a more historical approach in his valuable study. Bell (2000) also provides a great deal of detail. Cole (1990) evokes fond memories: the chapters by Knapp, Gaffney, Shields and Hainsworth are especially good. Clift (2003) is good on the Socialist Party, Knapp (1996) worth a read on the Gaullists. Courtois and Lazar (1995) is the best work on the Communist Party. The best published works on the National Front are in French: Mayer and Perrineau (1989) and Mayer (1999) especially.

Pressure politics in France, the subject of **Chapter 10**, has produced a burgeoning literature. Wilson (1987) is solid, if dated, as is Keeler (1987). Culpepper (1993) presents an alternative approach. Waters (2003) provides a useful English language study on new social movements. Neveu (2002) is very good on new social movements from a more theoretical angle. Barthélemy (2000) is succinct, but good on the characteristics of voluntary associations. More theoretical works are those of Jobert and Muller (1987), Le Galès and Thatcher (1995) and Fontaine (1996). There has been a spate of recent works on lobbying and European Union: Saurugger (2003) is very useful.

Issues of Citizenship, society and identity are raised in **Chapter 11**. Mendras (1989) and Mendras and Cole (1991) present an optimistic portrayal of the evolution of French society during the post-war period, one challenged by Todd (1995). A classic statement of republican citizenship is presented by Schnapper (1994). On immigration Weil (2001) presents a summary of current developments, but Hargreaves (1995) remains the standard English language study. Keating, Loughlin and Deschouwer (2003) place French regions in a comparative perspective. The debate over identities in contemporary France is well captured in French by Wieviorka (1997).

There are many, very good books on the French economy and patterns of economic governance, the subject of **Chapter 12**. Hall (1986) is path-breaking and remains the key reference. Schmidt (1996) is good on relations between government and business. Levy (1999) is very good in this area as in others. Hayward (1986) and Wright (1997) provide key English language references. The economic dimensions of French relations with the Euro are covered by Dyson and Featherstone's classic work (1999) and by Howarth (2001). Clift

(2002) gives a good overview of the political economy of the Jospin government. The standard work in French is that of Cohen (1996).

There is also a growing literature on France's relationship with the European Union, the subject of **Chapter 13**. Drake (2004) will, I believe, become the standard English language reference. Kassim (1997), Harmsen (1999), and Cole and Drake (2000) all present good accounts. In French the classic work remains that of Lequesne (1993). Costa (2001) is good on the European Court of Justice. A special issue of the *Revue Française de Science Politique* in 2001 deals with the European Union. Cautrès and Dennis (2002) present opinion poll evidence that demonstrates the limits of Euro-scepticism in France.

The debates over French exceptionalism in **Chapter 14**, finally, are especially well summarised in Lovecy (2000).

There are a number of **academic journals** with regular articles on aspects of French politics and policy-making. Two are specifically dedicated to French politics: *Modern and Contemporary France* and *French Politics*. The main French language journal is the *Revue Française de Science Politique*. Comparative journals often have articles on France or, better still, comparative articles placing France in a broader context. Two journals are especially useful: *West European Politics* and the *Journal of European Public Policy*. Other useful journals are the *Journal of European Social Policy, Comparative European Politics, Government and Opposition, Public Administration, Journal of Common Market Studies, Comparative Political Studies* and *Comparative Politics*.

The making of modern France

1 The making of modern France

1.1 Introduction

This introductory chapter places the evolution of the French polity in its broad historical perspective up until 1958. The chapter provides an overview of French political history, with particular emphasis on the role of the state in building a French identity and upon the legacy of the French revolution and its aftermath. The problem of political legitimacy is revealed as an essential problem throughout most of French history, the result of multiple social, economic and ideological cleavages and of territorial, linguistic and religious identities. Chapter 1 also highlights various sources of historical continuity between the pre-revolutionary monarchy (known as the *ancien régime*) and the post-revolutionary order, and puts into context the impact of political divisions upon the operation of French society.

By comparison with most of her European neighbours, such as Germany, Italy or the Netherlands, France is an old country. Modern France can trace its lineage back at least to the Capetian monarchy of the tenth century; Italy and Germany were only unified as independent national states in 1861 and 1870 respectively. But her relative age must not disguise the fact that the modern French nation is in certain respects an artificial creation. There was no natural empathy between the various provinces which came to form France. In the pre-revolutionary period, many provinces of France shared no natural common cultural or linguistic ties, but coexisted in a more or less autonomous manner, with a large degree of autonomy from the central government in Paris. Small rural communities throughout France were suspicious of all outside authorities, and lived a largely self-sufficient autarkic existence. The preponderance of agriculture in the French economy suggested why features of this social model survived until the early twentieth century. Identity was rooted in locality, or town, rather than the nation. The fact that French nationhood was imposed upon unwilling provinces (such as Normandy, Brittany, Acquitaine, Burgundy, Provence) by a succession of French kings, and later by the Revolution, served to reinforce this point. A city as French as Lille only became part of the nation in the late seventeenth century; Nice in the nineteenth century.

France was overwhelmingly a rural nation. Even in the pre-revolutionary period, there were marked regional variations in the economic prosperity of the peasantry, and in the political freedoms exercised by subjects. In certain regions of France, forms of traditional local self-government had existed for centuries. In other areas subjects were deprived of any political rights and tightly controlled by a zealous aristocracy. Regional differences were themselves linked to varying kinship and economic structures in different parts of the country.

In domestic terms, pre-revolutionary French history had usually appeared to turn around the attempts made by the central government in Paris to impose its will upon existing provinces, to conquer new regions and to extend the orbit of its competence. The attempt to impose central control was a constant feature of the pre-revolutionary French monarchs, most notably of Louis XIV (1648–1715), whose chief minister Colbert endeavoured (with mixed success) to expand the competence of the state into the economic sphere, as well as to impose a measure of political uniformity upon the provincial nobles.

| 1.2 | The *ancien régime* |

Political historians dwell correctly on the importance of 1789 and the French revolution as the fundamental reference point in French history. But many of the predominant traits of the French political tradition are older than the Revolution, rooted in the *ancien régime*, as the pre-revolutionary monarchy is known. The main historical legacy of the *ancien régime* was to have created a central institution in the form of the monarchy, which was able to impose a degree of authority upon the powerful feudal aristocratic landowners, and other particularistic interests (such as the church). In a number of key spheres, the Revolution built upon the centralising pretensions of the old absolutist monarchy:

- the origins of state economic interventionism lay with the *ancien régime*, although efforts at state-sponsored commercial and industrial development met with limited success. France remained a feudal society until the Revolution.
- French monarchs named officials (*intendants*) in each of the kingdom's provinces to administer the core functions of the state: public order, the raising of finances, and the levying of troops for military adventures abroad. In practice, these officials were forced to bargain with powerful vested interests, including the nobility and the clergy. The creation of the prefect by Napoleon represented a far more systematic application of the principle of central state direction.
- French kings claimed their legitimacy from divine right: they were answerable to God alone. They were supported in this claim by the Catholic Church, which thus derived its power from its role as an ideological legitimising agency for the *ancien régime*, as well as from the vast wealth it had accumulated. This undivided form of political legitimacy was echoed later by the Revolution, with the insistence on the general interest.

The heyday of the old monarchy was in the late seventeenth and early eighteenth centuries, when, under the influence of Louis XIV, France became the dominant power in Europe. The palace of Versailles remains until this day a testament to the glory of the old French monarchy. But throughout the course of the eighteenth century, the monarchy became steadily less effective and more corrupt, its authority challenged by the rising bourgeoisie in the towns, by the state's incapacity to control the feudal nobility, and by its diminishing international prestige.

1.3 The French Revolution: the making of modern France

The statist tradition in France certainly preceded the Revolution, but the case must not be overstated. The French Revolution, with its civil wars and its crushing of the power of the aristocracy and the clergy, created the conditions for the emergence of France as a genuinely unified post-feudal nation. The French Revolution was thus the fundamental reference point in the development of the French nation-state.

- The Revolution abolished the absolutist monarchy which claimed to rule by divine right, and replaced it with a Republic committed to the values of freedom, equality and brotherhood (*liberté, égalité et fraternité*). In spite of the restoration of the monarchical or imperial forms of government in 1815, 1830 and 1852, the Republic became firmly embedded in French political consciousness as the natural revolutionary form of government. It was durably re-established after 1875, although the republican form of government continued to be contested by powerful political forces until the aftermath of the Second World War.

- The French revolutionary settlement also satisfied the mass of the peasantry. It achieved this notably by the sale of lands confiscated from the Church and nobility, which created a class of prosperous small landowners indebted to the Revolution. Loyalty was further assured by the abolition of feudal labour obligations to the aristocracy. The revolution thus transformed the peasantry into one of the mainstays of support against any return to the pre-revolutionary social order, even after the monarchy had been restored in 1815. The conservatism and loyalty of the peasantry underpinned the stability of the Republic as a form of government after 1870.

- The Revolution crushed the political and economic power of the old landed aristocracy. More than anything else, this facilitated the creation of a more uniform centralised state, begun under the Revolution, but greatly developed under Napoleon. The key foundations of modern republican France might be traced to a curious synthesis of the parliamentary regime (*régime d'assemblée*), the revolutionary tradition, and the authoritarian centralising institutions created or consolidated by Napoleon.

The revolutionary-Napoleonic legacy continues to shape many of the institutions of contemporary France. These include (or included until recently):

- administrative uniformity throughout France, notably by the division of the country into departments, cantons and communes, each with the same legal responsibilities. Administrative acts were to be judged by a system of administrative courts, separate from the judicial system;

- central control over territorial administration and local government: the prefect was created as the representative of the central government in each department; the mayor was first and foremost an official of central government;

- a high measure of state interventionism in social *mores* by means of the civil code, a detailed regulation of family and property relations, and codes of moral conduct;

- a professional bureaucracy, conceived of as an elite to serve the state, to create order and enforce uniformity. The *école polytechnique* was created in 1804 to train an elite dedicated to state service.

The emergence of a strong central state during the revolutionary and Napoleonic periods was accompanied by a gradual but ruthless suppression of all linguistic and regional identities; the progress of the idea of nation thus became largely synonymous with that of the state itself. It is in this sense that modern France might be considered to be an artificial, or a state-led creation.

| 1.4 | The French Revolution: a divisive heritage |

The legacy of the French Revolution itself was highly divisive. This divisive heritage can be illustrated in relation to three spheres: the conflict between the Church and anticlerical movements; the legacy of political violence and the revolutionary tradition, and the lack of consensus over the form of government.

The Catholic Church, anti-clericalism and the republican state

The most divisive legacy bequeathed by the French Revolution related to the bitter dispute between the Catholic Church, the anti-clerical republican movement, and the French state. The close association of the Catholic Church with the *ancien régime* made it into an obvious target for the Revolution. The Church condemned the Revolution of 1789 as godless; in turn, the Revolution led a fierce attack on the privileges enjoyed by the Catholic Church under the monarchy, notably by confiscating Church lands and redistributing them to the peasantry. Church and state reached a new compromise under Napoleon's concordat of 1801, but they remained ideological rivals. The concordat recognised Catholicism as the religion of 'the great majority of French people', although Protestantism and Judaism were also tolerated religions. When the monarchy was restored in 1815, the Church recovered much of its former political influence, but by then it was probably too late. To be Republican became synonymous with an anticlerical stance; to be a practising Catholic automatically signified opposition to the notion of restoring a godless, secular Republic.

Les Invalides: burial place of Napoleon

The Church also became associated with defence of a hierarchical, conservative, pre-Revolutionary social order.

Once the Republic had been restored in 1870, it was natural that the ideological battle between Church and state should recommence. This took two forms. Firstly, there was an attack by the republicans on the continuing existence of powerful schools run by the Catholic Church; these schools were suspected by republicans of perverting the nation's schoolchildren with the anti-republican ethos of Catholicism. Secondly, the period from 1870 onwards was characterised by an uneven, but fierce ideological battle between the Catholic Church and the Republic, culminating in the separation of church and state in 1905, and the renewed *de facto* opposition of the Church to the Republic until 1944 (Ravitch 1990).

One of the principal battlegrounds between Church and state was in the sphere of education. The state's response to perceived clerical influence was to create its own echelon of republican primary schools. In the Ferry laws of 1881–2, the republican state created a secular rival to the powerful Church schools, which aimed to reproduce republican values. The conflict between Church and state schools has remained imbued in French consciousness ever since. The ideological conflict between Church and state (fanned by the Dreyfus Affair of 1899–1905) culminated in 1905, when the Republic decreed the separation of Church and state, which had been tied since Napoleon's concordat of 1801. Catholicism was no longer recognised as the official state religion; priests were removed from the state payroll, and many Church lands were again confiscated. Henceforth, the Republic was to be a secular one.

Until the First World War, religion was more important than social class in explaining political divisions within France. A party such as the Radical Party, which was fiercely anticlerical, was automatically placed on the left of the political spectrum, in spite of its basic social and economic conservatism. And Catholics were automatically considered to be on the right, even when they declared themselves to be socially progressive. This situation only gradually changed with the rise of the Socialist and Communist parties in the 1930s and the breakthrough of the politics of class and nationalism. Catholics became fully reconciled with the Republic as a result of their participation in the wartime resistance, despite the ambiguous role performed by the Church during the Vichy regime. The formation of a progressive Christian Democratic party in 1944 – the MRP – symbolised the final rallying of the Catholics to the

Republic. While this party started out as a left-of-centre party imbued with reformist notions of social-Catholicism, it became transformed into a recognisably conservative party, under the pressure of its Catholic electorate. As the Church schools example illustrated, vestiges of the clerical-anticlerical conflict remain today, and a practising Catholic is far more likely to support a right-wing party than a declared atheist.

The revolutionary tradition

The second sphere in which the Revolution left a distinctive legacy was in the creation of an ill-defined revolutionary tradition, perhaps better expressed as a revolutionary myth, which spurned its own antibody in the form of a powerful counter-revolutionary movement. The upheavals of 1789–99 were not unique: there were further revolutionary outbreaks on a smaller scale in 1830, 1848 and 1871, as well as various abortive attempts. There developed a disposition towards the use of violence and street protest to achieve political ends: relatively small groups of conspirators might succeed in toppling a regime, as occurred in the uprising of 1830. As the levers of power were so centralised in Paris, the capital became the theatre for countless confrontations, which then extended to the provinces (the pattern has not disappeared). In the nineteenth century, French people turned against each other with great ferocity: to take one example, the Paris Commune of 1871 was crushed with 20,000 deaths. The revolutionary tradition was itself highly ambiguous. It could mean either the tradition bequeathed by the French Revolution (which included a moderate Girondin phase, as well as the more violent and Messianic Jacobin phase), or else a commitment to using revolutionary means to seize power, a more specific connotation that would exclude most moderate republicans. One powerful strand in the French revolutionary tradition that was extremist, authoritarian and potentially violent, rather than committed to compromise, became legitimised. Yet the prevailing republican strand hardly fitted this description. By the early twentieth century, republicanism became synonymous with preservation of the existing social order (Anderson, 1977). The aspirations of moderate republicans were largely satisfied with the consolidation of the Third Republic after 1875; these men became transformed into conservative apologists of the existing political, social and economic order. With the consolidation of the Third Republic, the mantle of revolutionary challenge to the status quo shifted from republicans to anarcho-syndicalists, to Marxist Socialists and (after 1920) to Communists (Ridley, 1970; Tiersky, 1974; Kriegel 1985). For several generations, the PCF successfully articulated the aspirations of alienated industrial workers, and maintained a revolutionary tradition in French politics.

The existence of a revolutionary tradition on the political left was matched on the right by the preservation of a powerful anti-democratic strand in French politics, embodied by monarchist or Bonapartist political forces throughout the nineteenth century. Such forces held the ascendancy for most of the period from 1815–70, especially from 1815–30, and from 1852–70 (Rémond, 1982). They occupied a marginal place for most of the Third Republic, but were

Table 1.1 Post-Revolutionary political regimes

Years	Period	Regime type
1789–1815	Revolutionary-Napoleonic period	Monarchy/Republic/Empire
1815–30	Restored Bourbons	Monarchy
1830–48	July Monarchy	Monarchy
1848–52	Second Republic	Republic
1852–70	Second Empire	Empire
1870–1940	Third Republic	Republic
1940–44	Vichy	Dictatorship
1944–58	Fourth Republic	Republic
1958–	Fifth Republic	Republic

recognisable as part of the conservative anti-Dreyfus coalition at the turn of the century. During the twentieth century, the counter-revolutionary current found expression in the anti-parliamentary leagues of the inter-war years and later in the visceral hostility to republicanism by the wartime Vichy regime (Paxton, 1972; Jackson, 2001). Some would contend that J-M Le Pen's *Front national* is the latest manifestation of a counter-revolutionary strain in French politics.

The form of government

The correct form of government was closely linked to the Church–state dispute and the republican/anti-republican division. Throughout the 150 years following 1789, there was a basic lack of consensus in relation to the organisation of the political system, as there was, indeed, in relation to the organisation of society as a whole. Since 1789, France has experienced three periods of monarchy, five Republics, two spells of imperial rule and the reactionary wartime Vichy state.

Most transitions from one regime to another involved violence or the threat of violence. In comparative terms, the real comparison ought not, perhaps, to be drawn between France and Britain (the model of a relatively peaceful evolutionary transition, if we except Ireland), but between Britain and the major continental European states – France, Germany, Italy – all of whom experienced periods of intense political instability and disruption before achieving the status of relatively stable democracies during the post-1945 period. Excepting the brief wartime Vichy regime, the republican form of government finally prevailed after periods of monarchical and imperial rule. There remained a basic lack of consensus in relation to the political regime throughout most of the Third and Fourth Republics, however, which damaged the legitimacy of both regimes.

1.5 The Third Republic, 1870–1940

The Third Republic – which lasted for seventy years – was France's longest lasting post-revolutionary regime. A number of prominent features came to be associated with the operation of the political system, traits that reflected the divided state of French society throughout this period. In the seventy years of the Third Republic, France was a highly fragmented society, a society in which there was no natural majority for any particular course of action. The major sources of cleavage revolved around tensions between Paris and the provinces; the enduring influence of regional and local identities; the conflict between Church and state; republicanism, and challenges to the Republic; and the politics of social class and industrialisation.

As remarked above, there was a lack of consensus in relation to the political system, which reflected the divided ideological and social make-up of French society. The most powerful source of division was that which pitted devout Catholics, who detested what they considered as the godless Republic, against anti-clerical republicans, determined to defend the republican form of government against threats from monarchists and anti-republican clergy. This divergence between republican anti-clericals and Catholic anti-republicans dominated the first thirty years of the Third Republic, until the republicans definitively established control during the Dreyfus affair at the beginning of the twentieth century. During the inter-war period, the Republic again came under powerful attack from left and right. On the left, the PCF was created in 1920 to support the Russian Revolution and foster revolution in France. The 1930s witnessed, on the right, the challenge of the ultra right-wing Leagues, which aimed to replace the democratic republic with a more authoritarian regime. The anti-democratic undercurrent in French politics triumphed under duress in July 1940, when the Third Republic voted full powers to Marshall Pétain, who negotiated an armistice with Hitler after Germany's invasion of France. It provided a brief parenthesis before a return to the established republican form of government at the Liberation.

The Third Republic appeared on the surface as a fragile, parliamentary-dominated system. The principal characteristics of the Third Republic's political system bore scant reference to the constitutional provisions theoretically governing its operation. The constitution of the Third Republic was finally adopted in 1875 as a compromise between monarchists and republicans. Under pressure from the monarchist majority elected in 1871 at the end of the Franco-Prussian war, the 1875 constitution provided for a strong President, portrayed by the monarchists (who could not agree amongst themselves on who should be king) as a monarchical type of strong leader. The putative strong presidency was stillborn as a result of the MacMahon crisis of 1876–7. President MacMahon's dissolution of the Chamber of Deputies in 1876 did not succeed in its objective of producing a subservient Assembly. Rather, a more firmly republican majority was elected in the 1877 election, one determined to uphold the rights of parliament. This precedent enshrined parliamentary omnipotence, and disqualified presidential use of the weapon of dissolution (Hanley, 2002). By 1879, the republican forces had clearly established their ascendancy at all levels of government, with the result that the constitution of 1875 was never really applied as it had been intended.

Instead of being dominated by strong leaders, the Third Republic evolved into a political system dominated by a strong parliament, which ensured that – for the most part – governments remained weak and unstable. Throughout the seventy-year history of the Republic, there were 110 different cabinets. Governmental instability was a sign that deputies were performing their duty as collective guarantors of the national interest, and as defenders of civil society against the state. The republican tradition was thus interpreted to suit the reality of France as a divided, localist, society with no natural majority for any particular course of action. On the rare occasions when the nation was divided into mutually hostile camps – 1876–7, 1902–6, 1936–7 – governments could take firm decisions and rely on *de facto* parliamentary coalitions, but such occasions were short-lived. In the absence of cohesive political parties, deputies defended the interests of their constituents upon whom their political survival depended.

The manner in which parliament itself was organised during the Third Republic reinforced the tendency for the legislature to act as a block on effective governmental action. The lower house, the Chamber of Deputies, was composed of around 500 deputies, who, for most of the period, each represented a single-member constituency. The upper house, the Senate, was comprised of 300 senators, indirectly elected by electoral colleges within the departments, composed predominantly of local councillors. It was created to act as a conservative check on the Chamber. The Senate was overwhelmingly biased towards small-town and rural France, at the expense of the more dynamic, urban areas. With its right to veto bills passed by the lower house, the Senate could be counted upon to frustrate any efforts to enact social reforms, levy income tax or generally to disturb the interests of small-town and rural France (Anderson, 1977; Tombs, 1996). One such example occurred in 1912 when the Radicals finally pushed income tax through the Chamber, only to be vetoed by the Senate.

During the Third and Fourth Republics, a number of features combined to create apparently omnipotent parliaments and to make governments unstable. The first of these was a belief, ultimately derived from the French Revolution, in the supremacy of the elected Assembly as against the executive. A second feature was a fear of strong leaders, predicated upon the tendency of 'great men' to subvert the institutions of the Republic. During the Third and Fourth Republics, the fear of strong leaders usually meant that mediocre politicians were selected as premiers, by zealous parliamentarians determined to retain their own prerogatives. In periods of crisis, the Republican state had turned to 'great men', such as Georges Clemenceau during the First World War. But it rid itself of their services once normal circumstances had returned. The institutional consequence of this was to strengthen the negative capacity of parliament to unmake governments. Third, the fragmented nature of political representation, and the weakness of French political parties also contributed to the illusion of parliamentary omnipotence.

For most of the Third Republic, political parties were weak and poorly organised. The existence of universal male suffrage throughout the Third Republic meant that elections were fiercely and usually fairly contested. Yet the weakness of party structures reduced the election process to a myriad of local contests. As in the United States Congress, what passed for parties were clusters of individual deputies representing conflicting local interests, who refused to be bound to tight parliamentary discipline. The fundamental relationship was that maintained between a deputy and his local constituents, rather than with the party. This was especially true of the parties of the centre and right, although the parties of the left were far more disciplined. Party labels were often virtually meaningless: in line with the verbal leftism of French political culture, conservative candidates often attached to themselves revolutionary-sounding titles, which they discarded as soon as they had been elected. Furthermore, the pattern of electoral alliances varied greatly in different parts of the country; and there was no guarantee of electoral alliances being respected at a national level. The Radical Party during the early twentieth century symbolised this ambiguity. In the pro-clerical west of France, where the Church was strong, the Radicals were primarily an anti-clerical party, and attracted support from Socialist voters against conservatives. In the south-west, by contrast, where the Socialists predominated, Radical candidates were supported by conservative opinion as the only safeguard against the election of Socialist candidates. As Radical deputies owed their election to different electoral clienteles, they could not long be bound by party discipline at a national level. And the Radicals possessed more cohesion than most other parliamentary groupings of the centre and right.

The lack of a natural majority, the weakness of parties, the geographical diversity of France, and the weight of localism meant that it was virtually unprecedented – outside periods of war and national crisis – for governments to be able to rely upon the disciplined support of a majority of parliamentarians. Instead, deputies and senators jealously preserved what they deemed to be their rights, and ensured that the executive was kept in a position of weak subservience. The norm was that general elections would virtually never produce clear-cut majorities upon which governments could be formed. Governments tended to be formed as temporary coalitions to solve one or two outstanding problems, but they usually fell apart once these problems were solved.

There were several reasons explaining the decline of the Third Republic in the inter-war period. Firstly, certain social groups felt excluded altogether from the political system: this was notably the case for the new urban working class which developed with the industrialisation of the late nineteenth and early twentieth centuries. The Third Republic steadfastly avoided addressing the concerns of industrial workers, as it avoided those of urban society in general. Second, the challenges faced by and the demands placed upon the political system altered markedly after the First World War. During the period prior to 1914, the functions of government were relatively limited. In these circumstances, the shortcomings of the political system were tolerable, since national politics simply did not enter into most people's lives. French society – overwhelmingly rural – was largely self-sufficient and inward looking. But the political system became progressively less tolerable in the inter-war period, when international crises such as the depression, or the rise of fascism demanded governments which could take far-sighted decisions.

The rise of extreme internal and external challenges to the regime during the 1920s and 1930s further weakened the Republic, leaving it vulnerable to Hitler's aggressive designs. The polarisation occasioned by the victory of the left-wing Popular Front coalition in the 1936 election fuelled a mood of defeatism and revenge on the political right, symbolised by the slogan 'rather Hitler than Blum'. The breakdown of internal cohesion coincided with a period of aggressive expansionism on behalf of European fascism. The Third Republic finally collapsed in 1940, when the parliament elected to support the Popular Front in 1936 voted full powers to Marshall Pétain, who suspended the constitution, and signed an armistice with Nazi Germany.

The Third Republic has been much maligned, and yet it is not difficult to construct a defence of its political system. The system survived longer than any other since the Revolution, eventually succumbing to an external invasion. The impact of governmental crises in Paris were minimal on French society. Up until 1914 at least, loyalty to locality outweighed any loyalty to the nation. The effects of political instability were often exaggerated. The powerful Napoleonic administration provided much continuity of policy, notwithstanding biannual changes of government. Moreover, individual ministers occupied their posts for long periods in spite of governmental instability: to take one example, between 1906–32, Aristide Briand was Prime Minister on eleven occasions, and Foreign Minister in seventeen different governments.

Ultimately, the static political regime of the Third Republic reflected the static nature of French society. France remained a largely rural inward-looking society, at least until the 1920s, within which social and geographical mobility was rare. Only when there was a clear dysfunctioning in the 1930s between an immobile political system, a world-wide economic crisis and a chaotic international situation did the regime appear ill adapted to assume its responsibilities.

1.6 Vichy and the French Resistance, 1940–4

The Vichy regime lasted from 1940–4. The formal division of the French territory into two zones in 1940 – an occupied sector in the north, a free zone in the south – created the illusion of independence for the Vichy government. The German occupation of the previously free Vichy zone in November 1942 ended the illusion of independence.

The Vichy regime was, in reality, a personal dictatorship under Marshall Pétain, which ruled thanks to the tolerance of the Nazis. The initial belief that Pétain had safeguarded French national sovereignty, and secured the best possible deal for France conferred an aura of early legitimacy on the Marshall. The shortcomings of the Third Republic were blamed by many for the occupation of France; the clamour for more authoritarian government was a logical consequence of this. The ideological tenor of the Vichy regime was counter-revolutionary: in the discourse of Pétain's National Revolution, 'work, family and nation' replaced 'freedom, equality and brotherhood' as the leitmotifs of the regime. France reverted to being an authoritarian political regime which idealised a hierarchical, corporatist society of the type the Marshall believed to have existed before the French Revolution. The experience of the Vichy regime has been a subject of controversy in France ever since 1940, demonstrated by the continuing debate over the nature and extent of wartime collaboration, by the spate of trials of war criminals such as Klaus Barbie and Paul Touvier and by the controversy over former President Mitterrand's role as a minor civil servant of the Vichy regime (Péan, 1994). The place of anti-Semitism within the Vichy regime in particular has been the subject of fierce disputes (Jackson, 2001). Though it is convenient to excuse the anti-Semitic acts of the regime by the anxiety to please the Nazis, the French police were responsible for rounding up Jews and handing them over to the Germans (notably with the *Rafle d'Hel Viv* in November 1942). Moreover, there were strong justifications for anti-Semitism within the ideology of the National Revolution itself (especially the emphasis placed on *intégriste* Catholicism).

Resistance to the Vichy regime and to German occupation took two forms: internal and external. The external Resistance crystallised itself under the leadership of Charles de Gaulle, a young General in the French army who fled France upon the signing of the Armistice. In June 1940, de Gaulle called upon Frenchmen everywhere to join his Free French Resistance army, based in London. De Gaulle came unquestioningly to lead the French Resistance. Initially contested, his status as the key resistance chief was eventually recognised by the allies, and ultimately by the main internal resistance movements. The internal resistance consisted of various groups, divided to some extent along ideological lines, but united in its opposition to Vichy and to Nazi occupation. The main forces active in the internal resistance were Communists, Socialists, and Christians.

There were many tensions between the two branches of the Resistance. The internal resistance movement was dominated by the Communists, who were portrayed by de Gaulle as fighting an ideology (Nazism) rather than a country (Germany), leaving the external resistance fighters as the only true patriots. To some extent, the internal, Communist-dominated resistance dreamt of a new France; the Gaullist-led external resistance sought above all to restore the old France, with a satisfactorily reformed political system. While the internal resistance reasoned in terms of daily survival and was inclined to unrealistic dreams to stimulate the immediate resistance effort, the external resistance was more open to cultivating diplomatic contacts with the allies, to compromise and to concessions.

The evidence suggested that few Frenchmen were involved in acts of resistance, and that the imperatives of physical survival ensured a largely sub-jugated population until the liberation in 1944. The unification of the resistance forces under De Gaulle's control after the liberation of Paris most probably helped avoid any possibility of civil war (the Communists laid down their arms, in spite of their controlling large areas of France) and created a powerful coalition of forces anxious to rebuild and unify France. In August 1944, de Gaulle became the premier of a provisional government composed of the main resistance forces: the Communists, the Socialists, the Christian Democrats, and De Gaulle himself. A new progressive dawn beckoned.

1.7   The Fourth Republic, 1944–58

The liberation of France in August 1944 swept away the Vichy regime, and inaugurated a new period of French history in a spirit of near-universal optimism. From highly auspicious beginnings, however, the Fourth Republic was rapidly faced by a crisis of legitimacy in its mission. The period 1944–6 revealed a lack of constitutional consensus, which seriously weakened the political legitimacy of the new Fourth Republic. There was agreement amongst politicians that the form of government should be Republican. No one – not even the most pious Catholics – seriously contested this, as the anti-democratic, anti-republican forces had been discredited by the Vichy regime. In addition, the pre-war parties of the centre and right were widely distrusted either for collaborating with Vichy or failing to resist it (which, in immediate post-war eyes, amounted to the same thing). The strength of the left was revealed in the first three elections of the post-war period (October 1945, June 1946, November 1946), which witnessed major gains for the two left-wing parties – SFIO and PCF – and a breakthrough of the new Christian Democratic party, the MRP (Gildea, 1996).

In a first constitutional referendum in October 1945, the overwhelmingly majority of the French population invested the provisional government with responsibility for drawing up a new constitution, rather than reverting to the 1875 charter. Although it was clear that people did not want a return to the Third Republic, it was much less obvious what type of regime was to replace it. There were, essentially, three different points of view within the provisional government:

- De Gaulle believed in a rationalised democratic system, similar to the eventual Fifth Republic: grosso modo, he advocated a strong President who would stand above the petty quarrels of party politicians and incarnate the unity of the French nation. The parties of the left (SFIO, PCF and MRP) suspected de Gaulle of preparing a system that might lead to dictatorship. Unable to agree with his partners, and vigorously opposed to any return to a parliamentary-dominated regime, de Gaulle resigned as premier in January 1946. The loss of the prestige of the resistance hero was a severe blow to the young Republic.

- The two main parties of the left – the SFIO and the PCF – also called for strong disciplined governments, but they argued that these would have to base their authority on a single, powerful parliamentary Assembly. The left expressed its preference for the Jacobin tradition of a single directing Assembly, accepting few checks and balances to moderate the expression of the general will.

- The Christian Democratic MRP rejected de Gaulle's advocacy of strong personal leadership, but it was wary concerning the left as well. The MRP opted for a parliamentary system with checks and balances to prevent arbitrary executive rule.

Once de Gaulle had resigned, the PCF and SFIO (but not the MRP) proposed their version of the constitution for ratification in a referendum held in April 1946. In their draft constitution, the PCF and SFIO proposed to abolish the second chamber – the Senate – and to create a monocameral parliamentary system. The left was opposed to the continued existence of the Senate, which, representing the interests of rural and small-town France, had consistently frustrated social reform during the Third Republic. The left's proposed constitution was rejected in the April 1946 constitutional referendum. Quite apart from the predictable opposition of de Gaulle, this projected constitution was also fiercely contested by all other significant parties, including the MRP. A majority of French people feared that a single Chamber parliamentary system would be equivalent to handing unrestrained power to the left-wing parties.

The constitution of the Fourth Republic was narrowly adopted in a third constitutional referendum in October 1946, with 9,500,000 votes for, 8,500,000 against, and 9,000,000 abstentions (Williams, 1964). The constitution-makers hoped that the 1946 constitution would encourage the development of strong cabinets, based on the support of a few large parties, and would thereby end the chronic division which had characterised the previous French Republic. It aimed to emulate the British system of strong governments drawing their support from disciplined majorities in the lower Chamber. But in fact the Fourth Republican constitution established a parliamentary regime not fundamentally dissimilar from that of the Third. The idea that stable progressive governments would replace the transient coalitions of the Third Republic actually had little solid constitutional foundation: it depended for its reality upon the continuing political cooperation of the main resistance parties. This was called into question in 1947.

The principal features of the political regime created by the 1946 constitution were those of a parliamentary democracy. The supremacy of parliament was reaffirmed in the October 1946 constitution in a more overt manner than in the constitution of 1875: in so doing it reasserted traditions of the absolute sovereignty of parliament which dated back to the French Revolution. The powers of the Senate, renamed the Council of the Republic, were limited. It lost the power of veto over bills passed by the lower Chamber, and its rights were limited to those of delay and consultation, somewhat like the British House of Lords. The President of the Republic remained largely a symbolic figurehead, as in the Third Republic. The subordination of the President was to be ensured by an indirect method of election by the two houses of parliament. The rights of the executive were strengthened in certain respects, notably through the complicated provisions allowing the Prime Minister to call for a dissolution of the Chamber of Deputies, which Edgar Faure used to good effect in 1955 (the first time a dissolution had occurred since 1876).

The Fourth Republic has traditionally been judged a failure in most respects. It lasted a mere twelve years, before it collapsed in the face of a military insurrection in Algeria.

The immediate legacy of the French Resistance had been to strengthen the parties of the left (Socialists and Communists) and to reconcile the Catholic community to republican values. The three great parties of the Resistance (the PCF, the SFIO and the MRP) had believed that if they remained united, France would have a stable political system based on a progressive left-wing majority. This presupposition was unfounded: in May 1947, the tripartite governing coalition collapsed when the Socialist minister of the Interior, Jules Moch, expelled the Communists from government. The PCF's departure was dictated by a combination of internal and external pressures. The role of the US government, which made it clear that the removal of Communists from government was an essential precondition for France receiving massive financial aid under the Marshall plan, was primordial. In addition, the Cold War began in earnest in 1947, as Stalin began to consolidate his grip on Eastern Europe and as revelations of the nature of Stalinism began to filter through to the western democracies. The PCF reacted to its exclusion by declaring its fidelity to Moscow and reinforcing its control over a marginalised working class counterculture. From 1947, almost until the collapse of the Fourth Republic in 1958, the Communist party declared its total hostility to the regime.

The Fourth Republic also suffered after 1947 from the development of powerful new enemies on the right. The divisions of the left, the onset of the Cold War in 1947 and the electorate's disillusionment with the left-wing parties allowed the French right to recover a measure of influence. In 1947, the right found a new champion in General de Gaulle, who founded the Rassemblement du peuple Français (RPF) as a movement dedicated to replacing the Fourth Republic with a more presidential-style regime. From 1947 to 1951, the RPF rivalled the Communist party as France's best-organised and most popular party. From 1947 onwards, powerful enemies to its left (PCF) and its right (RPF) opposed the Fourth Republic. This forced the so-called centre parties (Socialists, Radicals, Christian Democrats, and moderate Conservatives) into a series of defensive 'third force' alliances from 1947–51, whose only rationale was to safeguard the Republic.

After the breakdown of tripartism, political instability returned after 1947, of a type that recalled that of the old Third Republic. Despite the fact that the centre parties combined to defend the Republic against its enemies, no party could resist manoeuvring to increase its influence in government. This led to the return of a pattern of governmental instability: from 1947–58, governments lasted an average of some six months, just as they had done in the Third Republic. In the eyes of the French electorate, the Fourth Republic, which had never benefited from a broad consensus in its favour, became discredited by the selfish games played by its politicians. An example of the perceived cynicism of politicians came in 1951, when, faced with the prospect of a negative, antiregime majority (PCF, RPF), the centre parties changed the electoral system in a way which deliberately discriminated against their rivals. As in the Third Republic, parliamentary supremacy came to be directly equated with weak executive government. Parliamentarians displayed a preference for rather uncharismatic, consensual personalities as premier, since strong leaders might attempt to limit the rights of parliament. When clearly exceptional leaders did emerge, with widescale support in the country – the best example being the Radical Pierre Mendès-France in 1954–5 – a majority of deputies crystallised in order to bring them down.

The political system appeared out of step with what was happening in the country as a whole, which, by the early 1950s, was experiencing an unprecedented industrial takeoff and social modernisation. One of the most telling critiques of the Fourth Republic was that, although France was modernising itself in a remarkable manner during the post-war period, this occurred in spite of the lethargy of the central politicians. This accusation appears somewhat unjust, but it contributed towards the discredit of the regime.

The result of this governmental instability was that central government gradually lost the authority necessary to take tough decisions in a period of rapid international change. For the post-war period was one of heightened international crisis, signalled by the movement towards the break-up of the French Empire with the outbreak of the Indo-Chinese rebellion in 1946, and the onset of the Cold War in 1947. France was gradually forced to accept that it could no longer sustain a far-flung empire, and that its interests lay in cooperating with others in Europe, and the Atlantic Alliance. Due to the weakness of its political system, foreign policy crises had a devastating impact upon the domestic political situation within the Fourth Republic. There was a direct and obvious relationship between permanent government instability within France, and the perception of weakness in the eyes of foreign governments. Furthermore, the inability of the state to control the activities of its agents in the armed forces and the colonial administrations proved a tangible sign of its weakness which, in a vicious circle, led to a further diminution of confidence in the capacity of the state to fulfil its functions.

The problem of decolonisation prevailed above all others. The retention of its extensive empire had been one concession obtained by Marshall Pétain in the armistice agreement with Hitler. France's post-war colonial headache began almost immediately after the end of the war, the most important conflicts being in Indo-China, Tunisia, Morocco and Algeria. The first of these was in Indo-China, where, from 1946–54, a bitter war was fought between the French army and the Vietnamese nationalists, with the French finally admitting defeat in 1954. The pride of the French army was severely wounded. The decision taken by the Mendès-France government to withdraw from Tunisia and Morocco in 1954 and 1955 added insult to injury, regarded by many army officers as another humiliation by the despised Republic.

The French army insisted that France must not cede in Algeria, regarded as a normal part of France even by most left-wing opinion. It had been a French colony since 1830, and was peopled by some 1,000,000 native French settlers, who were determined to resist demands for independence from predominantly Muslim Algerians. A nexus of political, cultural, economic and religious influences combined to make Algeria by far the most important of the colonial disputes faced by the Fourth Republic. Civil war and nationalist revolt raged in Algeria from November 1954 onwards. Successive attempts by French governments to promote greater autonomy without ceding to independence proved fruitless. Attempts to introduce even moderate reform (such as that of Gaston Defferre) were fiercely resisted by the colonial settlers in Algeria, secretly abetted by the armed forces. The civilian government in Paris became progressively less able to control the activities of the military, of the colonial administration, or of the native French settlers, with the effect that by early 1958 the authority of the Paris government had almost completely vanished. The army and the colonial administration in Algeria openly defied orders made by government departments in Paris: the problem of decolonisation was thus intricately linked with that of the lack of political authority of the government in Paris. The *coûp de grâce* for the Fourth Republic came in May 1958, when the French army sided with rioting French settlers in Algiers (the capital of Algeria) who organised themselves into a Committee of Public Safety and declared their autonomy from the Fourth Republic. The military authorities made it clear that their price for guaranteeing not to invade mainland France was a return of the wartime hero General de Gaulle to power. To all intents and purposes, the Fourth Republic was dead.

The achievements of the Fourth Republic were for long overlooked. They need to be reappraised and set against the regime's generally negative image. During the first fifteen years of the post-war period, France moved away from being a stalemate society, and entered a period of rapid socio-economic and demographic change, more rapid, indeed, than that experienced in any other west European nation (Fourastié, 1980). The French state succeeded in managing change in spite of (or perhaps because of) the Republic's weak political institutions. Political weakness left the administration free to fill the vacuum left by the feuding party elites. The introduction of elaborate planning mechanisms (the five-year plans), and the creation of the General Commissariat for Planning both testified to a powerful impetus in favour of economic and social modernisation on behalf of the state (Hall, 1986).

There was a rapid economic upturn: economic growth soon reached an average 6 per cent per annum after 1950, helped by the effects of Marshall aid, and, it has been argued, by active state interventionism in economic management in the form of a series of five-year plans. The seeds for the French economic miracle were sown in the Fourth Republic. Economic development had a radical impact on the nature of French society. There was a vast movement of population away from the land into the new urban areas. For the first time, France became a predominantly urban country, with a modern economy. The country also experienced a demographic explosion, in the form of a post-war baby boom. In 1939, France's population was barely forty million; by the end of the 1950s, it had reached fifty million. On balance this economic and social modernisation made the old cleavages based on religion and class less acute. The accelerated pace of secularisation in the post-war period, and the formation of the Christian Democratic MRP also lessened the traditional importance of the clerical-anti-clerical cleavage.

The Fourth Republic could point to its own political achievements. The most notable of these lay in the sphere of European policy. The main initiatives culminating in the Treaty of Rome in 1957 were of French or Franco-German inspiration: the European Coal and Steel Community of 1951, the abortive European Army of 1954, the Treaty of Rome of 1957 (Dedman, 1996). The complexity of French European policy was revealed by the proposed European Defence Community (the 'European Army'), first proposed by premier René Pleven in 1951, as a means of providing a European safeguard over German rearmament. Although a French initiative, the European Defence Community treaty was finally defeated by the French National Assembly in 1954. A bitter legacy of anti-Germanism continued to manifest itself across the political spectrum; this resurfaced to sink the EDC treaty in 1954 (Rideau, 1975).

Despite this powerful anti-German sentiment, the principal driving force of post-war closer European integration was that of Franco-German reconciliation, symbolised by far-sighted French and German statesmen, such as Robert

Schuman, Jean Monnet and Konrad Adenauer (Cole, 2001a). The European Community was created in 1957 on the basis of a new Franco-German partnership, symbolising not only reconciliation between the two nations, but also cold-headed assessments of national interest on either side. From a French perspective, the EEC itself was envisaged as a corset to prevent Germany from dominating the continent. The choice of European cooperation, at the same time realistic and idealistic, was made by visionary statesmen during the Fourth Republic, a choice called into question in the 1960s during de Gaulle's Fifth Republic.

As far as the effectiveness of the political system per se was concerned, however, the conclusion must be a globally negative one. Parliamentary domination led to a return to the pattern of unstable governments, just as in the Third Republic. The most pressing issues of the 1950s – with the exception of Europe – found no real response from French governments because there was a power vacuum. Where progress was made in post-war France, it came about largely as a result of the professionalism of its bureaucracy rather than of its politicians. The weakness of the political system damaged France's international reputation during this period. For these various reasons, the restoration of effective government was a key priority for the constitution-makers of 1958.

1.8   Concluding remarks

A number of salient themes emerge from this brief overview of French history until 1958. The first relates to the crucial role performed by the state in building modern French identity and in imposing cohesion upon a divided society. This process began during the *ancien régime*, advanced during the French Revolution and Napoleonic periods, and consolidated itself in stages thereafter. The state justified its universal mission in terms of the general will, as French kings had previously evoked divine right in support of their rule. Throughout the nineteenth century, an ambitious state coexisted alongside a largely self-sufficient society. The French nation remained extremely diverse prior to the Second World War. French remained a minority language in many French regions until the twentieth century.

The problem of political legitimacy was a consequence of the divisive legacy of the French Revolution. Disagreement over fundamental features of the political system pitted republicans against monarchists, Catholics against anti-clericals, and later nationalists against internationalists. As a result of multiple social, economic and ideological divisions the problem of political legitimacy was a genuine problem throughout most of the period preceding the Fifth Republic (1958). The impact of such divisions should not be exaggerated. Throughout the nineteenth century, political conflicts were often limited to competition between rival Paris-based elites, with French society remaining relatively unaffected. This testified to a more pervasive division between Paris and the provinces, a recurrent feature of French political history inherent in the nature of the state-building process itself. Despite the persistence of a revolutionary political discourse, the capacity of the political system to deliver peace and prosperity only appeared seriously threatened during the 1930s, and again after 1947.

2 France since 1958

2.1 Introduction

Chapter 2 considers the evolution of France's political system during the Fifth Republic (1958–2003), paying particular attention to the terms in office of the five Presidents since 1958. The events surrounding the creation of the Fifth Republic had their origins in the Algerian crisis, which had sapped the energy of the Fourth Republic since November 1954. On 13 May 1958, rebellious military officers, backed by rioting European settlers, finally overthrew the legal government in Algiers. The conspirators threatened to extend the rebellion to mainland France, unless General de Gaulle was called upon to lead the nation's affairs. To reinforce their point, French paratroopers invaded Corsica on 28 May 1958 and plans were advanced for a military movement on Paris itself. Under threat of military invasion and possible civil war, the National Assembly invested Charles de Gaulle as the last premier of the Fourth Republic on 1 June 1958. De Gaulle immediately suspended the constitution of the Fourth Republic, and was granted authority to draw up a new constitution, which was overwhelmingly ratified by constitutional referendum in September 1958. General Charles de Gaulle became the Fifth Republic's first President in January 1959.

The allegation of an illegal seizure of power, made by Mendès-France, Mitterrand and others, deserves brief attention; de Gaulle's investiture took place against the backdrop of a possible military *coup d'état*. Yet powerful forces within the old Fourth Republic aided de Gaulle's accession. De Gaulle was invited to form a government by the incumbent President, Réné Coty, underlining that even men who swore by respect for the Republican tradition were anxious to avoid the prospect of civil unrest and political collapse. This move was supported by public opinion.

2.2 De Gaulle's Republic

The related problems of Algeria and the consolidation of de Gaulle's authority dominated French politics from 1958 to 1962. With dubious constitutional legality, de Gaulle called referendums on four occasions between 1958 and

1962 to appeal directly to the French electorate, above the heads of the parties and other intermediary institutions. The transitional political circumstances of the period 1958–62 enabled de Gaulle to rule in a manner which opponents denounced as personal rule (*pouvoir personnel*). By governing in such a largely personal manner, de Gaulle created the bases for the emergence of the presidency as the most powerful institution in the new regime.

Propelled to power to maintain Algeria in French hands, General de Gaulle came to accept the case for Algerian independence. Why did this occur? We can identify domestic and foreign policy explanations. In terms of foreign policy, de Gaulle soon became conscious that France's new anti-imperialist discourse (see below) rested uneasily alongside the continuing French colonial presence in Algeria. The prospect of Algerian independence fulfilled domestic political functions as well. De Gaulle was determined to reduce the weight of entrenched interests preventing the state from representing national unity. No interest was more powerful than the army, which had brought the Fourth Republic to its knees. The Algerian conflict was finally resolved in April 1962, when the French electorate ratified the Evian agreements granting Algerian independence.

The various actors involved in the crisis of May–June 1958 each assumed that de Gaulle could be moulded to their own designs. Most deputies were convinced they could control de Gaulle once the immediate crisis over Algeria had passed. The French army and the settlers both believed that de Gaulle would never cede independence to Algeria. Subsequent events revealed that each was misguided. By granting Algerian independence, and by repressing attempts to reassert the army's power, de Gaulle crushed the political power of the military in French politics. With the resolution of the Algerian crisis, many politicians saw no reason to retain de Gaulle's services. Recognising the threat, de Gaulle provoked a conflict with the old parties by organising a referendum to introduce the direct election of the French President. By obtaining popular support for the direct election of the President in October 1962, de Gaulle inflicted a severe political defeat on the parliamentarians nostalgic for the Fourth Republic. The October 1962 referendum was followed by the Fifth Republic's second parliamentary elections, held in November 1962, provoked by President de Gaulle's dissolution of the National Assembly elected in 1958. Gaullist control was further strengthened when an overall pro-Gaullist (UNR and RI) majority was elected to support him. The events of October–November 1962 thus reinforced the model of the strong presidency which commentators for long considered a defining feature of the Fifth Republic.

The October 1962 constitutional referendum on the direct election of the Presidency was of great importance for the future development of the regime. The directly elected President could now boast a popular legitimacy at least equal to that of the National Assembly. Direct election would give the President the necessary popular legitimacy to be able to ensure that other institutions fell into line with presidential wishes. Invigorated by a direct bond with the French people, the presidency was to act as the key element of legitimacy underpinning the Fifth Republic's political system. This presidential reading of the Fifth Republic held sway largely unchallenged until 1986. The emergence of a strong

Beauborg, or the Pompidou Centre: symbol of the cultural and architectural ambition of French Presidents and of the significance of Paris as a capital worthy of avant garde modern art

presidential leadership provided a focus around which other features of the emerging political system became organised. Paradoxically, however, by subjecting the President to direct election, de Gaulle succeeded in politicising the presidency, subjecting the office to political competition, rather than protecting the institution from partisan rivalries.

The period spanning from June 1958–November 1962 was of fundamental importance in understanding the future evolution of the regime. In key areas of policy, the standard was set not only for the remaining years of de Gaulle's presidency, but for those of his successors as well. By any comparative measurement, de Gaulle must rank as the most important President of the French Fifth Republic, as well as one of Europe's leading statesmen during the post-war period. Amongst the many aspects of de Gaulle's legacy, we should mention: the creation of a strong presidency, the realignment of the French party system, the resolution of the Algerian conflict, the adoption of a more independent foreign policy, the consolidation of the Franco-German alliance at the heart of the European Community and the fostering of a new spirit of national self-confidence and economic prosperity.

At the heart of Gaullism lay a certain idea of France, with clear implications for how the political system should be organised (Lacouture, 1965; Shennan, 1993). De Gaulle's patriotic, even nationalistic beliefs required a form of Republican government sufficiently strong enough to enable France to regain international respect after the divisions of the Fourth Republic. In de Gaulle's terminology, this was a pre-condition for France 'being herself'. Ever since his Bayeux speech of 1946, de Gaulle had consistently advocated a strong presidency, able to represent the interests of the whole French nation, above what he portrayed as the particularistic interests represented by political parties. The first aspect of Gaullism was thus a reformed political system based on a strengthened executive, embodied by a strong President. The presidency lay at the central core of the political system; all other features depended upon presidential impulsion, initiative or approval.

A second key feature of Gaullism lay in the sphere of foreign policy. At the heart of de Gaulle's foreign policy lay a belief in greater national independence and a determination that France should be recognised as a great power. The decision to produce an independent French nuclear deterrent; the attempt to reassert French national sovereignty within a 'Europe of the Nation-States' and the efforts to adopt a more independent, pro-Third World policy with respect to France's former colonies in Africa and elsewhere all testified to de Gaulle's obsession with protecting the 'rank of France' as a great power. Under Gaullism, French foreign and security policy was much more distant from the Atlantic Alliance and the United States. In 1966, de Gaulle announced that France was withdrawing from the integrated military command structure of NATO, the military alliance between the US and the main West European countries (Menon, 2000). National independence was also evoked to justify de Gaulle's announcement in 1961 that France would build its own independent nuclear deterrent, rather than buy missiles from the Americans. These spectacular initiatives managed to fascinate and irritate France's allies at the same time, as did a number of rather eccentric French foreign policy initiatives in Eastern Europe, Africa, China and South America.

The counterpart to greater independence from the US was an attempt to strengthen France's role within Europe. This took two forms. Firstly, de Gaulle attempted to strengthen the Paris/Bonn axis as the driving force of the EEC. In 1963, a Franco-German cooperation treaty was a clear step in this direction. The other aspect of European policy was to promote France's interests at the expense of those of the United Kingdom, regarded as an American Trojan horse within Europe (Gordon, 1995). De Gaulle's vision of a dominant France within Europe depended upon frustrating the UK's desire to join the EC. De Gaulle vetoed British entry to the Community on two occasions, in 1963 and 1967.

The third aspect of Gaullism was the arrival of a period of economic prosperity, after the lean years of the late 1940s and 1950s. To attribute the economic take-off to de Gaulle is unfair to the Fourth Republic, which put into place the mechanisms for economic revival, but the figures were flattering for the French economy. French growth rates outpaced those of every EC country during the eleven years of de Gaulle's rule. Economic growth averaged 5.8 per cent in France during the period 1958–69, against 4.8 per cent in Germany, 4 per cent in the United States and 2.7 per cent in the United Kingdom.

2.3 May '68: the Fifth Republic in crisis

The Gaullist period is incomplete without an analysis of May '68, which almost overthrew not only de Gaulle but the Fifth Republic itself (Hanley and Kerr, 1989). The Gaullist regime claimed three great domestic achievements to its credit: political stability, social consensus and economic growth. In each of these areas, however, there existed reasons for dissatisfaction. The counterpart to political stability was the domination exercised by the Gaullist party at all levels of the state. The accusation that de Gaulle had presided over the creation of the Gaullist State (*l'État-UNR*) rang increasingly true with important sections of public opinion, as well as with non-Gaullist politicians. The 1958 Constitution might have produced a form of political stability, but the opinion was widespread that this stability equated with stagnation, or, worse, authoritarian government. Since 1965, de Gaulle had lost the aura of supra-partisan grandeur with which he had surrounded his rule, to become rather like any other political leader. Direct election of the presidency aggravated de Gaulle's problems: he had been re-elected in 1965, but only after being forced to a second ballot which had heralded the revival of the left-wing opposition (see Appendices 2 and 3). In 1967, the pro-Gaullist coalition (UNR and Giscard d'Estaing's RI) scraped a one-seat overall majority over the combined forces of the left and the opposition centrists. The political edifice constructed by de Gaulle appeared far from being invincible almost one decade after his accession to power.

The Gaullist claim prior to May '68 to have created social consensus was called into question by the May events. Economic growth had been real enough, but its fruits had been unequally distributed amongst different social classes. Above all, however, the events of May '68 reflected the spirit of the age, the outburst of one generation (the baby boomers) against the social and political values embodied by the ruling elites. The radical protest movement of May '68 was not confined to France; similar movements occurred across western Europe. France of the 1960s was a more open society than its predecessors, more receptive to influences from abroad. Nowhere in Europe did these protest movements overthrow existing political institutions. In France, the events of May '68 seriously damaged de Gaulle's authority and were followed by his retirement one year later; but 1969 also witnessed the peaceful transition of power to President Pompidou and the strengthening of the Fifth Republic.

What became known as May '68 was in reality a series of movements reflecting rather different concerns, but sharing in common a sense of frustration with the existing order and an ill-defined expectation of change. The May '68 events were initially a generational phenomenon; only later did they acquire obvious class overtones. When analysing the events of May '68, it is essential to distinguish between two separate movements: the student uprising; and the outbreak of mass strikes amongst French workers. The student events began on 3 May 1968, when police forcibly ejected protesting students from the Sorbonne. From 3 May onwards, confrontations between students and police became regular incidents; the student protest did not die down until mid-June 1968. Of greater importance, student activism acted as the catalyst for the outbreak of a series of spontaneous strikes amongst workers: by mid-May, over 10,000,000 French workers were on strike, with the country at a standstill. The motives behind these strikes were confused. Workers asked for a salary increase, but they also demanded more power within the firm, and expressed a sense of dissatisfaction at the authoritarian, Taylorian organisation of the workplace. The May movement reached its height in the confusing events of 24–30 May 1968, when there appeared to be a vacuum of power amidst rumours of de Gaulle's flight from the country. Thereafter the radical protest movement died down, and the conservative reaction set in. The turning point occurred on 30 May 1968, when de Gaulle returned from Germany, announced the dissolution of the National Assembly and called fresh general elections. A vast pro-Gaullist demonstration on the Champs-Elysée symbolically celebrated the turning of the tide. In the ensuing National Assembly election of June 1968, a landslide Gaullist victory was registered, symbolising the reaction of the provinces against Parisian radicals and a humbling of the left-wing opposition parties. The evidence from the counter-revolution of June 1968 suggested that more French people were appalled at the disorder manifested in May '68 than were supportive of the new demands formulated by the students and certain groups of workers.

The May '68 movement became a reference point, almost an ideology, for various new social groups created, or expanded by post-war social change. Representatives of these new social groups called into question traditional moral values, replacing them with calls for liberty, autonomy, the right to difference and anti-authoritarianism. The May '68-inspired movements served mainly to place new issues on the political agenda. Many of the demands formulated by activists in the 1960s found themselves in party programmes during the 1970s. Pacifist, ecologist, regionalist, feminist, extreme-left and other 'alternative' groups assumed considerable importance during the 1970s. The election of the socialist Mitterrand as President symbolised the hopes of these various radical movements. The crisis experienced by governmental socialism during the 1980s was in part also the crisis of May '68 inspired ideals. Since the mid-1980s, even successful social movements, such as the Greens, have been anxious to distinguish themselves from the legacy of May '68.

The short-term outcome of May–June '68 was a victory for the Party of Order over the Party of Movement. On a political level, de Gaulle survived for only one more year, and never fully recovered the public esteem he had enjoyed prior to May '68. The real Gaullist victor of the events of May–June '68 was premier Georges Pompidou, who, in contrast with de Gaulle, retained his calm throughout the crisis and organised the Gaullist electoral victory. His barely veiled intention of succeeding de Gaulle as President hastened his dismissal as premier in June 1968. Pompidou's performance meant that he was henceforth a credible successor waiting in the wings. For the first time, it appeared as if a vote against de Gaulle would not bring down the Fifth Republic.

The 1969 presidential election was caused by De Gaulle's resignation in April 1969, provoked by the electorate's rejection of a referendum on the dual, complicated and unrelated issues of the reform of the Senate and the creation of regional authorities. In the referendum of April 1969, a small majority of those voting refrained from supporting de Gaulle, thereby immediately precipitating the General's resignation. The events of May '68, and the subsequent evolution of the Fifth Republic revealed that even a leader as prestigious as General de Gaulle could not retain the confidence of the French people indefinitely.

2.4   Georges Pompidou: the acceptable face of Gaullism?

After de Gaulle's resignation, the Gaullist UDR immediately rallied behind Pompidou, whose election as President in 1969 helped to legitimise the transition to the post-de Gaulle phase of the Fifth Republic. The apparent ease of the succession was important for the regime, but misleading politically. Pompidou's political authority was contested not only by the left-wing opposition, but also from within his presidential majority. The problems encountered by Pompidou with his own parliamentary majority pointed to the frailty of the Gaullist coalition in the absence of de Gaulle. They also suggested that a President's political authority is only really established when a parliamentary majority has been elected to support his action as President.

Whatever his personal qualities, Pompidou did not possess de Gaulle's historic stature. From 1969–74, President Pompidou's principal political problem rested with his parliamentary majority. The fractious nature of the Gaullist party post-de Gaulle forced Pompidou to exercise a far closer supervision over the operation of the majority than had ever been necessary for de Gaulle (Charlot, 1970). This strengthened the belief that historic Gaullism had died with de Gaulle. Pompidou's majority was beset with contradictions. Historic Gaullists suspected Pompidou on account of his political past (the fact that he was not involved in the Gaullist resistance). Conservative Gaullists were suspicious of Pompidou's choice of the reforming Chaban-Delmas as Prime Minister in 1969. In addition to an independent-minded premier, and pressures from within the Gaullist party, President Pompidou had to contend with the political pretensions of Valéry Giscard d'Estaing, the leader of the Independent Republicans, the most important non-Gaullist formation within the presidential majority. Giscard d'Estaing was bitterly opposed by leading Gaullists, who rightly suspected him of wanting to strengthen his party at their expense.

The style which Georges Pompidou brought to the presidency was markedly different from that of de Gaulle. Whereas General de Gaulle was personally austere and withdrawn, Georges Pompidou brought a more relaxed attitude to the Elysée palace. While de Gaulle had been shaped by his Catholicism, his experience in the armed forces and the French Resistance, Pompidou, with his past experience in banking and industry, was far more open to French business interests. In his presidential practice, Pompidou was more openly interventionist than de Gaulle. This manifested itself in several manners: a closer supervision over the ruling (but fractious) Gaullist party; a more open intervention in election campaigns and candidate selection; a closer supervision over key aspects of domestic policy (notably industrial and urban policy), as well as continuing suzerainty over foreign policy. Presidential supremacy was recalled under Pompidou on several occasions, the most spectacular being his sacking of premier Chaban-Delmas in 1972 only days after the latter had received an overwhelming vote of confidence from the National Assembly. Pompidou's more interventionist style concealed a weaker political source of legitimacy. The 1973 National Assembly elections gave the first hints of the UDR's declining popularity with public opinion, a tendency that became fully apparent

Mitterrand window shopping

during the 1974 presidential election. Finally, death prevented Pompidou from exercising the full seven-year term of his presidential term-in-office.

The relationship between Pompidou and his first premier Chaban-Delmas testified to the complexity of the President–Prime Ministerial relationship in the Fifth Republic. Whereas Pompidou was unashamedly a British-style conservative, Chaban-Delmas was a progressive Gaullist. As premier, Chaban-Delmas baptised his government programme under the slogan of the New Society. The reformist tone of Chaban-Delmas' premiership rested uneasily alongside Pompidou's conservatism. Ultimately, Pompidou's will prevailed, but for a long time Chaban-Delmas acted as a role model of a strong premier backed by influential advisors (such as Jacques Delors) who held sway over key aspects of domestic policy. The contradictions inherent in Chaban-Delmas's premiership encouraged Pompidou to rid himself of his first Prime Minister in 1972, and replace him with the lacklustre, orthodox and conservative Pierre Messmer.

In key spheres of policy, the record of the Pompidou presidency was shaped by the legacy of de Gaulle's eleven-year rule, although there were departures from the Gaullist heritage as well. The main elements of continuity with Gaullism lay in the sphere of foreign policy and interventionist economic management. Under Pompidou, France continued to enjoy rates of economic growth superior to those of most of its European partners (Flockton and Kofman, 1989). The major policy evolution with respect to de Gaulle lay in the field of European policy. President Pompidou was far less enthusiastic than his predecessor about the Franco-German axis, although he was constrained to recognise its importance. Franco-German relations were soured somewhat by the difficult personal relations existing between Pompidou and the German Chancellor Helmut Schmidt. By contrast, Pompidou maintained a good personal relationship with British Prime Minister Edward Heath: one of the key decisions of his presidency was to remove de Gaulle's veto on British entry to the EC. A more sympathetic attitude towards Britian was combined with a more conciliatory tone towards the US. Pompidou made it clear, however, that there could be no question of France rejoining the integrated military command structure of NATO, demonstrating the weight of the Gaullist legacy on subsequent Presidents.

The left-wing opposition was transformed during Pompidou's presidency. The 1969 presidential election had represented the nadir of the French left: the official Socialist candidate polled barely more than 5 per cent, trailing well behind the Communist Duclos (21 per cent). In July 1969 the old SFIO finally transformed itself into the new Socialist party (PS) which began to revive in the 1970 local and 1971 municipal elections. In June 1971 at the congress of Epinay, François Mitterrand, the former united left presidential candidate in 1965, captured control of the new party with the help of allies from the old SFIO. Mitterrand finally defeated Mollet, the former SFIO leader, who had remained consistently hostile to the Fifth Republic. Under Mitterrand's leadership, the new Socialist Party (PS) committed itself to forming an alliance with the PCF. To achieve this alliance, Mitterrand agreed to the PCF's demand for a common programme of government, a detailed policy manifesto signed by the two parties. This committed the left to radical structural reforms, involving extensive nationalisations, decentralisation, and increased workers' rights. Mitterrand was convinced that in order to become electable the PS had to attract communist voters (as a credible new radical party) as well as centre voters (as the only alternative to Gaullism). In June 1972 the PS, PCF and MRG signed the common programme of government. With the common programme, the left alliance seemed the only credible alternative to the governing coalition. The left alliance made significant gains at the 1973 National Assembly elections, although insufficient to challenge the presidential majority.

On balance, historic Gaullism died with de Gaulle. The pitious performance of Chaban-Delmas in the 1974 presidential election provided the death knell of resistance Gaullism; Chirac's RPR was a different type of organisation altogether. The 1974 presidential election confirmed the declining fortunes of historic Gaullism: the UDR candidate Chaban-Delmas obtained 15.5 per cent, as against 32 per cent for his conservative rival Giscard d'Estaing and a strong showing for the united left candidate Mitterrand (42 per cent). Pompidou's greatest symbolic achievement as President was to have facilitated the peaceful transition to the post-Gaullist period, while preserving the Fifth Republic. The second President also ensured continuity with de Gaulle's legacy in most policy areas, while modifying their contentious aspects in a manner generally beneficial to France.

2.5 Valéry Giscard d'Estaing: the aristocracy in power, 1974–81

The narrow election of Valéry Giscard d'Estaing as the third President of the Fifth Republic (with 50.8 per cent, as against 49.2 per cent for Mitterrand) marked a watershed in the evolution of the regime. For the first time, control over the key institution escaped the powerful Gaullist party. Deprived of its control over patronage, and its monopoly of the most powerful office, the UDR collapsed, undermined by the manoeuvres of Jacques Chirac, who led a group of forty-three rebellious UDR deputies in support of Giscard d'Estaing from the first ballot of the presidential election.

Giscard d'Estaing's initial choice of Prime Minister was heavily influenced by the conditions of the presidential election. The new President named Chirac as Prime Minister as recompense for his assistance during the presidential election. President Giscard d'Estaing calculated that appointing Chirac would ensure him of the UDR's support, while at the same time allowing him to dismantle the 'UDR-state'. But Chirac remained a Gaullist, refused to be treated as Giscard d'Estaing's stooge and resigned from office in August 1976. He then took control of the UDR, rebaptised it *Rassemblement pour la République* (RPR) in December 1976 and concentrated on restoring the party's fortunes at the President's expense. Raymond Barre, a university professor with no formal party affiliation, who governed France until the 1981 presidential election, replaced Chirac as Prime Minister in August 1976. The internecine rivalries of the French right throughout Giscard d'Estaing's presidency were of fundamental importance in understanding why the Socialist Mitterrand eventually secured election in May 1981. We now identify several key features of Giscard d'Estaing's presidency, referring to themes that will be pursued in more detail in subsequent chapters.

The public face presented by Giscard d'Estaing was that of a liberal reformer, determined to modernise the French economy and society. This optimistic portrayal was outlined in detail in his 1976 work *La Démocratie française*. The President declared himself in favour of an 'advanced liberal society', a synthesis between a dynamic and open capitalist economy, and a society rejecting all forms of social exclusion, and relying on the participation of all social groups. Capitalism was portrayed as the ideal system for promoting consensus between social classes: it was important to reform capitalism, not to replace it, as argued by the united left alliance. For supporters, Giscard d'Estaing's formulation provided a decent, humane and reformist vision. For critics, however, these platitudes bore little relationship to the reality of spiralling unemployment, inflation and economic crisis. Whichever interpretation we make, Giscard d'Estaing lacked the means for his political ambitions. From the outset, the political foundations of the Third President's rule were fragile (Duverger, 1977). Elected by the narrowest of majorities, Giscard d'Estaing's firm supporters comprised a small minority of the pro-presidential coalition. Throughout his presidency, and especially after 1976, President Giscard d'Estaing was unable to rely upon a disciplined parliamentary coalition to back his governments. Essential measures had to be pushed through by relying on the use of restrictive articles of the 1958 Constitution designed to favour the executive over parliament.

During his 1974 presidential campaign, Giscard d'Estaing promised change with continuity, and without risk. In the course of the first two years of his presidency, the third President introduced several reforms tending to liberalise French society, and to modify the operation of its political system (Berstein, Rémond and Sirinelli, 2003; Frears, 1981). After 1976, this mild reformist spirit was replaced by a cautious social and economic conservatism. The predominance of conservative Gaullists within the presidential majority limited the social reforms that could be enacted in the months following his election. The key reforms of 1974–5 (abortion, divorce, reform of the constitutional council) depended upon the votes of left-wing deputies for their enactment. The hostility of the President's conservative supporters dampened his reformist ambitions from 1975 onwards. Several announced reform projects were never introduced: for instance on decentralisation, the reform of the judicial system, or a modification of state controls over the media. The onset of severe economic crisis after the oil crisis of 1973 greatly reduced the margins of manoeuvre available to French governments, as to those elsewhere. The need to manage the economy as effectively as possible became by far the most important issue governments had to face. After a failed economic relaunch under Chirac, premier Barre introduced a series of tough anti-inflation plans. On a comparative European level, the economic policies pursued by Barre's governments were similar to those being carried out by governments of comparable nations across Europe, whether controlled by conservatives, social democrats or socialists. Barre's deflationary economic policy was much maligned within France, however, especially by the Socialist-Communist opposition, but also to some extent by the Gaullist RPR.

The period 1974–6 represented an interventionist phase of the French presidency. President Giscard d'Estaing established a new precedent by addressing 'directive letters' to his Prime Ministers, outlining their duties for the following six months. The principle of presidential initiative was pushed further under Giscard d'Estaing than either of his predecessors; no sphere of policy was excluded from the possibility of presidential inolvement. Examples often cited included the President's decree that the tempo of the National Anthem should be speeded up in official meetings; the decision to intervene to halt the construction of a new motorway on the Paris left bank; the decision to replace the Prefect of Paris with a directly elected Mayor (Frears, 1981). This latter policy badly backfired when Chirac, by now a bitter rival, defeated the President's own candidate for the prestigious post of the Mayor of Paris in 1977. Whereas Pompidou had taken a keen interest in industrial policy, Giscard d'Estaing preoccupied himself with aspects of social and financial policy that previous Presidents had been content to leave to the Prime Minister and the competent ministers (Knapp and Wright, 2001). The appearance of hyper-presidential activism under Giscard d'Estaing disguised the fact that the political foundations of the third President's power were weaker than those of either of his predecessors. The more spectacular presidential interventions occurred during the early phase of his presidency, notably while he could still rely upon the support of the Gaullist premier Chirac.

From 1976 onwards, Giscard d'Estaing turned his attention to more traditional presidential interests: foreign policy, European affairs and defence. In foreign policy matters, Giscard d'Estaing appeared as the least Gaullist President of the Fifth Republic. The third President called into question de Gaulle's commitment to the nuclear doctrine of 'the weak's defence against the strong', and moved closer to NATO's rival doctrine of 'flexible response'. In other areas, President Giscard d'Estaing displayed a greater continuity of policy with his predecessors. One such area lay in the sphere of European policy and Franco-German relations. Distancing himself from Britain, President Giscard d'Estaing established a close relationship with Chancellor Schmidt of West Germany. The fruits of this renewed period of Franco-German collaboration were visible. The creation of the European Council in 1974 provided a regular forum for the heads of EC states to meet and take politically contentious decisions. The establishment of the European monetary system in 1979 provided a mechanism for closer European economic and monetary cooperation that made possible later moves to economic and monetary union.

President Giscard d'Estaing occasionally imparted an image of regal omnipotence, but his behaviour while in office led the third President to overestimate the strength of his position, especially after the left had failed to win the 1978 National Assembly election. His dealings with African heads of state were criticised for involving excessive peddling of influence. His acceptance of a gift of diamonds from Colonel Bokassa, the self-styled Emperor of the Central African Republic, was particularly ill-advised, as Bokassa had been implicated with serious abuses of human rights. As the 1981 presidential election approached, Giscard d'Estaing was so convinced of forthcoming electoral victory that he scarcely bothered campaigning for re-election. This attitude contributed to his unexpected defeat against Mitterrand in May 1981. The historical importance of the third presidency lay in its symbolic function of assuring the transition to the post-Gaullist phase of the Fifth Republic, at a period when a majority of the French were not prepared to envisage a full-blown left-wing alternative.

2.6   François Mitterrand 1981–8: the chameleon

François Mitterrand's election as President in May 1981 was the catalyst for a series of important changes in the political operation of the Fifth Republic. The political institutions of the Fifth Republic experienced a double evolution during the 1980s under Mitterrand's aegis: the first alternation in power between right and left in 1981; the first 'cohabitation' between left and right in 1986. The transfer of power from right to left in 1981 legitimised the Fifth Republic in two important senses. It proved that the regime could withstand the democratic alternation in power; it represented the final rallying of the left to the presidential institutions created by de Gaulle. The advent of 'cohabitation' in 1986 was equally significant, since the regime did not collapse under the pressure of competing political forces controlling the presidency and the National Assembly. For the first time, the 1958 Constitution was actually applied as it was written: the President presided, but the government governed.

The powerful presidency created by de Gaulle between 1958–69, and consolidated by his successors, was initially further strengthened by Mitterrand's election in 1981. By dissolving the conservative-dominated National Assembly immediately after his election, and securing the election of an absolute Socialist majority, Mitterrand was able to secure a more complete control over the main institutions of political power than had been enjoyed by his two immediate predecessors. During the period from 1981–6, Mitterrand mastered not only the presidency, but also the National Assembly, as well as the leadership of the presidential party. No President since de Gaulle had been able to claim as much. The early years of Mitterrand's presidency were characterised by a high degree of presidential interventionism. As personally representative of *le changement*, Mitterrand symbolised the arrival of a new political order, and was involved in many of the principal policy decisions of the early period in office. It was President Mitterrand himself, for example, who insisted that the government maintain its electoral commitments with respect to the nationalisation

President Jacques Chirac, 11 March 2004, delivers a speech at the Sorbonne University in Paris

programme of 1982, rather than moderate its provisions. Presidential interventionism was particularly marked during the early reformist years of the Mauroy premiership 1981–4, but gradually Mitterrand intervened less frequently in matters of domestic politics. His most critical arbitration occurred in March 1983, when the French President opted that France should remain within the European monetary system, at the expense of abandoning the Socialist government's Keynesian attempt to reflate the French economy.

Mitterrand was elected as President in 1981 committed to a break with capitalism. He was re-elected in 1988 advocating the merits of consensus, national unity and the modernisation of capitalism. The first two years of Mitterrand's presidency stand out as a period of reformist effort unprecedented in scope at least since the post-war tripartite government of 1946–7. The reforms undertaken by Pierre Mauroy's government combined classical redistributive left-wing policies in the sphere of social, economic and industrial policy; with quality of life reforms in other areas (notably decentralisation, enhanced workers rights, various liberal civil rights measures). The main reforms enacted included the nationalisation of leading industrial groups and banks, the decentralisation measures, and the accomplishment of wide-ranging welfare reforms (partly financed by redistributive taxation measures). Certain reforms were transient; the effects of others have only slowly become apparent.

Mitterrand came to office as a champion of the people of the left. In the French context this meant alliance with the Communist Party, Keynesian reflationist economic policies, nationalisation, and support for traditional industrial sectors. By 1984, there had been a change of direction. Economic reflation was rejected in 1983 for the strong franc policy. Traditional industries in areas such as coal and shipbuilding were forced to close or to make major lay-offs. There had been the first timid moves towards privatisation. These policy reversals indicated that governments do not act in isolation, especially in the economic sphere: the combined pressures of the international economy, spiralling trade and budget deficits, a sharp increase in inflation and diplomatic pressures from EC partners all pressurised the French Socialists to change course. Mitterrand's salvation lay in the fact that the fourth President was sufficiently adaptable as a political leader to make a virtue out of necessity.

From 1984 onwards, Mitterrand's attentions were increasingly focused on issues of foreign policy, defence, and, above all, Europe. In appraising Mitterrand's foreign policy, Stanley Hoffmann concluded that it was 'Gaullism by any other name'. In key areas of foreign policy, Mitterrand was more faithful to the model of national independence promoted by General de Gaulle than his immediate predecessor had been: his acceptance of the strategic doctrines underpinning the French independent nuclear deterrent was case in point. The importance placed by Mitterrand on bilateral Franco-German relations also recalled that of de Gaulle some twenty years earlier. The parallel with de Gaulle should not be overplayed, however. The Euromissile crisis of 1982–3 revealed Mitterrand as a stauncher supporter of the Atlantic cause than past French Presidents and current allies, far less prone to idealism in relation to the Soviet bloc countries. In European policy, in symbolic and substantive terms, Mitterrand's Europe was far more integrationist than that espoused by de Gaulle (Friend, 1998). From 1984 onwards, Mitterrand concentrated upon portraying himself as a great European statesman, with a coherent vision of Europe's future. Mitterrand was more genuinely convinced of the merits of a unified Europe than any of his predecessors, and proved more willing to sacrifice elements of national sovereignty in the interests of European integration than any of his precursors had been.

As the Mitterrand presidency progressed, the fourth President withdrew from the intricacies of domestic policy. This process preceded the 1986–8 'cohabitation', but expressed itself most fully during this episode. By calling upon Chirac, the leader of the victorious RPR-UDF coalition to form a government in March 1986, President Mitterrand respected the democratic logic that the victors of the most recent general election should be confided with the responsibility of governing the nation. Any other outcome would have been undemocratic. In the event, presidential supremacy disappeared once a determined Prime Minister armed with a parliamentary majority faced the President.

During the 1986–8 'cohabitation', Chirac's RPR-UDF coalition engaged in a radical programme of economic liberalism, combined with a strong dose of social and political conservatism, with obvious overtones of Margaret Thatcher in Britain or Ronald Reagan in the United States. Despite the popularity of certain measures (such as privatisation), in its haste to reform French society Chirac's government misread the state of French opinion, and created the impression of a government governing in the interests of one social class, symbolised by the decision to abolish the wealth tax introduced by Mitterrand in 1982. Chirac's mixture of economic liberalism and political conservatism failed in its central declared objective of reducing unemployment. Assisted by the political mistakes of Chirac's government and his own clever political positioning, President Mitterrand's popularity began to recover sharply.

During the 1986–8 'cohabitation', Mitterrand discovered a new role: that of 'arbiter-president'. The government was to be encouraged to govern, but as the arbiter of the nation, according to article 5 of the 1958 Constitution, Mitterrand reserved for himself the right to criticise government policies by speaking in the name of the 'French people'. This new stance worked: Mitterrand was easily re-elected against a divided right-wing challenge in the 1988 presidential election.

2.7	Mitterrand's second term, 1988–95

How Mitterrand won in 1988 was obvious: he attracted the support of a vital fraction of the centre-right electorate alienated by Chirac and unprepossessed by the other conservative challenger Barre. Why Mitterrand stood was more difficult to discern. His 1988 presidential platform contained no firm proposals in the sphere of domestic policy, limiting itself to justifications of past presidential actions. Mitterrand was more ambitious in respect of Europe, which the incumbent President made a leitmotif of his second presidential mandate. Mitterrand's European mission, which reached fruition with the negotiation of the Maastricht Treaty in December 1991, consisted of a steadfast vision of closer European integration, for which the French President deserved much credit or blame, depending upon one's viewpoint. At the same time, the political and diplomatic weight of the French President was challenged after the historic event of German unification in 1990, which appeared to alter the balance of European power in favour of Germany.

The pattern of presidential interventionism during Mitterrand's first mandate was curiously reversed during his second term. Whereas he had been highly active after his election as President in 1981, he was content, or at least constrained to allow his fourth premier, Michel Rocard, a relatively free hand in domestic policy-making from 1988–91. Rocard's enforced resignation in May 1991 temporarily recalled Mitterrand's pre-eminence as President, but it was a move from which he never fully recovered, not least because his move was misunderstood by public opinion. Under the premiership of Rocard's successor, Edith Cresson, President Mitterrand was forced to intervene more than he would ideally have liked, both in order to support publicly his beleaguered Prime Minister, and to ensure that her policy choices were not adopted. The succession of Prime Ministers during Mitterrand's second term increased public disquiet with the lack of a sense of purpose displayed by the Socialist governments. The economic policy of the strong franc, pursued vigorously by Socialist and centre-right administrations since 1983, appeared to deprive governments of much leeway in conducting policy elsewhere, especially if this involved raising public expenditure. The inability of either centre-right or Socialist governments to master unemployment in particular had a devastating effect upon their electoral fortunes. This was revealed in the 1993 National Assembly election, at which the ruling Socialists were reduced to under 20 per cent and sixty-seven seats. Combined with their perceived inability to master the economy, the Socialists suffered from a series of damaging corruption scandals, which did much to demolish their prior claim to moral superiority over the right. The tragic suicide in May 1993 of Pierre Bérégovoy, Mitterrand's sixth Prime Minister, appeared to many to symbolise the moral bankruptcy of the Socialists.

The final chapter in Mitterrand's long presidency began with the coming to office of the Balladur government in March 1993. During the 1993–5 period, Mitterrand's bargaining power appeared far weaker than at any other time, including during the first 'cohabitation' of 1986–8. This weakness stemmed in part because he was an obvious non-contender for a third presidential term; in part because the Socialists' electoral humiliation of March 1993 removed any real illusions of grandeur. In domestic policy, Mitterrand had little visible input during the second period of 'cohabitation'; his role was reduced to that of moral gatekeeper, whom no one really trusted. Mitterrand attempted to reinvent the role of the arbiter-president that had served him so well during the first 'cohabitation', but with much less effect. Presidential influence continued to manifest itself in relation to foreign policy, most notably with regard to Mitterrand's refusal to agree to renewed nuclear testing in the South Pacific, and in his continuing attachment to certain symbols of Gaullist nuclear policy that even RPR military advisers considered outdated.

Mitterrand shaped the Fifth Republic more than any other President apart from de Gaulle. France was a country rather less different from its European neighbours in 1995 than in 1981. His main achievements were in those spheres where his action had been least expected: he promoted European integration beyond the limits consented by former French Presidents; he contributed under pressure towards the modernisation of French industry and financial capitalism, he de-ideologised the left and partially reconciled it to the market economy. These real achievements bore only a tenuous relationship with his '110 propositions' of 1981, testament to the limited margins of manoeuvre for national political leaderships in an increasingly interdependent and global age.

The second episode of 'cohabitation' (March 1993–April 1995) was played out against a background of fratricidal rivalry within the Gaullo-conservative camp, in the form of presidential competition between premier Edouard Balladur, and Chirac, leader of the RPR. The division of the French right into two or three families is not new: in 1981 and 1988, right-wing divisions facilitated Mitterrand's victory. The original feature of the 1995 presidential campaign stemmed from the fact that both Chirac and Balladur came from the ranks of the neo-Gaullist RPR movement. This created an enormous dilemma for RPR deputies, especially until February 1995, when Balladur appeared the most likely victor. The fact that most RPR deputies supported Chirac even when his cause appeared forlorn is testament to the attraction he exercised over the RPR, a movement he had built up since 1976 (Knapp, 1996).

Balladur's nomination as Prime Minister in March 1993 formed part of an unwritten agreement between the two men: for Balladur the premiership, for Chirac the presidency. This understanding was rapidly undermined by the 'Balladur effect': consistently high opinion poll ratings led Balladur to envisage the presidential mantle for himself. In the event, the results of the first ballot left Balladur trailing in third place, behind the Socialist Jospin and the Gaullist Chirac. The election of Jacques Chirac as the fifth President of the Fifth

Republic (by 52.7 per cent, against 47.3 per cent for Jospin) witnessed the recovery of the Elysée after a period of twenty-one years in the wilderness for Gaullism. A new chapter in the history of the Fifth Republic had begun.

2.8   President Chirac, 1995–7: the abrupt presidency

Though Jacques Chirac's presidency has already lasted for over eight years (at the time of writing), to refer to the abrupt presidency is apposite (Colombani, 1999; Collovald, 1999). Elected comfortably in 1995, Chirac lost effective power two years later, after his dissolution of the National Assembly elected in 1993 backfired. President Chirac's difficulty partly lay in the manner of his election in 1995. Chirac's clever presidential campaign mixed and matched themes usually associated with the political left (such as employment and wages), with the desire for an end to '14 years of socialism'. Influenced by the theses of French sociologist Emmanuel Todd, Chirac diagnosed a 'social fracture' within French society, based on the exclusion of minorities, bad housing, low salaries, and – crucially – unemployment. The remedies to this situation, inherited from the harsh economic policies of the Socialists, involved stimulating economic growth and proposing measures to fight unemployment. Given the tenor of the campaign, it was always likely to be in the sphere of domestic policy that the new administration would be judged. Promising the reduction of unemployment, the healing of the 'social fracture' and an economic relaunch during the campaign, once elected President, Chirac attempted to navigate a delicate path between campaign promises and economic and international realities. There was, in some respects at least, a measure of incongruity between the substance of Chirac's campaign discourse, and his nomination of Alain Juppé as Prime Minister. A highly respected former Foreign Affairs minister (1993–5) Juppé was named as Prime Minister partly in order to reassure financial markets and foreign capitals, wary of Chirac's campaign promises. A firm supporter of European integration, Juppé reaffirmed straightaway France's intention of meeting the Maastricht convergence for a single European currency by 1999. Though his campaign had sounded a Euro-sceptical note, President Chirac himself made a strong commitment in October 1995 to preparing France to participate in the single European currency, and announced a package of economic austerity measures to accompany this choice. The perception held by many (especially his younger and working-class supporters) was that Chirac had abandoned his progressive message at the first obstacle.

This move was followed shortly afterwards by the publication of the Juppé plan to reform the health and social security systems. The Juppé plan, addressing intractable issues of health care and social security in a period of demographic change, was made public without any prior negotiation with the 'social partners'. By the end of 1995 the Juppé government was fighting for its survival. With hundreds of thousands of protesters taking to the streets to contest the Juppé plan, France reverted to one of its periodic crises. Though Juppé survived the strikes of November–December 1995, his government had to water down

Prime Minister Jean Raffarin, 10 February 2004, in the National Assembly when members voted to ban religious clothing and symbols from French state schools

proposed (necessary) reforms. Premier Juppé never recovered his prestige in the eyes of public opinion. Juppé suffered from an uncaring and arrogant image that his best efforts could not dispel and that contributed to the right's unexpected defeat in the 1997 elections.

During the 'abrupt presidency', Chirac's main activity was centred around his positioning as an international statesman. Early on, Chirac appeared to be guided by a vision of historic Gaullism, though it was debatable that he had the means to impose Gaullist-style policies. President Chirac's decision in June 1995 that France would resume unilateral nuclear testing in the South Pacific recalled earlier Gaullist episodes, as did the new President's refusal to bow to external pressures to cancel the decision. To the extent that Chirac chose a highly symbolic aspect of foreign policy to make his mark, this represented a sign of continuity with past Presidents. In other respects, however, President Chirac made his mark where least expected. Once the nuclear testing decision had been assumed, Chirac proved to be innovative in the sphere of foreign and defence policy. That a Gaullist President should announce the end of conscription, the slashing of defence budgets, and the partial reintegration of France into NATO marked a bolder break with the Gaullist legacy than any moves attempted by Chirac's three predecessors.

Why did President Chirac dissolve the National Assembly in 1997, one year ahead of schedule? With the benefit of hindsight, the decision seemed foolhardy. There was no obvious threat to the stability of the Republic, the President already had an overwhelming parliamentary majority, and the reason advanced – to qualify France for the euro – did not require the action proposed. The real explanation was linked to his reading of the presidential function and the need for a parliamentary majority to be elected to support the President. Upon his election in 1995 President Chirac took on an established large parliamentary majority, removing any pretext for dissolving the National Assembly. Chirac in 1997 was aware that an incumbent President's authority is only really established when a parliamentary majority has been elected in his name (as in 1962, 1981, 1988 and 2002). The National Assembly elections had originally been planned for 1998, but Chirac used his right to dissolve Parliament using the pretext of preparing France for entry into the euro. He failed. His action in 1997 demonstrated that the tool of presidential dissolution is a double-edged weapon to be used with caution. In 1997, the French right suffered from its own divisions, in the form of personality and policy-based factionalism, cutting across the division of the French right into the RPR and UDF. There remained the bitter legacy of the 1995 presidential election (setting Balladur supporters against Chirac loyalists). Policy-based disagreements regularly surfaced throughout the campaign, notably on the question of European integration, the single currency, and the franc–mark parity. Deeper ideological divisions remained not far from the surface; the statism of Philippe Seguin competed with the neo-liberal alternative advocated by former Economy Minister Alain Madelin. Neither had much sympathy for premier Alain Juppé. The unexpected defeat of the French right had immediate consequences, including the capture of the Gaullist RPR by President Chirac's opponent Séguin (aided and abetted by former premier Balladur). Most important of all, Chirac's abrupt presidency gave way to a new period of cohabitation.

2.9 Jospin and the plural left coalition

The government led by Jospin came to power rather unexpectedly in June 1997, after President Chirac's dissolution of the National Assembly elected in 1993 went badly wrong. The Jospin government was original in many senses. It was the first five-party 'plural left' government, operating within a novel institutional context: that of the first 'cohabitation' involving a Gaullist President and a Socialist-led government. It boasted a policy record that encouraged emulation from certain of her European partners (Italy), and aroused hostility from others (Blair's New Labour administration especially). Even its fiercest opponents acknowledged that the Jospin government had engaged in original experiments in economic, social and employment policy, of which the enforced reduction of the working week to thirty-five hours was the centrepiece (Milner, 2002). The Jospin government also undertook audacious measures to break down social and cultural blockages within French society (the civic contract (PACS) and professional equality (*parité*) reforms) and to modernise French politics. The discursive basis of Jospin's message was that politics does indeed matter; in the permanent compromise between politics and markets, economic imperatives must be counterbalanced with a respect for social justice. Whether in the domain of economic policy, the 35-hour week or European policy, the Jospin government believed in the virtues of affirmative state action. At the same time, the Jospin government adopted a reformist approach to state-society relations, marked especially by liberal reforms in relation to gender equality and sexual preference. Opinion polls suggested a mainly positive reception for the Jospin government and for the personality of Lionel Jospin in particular, who was more popular than Jacques Chirac for all but a few months of the 1997–2002 period.

From 1997–2002, there was a five-year long 'cohabitation', which confirmed the basic rules of this form of institutional coexistence between the two heads of the French executive. More resolutely than during the previous two episodes, the Jospin government dominated the domestic agenda, with President Chirac powerless to prevent the implementation of policies with which he was in major disagreement (such as over Corsica). On the other hand, attempts by premier Jospin to venture openly into the realm of foreign policy were unsuccessful. Jospin's deeply controversial visit to the occupied Palestinian territories while on an official visit to Israel in 2000 was a case in point. President Chirac publicly rebuked his Prime Minister for supporting the Palestinian cause, since he had no constitutional authority to do so. In the realm of European policy-making, the shared responsibility between Chirac and Jospin produced a good deal of confusion in other European capitals, as did their inability to define a coherent French position during the negotiations leading to the Nice treaty in December 2000. Most polls carried out during the 2002 presidential election campaign suggested that, other things being equal, the French would prefer not to have 'cohabitation'. Seasoned observers discerned bitter opposition and highly personalised conflict throughout the cohabitation experience, a rivalry that became obvious with the onset of the 2002 presidential election campaign.

The plural-left government was sometimes described in the French press as a 'dual cohabitation'. Alongside potentially conflictual relationships within the French executive, Jospin had to manage the differing political sensitivities of the five coalition partners (Socialists, Communists, Radicals, Greens and Citizens). Jospin's skills were, on the whole, effectively deployed in managing the plural-left coalition. For most of the 1997–2002 period Jospin proved an astute coalition manager and power-broker, though the coalition itself was always a fragile edifice that became more fragile as time wore on (Cole, 2002). Tensions within the plural-left coalition occurred across a range of policies – immigration, reform of the judicial system, the euro, Corsica – but none of these threatened the survival of the plural-left government. Jospin's uncontested leadership was a vital factor explaining the survival for five years of the plural-left coalition government. To Jospin's leadership, we would add the fortuitous combination of a pre-eminent (but not dominant) party, the ability to deliver political or symbolic side-payments to the main coalition partners (especially the Communists), the lack of an alternative and a common electoral necessity. The politics of accommodation was, however, time-bound and the cohesion of the plural-left coalition was eventually undermined by its internal contradictions. As time wore on, there were increasingly intractable policy divisions (over Corsica, the environment, Europe, jobs and many others), and a weakening of the personal ties that bound Jospin to the leaders of the other parties in the coalition. The forthcoming presidential election damaged the stability of the coalition, as did the shifting balance of power therein (the strengthening of the Greens and the weakening of the Communists). Whether a coalition-wide view ever prevailed is open to some doubt.

2.10   Chirac's second term, 2002–

Jacques Chirac was re-elected as President on 5 May 2002 with a crushing majority – 81.75 per cent – against his far-right rival Le Pen. We interpret the elections of 2002 as a return to sources of the Fifth Republic. A president genuinely representing the French nation was invested by the electorate in 2002 with a 'clear and consistent' majority, as he had requested. Better still, the electoral series was crowned by an overall majority in seats for the new style presidential party (the UMP), the best performance of a right-wing presidential rally since the heyday of Gaullism. The converging of the presidential and parliamentary majorities and the subordinate relationship of the latter to the former appeared to signal a return to a suitably modernised but pre-eminently presidential practice.

In other respects also, an interim evaluation of Chirac's second term would appear to suggest a return to Gaullist traditions. The primary focus of President Chirac's activity has been in the traditional presidential sphere of foreign policy, European affairs and defence. In foreign policy, the 2002 conflict in Iraq fully mobilised Chirac's energies. Opposition to the war provided a window of opportunity for Chirac to establish a direct relationship with the French people in the pure Gaullist tradition. President Chirac's refusal to engage in the war in Iraq was overwhelmingly supported by public opinion. Foreign policy convergence allowed a much closer relationship to be established with Germany and for the Franco-German partnership to be invested with renewed vigour in other areas of joint Franco-German interest (notably the negotiation of the new European constitution). A foreign policy tinged with anti-Americanism and multilateralism; a reinvigorated Franco-German partnership, closer European defence collaboration: all these features bore a striking resemblance to classic Gaullism.

In the domestic arena too, there were parallels with past Gaullist practice. President Chirac appeared removed from the day to day details of domestic politics, content to steer the direction of government policy from a distance. Invested with the support of over 80 per cent of French voters in May 2002, President Chirac was anxious not to dispense precious political capital in mundane domestic politics (but also, in line with tradition, to focus on specific areas of personal interest such as road safety and cancer). In the pure tradition of the Fifth Republic, the Chirac–Raffarin relationship was an uneven one: the President indicated the main orientations that the premier had responsibility to implement. While President Chirac concentrated upon defending the rank of France in the European and international arenas, Prime Minister Raffarin drove the difficult, politically unpopular dossiers, such as pensions reform (in June 2003). Prime Minister Raffarin publicly assumed the asymmetry in this relationship on several occasions. Raffarin was bound by Chirac's campaign promises, especially in relation to tax cuts and to the prioritising of domestic economic management over European solidarity. The one policy area associated with the Prime Minister was that of decentralisation, which we consider in Chapter 7.

| 2.11 | Concluding remarks |

The Fifth Republic is France's second longest surviving post-revolutionary regime. It has attracted a degree of elite and popular support that sets it apart from other post-revolutionary French regimes. While initially shaped in the image of its creator, de Gaulle, the Fifth Republic demonstrated its capacity to resist becoming a personalist regime. Certain early observers predicted that the regime was destined to disappear with the departure of its founder. This did not transpire. The transition to a post-Gaullist phase occurred gradually. Inaugurated by Pompidou's presidency of 1969–74, it was consolidated with the election of Giscard d'Estaing as the first non-Gaullist President in 1974. The final legitimisation of the Fifth Republic came in 1981, with the election of the Socialist Mitterrand as President. After more than forty years of existence, the Fifth Republic has thus demonstrated its longevity. The adaptability of the regime explains in part its longevity. The alternation in power between left and right in 1981 was followed in 1986 by the first experience of 'cohabitation', an experience repeated in 1993 and 1997. Henceforth, the alternation in power of rival left- and right-wing parties, or coalitions has become a banal occurrence.

Moving away from institutions, the period since 1958 has been one of relative prosperity (at least in relation to other comparable nations), of a strengthening of French influence within Europe and internationally, and of economic and social modernisation. While certain commentators favour an optimistic interpretation, others are less sanguine, pointing to the rise of the far-right, a sense of ongoing economic crisis, diminishing confidence in politicians, and widespread corruption to tarnish the reputation of the regime. The evidence presented in the following chapters might support either interpretation. It is a measure of how far the Fifth Republic has imposed itself in popular consciousness, however, that contemporary disputes are centred around particular policies, or practices, rather than overt challenges to the legitimacy of the political regime.

3 French political culture

3.1 Introduction

Chapter 3 introduces the reader to various interpretations of the French polity, namely those based on the revolutionary tradition, sub-cultural identities, centre-periphery relations, and patterns of authority. Concentrating upon some of the most influential French, American and British studies, the chapter aims to provide a broad understanding of the complexity of French political culture. This exercise is an indispensable preliminary to the wider context of institutional development engaged in Part 2.

3.2 Political culture in France: the traditional reading

We use political culture in this chapter as a loose, but useful overarching concept to attempt to capture different representations of Frenchness and distinct perspectives on the French polity in time and space. We are conscious of the dangers inherent in the concept and of the need to avoid some of the excesses associated with its use in political science. The main danger is that of the 'culturalist fallacy': that specific communities are, by their essence, unique. We are more interested in how communities construct their identities and shape their discourses than in affirming their essentialist character. When we speak of political culture, we agree with McMillan (1996: 69) that 'to study political culture is to study the beliefs, values, assumptions (spoken and unspoken) and modes of action to be found within a given polity'. We are convinced of the importance of history, geography, memory, language and discourse in shaping the 'beliefs, values and assumptions' that give meaning to contemporary France. These variables are not the only ones, but they are important and they elucidate aspects of the climate within which politics in contemporary France is carried out.

As developed in much of the literature, French political culture is highly ambiguous. The cultural portrayals of France have a tendency to vary depending upon the cultural preconceptions of the observer. American observers, for instance, have provided some of the most stimulating insights into French political culture, but these are not generally those highlighted by French analysts, in part because of different normative standpoints adopted (for instance, the definition of what constitutes civic or community behaviour). Furthermore, there is a very real difficulty in measuring cultural attitudes, especially in the period preceding the advent of opinion polls. This imparts a descriptive, impressionistic character to much of the early literature on political culture, especially textbook representations. To this extent, the notion of political culture can be misleading, since it disseminates potentially false images of modern and contemporary France.

At various stages in recent history, political culture has been advanced to explain a range of rather different obstacles to the smooth functioning of the French polity. Those studies undertaken before or immediately after the creation of the Fifth Republic looked for cultural causes of French political instability. The prevailing idea present in texts written in the 1950s and 1960s was that France had been prevented from becoming a 'modern' or 'stable' country on account of her uneven historical development and her idiosyncratic national character. As Safran (1999: 44) points out: 'American social scientists pointed to France's reluctance to marry her century – to the habit of ideological thinking, the prevalence of class distrust, the tendency to excoriate the political establishment, the absence of civic mindedness and an underdeveloped ethos of participation'. Even though France eventually developed democratic political institutions, and an advanced socio-economic infrastructure, certain analysts continued to refer to France as a 'delinquent' society, one marked by tax evasion, alcoholism, undisciplined motorists and a general lack of civic behaviour (Pitts, 1981). These 'delinquent' traits raised the question of the 'governability' of the French. As Hoffmann (1994) points out, 'most of these uncivic cultural traits no longer stand up to serious scrutiny'.

As formulated by classic political culture theorists such as Almond and Verba in *The Civic Culture* (1963), the notion of political culture has had difficulties in explaining political, or socio-economic change. In the French context, the cultural norms detected in the 1950s or 1960s appear ill-designed to describe France in the third millennium. *A fortiori*, the above remark applies even more forcefully to cultural stereotypes derived from the nineteenth century or earlier. The cultural perceptions developed when France was a static, economically inward-looking society are likely to be of limited assistance when attempting to assess how French politics and society has mutated under the impact of the dramatic economic, social, political and demographic changes of the post-war period. For political culture to be a meaningful concept, it has to transcend the cultural representations present at any one point in time. It has also to admit the importance of subcultures, either in addition to or against a prevailing national culture. As Berstein (1999) argues, also, we must admit the coexistence of rival intellectual currents of thought, more or less prevalent at given stages in French history, that impact upon the dominant beliefs, values and assumptions about the organisation of the political system. In the case of post-revolutionary France, Berstein identifies these prevailing intellectual cultures as comprising traditionalism, liberalism, republicanism, Marxism and Gaullism. Each political tradition has contributed in important ways to the 'republican synthesis' that comprises contemporary French political culture. As we see in Chapter 8, moreover, the main political traditions underpin the operation of the party system.

Traditional perceptions of French political culture have been shaped above all by two innovative surveys, *In Search of France* edited by Stanley Hoffmann (1965), and *The Stalled Society* (*La Société bloquée*) by Michel Crozier (1970). Common to both Hoffmann's 'static society', and Crozier's 'stalled society' lay the idea that the French nation was afflicted by numerous blockages, which prevented a normal democratic functioning of its polity. These blockages included a habit for overly ideological and abstract thinking (induced by France's education system), the persistence of class rivalries, a penchant for uncivic behaviour, a deeply ingrained anti-political strain within public opinion, a distrust of those in authority, an inability to compromise or to conduct civilised face to face negotiations, and a weak sense of political efficacy, leading to low levels of participation in voluntary organisations such as political parties or pressure groups. Such cultural portrayals partly influenced elite behaviour. This was true for General de Gaulle himself, for whom the French were an unruly bunch of individualists who could never agree on anything, and who needed firm leadership to overcome their disunity. The belief that French society was archaic and conservative; and that only the state represented the general will of the people was a powerful motivational force behind the state-led 'modernisation' drive from the late 1940s onwards. Given these cultural barriers, modernisation could only be carried out by a neutral, innovative and interventionist state.

In *In Search of France* Hoffmann contends, amongst other arguments, that relations between state and civil society are far more closed and less pluralistic than in the Anglo-Saxon countries. In Hoffman's opinion, French political culture combined extreme individualism and authoritarianism. On account of their individualism, French people were reluctant to participate in voluntary associations, such as political parties and interest groups. When they did join groups, such groups were weak, fragmented, and ill-disposed for compromise. In order to resolve inevitable disputes, they appeal to the state for arbitration. This provided the impetus for the development of a powerful bureaucracy, to arbitrate disputes. There was a weak bargaining culture of negotiation between the competing groups themselves, and between groups and the state. In a critique of this portrayal, Knapp and Wright (2001) demonstrate that relationships between pressure groups and the state were far more subtle than implied by Hoffmann.

Perhaps the most widely diffused exposé of the pessimistic appraisal of French culture was that provided by Michel Crozier, in two highly influential books, *The Stalled Society* and *The Bureaucratic Phenomenon* (Crozier, 1970, 1963). The essence of Crozier's thesis was that the French were afraid of 'face to face contact' and that they are 'unable to cooperate'. In order to resolve disputes, individuals appealed systematically to those in positions of higher authority, especially representatives of the state, rather than attempt to negotiate, bargain, or compromise amongst each other. This induced an exaggerated sense of hierarchy, but at the same time created the conditions for rebellion against this authority if unwelcome decisions were made. Thus French political culture combined a measure of routine authoritarianism, with sporadic rebellions against authority. Underpinning Crozier's analysis was the belief that French people are torn between submissive subordination to the state, and insurrectional outbursts against it. In normal circumstances, such cultural traits produce a bureaucratic defensive mentality and a lack of initiative.

Appraisals of French political culture have long been overshadowed by the work of Hoffmann and Crozier. At best, they described aspects of French society at a particular stage of historical development. Even if we accept their initial premises, which are difficult to substantiate or disprove, we would argue that French society has moved on since then. Critics of Crozier's thesis in particular have pointed to the development of voluntary groups and new forms of collective action, which point to a culture of negotiation and compromise. For Mendras (1989), for instance, Crozier's viewpoint is inadequate in analysing contemporary France. The opposition between Us and Them depicted by Crozier no longer accurately represents the structure of French society, nor the norm to be adopted towards authority. The creation of new social groups during the post-war period (the 'new middle classes') which insist upon a bargaining model of authority, and whose values are broadly post-materialist, has weakened the authority patterns evoked by Crozier. These developments are eloquently summarised by Gaffney (in Gaffney and Kolinsky, 1991: 18) who refers to a convergence of lifestyles, aspirations and social outlook, an assumed growing political consensus, a developing urbanisation, salarisation and tertiarisation, and the importance of a diffuse cultural liberalism as symbolising the cultural identity of the new France.

3.3 Traits of French political culture

The traditional portrayal of French political culture pointed to the persistence of cleavages inherited from the French Revolution. The divisions occasioned by disputes over Church, state and nation remained pertinent 150 years later: even today, they continue to provide the backdrop to many assessments of contemporary France. In their analysis of political culture, for example, Hanley, Kerr and Waites (1984: 109) emphasise the legacy of the French Revolution, the special status of Paris in French history, the slow rate of industrialisation, the role of the Church and anti-clericalism, the closed relationship between state and civil society and nationalism as 'the constants of French political culture'. These variables undoubtedly are of critical importance in understanding the evolution of French history, though they present a rather static portrait of contemporary France. The traditional portrayal of French political culture has emphasised the revolutionary tradition, the role of the state as an instrument of national unity, a tendency for uncivic behaviour and various characteristics attributed to France's status as a Catholic country.

A revolutionary tradition?

Republicanism in France traditionally declared its belief in the legitimacy of the revolutionary tradition. This tradition can have several meanings. At its most basic, it involved support for the French Revolution, avowed even by conservative republicans during the nineteenth century. For more radical republicans, the revolutionary tradition signified that French citizens had the right to overturn an unjust government, if its institutions affronted the ideals of the Republic and democracy. For the left during the early twentieth century, the revolutionary tradition involved a commitment to provide a social and economic counterpart to the political revolution of 1789: in other words, to replace capitalism with socialism, as 1789 had eventually replaced the monarchy with the Republic. This interpretation of the revolutionary tradition strongly characterised the activities of the French Communist Party during the inter-war years. A fourth version of the revolutionary tradition was that promulgated by the central state itself, channelled through the national education system. The revolutionary tradition was a justification for the actions of republicans in overturning monarchist governments during the eighteenth and nineteenth century. French children in state schools are saturated with the feats of their republican ancestors; an official revolutionary, republican tradition was inculcated by an interventionist state. Republican regimes have claimed the French Revolution of 1789 as the foundation of their own legitimacy; the presence of the 1792 Declaration of the Rights of Man and Citizen as the preliminary of the 1958 Constitution is a good example of this.

We must not overlook the fact that the French Revolution initially produced a divided political culture in France: for or against the Republic, the Church, the lay state. Whereas the French Revolution came to be accepted by most of the political elite, left and right continue to argue over whether the 1848 revolution, or the Paris Commune of 1871 were justified expressions of rebellion against unjust authority or not. The French revolutionary tradition is neither monolithic, nor accepted by everybody. The official celebrations of the bicentennial of the French revolution in 1989 were accompanied by counter-demonstrations on the part of those (ranging from regionalists to elements of the extreme right) contesting the legitimacy of events two centuries previously.

What remains of this revolutionary tradition in contemporary France? Until recently the main left-wing parties (PCF and PS) continued to refer to the French revolutionary tradition as a justification for their political activity. For the Communist Party, the notion of revolution formed an indelible part of the party's own political culture, however shallow that commitment revealed itself to be in May '68. In practice, ever since its creation in 1920, the PCF has fought elections like any other party and has eschewed any serious attempt at revolutionary upheaval, even when events appeared propitious, such as in 1944, or 1968. Despite its opposition to the 'personal power' it accuses the presidential system of promoting, the PCF has accepted working within the institutions of the Fifth Republic, rather than attempting to bring about a revolution. For the Socialist Party, it was sufficient that the Communist Party claimed a revolutionary heritage for it to define its own mission in terms of a revolutionary transformation of society. Invigorated by their own myths, the Socialists attempted to portray their victory in 1981 as being more a change of regime than a mere change of government. Such deception did not last for long. The failure of the Socialists' radical reform programme of 1981–2 destroyed many remaining illusions. The collapse of Communism in the late 1980s and early 1990s weakened the hold of Marxism over the mainstream French left. On the other hand, the rise of the far-left movements in the 1995 and 2002 elections demonstrated the persistence of a diffuse revolutionary tradition on the left of French politics.

On a slightly less exalted level, the French 'revolutionary tradition' has been invoked to explain the propensity of French citizens to take their protests to the streets. It does appear that certain social groups – such as farmers, fishermen and lorry drivers – have used the tactics associated with past 'revolutionaries' to forward their own corporate demands. But this is scarcely indicative of their desire to overthrow existing society. Henceforth, street demonstrations from unsatisfied social groups are openly attempts to press for concessions, rather than mythical insurrections aimed at overthrowing the government. Student demonstrations in 1986, 1990 or 1995 were indicative of this new public spirit. Unlike their counterparts in May '68, the young demonstrators never called into question the government's right to govern. Whatever its historical signific-ance, the revolutionary tradition has become a somewhat mythical aspect of French democracy. It is unclear what it signifies today, apart from a rather bland attachment to the slogans of the French Revolution and a propensity for direct action. The disappearance of the political discourse of revolution, in asso-ciation with the ideological discredit of Marxism, has been a further gauge of the weakening of the traditional model of French politics and policy-making.

Provincialism and the state

A celebration of provincialism is the counterpart of an excessively centralised state apparatus and a concentration of politico-administrative power in Paris. Provincial distrust of the state and of Paris is certainly deeply embedded (Mendras, 1989). *La France profonde* has always distrusted the centralising and corrupting influence of Paris. In traditional accounts of French political culture, emphasis was laid on the importance of the central state as a cohesive idea holding together French society. As surveyed in Chapter 1, modern France was created as an extension of the central state. This process had begun under the *ancien régime*, as the monarchy attempted to impose its control over feudal barons (McMillan, 1996). The process of state building was considerably strengthened by the Revolution, which supplanted the provincial *parlements*, smashed the autonomous power of the aristocracy and imposed the will of Paris on the provinces. After the revolutionary upheavals of 1789–99, Napoleon provided a further impetus towards the creation of the centralised nation-state: the Emperor relied on autocratic personal rule, backed by unrivalled control over military force, to impose a powerful and efficient type of state machinery, key features of which have remained unaltered until the present. A highly organised and regimented bureaucracy (selected by means of a centralised and elitist system of national education) was the key legacy of the Napoleonic period. Throughout the one hundred years following the Revolution, the central state attempted to ensure the lasting subordination of unruly provinces to its rule. The nomination of central state representatives (prefects) in France's ninety-six departments was a testament to the state's centralising mission.

This affirmation of central authority went alongside a reality of regional variation. Research from various disciplines – and at various stages of French history – has revealed a rich provincial diversity subsisting beneath an officially regimented system. Sociologists have emphasised the diverse patterns of kinship and family structures, as well as varying types of authority structures in different French regions (Todd, 1988; Le Bras, 1995). Linguists have revealed the survival of regional dialects and languages in spite of efforts to subordinate them in the nineteenth and twentieth centuries (Hoare, 2000). Social historians and geographers have insisted upon the importance of territorial identities in explaining lasting regional political allegiances (Le Bras, 2002). Political scientists, finally, have illustrated how the state machinery (the prefectures, notably) has functioned in specific ways in different parts of the country (Cole and John, 2001). Provincial diversity is the counterpart to centralisation. The construction of the French state was directly related to the endless variety of regional variations public policy-makers have to take into account. This accounts in part for the highly codified nature of the French legal system. Because regional variation was so strong across the nation, the state had to take positive action to affirm the revolutionary principle of equality.

The relationship with the state is highly complex, however, as French citizens, while firmly anchored in localist (and in places regionalist) identities, look to the state to enforce uniform treatment across the territory. Though we argue in Chapter 7 that a distinctive form of subnational governance has evolved, it has been bounded by a powerful coalition of centralising institutions (especially the Council of State), state-centred professional interests (in the teaching unions, for example, or amongst social workers or tax officers) and widely disseminated ideas, equating republican equality with uniformity. For many French citizens, decentralisation is synonymous with social regression, unequal provision, even a return to a pre-republican social order. Upstanding republicans equate territorial uniformity with ideas of progress, equal opportunity and citizenship. The building of France as a modern state-nation provides the key to understanding this equation of territorial identity and political reaction. Regional political formations are, almost by definition, suspected by a certain brand of republican of anti-republican intent. The French state building enterprise has, historically speaking, been remarkably successful in inculcating deeply rooted beliefs linking the national territory with social progress. We touch here at the core of state sovereignty which, in the French case, is intimately tied in with perceptions of national prestige and territorial hierarchy.

Challenges to the French state have come in several directions: from the European Union and the process of European integration (Chapter 14), from decentralisation (Chapter 7), from the globalising pressures of the international economy (Chapter 13) and from developments in public policy. The importance of the state as a reference point of national identity remains more marked in France than in most other European nations, however, alongside a tradition of central state innovative action and a particular conception of public service which relies heavily on affirmative state action.

An uncivic nation?

Critical observers have diagnosed French political culture as being responsible for a weak sense of civic responsibility. This is typified by a deeply ingrained anti-politicism, and a pervasive distrust of politicians (Perrineau, 2003). That there exists a deep distrust of most politicians might be verified even by occasional visitors to France. This distrust might be explained in terms of political culture, but other explanations are equally valid, notably those relating to political performance: anti-political sentiments within the French electorate are particularly marked when the political and economic systems are not performing as effectively as they should be, such as during the Fourth Republic, or since the mid-1980s. It is important not to take such developments in isolation: strong anti-political sentiments within public opinion have not been limited to France, but have been a more general phenomenon throughout western Europe and the United States. Indeed, by many comparative measurements (such as the degree of electoral participation) France is a model of civic pride. Moreover, while politicians in general might be subject to criticism, one's own local representative is usually spared excessive opprobrium. This is revealed by the rate of re-election of sitting mayors in the six-yearly municipal elections, even in cases of mayors being involved in criminal trials, as in the 1995 and 2001 contests.

A low level of political participation and a excessive penchant for individualism were classically highlighted as evidence of *incivisme*. This is difficult to substantiate. It sits uneasily with the proliferation of voluntary associations that have emerged during the post-war period. The fact is that one-half of French people claim to belong to voluntary associations, a comparable figure with other European countries. Levels of participation in elections, where even municipal contests can attract three-quarters of registered voters to cast a ballot, are amongst the highest in Europe. As measured by participation rates, the French electorate would appear to have a preference for two types of election – the municipal and the presidential. The presidential election involves a direct communion with a supra-partisan leader; the municipal contest allows close contact with a recognised local spokesman.

The suspicion of *incivisme* went alongside the absence of the regular alternations-in-power between social reformist and moderate conservative parties, of the type diagnosed in Britain, the Federal Republic of Germany or the US. In the political circumstances of post-war France (the unstable coalitions of the Fourth Republic, giving way to a right-wing monopoly from 1958–81), political discourse assumed a radical edge, a counterpart to a lack of face-to-face contact between political groups themselves. A tradition of ideological political reasoning appears to persist, especially on the left of French politics. There are several sound historical reasons why such a pattern should have prevailed for so long. The importance of ideology as a means of political competition can be related to the late development of an industrial working class, to the rivalry between the two left-wing parties, or to the revolutionary tradition we referred to above. But it is clear that classic ideological frameworks of reference are in decline. The experience of the left in government after 1981 discredited overtly ideological solutions to problems of public policy for the foreseeable future.

The collapse of the Berlin Wall had a critical effect upon what remained of traditional ideological frames of reference and posed a direct threat to the survival of the French Communist Party.

There is little firm evidence of a stronger incidence of anti-civic attitudes in France than in comparable democracies. Safran (1999) points to the alleged French tendency for tax-dodging as evidence to underline the lack of a civic culture in France. This is debateable. While no one perhaps likes paying tax, the high incidence of French tax evasion is more likely to reflect the structure of the taxation system rather than anti-civic attitudes. Viewed as a whole, the Fifth Republic appears as a regime enjoying a fairly high degree of political legitimacy. The acceptance by public opinion, and by the main political formations of the fundamental precepts of the regime is an unprecedented development in Republican France. Neither the Third Republic (1870–1940), nor the Fourth Republic (1944–58) could boast such an underlying consensus. While political choices divide French elites, the Republican form of government is less contested in contemporary France than at any period since 1789. Catholics have become fully reconciled to the regime, even more so than during the short-lived Fourth Republic. Republicanism has become banal, losing its mobilising force, but no longer inspiring intense hatred (Kriegel, 1992). Even Jean-Marie Le Pen, while courting the symbols of counter-revolution, and openly contesting 1789, is careful to portray himself as a republican.

A Catholic identity?

Certain cultural attributes have been attributed to France's heritage as a Catholic nation. A distinction must here be drawn between the cultural legacy of Catholicism *stricto sensu* and its impact upon political culture. In social terms, practising Catholicism appears to be in decline in France, as elsewhere in Europe, although France is still nominally overwhelmingly Catholic. In terms of political culture, France has never been a culturally homogeneous Catholic society. Indeed, the divisive and bitter struggle between Catholicism and anti-clericalism helped to shape contemporary political identities.

In political terms, the heritage of Catholic anti-Republicanism retarded the emergence of a modern Christian Democratic movement as a federating force of conservatism. The rallying of the Catholic Church to the Republic during the 1890s did not represent a fundamental compromise with the theological foundations of Roman Catholicism, which continued to refute the legitimacy of the republican form of government until after the Second World War. Catholics excluded themselves from the Republic until the emergence of French Christian Democracy, in the form of the MRP (*Mouvement Républicain Populaire*) and its participation in the post-war progressive tripartite alliance (Hanley, 2002). The failure of French Christian Democracy in the Fourth Republic stemmed in part from its ambiguous political message: MRP voters were far more conservative than its progressively minded leaders, who espoused social Catholicism and class solidarity. It also suffered from being a regime party of the Fourth Republic, with the discredit that this implied. Even before the fall of the Fourth Republic, organised political Catholicism had to cope with the emergence of Gaullism, as an alternative, pro-Catholic, federating force of French conservatism.

The influence of Catholicism might best be understood in subcultural terms: the existence of a powerful Catholic political subculture undoubtedly had a structuring effect on the political behaviour of France's most dedicated Catholics, rather similar to that exercised by the Communist Party over the industrial working class. This subculture was especially present in the French countryside, especially in certain regions: Brittany, Normandy, Vendée, Alsace-Lorraine. The weakening of this subculture has been closely tied to the decline of rural France, and the process of urbanisation, accelerated in the post-war period. In fact, as early as 1943, doubts were cast as to the real incidence of religious practice and belief amongst a majority of French citizens (Mendras and Cole, 1991). The decline in religious belief, and the diminishing saliency of religion-based political cleavages has reduced the differentiation between pious Catholics and other members of French society.

Traces of religious identification remain, however. More than any other issue, the defence of 'free' schools continues to mobilise Catholic opinion (and conservative opinion generally) in defence of its corporate identity. Deeply rooted in French history, this issue has an instrumental appeal that mobilises middle-class parents primarily in defence of the quality of education received by their children, rather than in terms of evangelisation. Religious identification also has a marked impact upon voting behaviour. Michelat and Simon's (1977) classic study revealed that voting patterns were closely associated with the degree of religious identity and practice. Regularly practising Catholics consistently supported right-wing parties; the strongest support for the left came from those professing no religion. This cleavage remained the most important indicator of voting choice in the second round of the 1995 presidential election (Cole, 1995). While religious identity continues to matter at the margins, most French citizens are neither pious Catholics, nor firm anti-clerical non-believers. The weakening of the significance of religious affiliation and partisan behaviour is another indication of France becoming rather less of a European exception.

The weakening of subcultures?

The above point is reinforced by the importance of subcultures, which exercise a far tighter influence over their members than a more diffuse national culture can possibly achieve. In several instances, analysis of subcultures has proved fruitful in explaining the persistence or otherwise of political phenomena. Subcultural analysis is essential for understanding the role of industrial workers in the politics of the French Communist Party and the trade union movement, as I shall illustrate below. The use of subculture might also prove useful in appraising the social organisation of France's immigrant communities, notwithstanding state-led efforts at 'integration' which go beyond those attempted in most other European countries. The weakening of subcultures has reduced differentiation between social groups and strengthened individualism, without necessarily increasing integration into a unified national culture.

The weakening of the proletarian subculture is of inestimable importance in understanding the decline of the Communist Party. Throughout the Fourth Republic, the PCF acted as a counter-community, in opposition to the rest of French society, in some senses a mirror image of the Catholic Church. The party was a highly organised community, which offered its members the emotional satisfaction of belonging to a cohesive, well-organised counter-society, with its own norms, duties and satisfactions. At its height, the PCF was a genuine tribune of the industrial working class, articulating the demands of alienated workers which other parties were incapable of expressing. The PCFs obsession with *ouvrièrisme* reflected its own position within the political system. Most of the party's electoral support came from industrial workers. With its conquest of the CGT in 1947, the PCF was the only party which could lay a genuine claim to be able to organise the working class politically. Communist Party cells proliferated in industrial areas throughout France, especially in the larger factories, the mines and the docks. The role of the Renault factory at Boulogne Billancourt in the Paris 'red belt' was of particular symbolic importance. The decline of this tightly organized and cohesive subculture began in earnest in the 1960s but it has accelerated greatly since the 1970s. The diminishing importance of traditional manufacturing industry, the enfeebling of class solidarity, the rise of unemployment, the breakdown of a specifically proletarian lifestyle and identity and the end of the Cold War have all contributed to the weakening of the Communist subculture.

Somewhat like industrial workers, today's immigrant communities have adopted many of the characteristics of defensive subcultures, against which the racist *Front national* has targeted its political appeal. The interaction of leading subcultures with overall society can have a dynamic effect on both. The breakdown of specific subcultures increases the fluidity associated with the prevailing values within wider French society, such as individualism. Evidence suggests also that the integrative character of subcultures can be lost once they no longer control their members. Is it any coincidence that the *Front national* has prospered in former working-class bastions controlled by the Communist Party, today polarised between the remnants of an indigenous proletariat and a high presence in the local population of second generation immigrant families?

3.4　The Fifth Republic and the new Republican synthesis

The creation of the Fifth Republic in 1958 challenged the traditional republican model in important senses: the role of political (presidential) leadership, the formal limitations upon parliamentary sovereignty, the creation of judicial counterweights to legislative and executive authority. As it has developed over almost fifty years, however, the Fifth Republic has developed its own republican synthesis based upon wide acceptance of the foundations of the political regime by political and popular opinion.

The Fifth Republic has managed to restore a measure of political stability generally unknown to past French regimes. It has also revealed itself to be more flexible than its early critics believed possible. The model of the French presidency established by de Gaulle and imitated by his successors has diminished the traditional republican distrust of strong leaders. The legendary figure of Napoleon III, the self-styled French emperor who ruled from 1852–70 after subverting the short-lived Second Republic (1848–52), has faded into a distant collective past. Direct election from 1962 onwards consolidated the authority of the President of the Republic as the *de facto* head of the executive (see Chapter 4). Until 1981, the left (PS and PCF) continued to regard 'presidential power' as illegitimate, at least in principle. Mitterrand's election as the first Socialist President of the Republic in 1981 and his exercise of full presidential powers provided a more consensual basis for the governance of France. For most of the period since 1958, the presidency has acted as the linchpin of the political system, although the practice of successive presidents has varied even outside periods of cohabitation. The three experiences of 'cohabitation' reveal the flexibility of the Fifth Republic's political system, and its capacity to adapt to changing circumstances.

The new republican synthesis is based on the lessening relevance of traditional ideological cleavages (those based on class conflict), while new ones (such as Europe, immigration and the environment) have cut across existing political parties. Put simply, the left/right cleavage is of less significance in French politics in 2004 than it was three decades earlier. The general ideological climate has changed, both in France and elsewhere, as have perceptions of the possibilities of governmental action. In fact, left and right in France have always been broad coalitions. In the same decade, the historian Réné Rémond referred to the 'three families of the French right' (Rémond, 1982) and the Socialist politician Michel Rocard diagnosed two cultures of the French left. The ambiguity of themes associated with left and right is scarcely new. The early twentieth century Radical party was on the left on anti-clerical issues and in defence of the Republic, but conservative in terms of preserving the socio-economic status quo. The cultures of the French left and right have always been plural.

Despite the plurality within both left and right, until (and including) 1981 each political camp was able to mobilise by referring to distinctive sets of values. Whichever side one was on, the sense of identity and of belonging to one camp or another was strong. Since the Socialist experience in office (1981–6, 1988–93), the ideological bearings of left and right have become far more confused. Each side has borrowed themes hitherto voiced by the other in order to justify its shifts in policy. With the weakening of traditional ideological bearings, left and right have moved closer together in some important respects. France was a country rather less different from its European neighbours in 2004 than in 1981, not least in terms of its ideological register, but also in terms of the content of its public policies. Beneath the clash of rival political programmes lay a *de facto* convergence on many areas of public policy. This was particularly the case in relation to economic policy (see Chapter 12). Whatever the professed ideological differences between the parties, external constraints weighed increasingly heavily on the freedom of manoeuvre of governments of both sides from the early 1980s onwards. In key sectors of domestic policy, difficult choices were imposed upon governments of all political hues. At the beginning of the third millennium, the parties of the mainstream left and right share a renewed reference to the Republic as the overarching national political community. On the left, the reference to republican values has become all-encompassing, reverting in many senses to the positivistic, rationalist culture characteristic of the republican left in the late nineteenth century (the emphasis on progress, *laïcité* and citizenship). If anything, left-republicanism has become less tolerant in 2003 of difference and cultural diversity than during the Socialist revival of the 1970s. For its part, the right has rediscovered the Republic as a means of marking its difference from the resurgent far-right.

There are a number of common themes underpinning the new republican consensus. Both left and right accept the political regime and share a common (though not identical) perception of the role of France within European institutions and international organisations. The large consensus supporting President Chirac's stance on Iraq in 2003 demonstrated the persistence of a foreign policy consensus in many important areas. Both left and right seek to defend a French model of social and economic development that is distinctive in its content and universalistic in its pretensions. Neither left nor right has embraced doctrines of neo-liberalism (as opposed to classical liberalism) except for short and exceptional periods in recent history (the RPR in 1986). Both left and right look to safeguard the state as an instrument of public service, and a means of preserving a French way of life faced with globalisation. Most fundamentally, as the 2003–04 debate on *laïcité* demonstrated, left and right are closer to each other in relation to defining the conditions of French citizenship than either are with the domestic far-left or the far-right, or, indeed, with rival Anglo-Saxon or Germanic notions of citizenship.

3.5 Conclusion

There is a plurality of political traditions in contemporary France, each of which feed into the nation's overarching political culture (Bréchon, Laurent and Perrineau, 2000). Along with Berstein (1999) we must admit the coexistence of rival intellectual cultures, more or less prevalent at given stages in French history. Berstein identifies these prevailing intellectual cultures as comprising liberalism in the mid-nineteenth century, republicanism from the 1880s to the mid-1950s, Marxism from 1945 to 1975 and a revitalised republicanism since the mid-1980s. Political cultures represent a dominant paradigm, but they are never uncontested within society.

France in the third millennium is a pluralistic society which contains a broad range of political orientations and cultural practices within its midst. Social and political change has been marked throughout the post-war period. With the weakening of traditional structures of power, there has been a move towards a greater autonomy in all strata of society, a move facilitated by the weakening of the influence of traditional institutions such as the church, the state, political parties, the military and the extended family (Mendras and Cole, 1991). The birth of new social classes during the post-war period has been accompanied by a transformation of attitudes towards hierarchy and authority. Crozier's stalemate society no longer corresponds to an accurate portrayal of contemporary France. Although it failed as a political movement in the short term, the longer-term cultural significance of May '68 should not be underestimated. The egalitarian, anti-hierarchical ethos present in May '68 has had a profound impact upon French attitudes towards hierarchy and authority. France has become a European society similar in most respects to its neighbours; this is eminently more important than its cultural specificity, which nonetheless continues to provide a sense of national identity that gives the French a distinctive place amongst Europeans.

Part

2

Institutions and power

4 Presidents and Prime Ministers

4.1 Introduction

The study of Presidents and Prime Ministers forms part of the staple diet of comparative politics. Along with the American President, or the British Prime Minister, the French Presidency has become one of the key political offices in western liberal democracies.

What sets the French case apart from the British and American cases is the existence of two powerful political leaders, the President of the Republic and the Prime Minister. The French 'dual executive' has long fascinated comparative political scientists hungry for neat typologies. As a semi-presidential regime, the Fifth Republic is an evolving constitutional and political reality, which fits neatly into neither of the traditional presidential or parliamentary models of executive power. The study of political leadership in the Fifth Republic has, understandably, concentrated upon the figure of the President of the Republic, testament to the model of the strong presidency created by President de Gaulle from 1958–69 and imitated by his successors (Berstein, 2002; Hayward, 1993; Lacroix and Lagroye, 1992). The role of the French Prime Minister tended to be overlooked and underplayed during the prolonged period of presidential ascendency (1958–86) (Elgie, 1993). Especially in the aftermath of repeated experiences of 'cohabitation' (1986–8, 1993–5, 1997–2002), the focus of leadership politics in France is no longer exclusively presidential.

4.2 Political leadership in the French republican tradition

During the 150 years following the French Revolution, a fear of strong leaders was an essential part of the French republican tradition. The 'Great Man' transgressed the norms of democratic republicanism on more than one occasion. The example of Louis Napoleon (1848–70) became the model to avoid for republicans. Once the republican form of government had become firmly established in 1875–6, the Third Republican elite was convinced of the need to safeguard against the threat of strong leaders. Thus defined, the republican tradition precluded strong political leadership, except in periods of crisis, when saviours were briefly resorted to as figures of national salvation. The collapse of

The Elysée Palace: official residence of French Presidents

the Third Republic in 1940, followed by the wartime Vichy regime and the cult around the authoritarian personality of Marshall Pétain, confirmed the worst fears of republicans.

The appropriate form of political leadership was strongly contested throughout the Fourth Republic. The post-war provisional government (1944–6) was headed by the wartime resistance hero de Gaulle. De Gaulle believed in a rationalised democratic system, similar to the eventual Fifth Republic: *grosso modo*, he advocated a strong President who would stand above what he considered to be the petty quarrels of party politicians and incarnate the unity of the French nation. The General attributed France's collapse in 1940 at least in part to the degeneracy of its parliamentary system. De Gaulle's advocacy of strong personal leadership revived the traditional republican fears of strong leaders. The parties of the post-war left (Socialists, Communists, and Christian Democrats) suspected de Gaulle of preparing a system which might lead to dictatorship. They advocated instead different variations on the parliamentary theme. The presidential alternative posited by de Gaulle in his Bayeux speech of November 1946 remained the unwritten option to the parliamentary regime of the Fourth Republic throughout its existence. By rallying to de Gaulle in May–June 1958, the French nation appeared to have reverted to the Great Man to resolve a crisis as it had on several previous occasions in its history. In many respects, de Gaulle lay squarely within the tradition of the providential ruler, convinced as he was that he represented the unity of the nation above the squalid compromises made by politicians and political parties. But de Gaulle, the hero of the French Resistance, was far from being a leader who relied upon the implicit threat of force alone. De Gaulle enjoyed a personal legitimacy in the eyes of the French people that none of his successors could aspire to.

The 1958 Constitution has been subject to many different readings. It was a compromise between efficiency, so lacking in the previous Republics, and democracy, a requirement of the French Republican tradition. Those involved in drawing up the Constitution invoked different criteria for supporting it. For Prime Minister Debré (who chaired the all-party Commission charged with producing a draft Constitution), it created a British-style system of rationalised parliamentary government. For the Socialist leader Mollet, the fundamental principle was that of government responsibility to parliament (the cornerstone of a genuinely parliamentary system). De Gaulle believed that the Constitution invested the President of the Republic with supreme authority. Such ambiguity reflected the haste with which the Constitution had been drawn up, as well as the conflicting objectives of its authors. The constitutional consensus broke down almost as soon as the Constitution had been overwhelmingly ratified by referendum in September 1958.

The Constitution of 1958 was arguably a compromise between two guiding principles: the need for strong executive leadership (whether of the presidential or prime ministerial variety) and the principle of a government responsible to an elected Parliament. The creation of a pure presidential system of the US variety (with a complete separation of powers between the executive and legislative branches) was explicitly rejected by the constitution-makers in 1958. The 1958 Constitution did contain a reference to the separation of powers and greatly strengthened the prerogatives of the President of the Republic. But the core principle of the 1958 Constitution was that of governmental responsibility to parliament, the canon of a parliamentary system. Michel Debré openly looked to the British parliamentary system, with a strong premier supported by stable cohesive majorities, as a model to imitate, a conception shared to some extent by the representatives of Fourth Republic parties, who feared that a strong President would subvert republican democracy.

The 1958 Constitution established a curious hybrid regime, immediately labelled by most commentators as a dyarchy, or a twin-headed executive. It appeared to create two powerful executive figures, the President of the Republic and the Prime Minister. Whether the latter or the former is invested with executive authority depends somewhat upon how the Constitution is read. The 1958 Constitution can be open to a presidential and a prime ministerial interpretation.

Certain articles in the Constitution lend themselves to a presidential reading. Article 5 proclaims that 'The President of the Republic shall watch to see that the Constitution is respected. He shall ensure by his *arbitrage* the regular functioning of the public authorities, as well as the continuity of the State'. The crucial word here is that of *arbitrage*: it could be interpreted in a weak sense as the President being an ultimate referee in times of crisis, but in normal circumstances remaining above politics. But it could also be interpreted in a strong sense: that the role of the President was to give direction to government action.

Table 4.1 Ten selected articles of the 1958 Constitution

Article	Feature	Comments
5	The President is arbiter of the Constitution	Open to several interpretations
8	The President names the Prime Minister	No mention is made of dismissal
11	The President can call a referendum on matters 'relating to the nation's economic and social policy, and public services', and on 'the organisation of public authorities'	
12	The President can dissolve the National Assembly	Only once every twelve months
16	The President can assume 'emergency' powers, by suspending the Constitution for a six-month period	President alone determines conditions for this. Parliament sits as of right
20	'The Government shall determine and conduct the policy of the nation' and 'it shall be responsible to parliament'	
21	The Prime Minister 'shall direct the operation of the Government'	
34	Parliament is concerned with 'matters of law'. 'Matters of regulation' are the government's responsibility alone.	Constitutional limits to parliamentary sovereignty
38	Government can request parliament for authority to rule by decree in those policy sectors falling within the normal legislative domain	Speeds up the policy process. Avoids parliamentary blocking tactics
49 (clause 3)	'The Prime Minister may, after deliberation by the Council of Ministers, pledge the government's responsibility on the vote of a text. The text shall be considered as adopted unless a motion of censure is carried'	This clause forces deputies to support a particular bill, or else to bring down the government. It has mainly been used to prop up minority governments, and those with small majorities

De Gaulle used this article to justify the extension of presidential authority after 1958. There was a strong element of personal rule during the early formative years of the Fifth Republic. De Gaulle envisaged his action as that of a positive arbiter, deciding what was in the best interests of France.

In addition to traditional presidential powers under previous French republics, the President was invested with a series of new powers whose application did not require a prime ministerial counter-signature (Wright, in Hayward, 1993). The most important of these were:

- The right to dissolve the National Assembly, after consultation with the premier (Article 12).

- The right to call a referendum on issues not involving constitutional change (Article 11), or as the final stage of a constitutional amendment (Article 89).

- The right to nominate (but not to dismiss) the Prime Minister (Article 8). Article 8 also stipulates that the President nominates and dismisses ministers 'on the proposal of the premier'.

- The right, under Article 16, to declare a state of emergency should circumstances require it. These circumstances were to be determined by the President alone.
- The right to address written messages to the two Houses of the French parliament (Article 18).

All other presidential powers require a prime ministerial counter-signature, which, in terms of constitutional theory, curtails their autonomous manipulation by the President. The constitution definitely strengthened the role of the President, who had occupied a relatively minor position in the Third and Fourth Republics. On a strict reading of the constitution, however, power was vested in the hands of the Prime Minister and government, rather than the President. Two articles of the 1958 Constitution clearly stipulated that the Prime Minister, although named by the President, was the head of the executive in his or her own right:

- Article 20 asserts that 'the Government shall determine and conduct the policy of the nation' and that 'it shall be responsible to parliament'.
- Article 21 stipulates that 'the Prime Minister shall direct the operation of the Government'.

The Fifth Republic thus appeared to have an executive with two heads, the President and the Prime Minister. This potential conflict situation probably required either the President or the Prime Minister to assume a leading role. Developments after 1958 illustrated that de Gaulle conceived of the presidency as the ultimate source of legitimacy within the political system. The presidential interpretation of the Fifth Republic prevailed, with somewhat varying rhythms and emphases, until the onset of cohabitation in 1986. We now consider in some detail the office of the presidency.

4.4 The French presidency

During the period from 1958–86, there was little doubt that the presidency was the pinnacle of legitimacy giving coherence to the political system of the Fifth Republic. The strength of the French presidency lay in its combination of the monarchical trappings of power associated with the Head of State, with the real executive authority conferred by direct election, by a strengthened constitutional position, and by the political precedent established by de Gaulle from 1958–69. After an initial period of uncertainty and confusion, de Gaulle was able to impose his model of a strong presidency upon an initially hostile political class. This was possible for several reasons:

- The pressures created by the Algerian war and the lack of a serious alternative to his stewardship strengthened de Gaulle's position. The key national elites might have regarded de Gaulle with suspicion, but their imagined alternatives were far worse: civil war, military dictatorship, or political anarchy.

- In the absence of a clear-cut parliamentary majority from 1958–62, de Gaulle relied on a repeated use of referendums to consolidate his political authority: electors were invited to support de Gaulle, or hasten a return to chaos. The plebiscitary element in these early referendums was manifest.

- The sacking of premier Michel Debré in April 1962, followed by the October 1962 referendum establishing direct election of the President, consolidated a *de facto* evolution in favour of the President within the French executive.

- The emergence of the majoritarian presidential coalition in November 1962 completed the process of presidential pre-eminence.

The existence of disciplined, pro-presidential coalitions controlling the National Assembly during the period from 1962–86 was in stark contrast with the chaos of the Fourth Republic, where governments were short-lived and multifarious. Presidential power was built upon propitious political circumstances, the balance of political forces, and the legacy of personal power moulded by de Gaulle and bequeathed to his successors. These political factors were of greater importance than any undisputed constitutional provisions. Political circumstances enabled de Gaulle to interpret the ambiguities in the 1958 Constitution to his own advantage. Ever since de Gaulle's famous press conference of 1964, the 'principle of presidential initiative' (a phrase coined by Jean Charlot) has aptly described the underlying legitimacy of the Fifth Republic's political system, with the exception of the periods of 'cohabitation'. Presidents have not only defined the broad parameters of governmental action; they have also reserved the right to intervene in any policy sphere. Except during periods of 'cohabitation', policy arbitration on exceptionally divisive issues has occurred at the Elysée. When conflicts have arisen between Presidents and their Prime Ministers, the former's views have usually prevailed. The unpredictability of presidential interventions infuriated unsuspecting ministers as much under Chirac, as they had under Mitterrand, Giscard d'Estaing, Pompidou and de Gaulle.

It should not be assumed that all Presidents have been equally interventionist, nor that Presidents have been consistently interventionist. Presidential practice has varied with each incumbent, as well as at different stages of each presidency. French Presidents have been able to choose the scope and nature of their intervention in domestic politics. Each President has had a rather different appreciation of what this entails. All have paid a special attention to spheres of action, such as culture and architecture, which are likely to enhance their personal standing with posterity. Each President has also claimed primary, if not exclusive, responsibility in matters of foreign policy, defence and European affairs. Presidents are not the only actors in determining French policy in these arenas, but they are the most important. Under Giscard d'Estaing and Mitterrand, presidential involvement in domestic political priorities was stronger at the early stages of the presidential mandate. The primary mission of the Chirac (1974–6) and Mauroy (1981–4) governments was to transform the President's electoral programme into legislation; prime ministerial activity was supervised closely by the President.

Evaluating Chirac's presidency is made difficult by the five-year 'cohabitation' from 1997 to 2002, when the Socialist premier Jospin and the plural left government exercised most powers. Insofar as we can make generalisations across his presidency, President Chirac favoured the classic presidential domain of intervention – foreign policy, defence, European affairs – whether under cohabitation or not. Chirac's intervention in domestic policy has been random, even trivial. From 1995–7 and since 2002 President Chirac has paid close attention to relatively minor appointments, but allowed his Prime Ministers to occupy the domestic limelight. Chirac has generally stood aloof from the details of domestic policies, publicly affirming that while the President presides, governments should govern. This semi-detached attitude was best illustrated by the President's response to the mass strikes that followed premier Juppé's proposed social security reform in November–December 1995. Chirac intervened publicly only once during this period – and this on a matter relating to foreign policy! More recently, Chirac was careful to remain above domestic politics in 2003, leaving Prime Minister Raffarin to pilot difficult reforms in the area of pensions and social security, while the President occupied the international limelight during the Iraq war.

This division of labour (high politics for the President; the management of contentious policy dossiers by the Prime Minister or ministers) recalled more than any other the relationship maintained between De Gaulle and his Prime Ministers. The classic role of the French Prime Minister is to act as a *fusible*, a fall guy for the President. The Chirac-Juppé relationship provided a good example. After one year in office, premier Juppé's political credit appeared virtually exhausted by unpopular, but essential reforms of the social security system, and by austerity measures taken to prepare France to meet the convergence criteria for participation in the single European currency. Though Prime Minister Raffarin fared rather better in 2002–3, the nature of the relationship was similar, with the Prime Minister shouldering the burden of implementing unpopular reforms in the fields of pensions or social security, while effacing himself behind the President and his Foreign Minister (de Villepin) in foreign affairs.

French Presidents are assisted by their own presidential office, composed of three main components: the *cabinet*, the *secrétariat général* and the *chef d'état major particulier*. Under Mitterrand, the press office and the President's special adviser also became important actors. The *cabinet* is involved in controlling the President's diary and managing his mail. The General Secretariat of the Elysée is the body that engages in strategic policy reflection and whose advisers, where appropriate, represent the President in the inter-governmental arbitration committees chaired by the Prime Minister. Presidential policy advisers typically each oversee several broad areas of presidential interest. Their role is not to implement government policy directly, but to ensure that the presidential interest is paramount, especially at the decision-making phase of the policy cycle. All in all, French Presidents are assisted by thirty to forty civilian and five to ten military advisers, a modest infrastructure by comparison with that of the tentacular American presidency. Though they do not usually manage specific items of government policy, the role of advisers has been more affirmative at certain stages than at others (see Elgie, 2003; Stevens, 2003 for good accounts). This light presidential infrastructure has to be set in the context of the extensive bureaucratic machine officially coordinated by the French Prime Minister, as well as the administrative capacity at the disposal of the larger government departments (Seurin, 1986). A specific role within the presidential office is performed by the *chef d'état major particulier*. This military cell advises the President on aspects of foreign policy, defence and security. The unit is highly sensitive and each president has endeavoured to ensure total loyalty on behalf of the armed forces.

The role of the staff varies somewhat with presidential incumbent. Staff members are usually young civil servants, seconded to work in the presidential staff from their ministries. Under Mitterrand, the evolution of presidential staff followed the general direction of the presidency: early *compagnons des routes* (political allies from various stages of Mitterrand's career) were later replaced by career civil servants. In a novel departure, President Chirac accepted several close confidants of premier Juppé into his presidential office. The General Secretary of the Elysée staff from 1995–2002, Dominique de Villepin, had previously headed Juppé's office in the Foreign Affairs ministry from 1993–5. In 2002, de Villepin made the transition from adviser to full minister when he was named as Foreign Affairs Minister in the Raffarin government. This trajectory – from civil servant to adviser to full-time politician – is not unusual in Fifth Republic France.

The Elysée is not the Whitehouse. It is a relatively light infrastructure. Its proximity to the centres of decision-making, however, inevitably fuels accusations of the office exercising power without responsibility. There have been occasions when presidential advisers have appeared to exercise a powerful role. Under Pompidou, for instance, the influence exercised by Marie-France Garaud and Pierre Juillet received much critical attention. Under Mitterrand, more recently, the involvement of presidential advisers in various major scandals (notably concerning illegal phone tapping, and insider-dealing on the Paris stock exchange) revived accusations of power without responsibility. Under Chirac, the General Secretary de Villepin was credited with much influence over presidential decision-making, including in the sensitive decision to dissolve the National Assembly in 1997 (Colombani, 1999). The poor state of relations between M. de Villepin and M. Schrameck, the head of premier Jospin's office, was an open secret acknowledged by the latter in 2001 (Schrameck, 2001).

Presidents have controlled key political and bureaucratic nominations. They have exercised their constitutional duty (Article 8) to nominate the Prime Minister. The first four Presidents also exceeded their constitutional brief and insisted upon their right to dismiss incumbent Prime Ministers. The model of presidential dismissal established by de Gaulle with Debré in April 1962 was repeated on numerous subsequent occasions, most notably with Pompidou in 1968, Chaban-Delmas in 1972, Rocard in 1991, and Cresson in 1992. Presidents have also intervened closely in the nomination of individual ministers. Some key ministers have in the past been encouraged to bypass the formal governmental hierarchy headed by the Prime Minister, and deal directly with the President. Such a pattern occurred at various stages of Mitterrand's presidency, notably with respect to the Finance Minister Bérégovoy. Presidential patronage traditionally extended beyond the *de facto* selection and dismissal of the political elite, to include top civil servants, the heads of nationalised industries and banks, prominent positions within the media, rectors, prefects, judges, ambassadors and appointments to a myriad of governmental agencies. One side effect of state retrenchment has been to reduce the scope for political appointments, especially in the economic and financial sphere. As a rule, the model for political appointments has been one of bargaining and compromise between President and Prime Minister, with the former exerting a greater degree of influence than the latter. The pattern of appointments is reversed during periods of cohabitation. During the first period of 'cohabitation' (1986–8), Mitterrand reserved a right of oversight over certain defence appointments, but elsewhere deferred to the wishes of the Chirac government. The president's oversight over nominations was even less effective during the second and third 'cohabitations'.

All Presidents have used referendums to appeal directly to the French people. The 1958 Constitution provides for various scenarios when referendums can be used. During the early period of regime consolidation (1958–62), General de Gaulle repeatedly used referendums to impose his authority on parliament, the political parties and the nation. The referendum was a device to impose de Gaulle's *de facto* executive authority to fill what might otherwise have proved a power vacuum. De Gaulle valued the referendum, insofar as it initiated a personal relationship between the providential ruler and the nation, by-passing the intermediaries of party, parliament and pressure groups. De Gaulle's success in these early referendums established his presidential ascendancy more solidly than in the ambiguous Constitution of 1958, and helped to legitimise and stabilise the new regime. The October 1962 referendum on direct election of the president was of crucial importance, for it helped to provide the necessary peacetime legitimacy for the presidentialisation of the regime that had occurred during the Algerian emergency. This fundamental change was highly controversial, however. Not only was de Gaulle's manner of calling the referendum unconstitutional, but this final result was approved by less than a majority of the overall electorate (62 per cent of voters, 46 per cent of registered voters). De Gaulle finally quit in April 1969 after the electorate refused to support his proposed constitutional reform of the Senate and the regions. The failure of the General's political blackmail provided a salutary lesson to his successors.

Although Pompidou, Mitterrand and Chirac all held referendums, they were careful not to hedge their future survival on the results of these contests. The diminishing use of the referendum also reflected its limited efficacy as a weapon of presidential control. In 1972, President Pompidou's referendum on the accession of the UK, Ireland, Denmark and Norway to the EEC was widely portrayed as a political manoeuvre designed to restore the President's falling fortunes: the high level of abstention (46 per cent) ruined the presidential effect. The referendum organised by Mitterrand on the New Caledonia agreements of 1988 was far less controversial. But it singularly failed to mobilise French voters to participate; on this occasion abstentions reached 65 per cent. In September 1992, President Mitterrand's referendum on the ratification of the Maastricht Treaty so nearly backfired that he was unable to claim the hoped for political credit. The margin of approval (51 per cent/49 per cent) was far too close. The only other national referendum – that of September 2000 on reducing the presidential term-in-office to five years – was organised in the context of 'cohabitation' with the joint agreement of President Chirac and Prime Minister Jospin. Though the proposal was easily passed (73.2 per cent), turnout was only just over 30 per cent. The referendum has revealed itself to be a double-edged political tool, an unreliable means of manufacturing artificial political consensus.

The case of the referendum underlines that the power of any President depends ultimately upon political circumstances, the results of elections and the party system. The most favourable political circumstances for a President are those where a presidential election or a successful referendum is followed shortly after by a parliamentary contest, as in 1962, 1981, 1988 and 2002. Once re-elected in April 2002, President Chirac called upon the French people to give him 'a clear and coherent majority' in the parliamentary elections of June 2002. Previous Presidents de Gaulle, Giscard d'Estaing and Mitterrand had acted similarly in comparable circumstances. Chirac's call was answered by the election of a majority of deputies for the UMP, at the time an umbrella organisation for the various parties supporting the President. The existence of a majority elected to support the President is the most fundamental underpinning of the French version of presidential power. The reduction of the presidential term-in-office to five years in 2000, and the provision that parliamentary elections will normally follow presidential contests were both intended to consolidate the position of the presidency as the key political institution. Though there is no guarantee that parliamentary elections will always deliver a majority for the President, coinciding five-year terms will probably make incidences of 'cohabitation' rarer than in recent years. The converging of the presidential and parliamentary majorities in the 2002 elections signalled a return to a pre-eminently presidential practice, not least because premier Raffarin embraced the traditional role of the subordinate Prime Minister.

The fundamental dynamic of the Fifth Republic is one of contingent semi-presidentialism. The 'principle of presidential initiative' depends for its effective functioning upon the complicity of other players, first and foremost the democratically elected National Assembly (itself a reflection of the party system). When Presidents lose the support of a compliant Assembly elected in their name, their power and authority are diminished. We now consider relations within the executive during cohabitation.

Presidents and Prime Ministers during periods of 'cohabitation'

The model of presidential pre-eminence outlined above depends upon a coincidence of presidential and parliamentary majorities. After a long period (1958–86) which commentators generally viewed as one of encroaching presidentialism, the election of a narrow centre-right RPR-UDF majority in 1986 inaugurated the first period of 'cohabitation', between the Socialist President Mitterrand, and the Gaullist premier Chirac (Cohendet, 1993). From being the potentially omnipotent and omnipresent chief executive, the French President was reduced to a rather more modest role as an arbitral observer. For once, the constitution was applied as written in 1958. The Prime Minister led a government responsible to the RPR-UDF parliamentary majority, rather than to the President. By nominating Chirac as Prime Minister in 1986, Mitterrand recognised that power had to be vested in the victors of the most recent decisive election. During the period from 1986–8, President Mitterrand withdrew from detailed policy-making in the arena of domestic politics, although he did make use of those weapons reserved for the President in the 1958 Constitution, notably by delaying certain pieces of legislation. Mitterrand insisted on preserving his constitutional prerogatives in matters of foreign policy and defence, and was by and large successful, in spite of a powerful push on behalf of premier Chirac. One expert concluded that presidential pre-eminence was retained in high diplomacy and defence policy, whereas the government held the upper hand in relation to African affairs, with European policy resulting from carefully prepared compromises between the two (Cohen, 1989).

A similar pattern reproduced itself in 1993, when the RPR-UDF coalition won a crushing victory at the expense of the incumbent Socialists. During the second cohabitation, Mitterrand no longer had either the energy, or the political prestige to intervene in domestic politics, but retained a measure of influence in European affairs, defence and foreign policy. From 1993–5, President Mitterrand and Premier Balladur spoke of foreign policy being 'a shared sector'. In his memoirs, Balladur admitted that he had been unable to resume French nuclear testing while Prime Minister because of the President's opposition. From 1997–2002, there was a third, five-year long 'cohabitation', which confirmed the basic rules of this form of institutional coexistence between the two heads of the French executive. More resolutely than during the previous two episodes, the Jospin government dominated the domestic agenda, with President Chirac powerless to prevent the implementation of policies with which he was in major disagreement (such as over Corsica [which he delayed for one week] or the 35-hour week). On the other hand, attempts by premier Jospin to venture openly into the realm of foreign policy were unsuccessful, as we saw above with the example of Palestine. In the realm of European policy-making, the shared responsibility between Chirac and Jospin produced an ambiguous and inconsistent French position during the negotiations leading to the Nice Treaty in December 2000.

Presidential styles

Each presidential incumbent has portrayed his office as being the supra-partisan embodiment of national unity. Upon election, the successful presidential candidate claims to be the President of all the French, though each President is initially a representative of a party, a coalition, or a set of interests. This monarchical style of presidential political discourse is essential, in order to facilitate the transition from being a presidential candidate to being President. Only Jacques Chirac, in the exceptional circumstances in 2002, could claim to be President of (nearly all) the French.

The two prevailing images of the French President are as a supra-partisan republican monarch, and as an interventionist and partisan political leader. The ability to combine the monarchical and partisan functions of the presidency has become a test of political strength for French Presidents. A partisan identity is an indispensable precondition for building an electoral coalition to fight a presidential election, and for establishing a presidential party, or pro-presidential coalition to provide disciplined support for presidentially inspired policies. As any other political leader, a President needs a partisan base of support, notably a supportive parliamentary majority. The President is the key executive leader, involved in the overall conception of government policy and selection of governmental personnel. The monarchical posture, on the other hand, is essential for posing as a head of state embodying national unity, rather than as any run-of-the-mill Prime Minister. The diplomatic precedence accorded to the French President as head of state in international summit meetings should not be underestimated in its domestic political importance.

The role model of presidential political leadership was that provided by de Gaulle, whose lofty presidential style was imitated to a greater or lesser extent by his four successors. A strong sense of national identity underpinned President de Gaulle's presidential practice. The General's concern with restoring French diplomatic and political prestige coloured his practice as President: his priority areas of interest lay in foreign policy, European affairs and defence. De Gaulle's primary preoccupation with restoring France's greatness also had clear implications for the organisation of its domestic political system. The Republic must be a form of government sufficiently strong to enhance France's international prestige, and to allow France to re-enter the group of 'first-rank' nations. By consolidating the presidency first as a form of heroic, then as a type of institutionalised strong leadership, de Gaulle inaugurated a new style of political leadership that had a profound impact on the subsequent evolution of the Fifth Republic. When performing certain key rituals (for instance, official televised addresses to the Nation) associated with the presidential office, each subsequent President has, to a greater or lesser degree, consciously imitated de Gaulle. The strong personal element of legitimacy underpinning de Gaulle's leadership allowed the first President to present himself as the embodiment of national unity more effectively than any of his successors. De Gaulle came closest to disguising the partisan function behind his public display of monarchical aloofness.

None of de Gaulle's successors were able to boast a personal legitimacy in the least comparable to that of the General. Whatever his qualities, the next President Pompidou lacked de Gaulle's historic stature and relied upon far tighter control over the governing Gaullist party to provide a personal source of legitimacy. The different backgrounds and political upbringings of the first two Presidents of the Fifth Republic were reflected in their political styles and preoccupations. As a strong patriot and former military commander, de Gaulle was primarily interested in foreign policy. While unable to ignore foreign policy issues (and while actively engaged in French European policy), President Pompidou's real interests lay elsewhere (Roussel, 1984; Muron, 1994). The second President entered politics after a successful business career and one of his principal preoccupations as President was in the sphere of industrial policy, over which he imposed a large measure of presidential control.

The third President, Giscard d'Estaing, possessed neither a strong majoritarian party support, nor a political personality of historic proportions. The third President compensated for his political weakness with an attempt to move towards a more overt presidential interpretation of the regime (see Chapter 2). Giscard d'Estaing's presidentialist aspirations were based on fragile foundations. The increasingly regal image dispelled by Giscard d'Estaing contrasted with his growing political isolation after 1976. Herein lay another facet of the French presidency. The republican monarch aspect of the presidency can have negative as well as positive dimensions. In the case of Giscard d'Estaing, the dissemination of the image of the unresponsive, secretive and arrogant monarch contributed to the image of decadence, scandal and impetuosity that surrounded the end of his presidency. An analogous conclusion was drawn by many commentators in relation to the final years of Mitterrand's presidency.

President Mitterrand's style varied according to events, opportunities, personal evolution and political strength. Mitterrand's presidential practice demonstrated the apparent paradoxes and contradictions imposed on any French President. Arriving in office as the most openly partisan President of the Fifth Republic, for instance, Mitterrand was re-elected in 1988 as the embodiment of supra-partisan consensus. By 1993, the Socialist president had been deserted by his formerly stalwart lieutenants in the Socialist Party (Cole, 1994). By 1995, Mitterrand was an isolated, lonely figure: it was difficult to recall the highly interventionist President of the early Mauroy premiership (1981–2). Both Mitterrands were accurate reflections of the presidential functon and style at a given point in time. The longevity of Mitterrand's rule as President gave occasion for several legitimate portrayals of his presidential style and practice, more so than for any other President.

Jacques Chirac adopted a far more direct and popular presidential style than that of his predecessor. Even though opinion polls showed a majority being dissatisfied with government policy as early as November 1995, President Chirac was personally appreciated as being 'sympathetic' and 'close to the people'. Chirac's popular touch lessened the impact of ongoing corruption investigations throughout his first presidential term. Chirac's repeated visits to the French provinces surprised certain observers, as did his practice of public walkabouts. At the same time, while early pronouncements revealed inexperience (especially in foreign policy), Chirac also demonstrated an ability to internalise the gravitas of the presidential function, notably with his funeral oration for former President Mitterrand in January 1996. During his second term-in-office, Chirac cultivated a lofty, Gaullien, supra-partisan style, reflecting the conditions of his re-election in 2002. Being President is a learning process, with individual skill gradually increasing over time, and with a particular political style emerging as much as a result of trial and error, as of conscious design.

Each presidential incumbent has left his distinctive mark upon the presidency. All French Presidents have been subjected to a tendency for diminishing political returns as their presidencies have progressed; this suggests a natural threshold (variable for each incumbent, but not surpassing ten years) beyond which the effectiveness of presidential political leadership is seriously impaired.

4.5	Prime ministerial political leadership

Whether under 'cohabitation' or not, the hybrid nature of the French executive is very much in evidence. The obvious alternative model of national political leadership to the presidency is that offered by the Prime Minister. We will now consider the evolving role of the French Prime Minister. Of course, the relationship between President and Prime Minister does not encompass the totality of relationships within the French executive. Following from the insights of core executive theory (Hayward and Wright, 2002), we can identify various types of actor within the French executive. Apart from Presidents, Prime Ministers and their advisers, these would include ministers (notably the Finance and Interior Ministers), differing grades and types of civil servants (spread across multiple *directions* and *corps*), members of ministerial cabinets, unofficial advisers. In a comprehensive study of the community of central government policy-makers, attention would be drawn not only to various types of actor, but also to their differing sources of legitimacy and expertise (for instance political, bureaucratic, or professional). Processes of governance do not limit themselves to an isolated space (central government) but are increasingly multi-layered and interdependent in character. A full overview of patterns of governance lies beyond the scope of this chapter, but this diversity should be kept in mind when considering French political leadership.

Relations between Presidents and Prime Ministers have been the subject of many rather simplistic assessments, which betray a complex reality. No single model can account for the complexity of the President-Prime Minister relationship, which is simultaneously conflictual and cooperative, routine and non-static. There is an institutionalised tension between the Elysée (the President's official residence) and Matignon (that of the Prime Minister). As the chief presidential representative, the Prime Minister is expected to defend presidential policy priorities and translate them into legislation. As a transmission belt for the President, the premier has been expected to assume responsibility for unpopular policies. But he is also anxious to assert his political identity, not least because the premiership has occasionally been a pedestal for a later bid for the presidency itself. The attempt to reconcile the conflicting roles of faithful presidential lieutenant and policy initiator has proved too difficult for several ambitious premiers.

The chief roles performed by a French Prime Minister are those of political leader, of government manager, and of presidential lieutenant. As a political leader, the Prime Minister is responsible for guiding the government's policy programme through Parliament, and smoothing relations with the parliamentary majority. This task is often arduous; Barre or Rocard had to rely on restrictive constitutional mechanisms to ensure their survival. Each Prime Minister suffers the indignation of quasi-permanent media speculation on his personal relationship with the President, and on the identity of his likely successor. As a governmental manager, the Prime Minister possesses powerful resources, but is aware that presidential support is required for maximum impact. Unlike in most parliamentary systems, it is rare for the premier to head the main political

Table 4.2 Prime Ministers in the Fifth Republic

Prime Minister	Office	Party
Debré	1959–62	Gaullist
Pompidou	1962–8	Gaullist
Couve de Murville	1968–9	Gaullist
Chaban-Delmas	1969–72	Gaullist
Messmer	1972–4	Gaullist
Chirac	1974–6	Gaullist
Barre	1976–81	UDF
Mauroy	1981–4	PS
Fabius	1984–6	PS
Chirac	1986–8	RPR
Rocard	1988–91	PS
Cresson	1991–2	PS
Bérégovoy	1992–3	PS
Juppé	1995–7	RPR
Jospin	1997–02	PS
Raffarin	2002–	UMP

party, thus to enjoy the legitimacy of popular election. As a presidential lieu-tenant, the Prime Minister is conscious that his legitimacy stems primarily from the fact that he is the President's appointee.

Being the President's man (or woman) is a mixed blessing, as two of Chirac's three Prime Ministers discovered. The case of Alain Juppé illustrates well the limited room for manoeuvre of the French Prime Minister. Named as premier after Chirac's election as President in May 1995, Juppé only partially controlled the nomination of his own government. The Prime Minister had to respect a delicate dosage between RPR and pro-Chirac UDF ministers, as well as fulfilling Chirac's campaign promises in relation to female representation (twelve ministers out of forty-two), and the rejuvenation of political personnel. As a result, Juppé led an overmanned and inexperienced government team, whose indiscipline and amateurism contributed towards record unpopularity ratings for both President and Prime Minister after only five months in office. The nomination of Jean-Pierre Raffarin as premier in April 2002 was worthy on at least three counts. It was the first time since Raymond Barre (1976–81) that a Prime Minister had been selected from outside the ranks of the Socialist or Gaullist parties, the President acknowledging the very broad basis of his second round majority. It was also the first time that the head of one of France's regional councils (Poitou-Charentes) had been selected as premier, presaging closer attention to the concerns of provincial France ('La France d'en bas'). Most significantly, however, Chirac exercised a very close control over the composi-tion of the Raffarin government, with most appointments either suggested or directly imposed by the President. Most of the key positions in the government were held by Chirac loyalists, with Raffarin holding out for a small number of symbolic appointments such as Luc Ferry, the Education Minister.

As a political leader, the Prime Minister must navigate the horns of a dilemma. A successful Prime Minister is likely to arouse presidential jealousy, inviting dismissal, or at least an effort to claim presidential credit for successful prime ministerial policies. This was the case notably for Pompidou under de Gaulle (1962–8) and Rocard under Mitterrand (1988–91). A Prime Minister who fails to protect the President from unpopularity – or who contributes to executive unpopularity through inept management – is likely to suffer even greater indignity. Edith Cresson, Prime Minister for barely eleven months, was exemplary in this respect. Premier Juppé's rapid descent in popularity from May–November 1995 demonstrated the existential problems faced by French Prime Ministers. As Prime Minister, Juppé was expected to manage the contradictions of Chirac's own presidential campaign, to implement policies with which he was in partial disagreement (notably over Europe) and to take the blame if things went wrong. A similar pattern reasserted itself in 2002. While Raffarin was able to ensure that decentralisation would be the flagship reform of the new government, most laws passed and regulations enacted during the first twelve months related to commitments made during Chirac's 2002 campaign. The political saliency of insecurity and immigration, in particular, was acknowledged by the passing of tough new laws in these areas, piloted by Interior Minister Nicolas Sarkozy.

During the periods of presidential ascendancy (especially from 1958–86) French Prime Ministers suffer from several accumulated disadvantages which limit their capacity to exercise the *political* role that their status as head of government requires. These include their insecurity of tenure; presidential control over the composition of the government; the special relationship maintained by individual ministers with the President; the sporadic nature of presidential interventions; presidentially-inspired policy-agendas; the inputs of the presidential party, and rivalry with the President in relation to public opinion. The constraints on the freedom of manoeuvre of French Presidents (such as public opinion, the economic and social environment, or the foreign policy climate) apply all the more forcefully to Prime Ministers on account of their insecure position and their dependency on the President. As illustrated above, the success of the Prime Minister as a policy-maker does not ensure his political longevity. Arguably the three most successful policy-makers (Pompidou, 1962–8; Chaban-Delmas, 1969–72; Rocard, 1988–91) were negatively rewarded for their services with dismissal by a resentful President. Their political dependency does not, however, deprive French Prime Ministers of all substantive leadership functions. From the inception of the Fifth Republic, various key functions have (with greater or lesser efficiency) been performed by the Prime Minister.

The Prime Minister is usually more involved than the President with the coordination and formulation of detailed government policy and the arbitration of inter-governmental disputes. In particular, the premier (along with the Finance Minister) is in control of arbitrating between spending departments in the annual budget negotiations. In broad areas of domestic policy, most French Presidents have refrained from consistent intervention, except during periods of crisis, or immediately after coming to office. Economic and social policy typically falls into this category. Even in this mainly 'non-presidential' sector, however, each President periodically defines broad directions that governments are invited to follow, and occasionally intervenes directly. Set-piece occasions, such as the annual 14 July interview or the New Year address, allow the President publicly to set the guidelines for government policy.

As Head of Government in the 1958 Constitution, the Prime Minister is vested with a coordinating role. Most government agencies with a clearly inter-ministerial function are placed under the official tutelage of the Prime Minister's office. The constitutional role of the French Prime Minister in coordinating government policy is undermined by several cross-cutting pressures. The appeal against the Prime Minister to the President by disgruntled ministers provides one example; the powerful position occupied by the Finance or Interior Ministers is another. Policy initiatives undertaken by ambitious premiers have frequently run up against the opposition of the Finance ministry in particular. The example of Mme Cresson was indicative in this respect. France's first female premier was deprived of the means of effectively coordinating government policy, since President Mitterrand and Finance Minister Bérégovoy formed an insuperable coalition to prevent her interventionist industrial ideas from being put into practice.

The Prime Minister possesses far greater administrative resources than the President to assist in the task of policy coordination and formulation. The President's Elysée staff is relatively small in comparison with the expertise available to the Prime Minister. The Prime Minister is in a stronger day-to-day position in relation to the permanent bureaucracy than the President. As the official head of government, he controls the services responsible for evaluating and monitoring government policy (notably the General Secretariat of the Government), and maintains close relations with key politicians and bureaucrats within the ministries. The General Secretariat is composed of career civil servants, who attempt to minimise bureaucratic rivalries, and to coordinate government policy, before and after decisions are ratified by the Council of Ministers (Py, 1985; Elgie, 2003). As its name implies, the General Secretariat assists the Prime Minister in the preparation of the government's work. It prepares meetings of the Council of Ministers, and of interministerial committees, and – crucially – writes up the minutes of these meetings.

The General Secretariat is formally attached to the Prime Minister, as are most other interministerial structures, whose role is to coordinate between various government departments. In theory, it is above political conflicts, being headed by a senior civil servant. In practice, as with its British homologue the Cabinet Office, the General Secretariat is responsible to the incumbent government, to the extent that incoming governments have replaced the head of the General Secretariat with one of their own. The General Secretary is a key politico-administrative actor, who derives his influence from formal control over the government machine and the information that this provides. The close contacts maintained between the General Secretary, and the key political decision makers (the Prime Minister, but also the President) enhance the influence of the General Secretariat.

The Prime Minister is assisted by a powerful private office (*cabinet*), responsible for intervening on his behalf in the work of other government departments and in assisting the head of government in the process of interministerial arbitration and policy formulation. As with ministerial *cabinets*, each *cabinet* performs rather different functions according to the personality of the Prime Minister, and the individuals involved. Certain prime ministerial offices have enjoyed a reputation as fearsome defenders of a Prime Ministers' political and policy interests (Huchon, 1993; Schrameck, 2001). The staff available to the premier (between fifty and a hundred advisers in his office) facilitates a detailed oversight of prime ministerial initiatives. The information provided by these advisers is one of the premier's most valuable resources. Even outside of periods of 'cohabitation', the Prime Minister disposes of significant sources of patronage, to some extent in competition with those of the President. Nominations falling within the prime ministerial sphere have included appointments to the position of Legion of Honour, to the Court of Accounts, and to the Council of State, and the Prime Minister will usually be consulted over all senior bureaucratic appointments.

As with the President's Elysée staff, the Prime Minister's office has no official legal existence, leaving the premier free to determine its missions. As a rule, his advisers mirror the principal spheres of government activity, with a particular interest in matters of current and forthcoming legislation. Most members of the prime ministerial office are young civil servants on secondment from their own departments. Some are always close political allies of the individual Prime Minister concerned, which can also complicate relations between President and Prime Minister. This system also produces tensions between permanent civil servants working in the government departments and those serving the President or Premier.

The Prime Minister performs an important role in arbitrating interministerial conflicts. Such conflicts are a routine feature of government activity, few policies lying exclusively within the sphere of one ministry. When conflict arises, arbitration between conflicting demands is necessary, in the interests of the coordination of government policy. Arbitration occurs both in a formal and an informal sense. The bulk of formal arbitration takes place in meetings chaired by the Prime Minister, or one of his representatives. Although the President defines the general parameters of policy and can intervene at random, the Prime Minister usually performs a more important role than the President in coordinating specific governmental policies. Alongside these formal mechanisms, many intergovernmental conflicts are solved in an informal manner: by the interministerial telephone; by *ad hoc* meetings of all sorts, by corridor discussions and around the dining table, a privileged instance for the resolution of conflicts in the French case. Only occasionally are disputes resolved in the full Council of Ministers, which meets weekly under the chairmanship of the President of the Republic.

4.6 Concluding remarks: what type of political system is the Fifth Republic?

Constitutions are drawn up at specific moments in history. Almost inevitably, they reflect social conditions prevailing at particular points in a nation's history. The American constitution, for instance, refers to a social and economic system that has been largely superseded. One measure of the success of a constitution lies in its adaptability to changing circumstances. By this measurement, the American written constitution, and the British unwritten constitution have both fared relatively efficiently. The sanctity of the American constitution has had no equivalent in French history. In keeping with tradition, the 1958 Constitution was partially shaped by the conditions surrounding its elaboration. The 1958 Constitution refers, for example, to the French Community as a political union linking metropolitan France and her overseas colonies, although the decolonisation of French African states from 1958–62 meant that this institution was stillborn.

The political system created by the constitution of the Fifth Republic was a constitutional hybrid, containing recognisable elements of a presidential system, as well as those commonly associated with a parliamentary model. The constitution-makers specifically rejected a presidential system along the lines of the American model, but there was a marked evolution away from the (theoretical) parliamentary omnipotence that had characterised the Third and Fourth Republics. Probably the most significant feature of the Constitution was to strengthen the executive branch of government, by severely curtailing the rights of parliament, to such an extent that practices of executive manipulation became commonplace.

In order to gauge the confused reality of the constitutional system established in 1958, it is useful to portray it in a comparative perspective. The French Fifth Republic, *as established by the 1958 Constitution*, lies somewhere between the two liberal democratic poles of the American presidential system, and the British parliamentary model. The kinship with the American system is obvious, though limited. The most obvious similarity between the two systems relates to the irresponsibility and irremovability of both Presidents. Neither the American, nor the French Presidents can be ousted by a rebellious cabal in parliament, in stark contrast with the French premier during the Fourth Republic, or the Italian Prime Minister today. The differences between the constitutional positions of the two Presidents, however, are more significant than their similarities. Whereas the French system introduces a strict system of direct election, the US system is based on an electoral college, where the leading candidate takes the totality of college votes in each state. The French President's power of dissolution accords the head of state a formidable power of leverage over the elected Assembly, in a manner quite alien to the American system of government, where the function of Congress is to check the exercise of executive power. The reference to the separation of powers in the French constitution bears little relationship to the spirit of the American constitution. In the French instance, the 'separation of powers' meant that certain policy spheres were to be removed from the competence of parliament. In the spirit of the American constitution, on the other hand, the 'separation of powers' indicates the possibility for each branch of government to check and balance each other, thereby ensuring a system of limited and divided government.

The prospect offered by the 1958 Constitution of a direct relationship between the President and the nation is the antithesis of the interest intermediation and bargaining model underpinning the American federalist constitution. The referendum in particular stands out as a powerful presidential weapon even on a strict reading of the 1958 Constitution. The American President's constitutional status as the chief executive, combining the functions of head of state and head of government, does not apply to the French President. On a strict reading the 1958 Constitution clearly vests executive authority with the Prime Minister.

The kinship with the British system of government is more apparent than with the American. The constitution provides for a government responsible to parliament, a government which, as an ultimate sanction, can be revoked by parliament. Indeed, the restrictive clauses of the 1958 Constitution were intended artificially to manufacture political stability, by allowing even minority governments to survive; the modelling on the British system was obvious (Frears and Morris, 1992).

The French system forms part of the small family of semi-presidential regimes, where 'a popularly elected fixed-term president exists alongside a Prime Minister and cabinet who are responsible to parliament' (Elgie, 1999: 13). The logic of this hybrid regime is majoritarian. It is designed to ensure that governments can govern, whether these governments are drawn from elected Assemblies supportive of the President or not. This majoritarian logic ought to produce stability. Since 1986, however, the political regime has been driven by conflicting pressures. 'Cohabitation' has proved that the political regime has the capacity to withstand systemic pressures that many had predicted would hasten its demise. Indeed, there is an argument that the hybrid nature of the regime allows the flexibility and adaptability required of modern political institutions. On the other hand, the fundamental dynamic is political: power resides with the victors (individual or coalition) of the most recent decisive election, presidential or parliamentary. There has also developed a tendency for incumbent governments to lose elections. Given this 'iron law of anti-incumbency', this has tended to mean that governments have once again become short-lived. Because incumbent governments invariably lose elections (on every occasion since 1978), 'cohabitation' has become an increasingly regular occurrence. The Fifth Republic's claim to have restored political stability has to be seriously challenged.

5 Checks and balances?

5.1 Introduction

One of the principal themes of Chapter 4 related to the strengthening of executive government in the Fifth Republic is what are the checks and balances on the executive in France? In Chapter 5, we begin by focusing upon the role performed by the French parliament, the specific angle being to highlight the weakness of parliamentary checks and balances against uncontrolled executive power within the Fifth Republic. We then consider the judicialisation of French politics, concentrating on the Constitutional Council, the Council of State and the role of the investigating magistrates. We conclude that legal, constitutional and supranational factors have provided some checks and balances against the uses and abuses of executive authority that were not initially envisaged in the 1958 Constitution.

A belief in parliamentary supremacy against arbitrary executive government guided republicans from the eighteenth century onwards. During the Third and Fourth Republics, deputies referred constantly to this parliamentary republican tradition to resist attempts to encroach upon their power. The particular devices used by parliament to shackle the executive fascinated observers such as Philip Williams (1964, 1969). Private members' bills were a favoured means of securing favours for constituents and pressure groups, so much so that individual deputies became hostages to entrenched interests, such as the notorious wine-growers. Powerful parliamentary committees performed a major role in determining the fate of government bills. The presidents of these committees were leading political players in their own right. It was not unknown for ministers to resign their portfolios in order to take charge of the ranking parliamentary committee, since committee chairmen were regarded as being more powerful than ministers. Parliament retained control over its own timetable, which, put simply, meant that a government had to barter with the party leaders to ensure that its own proposals were placed on the agenda. Some measures were especially blunt. According to the rule of 'interpellation', for instance, deputies could demand an explanation on any aspect of government policy at any time: this would be followed by a vote which, if it went against it, could bring down the government.

The rhetoric of parliamentary supremacy was accompanied by a lessening parliamentary influence over policy-making throughout the twentieth century.

The diminished centrality of parliament was in part structural, in France as elsewhere. Parliamentary sovereignty had to confront the growing role of the state in economic management, the post-war creation of the welfare state, the increasing technical complexity of policy-making, the input of well-organised interest groups and the emergence of new actors such as the European Union. Many of these developments were underway before the creation of the Fifth Republic in 1958. Faced with these pressures, added to their unwillingness to take responsibility for unpopular decisions, deputies delegated responsibility for policy-making to the executive, notably by allowing governments to issue 'decree-laws' to settle contentious and unpopular decisions. The appearance of parliamentary sovereignty was preserved, but the reality was one of progressive disengagement from detailed policy-making before 1958.

| 5.2 | The organisation of the French parliament in the Fifth Republic |

The French Parliament is composed of two chambers, the National Assembly and the Senate. The French Parliament meets for a minimum of 130 days per annum, in one continual session of nine months.

The National Assembly

The National Assembly presently consists of 577 deputies. This figure has varied throughout the Fifth Republic. Deputies are currently elected to represent single-member constituencies under the second-ballot system. All elections except one (1986) have been fought under this electoral system. To secure election on the first round, candidates require over 50 per cent of valid votes cast, and over 12.5 per cent of registered electors. Most constituencies require a second ballot: candidates having polled the support of over 10 per cent of the registered electorate on the first ballot are eligible to contest the run-off. The candidate with the most votes wins the second-ballot election. Unlike the presidential election, the parliamentary contest does not require that a candidate obtain an absolute majority of second round voters to secure election. With the rise of parties such as the *Front national* and the Greens, three- or four-cornered second-ballot contests have become more frequent.

The National Assembly is the popularly elected first chamber. Elections to the National Assembly take place at least once every five years, more frequently if the President exercises her right of dissolution. The National Assembly disposes of clear advantages over the Senate, in that it is vested with popular sovereignty. In disputes between the two Chambers, the National Assembly has the last word. The National Assembly is more important than the Senate in the process of passing legislation. Both government bills (*projets de loi*) and private members' bills (*propositions de loi*) can begin life either in the National Assembly or the Senate. After a first reading, bills are then sent to one of the six standing committees existing within both houses. Committees prepare reports on each

The French National Assembly: seat of France's lower chamber

bill, attempting to ameliorate proposed legislation by way of proposing amendments. These reports are eventually presented to the full house. Committee reports are either accepted by the Chamber concerned, or are sent back to committee, after which they are again presented at a later date. After completing their passage through the first house, bills are then sent to the second, where this procedure is repeated. In the event of the two houses failing to agree upon an identical text, the government has several available options at its disposal. It will usually establish a Mixed Parliamentary Committee with representatives of the National Assembly and the Senate with a view to arriving at an acceptable compromise. Should this body fail to agree on a text admissible by the government, the latter will invite the National Assembly to decide.

The Senate

The second Chamber is known as the Senate. It is currently composed of 321 senators, each serving for a nine-year term. Senatorial elections are held once every three years, to replace one-third of the Senate. The role of the second Chamber has been somewhat controversial throughout its existence. Due to its mode of indirect election, the Senate has traditionally over-represented small-town and rural France, at the expense of more dynamic urban areas. Senators are indirectly elected by electoral colleges based on the one hundred departments (metropolitan France only). Each department returns, according to its size, a minimum of two senators. The electoral college for each department is formed of the deputies, members of the departmental council, and delegates from each commune, depending upon its size. The changing balance of power within France's local councils is a useful guide to understanding the changeable composition of the Senate. Shifts in local election results are usually reflected shortly afterwards in the composition of the Senate. The 1958 Constitution clearly assigns the Senate as the subordinate parliamentary institution, but the second chamber retains certain delaying and ratifying powers. On occasion, the Senate can have an important political impact by becoming a focus of opposition to government policy: it performed this role *par excellence* during the resistance to the 1984 Education bill, for instance. The Senate has proved its political existence on several occasions, most notably through its resistance to General de Gaulle's attempts to reform it in 1969. The most powerful resource possessed by the Senate is that its consent is necessary before constitutional reform can be engaged under Article 89, giving the second Chamber an effective right of veto over constitutional reform. The Senators have used this power effectively, most recently in 2000, when the second Chamber blocked the constitutional reform project, supported by President Chirac and Prime Minister Jospin, to guarantee the independence of the investigating magistrates.

5.3	Parliament in the Fifth Republic: an emasculated legislature?

The 1958 Constitution explicitly set out to ensure that governments could govern without undue parliamentary interference, through strengthening executive control over parliamentary business, restricting parliamentary sovereignty and limiting opportunities for parliamentary oversight.

Executive control over parliamentary business

During the Third and Fourth Republics, control over the parliamentary timetable was vested in a parliamentary committee representing all the political parties present in Parliament. Governments had to make concessions to secure consideration for their proposals by Parliament. Executive control over the parliamentary timetable since 1958 has been of major importance in regulating the operation of parliament. It enables a government to pursue its business with minimal regard for parliamentary harassment. Government bills (*projets de loi*) account for some 80–90 per cent of the legislative timetable, with private members bills (*propositions de loi*) completing the shortfall. Government bills have priority over private members' bills. Private members bills can no longer propose to increase or reduce government expenditure, which limits their scope. This change was in response to the inflationary impact of such bills during the Fourth Republic.

The length of the parliamentary session is another aspect of executive control over the legislature. Whereas parliament used to sit for at least nine months during the Fourth Republic, from 1958–95 there were two statutory sittings of the National Assembly lasting for no more than a total of five and a half months. Parliament convened as of right in April and October. Special sessions could be convoked, but only on the initiative of the executive. The short duration of parliamentary sittings proved inconvenient for the executive itself, since it left scant time for the passage of necessary legislation. In July 1995, a constitutional reform reintroduced a single parliamentary sitting of nine months, from October to June. In order to speed up their legislative programme, governments have continued to invoke Article 45 of the 1958 Constitution, which allows them to declare a bill to be 'urgent'. In the case of urgency, the bill requires only one reading in each Chamber before a Mixed Parliamentary Committee (CMP) is convoked. This speeding up clause is rather similar to the guillotine in the United Kingdom.

Limitations on parliamentary sovereignty and motions of censure

A chief feature of the French republican tradition was that popular sovereignty should be vested in an elected Assembly. The Fifth Republic Constitution of 1958 directly challenged this principle. In Article 34, the Constitution draws a fine distinction between 'matters of law' requiring parliamentary approval and 'matters of regulation', for which the government alone has responsibility. Furthermore, those matters deemed to fall within the 'sphere of the law' are subdivided into two categories: those where detailed parliamentary legislation and scrutiny is needed, and those where Parliament was only required to approve general principles, allowing government departments to fill in the details of implementation. Those areas of policy in which Parliament decides upon general principles only include such key matters as defence, local government, education and social security.

Articles 37, 38 and 41 of the 1958 Constitution reinforce the pro-executive battery of weapons. Article 37 sets out that 'Matters other than those which fall within the domain of legislation shall have the character of regulations', with no parliamentary approval needed for these executive orders. Article 38 allows the government to request Parliament for authority to rule by decree even in those policy sectors falling within the normal legislative domain. This provision has allowed governments to speed up the process of policy-making when faced with an abnormally charged timetable. Juppé used it, for instance, in 1995 to push through sweeping reforms of the social security system. Article 41 forbids parliamentarians from proposing any bill on an issue falling within the 'executive sphere', as determined by Article 34. The provisions of Article 16 are the most draconian, in that they assign emergency powers to the President to rule by decree throughout the duration of an emergency that the President himself defines. The only safeguard is that Parliament sits 'as of right' throughout the emergency. On the one occasion that such an emergency was declared (in 1961), Parliament sat as usual, but President de Gaulle challenged its right to take any policy decisions.

The constitutional provisions relating to *motions of censure* are particularly severe. Along with Article 16 (the emergency powers clause), Article 49 must be a strong contender for being the most draconian in the 1958 Constitution. The fundamental defining feature of any parliamentary democracy is the right of the elected Assembly to overturn the incumbent government. This right is formally assured by Article 49, which provides in its second paragraph that a motion of censure may be tabled against the government on the signature of one-tenth of deputies. An absolute majority of the National Assembly is required to carry the motion of censure. Only votes in favour of a motion of censure are counted for the motion. Whatever their cause, abstentions and absentees are counted as being votes for the government. Only one successful motion of censure has been carried in the Fifth Republic: in 1962, against the government of Georges Pompidou.

The most sweeping aspect of Article 49 relates to its third paragraph, which stipulates 'the Prime Minister may, after deliberation by the Council of Ministers, pledge the government's responsibility on the vote of a text. The text shall be considered as adopted unless a motion of censure is voted under the conditions laid by the preceding paragraph (i.e. abstentions being counted as votes for the government)' This allows governments to stake their survival of the passage of a particular bill. Article 49, clause 3 (49.3) has been used for several distinctive reasons:

- To speed up parliamentary debate of contentious government bills. This occurred regularly during the 1981–6 Socialist government, despite the Socialists' past criticism of the undemocratic character of the Article. The use of Article 49.3 has also been used to stifle dissent from amongst the ranks of the government's own supporters. In 2003, premier Raffarin used Article 49.3 to push through reform of the electoral system for the 2004 regional elections, a measure contested by elements within the ruling UMP party.

- To preserve a minority government in office. An explicit consideration of the 1958 Constitution-makers, this use was endemic to the experience of the 1988–93 Socialist governments. With only a relative overall majority, the governments led by Rocard, Cresson and Bérégovoy were forced to apply Article 49.3 fairly systematically in order to ensure passage of vital government legislation.

- To coerce an unwilling coalition partner into line. This occurred most notably during the premiership of Raymond Barre. With Chirac's RPR in a situation of semi-opposition, Barre repeatedly invoked Article 49.3 to force the Gaullists either to support the government, or to take the responsibility for precipitating a general election. On each occasion, the RPR fell into line.

A limited capacity for parliamentary scrutiny

The means at the disposal of the French parliament to oversee the executive are weak by comparison with past Republics. In part, this reflects a more general evolution away from legislatures in developed liberal democracies: even the most powerful American congressional committees cannot realistically expect to be kept informed on every aspect of executive policy. There is a specifically French angle too. The 1958 Constitution reduced the number of permanent standing committees of the National Assembly and the Senate from nineteen to six. Standing committees consider all *propositions de loi* and *projets de loi* once they have received their first reading in either the National Assembly or the Senate. Their size is such that they are unwieldy instruments of public policy: the two largest committees contain up to 121 members, with four smaller committees composed of a maximum of sixty-one deputies.

Even governments with no overall working majority (such as the Socialist administrations of 1988–93) are under no constitutional obligation to accept amendments proposed by committees. Article 44.3 allows a government to demand a single vote on all amendments, and to insist that parliament debate the government's text. Article 47, finally, gives both Chambers a maximum of seventy days to agree upon the government's budget, after which the government's text can be enforced by decree. By comparison with past French regimes, budgets are no longer held to ransom by the pork-barrel demands of key deputies.

Scrutiny of the executive is limited because the French parliament is not seen as a forum for great national debates. Written questions to ministers have proved to be a damp squib: overwhelmingly they concern local constituency issues of interest only to individual deputies and – possibly – their electors. Oral questions have had little more impact. The procedure of 'questions to the government' was established during the Giscard d'Estaing presidency. Government ministers respond to prepared questions delivered by deputies. These sessions have proved ineffectual, partly because no supplementary questions are permitted, partly because of a lack of public and media interest. The political irresponsibility of the French presidency has something to do with this. French Presidents have repeated at will that they are responsible only to the people, not to the intermediaries gathered in parliament. The sense of drama aroused by Prime Minister's Question Time, or by the great parliamentary debates in the UK is quite absent in France. French national political debate occurs in television studios more than in other west European nations, where parliamentary debates can have an important political impact (Kuhn, 1995).

The other form of executive scrutiny is that provided by special parliamentary committees of enquiry or control. They are pale imitations of the powerful US congressional committees, with freedom to information and officials. They can be established only if a majority of deputies or senators supports their constitution. Only a small proportion of requests for the creation of committees are agreed to by the Legislative Committee (*Commission des lois*), usually dominated by the government's supporters. The incumbent government invariably establishes the framework of reference of these committees. Most pertinently, access to official information is limited, ministers can refuse to cooperate and civil servants are not required to attend meetings. On occasions, however, these committees have made a difference and uncovered abuses of executive power.

| 5.4 | Political dynamics and the operation of parliament |

Political dynamics underpin the constitutional devices we have explored above. Any government is secure as long as a hostile majority can be prevented from forming against it. Even minority governments, such as those of 1976–81, or

1988–93 have generally been safe. Unlike in the Third or Fourth Republic, changes of government have occurred either as a result of general elections, or as a consequence of presidential manoeuvring; changes of government as a result of shifting parliamentary alliances between elections are virtually unheard of. The emergence of majoritarian governing coalitions has provided a solid political underpinning for the constitutional subordination of parliament, especially during periods of presidential pre-eminence. The French parliament is not devoid of influence, however. Governments are sensitive to party, especially when the executive relies upon a broad-based coalition for support, as during the 1997–2002 plural left government. Wherever possible, governments will attempt to appease their own backbenchers, usually by adopting a carrot and stick approach, balancing the threat of sanctions with the promise of sympathetic concessions. Regular caucus meetings between the parliamentary groups of the governing parties, and representatives of the government ensure that backbench demands are filtered to key decision makers in office.

Taking the period 1958–2003 as a whole, there is little doubt that a rationalised party system within parliament has facilitated the emergence of stronger governments, just as much as the constitutional devices within the 1958 Constitution. But the character of the parliamentary majority has also had an impact upon the type of legislative programme envisaged by the government. This was revealed in Chapter 2 with our appraisal of the governments presided over by Chirac (1974–6) and Barre (1976–81). The lack of a reform-minded parliamentary majority, as well as the weakness of the presidential party, had a constraining effect on the type of policies that could be pursued during this period. President Giscard d'Estaing's early reformism was quietly shelved after one year, on account of the fundamental conservatism of his parliamentary majority. Premier Chaban-Delmas (1969–72), whose radical intentions were frustrated as a result of a tacit alliance between a conservative President Pompidou and an even more conservative parliamentary majority, had provided an earlier example.

The plural left government headed by Lionel Jospin (1997–2002) offered the best example yet of the bargaining, compromise and adaptation of coalition government. Respectful of parliamentary procedure, the Jospin government refrained from using the restrictive clauses in the 1958 Constitution (Article 49.3 especially). Coalition politics undoubtedly made a difference during the 1997–2002 government, when Jospin had to manage the differing political sensitivities of the five coalition partners (Socialists, Communists, Radicals, Greens and Citizens). The Jospin method of coalition management relied upon maintaining close personal relationships with the leaders of the five parties, rewarding each party leader with an important ministry and respecting minimal political demands in each case. Consistent with his pedagogic governing style, the Socialist premier made a virtue out of necessity and allowed the governing parties to express their differences over policy in parliament. The agreement to differ was most explicit in European affairs. Though the Communist Party (PCF) opposed the single currency during the 1998 parliamentary vote and voted against the Amsterdam Treaty in March 1999, no sanctions were taken against Communist ministers. Abstentions, or votes against the government by

The Senate: seat of France's second chamber

deputies from the governing parties were a routine feature of the 1997–2002 experience. After the left's setbacks in the 2001 municipal elections, Jospin attempted to prop up the ailing Communist partner on several occasions, most notably in May 2001 when, after intense PCF pressure, the government made it much more difficult for employers to lay off workers than it had originally intended.

In their detailed study of the operation of parliamentary dynamics, Knapp and Wright (2001) refer to a *resurgent* parliament. To back up their claim, they point to the increasing number of amendments tabled and the increasing success of committee amendments in particular; the growing importance of special committees of enquiry; the improved chances of success of private members' bills and the ability of opposition parliamentarians to refer government bills to the Constitutional Council. Though it is difficult to disentangle cause and effect, the effectiveness of these various indicators is mainly dependent on the operation of the party system, rather than the effectiveness of parliament as an institution. Parliament operates more effectively – in its own terms of reference – in situations of multi-party coalition government, than when there is a single 'presidential party' majority, again the case since June 2002. On the other hand, recent legislatures have displayed much less discipline within all main party groups, testament to the desire of parliamentarians of all complexions to be taken seriously. That premier Raffarin felt forced to use Article 49.3 in 2003 to change the electoral system for the 2004 regional elections recalled that the bluntest weapons of executive control are often used against one's own side. The 2003 episode also demonstrated that, on the issues that really matter such as elections, the government of the day will not risk parliamentary disapproval.

As in other parliamentary systems, the National Assembly is a breeding ground for political talent. Many politicians make their political reputations in parliament, although other avenues, such as party and local government are probably more important than in most comparable democracies. In this context, we consider the French tradition of multiple office-holding – *cumul des mandats* – in rather more detail in Chapter 7. Important strategic positions occupied within both houses of parliament are coveted by leading politicians. The President of the National Assembly is one such position: the post has been occupied by former-premiers such as Chaban-Delmas and Fabius, as well as by former President Giscard d'Estaing. The post is the fourth in the official state hierarchy, and offers its occupant a measure of influence over parliamentary procedure, the right to nominate one-third of the members of the Constitutional Council, the occupancy of a splendid official residence and permanent contact with ministers. To a lesser extent, the presidency of the Senate is a comparable position of influence. The presidents of the parliamentary committees, while no longer the barons of old, are assiduously courted by government ministers. The leverage of such positions can be considerable.

Despite the constraints placed upon it, the French parliament is a conscientious legislative body. There has been a steady increase throughout the Fifth Republic in the proportion of successful amendments to government bills, and governments have become increasingly reluctant to use the most restrictive constitutional articles against parliament. As in other liberal democracies, however, classic parliamentary functions have either been ceded to the executive (in terms of policy-making), or are more convincingly performed by other bodies (those of scrutiny and political communication). Certain representative functions are in practice devolved to the party system (Chapters 8 and 9); others are performed by interest groups and voluntary associations (Chapter 10). The principal function that remains with parliament is that of democratic legitimisation: no government would survive for long without the confidence of the democratically elected Assembly.

| 5.5 | The judicialisation of French politics? |

Politics in France operates within a strongly legalistic tradition. Knapp and Wright (2001) argue that there has been an increased legalisation of public policy as France has become more embedded in European and international structures. Respect for the law, and more specifically for the precise rules emerging from particular laws, is characteristic of the new French polity. The development of the European Union has reinforced existing tendencies, in that it requires legal conformity. There are three distinct branches of the law in France. The Constitutional Council regulates constitutional law. There is a separate system of public (administrative) law, wherein the Council of State is the key institution in setting norms and determining procedure. Matters of civil and criminal law (matters of contract, civil relations, property, criminal misdemeanour and so on) lie within the domain of the judiciary, with the Court of Cassation as the final court of appeal. Consideration of the judiciary, *stricto sensu*, lies outside this book, but the interested reader can consult a number of good recent studies (Knapp and Wright, 2001; Feuillée-Kendal, 1998).

Increasingly, the French legal system is also subject to the judgments of the European Court of Justice for matters of community law and the European Court of Human Rights for issues of civil liberties (because France is a signatory of the European Charter of Human Rights). The interested reader will find thorough treatment of the impact of these supranational jurisdictions in several recent works (Elgie, 2003; Knapp and Wright, 2001). In the ensuing section, we consider the Constitutional Council and the Council of State, two French institutions of primordial importance.

The Constitutional Council

The creation of the Constitutional Council was one of the major innovations in the 1958 Constitution. Setting up a Constitutional Council was intended to give substance to the reference to the separation of powers in the 1958 Constitution. Its nine members (who normally each serve for one non-renewable term of nine years) are appointed in equal measure by the President of the Republic, the President of the National Assembly and the President of the Senate (Stone, 1992). The President of the Republic chooses the President of the Constitutional Council from amongst its nine members. As appointees are replaced at very irregular intervals, at any one time there is likely to be a political imbalance within the Council. As the composition of the council only slowly changes, however, the effects of imbalance are delayed. During the early 1980s, the left-wing government was forced to retreat on a number of occasions faced with a solidly right-wing dominated Council. By the mid-1990s, after over a decade of mainly left-inspired appointments, the Council had a slender left-wing majority (coinciding with the 1993–5 Balladur government). For most of the Jospin government (1997–2002), a recognisable 'stato-conservative' majority in the Council struck down a number of government reforms.

The early history of the Constitutional Council was hardly auspicious. De Gaulle openly mocked the institution. The Council itself lacked sufficient confidence to challenge the executive, even when the executive branch blatantly transgressed the Constitution. In 1962, for instance, the Council proclaimed its inability to nullify the result of the referendum on the direct election of the President (of dubious constitutionality) because it had already taken place. Its timid beginnings notwithstanding, the Constitutional Council has grown steadily in prestige. In 1971, it ruled for the first time against the government of the day. In 1974 President Giscard d'Estaing introduced a reform whereby (sixty) opposition deputies or senators could petition to refer any government bill to the Council for arbitration on its constitutionality. Opposition parties have regularly referred government bills for adjudication to the Council. In a series of judgements in the course of the 1980s and 1990s, the Court revealed its real political muscle, constraining governments, amongst other decisions, to review nationalisation programmes (1982), redraw constituency boundaries (1986), revise the constitution to permit ratification of the Maastricht treaty (1992) and abandon certain contentious articles of an anti-terrorist law (1996). In 1990, President Mitterrand attempted to extend access still further to include individual citizens, but ran against the opposition of the Senate. Against the trend running in favour of the Council since 1974, President Chirac's constitutional reform of July 1995 limited the possibilities open to the Constitutional Council to oppose presidential initiatives, notably those taking the form of referendums under Article 11.

The Constitutional Council performs a number of important roles. It is in charge of the practical details of organising election campaigns and referendums. The Council ensures that elections are fought in a free and fair manner and that campaign rules are respected. After each election, the Council considers whether there have been any electoral irregularities (typically over finance or canvassing rules), usually forcing a spate of by-elections. Though this work might appear of secondary importance, it occupies a lot of the Council's time. The consent of the Council is also required before treaties can be ratified (for example the Treaty of Amsterdam in 1999).

The major area of responsibility for the Council is that of a constitutional arbiter. The Constitutional Council considers all organic laws (those relating to the working of the Constitution), as well as those ordinary laws referred to it by the opposition parties. In practice, most major bills will be referred to the Council. Under the Jospin government, for example, the Council considered the 35-hour week, gender parity, Corsica, the Civil Action Pact (PACs) and many other reforms. The Council must make known its decisions on a bill within one month of being asked. In the case of the budget, the council has 'eight days, for over one million documents' (interview).

Once a law has been referred to the Council, how do the judges make their decisions? The judges are guided by the principle of the constitutional block (*'bloc de constitutionalité'*). The judges must determine whether the law infringes any one of a number of texts with a constitutional force. The first, and most important of these, is the text of the 1958 Constitution itself. Somewhat below the Constitution are a number of other texts with constitutional force. These are:

- the preface to the 1958 Constitution;
- the 1789 Declaration of the Rights of Man and Citizen (which is mentioned in the preface to the 1958 Constitution);
- the preface to the 1946 Constitution (also mentioned in the 1958 preface);
- a number of established republican principles that are recognised to have constitutional status by the Council itself and that are drawn from constitutional jurisprudence.

Most of the time, the judges are faced with contradictory principles that can inform their decisions. There are obvious contradictions between the 1789 Declaration of Rights and the preface to the 1946 Constitution: the former established bourgeois property rights and celebrated the principles of economic liberalism; the second was of Socialist inspiration. When property law and labour law come into conflict, there is no obviously 'right' constitutional response. The Council claims to interpret the will of the legislator. If the bill has a social content, it will use the 1946 preface as its benchmark; if it is involved with property rights, it will draw its inspiration from the 1789

Declaration. The Council defends itself strongly against the charge of 'wanting to become a third chamber' (interview), though the evidence presented above suggests that its political composition does influence its behaviour.

In attempting to place itself in the position of the legislator, the Council can adopt a more flexible position than the Council of State, which we consider below. The 'parity' reform under the Jospin government was a good example. According to the criteria of formal equality under the law, the Council was tempted to declare parity to be against the Constitution. Placing itself in the role of the legislator, however, the Council accepted that a respect for formal equality could produce unequal outcomes. Ensuring equal treatment for men and women by 'quotas' required accepting a law that might be interpreted as contrary to formal equality of opportunity. This particular decision was the subject of much controversy within the Council itself.

The Council of State and the system of public law

There is, in France, a separate system of public (administrative) law, which is concerned mainly with the French administration itself. The branch of public law deals with all matters relating to the operation of public authorities, as well as to complaints levelled by citizens against the state. The Council of State is at the apex of this administrative law system, which includes five regional appeals courts (*cours administratives d'appels*), as well as thirty-three local courts (*tribunaux administratifs*) (Hérard and Maurin, 2000). The Council of State is the most prestigious of the *grands corps*, one of the prize placements for ENA students. The Council is composed of some 300 members, divided into six grades according to length of service. The collegial identity of members of the Council of State is one of its most significant features. Each member is conscious of belonging not only to a venerable institution, but also of forming a part of the inner circle of the French elite.

The Council of State is at the forefront of the French state tradition. It performs two distinctive roles: as an adviser to the government of the day; and as the highest administrative court in the land.

As an adviser to the government, the Council of State discharges a key role in the preparation of government laws. Before French government bills (and decrees) are considered in the Council of Ministers, or the National Assembly, they must be submitted to the Council of State for an appreciation of their legality and administrative feasibility. The Council of State considers all government bills, decrees and *ordonnances* and all EU acts having a legislative character (Knapp and Wright, 2001). Although Council of State judgements are not binding, governments of all persuasions listen attentively to its deliberations. The Council of State also intervenes when called upon to give general advice to governments on a broad range of issues (for example electoral reform). In the opinion of a former Vice-President (Long, 1992), the Council of State lies at the heart of the French governmental system. It is 'an obligatory reference point before any important decision is taken'. Because of the prestige of its function and membership, 'its recommendations, though non-imperative, are at the intersection between advice and decisions'. This advisory role can, on occasion, develop very political overtones. During the Jospin government (1997–2002) the Council of State made several hostile rulings in advance of the government presenting bills or decrees to the council of ministers (over Corsica, or regional languages, for example). The Constitutional Council then struck down government bills or decrees, pointing to the Council of State's rulings as lending support to its own interpretation. As the Constitutional Council manifestly values the viewpoint of the Council of State, the two judicial bodies appeared to form a powerful coalition against the reforming government of the day.

In terms of administrative jurisprudence, the Council of State is the highest authority in the land and all other public authorities are expected to follow its rulings. As the pinnacle of the French system of administrative courts, the Council of State operates at various different levels: as an administrative court of first instance, as an appeals court, and as a court of cassation. For most of its activity, it operates as an appeals court for contested decisions from subordinate courts. Only in a few instances does it act as a court of first instance, generally in relation to major disputes involving the legality of ministerial regulations or government decrees, and potential major abuses of public authority. As a court of cassation, the Council of State exercises judicial and administrative control over other key administrative bodies such as the Court of Accounts, the Higher Council of the Magistrature and the Higher National Education Council. It is also called upon to arbitrate in disputes between public authorities (Stirn, 1991).

Through its use of case law, the Council of State has adopted a standard-setting role. Rather like the Constitutional Council, the Council of State edicts 'general principles of law', which go beyond the provisions of any particular legislative act or decree. The effect of this case law is to enshrine a system of judicial review. In practice both the Council of State and the Constitutional Council reserve for themselves, under certain circumstances, the right to act in a quasi-legislative capacity. The Council of State advises on proposed legislation, lays down general principles and interprets EU directives. Even more overtly, the Constitutional Council not only strikes down government bills, but has claimed the right to decide the conditions under which a bill will or will not be declared constitutional.

Its critics accuse the Council of State of perpetuating an archaic vision of contemporary France. During the 1997–2002 Jospin government, for example, the Council of State made a series of judgments that were hostile to recognising the rights of regional and linguistic minorities and that appeared openly to challenge the will of the elected government. As the guarantor of the integrity of French administrative traditions, the Council of State has been critical of many aspects of moves towards closer European integration, especially insofar as this process threatens the pre-eminent role it performs within the French administrative system. The Council only finally accepted the primacy of European over French law in 1989, though this primacy is explicitly mentioned in the Treaty of Rome (Picard, 1999). More than any other organisation, the Council of State derives its legitimacy from safeguarding the myth of the unity

Jardin du Luxembourg: in the grounds of the Senate

and indivisibility of the French State that appears to many out of kilter with the reality of contemporary France.

The Constitutional Council, the Council of State and the European Court of Justice (Chapter 13) all offer evidence for the growing judicialisation of French politics. Other new judicial actors came to the fore in the 1980s and 1990s. Much attention was focused on the role of the investigating magistrates, the *juges d'instruction*. In the French legal system, these magistrates are instructed by the representative of the Justice Ministry (the *procureur-général* or the Parquet) to enquire into alleged breaches of the law and to present reports recommending (or not as the case may be) further action to the Justice Ministry. To carry out their functions, they are invested with certain powers: such as the right of search, the confiscation of documents and the interviewing of suspects. Inspired by their Italian counterparts, French investigating magistrates have meticulously uncovered abuses of executive and municipal power, as well as widespread but illegal practices of financing political parties. Their fervour has made a handful of magistrates into household names, such as Van de Rumbeyke, Thierry Pierre and Eric Halphen. These figures have used their powers to the full, including making spectacular visits to headquarters of the main political parties (PS, RPR and PR) and even conducting investigations inside the Prime Ministers' office. In at least one case – the 1990 law on the Financing of Political Parties – the activities of the investigating magistrates led to important legislation being enacted, as well as legal sanctions being taken against several party treasurers, and a handful of former government ministers.

Alongside these well-publicised cases, however, insiders complain of executive pressures being brought to bear against magistrates who are too meticulous in their enquiries, especially when these touch political parties, the inner workings of the state, or the murkier sides of state activity, such as the secret services, or government slush funds. Faced with the refusal of the Senate to agree to constitutional reform in 2000, the Jospin government failed in its attempt to ensure the complete independence of the investigating magistrates. The influence of the executive branch on the judiciary remains primordial. Most important judicial appointments (notably the public prosecutors) are made by the executive branch (either by the President of the Republic, or by the Justice Minister) after consultation with the Higher Council of the Magistrature, a body representing both the political executive and the legal profession. The investigating magistrates have demonstrated, in the circumstances, a resolute determination to conduct their enquiries without undue executive interference.

5.6 Concluding remarks

Though the 1958 Constitution refers to the separation of powers, the Fifth Republic constitution establishes a unitary system of government that is closer in its operation to the British fused parliamentary model than the mix of presidentialism and active legislature represented by the United States. The limited sovereignty accorded to parliament in the 1958 Constitution marked a real break with republican traditions of government by assembly. The Fifth Republic is also an evolving and changeable political entity. The evidence presented in Chapter 5 suggests that legal, constitutional and supranational factors have provided some checks and balances against the uses and abuses of executive authority that were not initially envisaged in the 1958 Constitution. These institutional innovations are essential if France is to function effectively within the emerging European polity.

6 The immobile state?

6.1 Introduction

Metaphors of bureaucratic power in France abound, typified by references to an *énarchie*, to the ubiquitous influence of 'technocracy' and to the administrative state. In Chapter 6, we begin by setting out the legalistic context within which French politics and policy are conducted. We then study in some detail the recruitment of elites, the principal characteristics of the French civil service and the shifting boundaries between politics and the administration. We investigate elements of continuity, conflict and cohesion within the French state. We conclude by charting efforts since 1981 to reform the over-elaborate state and by considering whether there is a French-style New Public Management.

6.2 The French civil service: characteristics, context and culture

Politico-administrative activity in France is embedded in a strong legalistic tradition, theorised at some length by the French Organisational Sociology school since the 1960s. Certain of the themes associated with new institutionalist thought in Anglo-American political science were preceded by the French organisational sociologists, who lay great emphasis upon the importance of rules, rule-bound behaviour and normative beliefs amongst civil servants. If only for the subsequent criticism it raised, Michel Crozier's *The Bureaucratic Phenomenon* (1963) was the most significant early contribution to the study of the French 'bureaucratic mentality'. The key theme of Crozier's portrayal was that of compartmentalisation (*cloissonnement*), referring to the compact, impenetrable character of different bureaucratic divisions, and the lack of communication between them. Taking issue with Max Weber's belief in the 'absolute superiority of a regimented, hierarchical form of organisation', Crozier affirmed that each level of a bureaucratic hierarchy operates in accordance with its own norms, usually in complete ignorance of the overall objectives of an organisation. The term *cloissonnement* became used as a code to depict the inward looking, defensive character of French bureaucratic actors, and, more generally, of French society. In spite of its dysfunctional character, for Crozier the French administration has retained the features of a classic bureaucratic organisation, governed by impersonal rules, a centralisation of decisions and a lack of initiative by middle-ranking officials.

Studies of France's legalistic culture have emphasised the cognitive universe within which civil servants operate. Civil servants are prone to rule-driven behaviour, as well as the acceptance of overarching norms, such as equal treatment and equality of outcomes (Knapp and Wright, 2001). French officials draw their legitimacy from their ability to interpret and filter circulars, directives and regulations. Vested with a belief in their public service mission and their role as guardians of the rules, French officials will only 'break the rules' in order to provide better services for citizens (Dupuy 1990) or to increase their bargaining resources within an organisation (Crozier and Friedberg, 1977). The bureaucracy sometimes functions efficiently only because rules are not enforced, but maintaining the fiction of uniformity and equal treatment for everybody is a core belief.

The metaphor of the administrative state and the bureaucratic society implies a strong unitary state and a complacent society. Though administrative procedures are formalised and codified to a high degree, uniformity in the French administration is more apparent than real. There is disagreement about the degree of unity amongst public officials. For Jones (2003) French civil servants share a common frame of reference about what public service comprises and what their forms of appropriate behaviour should be. Others doubt whether French public officials adopt such a cohesive worldview, as the administrative system is fractured into rival corps, divisions, and ministries (Clark, 2000; Bézès, 2000). To investigate in more detail, we need first to understand some basic facts about the public sector in France.

- Who is a 'civil servant' in France? There are various ways of counting the number of public employees. In 2001, the French state directly employed 2,313,700 civil servants. In addition, the local authorities employed 1,767,600 and the health service 887,000 (INSEE, 2003). These numbers rise to 7,000,000 if we include those workers that enjoy a public service statute (in EDF-GDF, SNCF and France Telecom), or to 9,000,000 people if we include those on public sector pensions. By any standard, civil servants and public sector workers represent a powerful lobby, organised into strong public sector unions.

- What does the title civil servant cover? There are over 1,700 different grades (*corps*) of civil servant. As the public sector professions are classified as belonging to the civil service, this is a greatly inflated number in contrast with other European countries. Schoolteachers (over 1,000,000) are the single most populous group. The category is a broad one. Senior civil servants are heavily concentrated in the Parisian headquarters of the various ministries, or in certain key posts in the provincial prefectures and ministerial field services. Most workers in the state railways (SNCF) or the gas and electricity companies (EDF/GDF) also have a public service statute.

- Entry to the civil service at all levels is based on competitive public examination and carries with it security of employment, and specific rights and duties. In 1946, a general statute of the public service was created setting out the rights and responsibilities of public servants and offering them legal immunity. The 1946 statute also lays down procedures for promotion and recruitment. The conservative public sector unions closely monitor conformity to the provisions of the 1946 statute.

Many of the observations we make below are valid for any system of public administration, but we focus upon aspects that are the most closely associated with the French model, namely the pattern of elite recruitment, the system of administrative corps, the role of political appointees, politico-administrative linkages and public–private spillage ('*pantouflage*').

Recruiting the elite

Nominations to top administrative positions are determined on the basis of competitive examinations, internal promotion procedures and political appointments. Prior to 1945, civil servants were recruited according to the norms in operation in different *corps* and ministries, which each operated their own entry examinations. Since 1945, ENA (the National Administration School) has been the privileged channel for recruitment to top civil service positions (Howarth and Varouxakis, 2003). The School was created in 1945 as a means of democratising the recruitment to senior levels of the French administration. The mission of ENA is to recruit the best and the brightest to the senior administrative ranks. The annual intake of ENA students is of the order of 120, with the most frequent entry route being the School's competitive examination taken on completion of a university degree, or (usually) a diploma from one of France's leading schools (*grandes écoles*). Each individual is classified in relation to his or her performance, and compared with co-students. The individual performance of each ENA student determines the civil service posts to which he or she can aspire:

- High flyers strive for the Council of State, the Court of Accounts or the Financial Inspectorate.
- Other postings open to ENA graduates are the administrative inspectorates of the various government departments, the prefectoral corps, the Foreign Affairs ministry, overseas commercial attachés, administrative postings in a range of government departments, the Regional Courts of Accounts, and the Paris town hall.

Entry to ENA secures a prestigious civil service post, with the possibility of a lucrative transfer to the private sector at a later date. Rapid promotions within the civil service are usually restricted to the small core of ENA high performers. The end product of this system is sometimes contemptuously referred to as an *énarque*, with the same mixture of enmity and admiration reserved for Oxbridge graduates in the UK. This system is resented in the provinces for producing out of touch Parisians from narrow educational backgrounds. In deference to such views, the Socialist government of Edith Cresson partially transferred the school to Strasbourg in 1991, causing furore amongst ENA students for whom study in Paris was the height of social achievement. ENA is not the only route for access to the higher echelons of the civil service. It tends to attract general-ist administrators with political ambitions. The highest technical grades (*grands corps techniques*) are recruited from graduates of the three top engineering schools: Polytechnique (created by Napoleon in 1804), the Highways and Bridges, and the Mining schools (*Écoles des Ponts-et-Chaussées et des Mines*). These schools have an identity just as strong as ENA and they feed the main technical administrative corps (Highways and Bridges, Mines).

There is an inherent hierarchy in this model. Senior civil servants in Paris issue directives and circulars to officers in the field services. As the supposedly brightest are selected to serve in Paris, they are distant from and distrustful not only of civil servants working in the provinces, but also of local and regional politicians and officers. Outside of the charmed circle of the *grands corps*, the prospects for internal promotions based on performance are fairly limited, a theme to which we return later. Promotion within the civil service is generally based on rank and seniority, rather than performance.

The Civil Service Corps

The most distinctive feature of the French civil service is the system of adminis-trative corps. The *corps* are bodies without obvious parallels in the British or American contexts. Rather than designating an institution or a government department as such, the term is used to describe the different state grades to which all civil servants must belong. Entry to each *corps* in based on compet-itive examination, and carries with it rights, responsibilities and prospects for career development. The *corps* structure is vital for career mobility. Membership of a *corps* qualifies an individual to carry out a range of jobs. As individuals are recruited to ranks within the corps, not to specific posts, promotion depends on standing within the *corps* structure. Promotion is by rank and seniority rather than performance. The model is innately conservative. It fosters a strong corporate identity, an aversion to performance-related pay or targets, a cult of written rules and a strong inner-corps rivalry. Civil servants are primarily loyal to their corps, rather than to individual government departments, and are gener-ally well organised to defend their interests. Mobility within the civil service is very rare – except at the top levels. Political or public management reforms that are perceived to threaten the role of the *grands corps* – such as the creation of regulatory agencies or decentralisation – invariably attract opposition from top civil servants.

Each *corps* has its internal management procedures that are not covered in the General Statute of Public Servants. There are 1700 such corps. Such a large number of distinctive statutes make any attempt to reform the workings of the state inherently difficult, especially if the purpose of reform is to change work-ing practices.

A strict internal hierarchy exists within the French civil service (Kessler, 1986). Three administrative and two technical *grands corps* are the most prestigious.

The three administrative *grands corps* are the Council of State, the Financial Inspectorate, and the Court of Accounts. Competition to enter these *corps* is fierce, and they attract the best ENA graduates. Their combined membership of under 1000 individuals is tiny: there is no surer sign of belonging to the French elite. Stevens (2003) points out that the three leading administrative *grands corps* are all concerned with controlling and checking the work of other civil servants. The Council of State lies at the apex of France's system of public law. Its decisions establish administrative jurisprudence and lower administrative bodies are expected to comply with its rulings. Governments of all political persuasions listen attentively to the Council of State, even when (as in most instances) its advice is only indicative. The Financial Inspectorate undertakes rigorous financial inspections of government departments and other public administrations. The Court of Accounts publishes annual reports on the uses (and especially abuses) of expenditure by organisations and programmes funded from the public purse. Though it enjoys great prestige, the finite range of sanctions it possesses limits its effectiveness (as does the rivalry with the Financial Inspectorate). The prefectoral corps and the diplomatic corps fall slightly lower in the administrative hierarchy, but retain considerable prestige.

Alongside these administrative corps, two technical corps – Mining, and Highways and Bridges – recruit engineers to serve in the more technical government departments (Infrastructure, Agriculture, Industry) and their field services. The Highways and Bridges corps has traditionally performed a lead role in public infrastructure projects (road building and bridges especially). The Mining Corps has provided executives to manage and lead France's main companies. Members of the mining corps are heavily over-represented at the head of French firms (Lafarge, Saint-Gobain, Total, Matra, Cegetel) though the current trend is to recruit those with Master in Business Administration degrees. Membership of different corps can affect relationships at all levels of the governmental machine. Thus, one regional prefect interviewed in 1995 complained of being ignored by the lead field officials from the Infrastructure ministry on account of their belonging to a separate corps (Highways and Bridges, rather than the prefectoral corps). In this case, membership of a corps dictated 'appropriate behaviour', rather than the written rule (since 1992, regional prefects are supposed to have a responsibility to coordinate all government services in their regions).

The system of *grands corps* sets the French administration apart from others in Europe. However, we must be careful not to espouse a thesis of bureaucratic power based on membership of a *grands corps* alone. Membership of a corps is often a powerful source of identity, but members of the same corps can adopt widely divergent political and policy stances. Members of *corps* are usually spread across separate government departments and public or private organisations. According to Suleiman (1974) their viewpoint will be influenced in accordance with the role or function they perform.

A politicised administration?

If it is true, as Wright (1974) pointed out, that the first political nominations occurred in the Fourth Republic, the movement has gathered pace in the Fifth

Republic, notably with the repeated changes of government since the early 1980s. Around 300 or so top administrative appointments are decided in the Council of Ministers, allowing the government of the day to select its top officials according to political criteria. Prefects, rectors and ambassadors are regularly moved when governments change, along with the heads of the state-controlled gas and electricity company, the national railways and the post office. The vast majority of positions are not available to political interference, however, being determined uniquely by internal administrative promotion procedures (Le Pourhiet, 1987). Though political appointments within the French bureaucracy are limited to the top elite, rather than reaching the middle ranks as in the United States (or, even more so, Italy), the principle of political appointment arguably contravenes the neutrality of the state.

The politico-administrative nexus

More important than overt politicisation, there is a very close relationship between politicians and officials, leading some experts to refer to an interpenetration of political and administrative personnel (de Baecque and Quermonne, 1981). The boundary between politics and administration has become blurred. A common career trajectory for members of the political elite involves a passage through ENA, attachment to a *grand corps*, followed by service in a government department, or a ministerial *cabinet*, succeeded by an overt political engagement. This phenomenon is less surprising than it appears at first sight. Politicians and top civil servants are drawn from the same talent pool, with both often having followed the same educational path – 'Sciences Po', then ENA. Far from being merely a training ground for France's civil service elite, ENA has become a nursery for France's political elite as well, in a broad sense that surpasses political cleavages. ENA attracts the best students, who, naturally ambitious, are often driven towards pursuit of political office. There exists a powerful network of relationships between former ENA students, who maintain contact with each other. ENA graduates are to be found in the ministerial *cabinets*, in government departments, amongst cabinet ministers, as well as on the boards of private industries. Because civil servants enjoy security of tenure, they are able to take time out of their administrative careers in order to engage in political activity. Should they suffer an electoral setback, they can usually re-enter their *corps* at a later date. For some, this overlap of politics and administration lends support to a bureaucratic power thesis. The permanent administration in France has proved remarkably effective at diffusing an administrative ethos amongst politicians.

Pantouflage

By *pantouflage*, we mean the transfer of personnel between top civil service or political positions, and lucrative posts in private industry. As in other European democracies (such as Britain), the evidence points to a regular transfer of former government ministers to lucrative posts within state or private industry.

Nominations to leading positions in state industry are often barely concealed 'golden handshakes' for former ministers or presidential advisers. The French government's privatisation programme has added a new dimension to this traditional practice. A furore was created in 1986–7, when the Chirac government was accused (rightly) of ensuring that industrialists close to the Gaullist RPR were placed in key positions on the boards of the industries to be privatised. The involvement of key French companies in repeated corruption scandals has made it a hazardous exercise for former politicians to embrace a practice that was for long accepted as one of the perks of state service.

Economic globalisation and the attractiveness of the private sector for the brightest civil servants have challenged the French model of disinterested public service. In 1999, it was estimated that 85 per cent of members of the mining corps would finish their career in the private or public industrial sector, a figure falling to 47 per cent for Financial Inspectors, 37 per cent for the Bridges and Highways corps and 22 per cent for the Court of Accounts. Almost all leading positions in large French companies are occupied by members of the *grands corps*. The realisation that the 'best and brightest' will no longer automatically look to serve the state has come to a shock to more traditionally minded civil servants.

| 6.3 | The French state today: continuity, conflict, cohesion |

The omnipresence of the French state is real; its omnipotence and unity is far less certain. Several types of differentiation exist within the French administration. Certain of these are present in all liberal democratic political systems, whereas others are more specifically French. In a rather schematic manner, we might identify at least seven sources of potential and real conflict within France's one and indivisible state.

Competition between ministries

As in other western European nations, there is an inbuilt tension between the Finance ministry, and the spending ministries. The annual budget round bears testament to this. In his study of the French Prime Minister, Elgie (1993) illustrates how the budget division (*direction du budget*) of the Finance ministry exercised a tight control over the budgetary process, marshalling all means at its disposal to resist spending increases by ministries such as Education, Defence, and Health. The budget studied by Elgie (1989) provided limited evidence for a bureaucratic model of the policy-making process. The key resources at the disposal of the budgetary division were essentially financial and technical. But they were also political, in the sense that they were charged with implementing tough government guidelines ultimately determined by the President (guidelines that the Finance ministry itself was instrumental in pressing upon the incumbent government).

Competition between ministers and civil servants

Tensions between high-ranking civil servants and ministers are obvious, although they should not be overstated. In spite of their common outlook in many respects, political and administrative actors pursue rather different logics. The bureaucratic logic is justified by reference to the general interest and the service of the state, an appeal with a particular resonance in France. From a bureaucratic perspective, politicians look to their particularistic interests, notably to the need to get re-elected. The need for continuity in public policy is used as a powerful argument by bureaucrats to justify attempting to shape decisions in particular directions. From a politician's perspective, bureaucrats often reason in terms of longer-term departmental agendas, which take inadequate account of political realities and the democratic legitimacy of politicians. These diverging outlooks should not be overstressed, however: the defence of specific sectoral interests (such as Health, Education, or Defence) usually unites the ministers and civil servants within a particular government department, since their mutual interests are tied up in maximising their resources and influence.

One specific mechanism adopted in the French case is that of the ministerial office (*cabinet*). Each minister is assisted by a team of advisers, whose function it is to follow particular briefs, write speeches, and provide advice. The size of ministerial cabinets vary from four to five advisers to fifty or more in the case of the Prime Minister. The status of the *cabinets* is rather ambiguous; with no statutory existence, they tend to mirror the qualities and priorities of the minister involved. The activities of the *cabinets* can cause resentment from career civil servants, especially the top officials, the Directors. They are often composed of young ENA graduates. Ministers usually nominate junior civil servants to serve in their *cabinets*, despite the fact that one of the functions of the *cabinet* is to attempt to control the civil service. Because individuals generally serve in *cabinets* at the beginning of their careers, and because they are identified with particular ministers, they rarely remain in any one *cabinet* for more than two years. There is no settled pattern of relations within the *cabinets*. Certain *cabinets* are dominated by representatives of the chief divisions (*directions*) within the ministry; others are openly political, determined to impose the will of the minister, still others lie somewhere between these two examples.

The attempt undertaken in 1995 by the Juppé government to reform the operation of the *cabinets* revealed a sense of unease at their political irresponsibility, as well as the financial improprieties involved in certain cases. In theory, no minister is henceforth able to employ more than five advisers in her office. In practice, a detailed investigation proved that most ministers continued to employ far more than this number, relying on the indulgence of government departments to second their officials to serve on *cabinets* (Favereau, 1995).

Departmental interests and governmental coordination

As in all unitary liberal democracies, there are tensions between the interests of particular ministries, and the overall cohesion of the government machine, requiring efforts at government coordination. This coordinating function is performed at different levels and rhythms by the presidential Elysée staff, the Prime Minister's *cabinet*, the General Secretariat of the Government and various interministerial committees.

The role of interministerial structures

Tension between individual ministries, and interministerial structures can be extremely significant. Each government department has its own traditions, policy concerns and budgetary priorities, often cultivated by career civil servants whose longevity of service surpasses that of any individual government. However much it might resist, coordination by the Finance ministry, the Prime Minister or the President is accepted as inevitable. Less welcome is coordination by specifically created interministerial structures, designed to demonstrate the government's commitment to a particular policy area. The creation of an Interministerial Delegation (*Délégation interministérielle*) is a means of attempting permanent coordination in a policy sphere which falls between several ministries, but which has a high governmental priority. They have existed in areas such as training policy, drug prevention campaigns or regional policy. It is a classic problem of public administration that horizontal interministerial delegations suffer from bureaucratic resistance from vertically organised government departments. From the point of view of government departments, the interministerial organ will always make unacceptable demands that deflect the ministry from its mission. Departments wish to determine where and when their expenditure takes place, rather than being forced to finance programmes they do not completely control.

A long-standing example of such an interministerial structure is the DATAR, the tool of central regional policy since the 1960s (Biarez 1989). In theory, the DATAR exists as an interministerial organ for coordinating all policies that have an effect upon spatial planning (*aménagement du territoire*). In practice, its power tends to vary according to the political support it receives at any one moment. The DATAR is resented not only by individual ministries, but often by local authorities as well, since its existence symbolises the state's interest in local affairs. A more recent example is that of the Interministerial Delegation for the City (*Délégation interministerielle de la Ville* (DIV)). This was created in 1989 in order to stress the Rocard government's commitment to an audacious urban policy: the invention of an interministerial structure was intended to give urban policy greater importance within the administrative apparatus. The efficiency of such structures depends upon a strong political will in order to facilitate their coordinating task: the DIV had to deal with over forty divisions spread across several ministries (Le Galès and Mawson 1994).

Tensions exist between different interests within a single sector

Government departments are highly complex entities. Competition between rival divisions (*directions*) can be acute, as each attempts to maximise influence and budgets against the claims of rivals within the same ministry (as well as against similar divisions in other departments). Within the French Education sector, for instance, competition for resources between the secondary and higher education divisions is endemic. These divisions are sometimes called upon to cohabit in the same department; on other occasions they form separate ministries. In his study of the Industry ministry, Friedberg (1974) pointed to the minimal contact between the heads of rival divisions, and to their preference for cultivating outside contacts rather than seeking compromise with each other.

Paris and the provinces

Tensions within a single ministry can also arise from conflicts of interest and appreciation between the Parisian headquarters of a ministry, and the regional and departmental field services of the same ministry. This has always existed, but the situation has become immensely more complicated since the *déconcentration* reforms of the 1980s and 1990s. By *déconcentration*, we mean the granting of greater autonomy to the regional and departmental offices of the main ministries. To some extent, these agencies can decide how they implement laws and decrees issued from Paris. Their autonomy is – in theory – counterbalanced by the requirement that they submit to the coordinating role of the prefect, rather than the hierarchical command of their Parisian headquarters. In practice the field services still have closer contacts with their own ministries, than with the prefectures, whose coordinating appetites are resented by the field services in a similar manner to the oversight role exercised by the Prime Minister on a national level.

Cross-cutting pressures

Finally, several sources of tension cut across those explored above. They include rivalries between members of the administrative *grands corps* and others; between *énarques* and others; between different territorial levels of administration (the centre, the regions, the departments), between the prefectures and the ministerial field services. The omnipresence of the state gives these rivalries an intensity in France that is absent in such an obvious form in most other European nations. Far from representing an administrative monolith, this situation has been likened to a bureaucratic jungle with few fixed ground rules (Dupuy and Thoenig, 1985). This is to overstate the case: there are several key elements of cohesion in the system. The sense of duty possessed by a caste of high-ranking civil servants is no less marked in France than it is in Britain and in both instances certainly more so than in the United States. The existence of a unitary system of government, and the concentration of most bureaucratic resources with the central government is another source of cohesion. The financial and technical resources possessed by the central ministries – and their field services – continues to give the state real presence at all territorial levels of administration. But it is probable that the uniform character of the French state has been overemphasised.

6.4	The reform of the state

From the perspective of the politicians – outside of election periods, at least – the case for reforming the operation of the French state is overwhelming. The external context within which the French administration functions is one of growing Europeanisation, a theme we develop in Chapter 13. The direct impact of the European Commission (and the European central bank) upon levels of public expenditure has become more obvious with the launch of the single currency in 1999 (though, as we see in Chapter 13, French governments have refused to be bound too tightly by the rules). Had the EU or EMU not been invented, French governments would still have been under pressure to rein in public expenditure and to reform working practices. More pressing in the early 1980s than the external context was the process of budgetary retrenchment. The Socialist economic U-turn of 1982–3 came after a period of unprecedented expansion in the economic and administrative public sector in 1981–2. Efforts to reform the state after 1983 formed part of the general effort at budgetary restraint imposed upon France's Socialist rulers. Rather unexpectedly, given its beginnings, the Socialist government of 1981–6 marked a watershed in the process of administrative reform. Budgetary cutbacks encouraged 'a move away from the traditional quantitative approach of seeking growth in the public sector to a qualitative strategy that emphasised the most efficient use of existing resources'. (Jones, 2003: 54) The Socialist government was also influenced by new ideas about public management that surfaced in the 1980s and that found favourable echoes from elements within the Socialist Party. Each subsequent government has sought new ways of ensuring the most efficient use of existing resources and of adapting the weighty French state machine to the complexity of modern governing tasks.

When we refer to the reform of the state we allude to (at least) two separate, though linked, objects of analysis. The reform of the state refers to a process of modernisation within the civil service, defined narrowly in terms of central departments, their field services and the processes of management reform therein. Reforming the state also involves attempts to modernise the delivery of public services in areas of traditional state involvement, such as education, taxation and the public industrial sector. The first process mainly concerns career civil servants working in public administration. The second involves attempts to intervene in the working practices of public sector professionals and workers. While there are many similarities between the two processes, the actors mobilised by state reform are different in the two cases. Reform of the civil service involves a fairly small number of professional administrators. Reform of the public sector, on the other hand, brings into play powerful public sector unions with the capacity to cause major disruption.

Reforming the state: the modernisation of the civil service

The reform of the state has been a preoccupation of all recent governments. No fewer than six different reform programmes have been implemented since

1981, with varying degrees of success, the most influential being that of Socialist premier Rocard in 1988–9. Though each reform programme has had its own characteristics, a number of common themes have resurfaced. The most important of these are the 'responsibilisation' of lower units, the use of contracts between central ministries and the field services, the introduction of more budgetary autonomy for lower administrative units, more user friendliness and the timid introduction of private sector techniques within French public administration.

Reforms have all centred upon the need to 'responsibilise' lower administrative echelons. There has been an acceptance by central governments from at least the early 1980s that the top-down hierarchical model is not the most efficient manner of delivering services. Central governments have attempted to transfer more functions to lower administrative units (or to local authorities), closer to the populations they are supposed to serve. Moves to enhanced political and administrative decentralisation from the early 1980s onwards were driven in part by ideas of modern management, namely that proximity allows more efficient service delivery. Reforms in the state machinery during the 1980s and 1990s were intended to strengthen and make more autonomous the regional and/or departmental units of the major ministries, the so-called field services. The field services were strengthened in part to allow them to deal with the newly empowered local and regional authorities, but also to provoke innovation at the local or regional levels of government departments.

Devolving responsibilities to lower levels in theory allows decisions to be taken closest to recipients of services. Under the Rocard programme (1988–9), there were two principal methods through which lower levels (the field services) would be empowered: service plans (*projets de services*) and cost centres (*centres de responsabilité*). Service plans would involve all staff in ministerial field services in defining key functions and performance indicators by which their action would be judged. Though agreeing service plans would not produce additional resources, they were intended to encourage dialogue within field units. By 1991, 470 service plans had been signed (Jones, 2003). The cost centre scheme gave lower units more flexibility in staff management, as well as more control over local budgets. Both schemes were voluntary and each met with internal resistance from the middle ranks of the bureaucracy, for reasons we consider below. Juppé's government in 1995 introduced a rather similar scheme, in the form of the service contracts.

Contractualisation between the central administrative divisions and their field services was the counterpart to their 'responsibilisation'. The Rocard circular of 1988 contained the recommendation that relations between a field service and its central ministry should be codified in the form of three-year contractual agreements. Officials within the field services were invited to develop medium-term projects and to sign contracts with their lead divisions within the central ministry. These contracts were not legally binding. They would be separate from the annual budgetary negotiations and would not produce additional sources of financing. The real significance of the Rocard reforms was to introduce the notion of contractualisation between a ministry and its field services, a theme that has resurfaced in various guises and in different ministries since then. As a counterpart of more devolved powers, field services would be made more accountable for their actions and be subject to processes of audit and evaluation.

Financial reforms, introduced by Rocard and Jospin especially, were potentially the most important innovation. With the cost centre scheme, Rocard introduced the notion of enhanced budgetary flexibility. Provisions for financial globalisation were developed further during the Jospin government (Dreyfus, 2002). Financial reforms have centred around the introduction, then generalisation of 'global' budgets. Rather than the older device of budgetary chapters (where credits had to be approved by Paris for minor elements of expenditure and funds could not be transferred across budgetary headings) global budgets allow much more discretion. Field services receive block grants that – within limits – they can put to use as they see fit. For those interviewed in 2000 in the Education ministry, however, enhanced budgetary autonomy was more apparent than real, since budgetary choices still had to be approved by the Budget Division of the Finance Ministry. The field official of the Finance Ministry (the *Trésorier payeur-général*), moreover, has to approve any changes to planned budgets, which civil servants interviewed found a very burdensome procedure.

Another important theme in the reform of the state programmes was to encourage public administrations to become more user friendly. A Charter for Public Services was created under Rocard in 1992. Premier Juppé (1995) insisted upon the need to simplify administrative procedures, notably by creating One-Stop Shops (*Maisons des services publics*) for citizens to deal with the administration. In a major symbolic reform, the Jospin government abolished the *État-civil* in 2002. Civil servants are encouraged to see their role not only as those vested with public authority, but also as efficient service providers.

Some observers have concluded that a French-style New Public Management has evolved (Demaillie, 1993). As Wright (1994) argued, any country is likely to 'select those aspects of the New Public Management agenda that correspond to its own specific institutional context', which makes agreeing to the proposition rather easier. Stevens (1996) contends that internal administrative controls are used primarily to ensure consistency with procedures, not evaluation of results and performance. Nonetheless, themes of contractualisation, evaluation, performance targets and enhanced budgetary autonomy all contribute to a new management ethos within public sector organisations that bears some similarities with New Public Management (Breuillard and Cole, 2003). The culture of evaluation is certainly different from that in the UK, but, as Dreyfus (1994), Oberdorff (1998), Elgie (2003) and others demonstrate, independent administrative agencies (such as the High Council for Broadcasting (CSA), the Telecommunications Regulatory Authority (ART) or the National Commission for Freedom and Information (CNIL)) have performed an increasingly important role. The French administration has also gone some way down the road of introducing management techniques from the private sector (such as quality circles, audit and human resource management) into the management of public organisations. Though the mode of operation of French public administration remains hierarchical, corporate and rule-driven, the complexity of policy challenges has forced the French administration to imagine innovative responses.

There are a number of fundamental ambiguities with the reform of the state programmes. The reforms were not integrated into the French administrative framework. No government attempted to call into question the 1946 civil service statute, for example, or seriously to challenge the system of administrative corps. Until the Raffarin government, negotiating working conditions (the system of *corps* and the 1946 statute) did not form part of the agenda. Social peace was a prelude to more organisational efficiency.

Reforming the state II: the public sector

Reforming the state also involves attempts by central government to modernise the working conditions and improve the service delivery of public sector professionals and workers. The difficulties encountered by governments of all persuasions in implementing reform point to powerful structural constraints. In spite of three decades of attempts to reform the state, the weight of the public sector in France has actually increased. In contrast, all other developed countries have reduced their public sector. In recent years, there have been many examples of unsuccessful reform attempts by ambitious ministers. Premier Juppé's attempts to reform the employment statutes of public sector workers provoked mass strikes in November–December 1995 that brought the country to a standstill. More recently, premier Raffarin's attempt in 2003 to equalise pension provision between public and private sectors provoked a furious backlash from the public sector trade unions. In between these two examples, the Jospin government (1997–2002) provided some excellent examples both of the scope of reformist ambition and the meagre results achieved. Two examples were particularly illustrative of the difficulties in reforming the public sector in France.

The failure of the Finance Ministry to reform itself in March 2000 provided one example. France has a particularly costly and inefficient system of tax collection. One bureaucratic unit (DGCP – Public Finance Directorate) is responsible for assessing tax liabilities, another (DGI – General Directorate for Taxes) for collecting taxes. This anachronistic separation between tax assessment and tax collection dates back to Napoleon. In 2000, the Finance Minister Christian Sautter announced his decision to merge the two divisions, with the aim of simplifying France's costly system of tax administration. His reformist intent encountered determined resistance from both divisions, each with its own distinctive culture and with different patterns of Union strength. The Public Finance Directorate – dominated by Force Ouvrière – argued against the reform because it would threaten the existence of the tax offices (and therefore jobs) in many of the smallest French towns. Faced with fierce mobilisation from the public sector unions, Sautter abandoned his reform. The present (at the time of writing) incumbent of the Finance Ministry, Francis Mer, has backed away from several important reforms: such as the pay as you go system of income tax collection; the non-suppression of the TV licence (which costs more to collect than it brings in public revenues) and the suspension of further administrative decentralisation of the Finance Ministry, as initially promised.

If Finance is unable to reform itself, there is little chance that other ministries will follow.

The Education Ministry provides an equally cogent example. Jospin's first Education Minister, Claude Allègre, aroused fierce passions by calling for thoroughgoing reform of the 'Mammouth', as he delicately described the Education Ministry. One of Allègre's first acts was to reorganise the central administration at the Rue de Grenelle, the Ministry's Parisian headquarters. The Minister announced the suppression of eight (out of nineteen) central divisions, and decreed that there must be much greater administrative decentralisation. Some lasting reforms were implemented. Since 1999, for example, staff transfers within the regions have no longer been managed by Paris, but have taken place at the level of the Academies (the field service of the Education Ministry). This measure posed a real threat to the power base of the SNES, the main secondary teachers' union, since the union dominated the committee in the rue de Grenelle that determined staff transfers. As Claude Allègre discovered to his cost, the successful implementation of educational policy still depends upon the acquiescence of the teaching unions. Though Allègre 'won' on staff transfers, he lost on a raft of other issues that the teaching unions opposed (teaching methods, school governance, the decentralisation of some technical staff). Reforms that threaten the core interests of the teaching profession encounter the determined and usually effective opposition of the teaching unions. The succession of Education Ministers during the 1990s (Jospin, Lang, Fillon, Bayrou, Allègre) illustrates the point.

The reshuffle of March 2000 appeared to lend weight to the failure of state reform under Jospin. Allègre was forced to go as Education Minister and the Finance Minister, Sautter, abandoned his attempt to streamline France's tax system, being replaced shortly after as Minister. In the absence of successful reform, the progression of the French state continues relentlessly and there is an automatic growth in the number of civil servants. Thus, the number of civil servants increased by 17,000 in the last year of the Jospin government. The demand for additional public services – in the area of security especially – increases the importance of public sector employment.

6.5	Concluding remarks

When Clark (2000) refers to the 'institutional and cultural constraints on the capacity of the French administrative system to move towards a more managerial model of administration', he is articulating the mainstream view about the innate conservatism of the French administration and its contextual incapacity to change. The French state consists not merely of a set of institutions, but also represents a core of beliefs and interests. Habits of centralised thinking remain very strong. National state traditions underpin norms and rules, as well as remaining deeply embedded in the consciousness and the behaviour of the actors. Powerful trade unions and civil service corps form a coalition to bar the route to many UK-style developments. There is strong resistance to reform, stemming from a combination of institutions, ideas and interests. The causes of resistance and institutional stability are certainly very strong. The terms of working conditions of the civil service, the role of the civil service statute and the system of administrative corps all contribute to institutional lethargy. Established positions are backed up by ingrained ideas, especially about the nature and importance of public service. The mobilising myth of social progress through public service has come to form part of modern French political culture (Cole, 1999). On the other hand, the French state has had to adapt to significant changes in its internal and external environment. How it has adapted has varied somewhat according to level (local, regional, national, European) institution and issue-area, a theme we revisit in the final chapter of the book.

Insofar as the civil service is concerned, the administrative reforms first introduced by the Rocard government (1988–91) have produced a great deal of organisational innovation. If anything, they have added to the fragmentation of the French state, a conclusion that is equally valid with respect to France's local and regional authorities that we now consider.

7 Local and regional government

7.1 Introduction

One of the most apparent paradoxes of the French polity lies in the coexistence of rigid centralised judicial norms and rules, and a rich diversity of local and regional situations and practices. This diversity exists in spite of (or because of) the uniform presence upon the territory of metropolitan France of three levels of subnational government and administration: the commune (36,500), the departmental council (96) and the Regional council (22). Following on from the discussion of the French state in the previous chapter, here we study political and administrative decentralisation and the organisation of local and regional government. The main body of the chapter focuses upon the decentralisation reforms of the early 1980s and their lasting consequences. We also present brief commentary of a much more recent effort to deepen decentralisation, that undertaken by the Raffarin government of 2003–4. An attempt is made to formulate some conclusions in relation to the impact and consequences of the decentralisation reforms and to identify underlying continuities in French subnational administration.

7.2 The French model of territorial administration

French subnational authorities have traditionally operated within the confines of a highly centralising state tradition, which emphasises the indivisible nature of political legitimacy and the organisational pre-eminence and legitimacy of the state. The revolutionary and Napoleonic periods established the republican model of territorial integration that remains important even today. The orthodox French model of territorial administration rested upon the principle of administrative uniformity across the nation. It formed part of a hierarchical mode of public policy formulation, whereby public policies originated within government departments or administrative corps, were implemented in localities by state field agencies and local authorities and were coordinated by the prefect, the representative of the French state in the departments. The prefect was charged with controlling local authorities, implementing central government policies and maintaining public order. Underneath the prefect, the subprefects exercised an even closer control over local authorities. Government departments were organised in an analogous manner, with decentralised units often operating at the departmental and subdepartmental levels. Thus, the taxation offices were arranged around a departmental division, with subdivisions at the level of the *arrondissement* (electoral constituency) and officers at the level of the commune (Mabileau, 1991). This tentacular organisation of the French state in the localities brought forth metaphors of the 'Honeycomb state' (Dupuy and Thoenig, 1983).

As the Republic was one and indivisible, so local government units were long considered to be the antennae of central government. The ninety-six departments were sufficiently large to allow for the efficient territorial administration and implementation of central state policies, but they were sufficiently small not to pose a challenge to central state direction. Subservient departments were favoured over more independent-minded communes. In practice, the pattern of subnational politics contained a rather more subtle mix of centralising ambition and local influence than implied by this top-down model. The 38,000 French communes were based on the parishes of the pre-Revolutionary *ancien régime*. The communes were usually the foci of local identities and community interests that persisted in spite of the centralising ambition of the Republic. The 1884 Municipal Government Act recognised the responsibility of municipal government for 'the affairs of the commune'. The Act endorsed municipal councils as entities with their own legal character, with the right to raise budgets. The pre-eminent figure in French small-town society was the mayor, the head of the commune and the personification of local identities.

The dependency of local democracy on the central state attracted academic attention in the 1960s and 1970s. Specifically related to local administration, Crozier and Thoenig (1975) developed the 'cross-regulation' approach to describe relations between local political and administrative actors in this state-centric and bureaucratic system. Three pillars supported the system. First, the rules governing centre–periphery relations were defined by national politicians and officials. In the state-centric view, the control of society required uniform administrative rules and a hierarchical method of making and implementing public policy. While local politicians and officials could negotiate concessions and exceptions, the rules had to remain intact. Second, there was a long-term dialogue between state officials (notably the prefect) and local *notables* to allow for adjustments to nationally defined rules to reflect local circumstances. Third, local relationships were limited to a 'dual elite' of political and administrative actors. The principal local relationships were between political *notables* (parliamentarians, mayors, departmental councillors) and state officials (either prefects, or officials from the ministerial field services).

The practice of multiple office holding (*cumul des mandats*) was for long (and to some extent still is) a central feature of this system of cross-regulation. The logic of this practice preceded the decentralisation reforms of the early 1980s and, indeed, was especially important during the Third Republic, where the presence of the deputy in Paris presented physical opportunities for accessing favours and resources. Given the dispersal of decision-making authority across a range of separate institutions, individual politicians felt compelled to accumulate

Hotel du Ville in Paris: the seat of France's most influential local council

political offices in order to consolidate their own political positions and to strengthen their bargaining position in relation to others, especially the departmental prefect. A classic example would be that of a mayor, who is elected deputy. As a simple mayor, he occupied a relatively weak bargaining position *vis-à-vis* the departmental prefect, or other local authorities. As a deputy and a mayor, local interests could be more effectively defended, since national connections could be called upon to overcome the resistance of a departmental prefect. Any genuine *notable* could usually ensure the defence of his essential interests against the prefect, the state's departmental representative.

The effects of *cumul des mandats* and of local adaptations to national rules ensured a space for negotiation, compromise, even for the building of local coalitions between mayors and prefects in 'local politico-administrative systems'. For all of their flexibility, however, centre–periphery relations remained bureaucratic and hierarchical. Post-war innovation occurred, by and large, outside local government, in the technical services of central ministries and within the regional planning agency, the DATAR. During the 1970s, the localist case began to be won at the level of ideas. The Guichard (1976), Peyrefitte (1976) and Bonnet (1978) reports gave support for more decentralisation, as did the Barre government's Green Paper of 1978 (Cole and John, 2001). There was a measure of elite-level consensus in favour of change, though powerful opponents persisted within the Interior Ministry, the Senate and amongst the *grands corps*.

| 7.3 | The decentralisation reforms, 1982–3 |

In the decade ensuing their implementation, the Socialist decentralisation reforms attracted a good deal of attention, both in France and amongst external observers (Ashford, 1982; Schmidt, 1990; Biarez, 1989; Dion, 1986; Rondin, 1986; Keating and Hainsworth, 1986). The decentralisation reforms of 1982–3 were highly complex. The reforms created twenty-two elected regional councils, replacing previously co-opted institutions, and greatly enhanced the decision-making powers of the ninety-six departmental councils and of the larger communes. The decision-making responsibilities of a range of local actors were increased, with the extension of their influence into policy sectors within which they previously exercised a marginal influence, or from which they were excluded altogether (such as social affairs, economic development and education). The three layers of French subnational government – the region, the department and the commune – were all strengthened, with increases in budgets, staff and powers. Amongst the numerous laws and decrees, the most prominent decisions involved:

- the creation of directly elected regional authorities as a separate tier of sub-national government;
- the transfer of executive authority from the prefect to the elected heads of the ninety-six departmental councils and 36,500 communes;
- the right of communes and departmental councils to set their budgets without prior prefectoral oversight;
- the transfer of some staff from the prefectures and the ministerial field services to the departmental councils.

The general principles underpinning decentralisation were vague and generous. Greater democracy and citizen participation were the declared objectives of the 1982–3 reforms. In opposition in the 1970s, the Socialists had called for an increase in citizen participation and self-management. The Socialists argued that the proximity of municipal, departmental and regional authorities made them the appropriate suppliers of an extensive range of services. Proximity was more democratic. It was also more efficient, since it avoided unnecessary bureaucratic delays, and allowed local authorities greater choice in prioritising their activities. Arguments of proximity thus encompassed expectations of greater democracy and the more efficient delivery of services. For some critics, however, the real issue at stake involved not democratisation, but the removal of constraints on the power of entrenched municipal *notables*, especially prominent within the ranks of the Socialist Party.

The 1982 reforms were guided by two rather contradictory operational principles. First, that decision-making responsibilities should be attributed to specific 'levels' of subnational authority. Second, that all authorities should enjoy the freedom of initiative to make policies in areas they deemed to be important for their constituents. The first of these principles enshrined the so-called '*blocs de compétences*', particular responsibilities carried out by the different levels. As a general rule, matters of immediate proximity (low-level social assistance, administrative port of first call, planning permission, waste) are the preserve of the communes and the various inter-communal bodies – SIVU, SIVOM, EPCI – to which they delegate authority. Matters of intermediate proximity are the policy province of the ninety-six elected departmental councils (the *départements*) which manage large budgets and are major service delivery agencies (in social assistance, some intermediate education, social services, roads, minimal income (RMI)). Matters deemed to be strategic are, in theory, the preserve of the elected regions: economic development, vocational training, infrastructure, some secondary education, some transport (and regional rail services since 2002), with additional responsibilities in culture and the environment.

The second principle – that of the 'free administration of local authorities' – cuts across the apparent clarity of the first. In practice, the various subnational authorities have overlapping territorial jurisdictions and loosely defined spheres of competence. Even when responsibilities are clear, they are not respected. Communes, departments and regions compete openly with each other and adopt policies designed to appeal to their electorates. Moreover, there is no formal hierarchy between them. In theory, no single authority can impose its will on any other, or prevent a rival authority from adopting policies in competition with its own. Unlike in genuinely federal systems, the French regions do not exercise leadership over other local authorities; if anything, the French regions are dependent upon the cooperation of lower-level authorities – the *départements* in particular – for the successful implementation of their own policies.

7.4	Local and regional government after decentralisation

However consequential, the decentralisation reforms did not alter the basic, highly fragmented structure of French local government. In contrast to the pattern of ongoing change in the United Kingdom, there has been no root and branch structural reform of local government in France. Rather a process of incremental accretion has taken place. New structures have been added to existing ones, without a fundamental overhaul of the territorial system as a whole. This observation remains as true in 2004 as it did twenty years ago. In the main body of the chapter, we now explore in some detail the functioning of local and regional governance in France. We consider in turn the commune, inter-communal structures, the departmental councils and the elected regions.

The commune

As the oldest and most revered territorial unit in France, the commune imposes attention. With the commune, France has probably the smallest local politico-administrative structure of any country. France's 36,500 or so communes elect 550,000 local councillors, almost 500,000 of whom represent 34,000 rural or small-town communes with less than 1500 inhabitants. The modern commune is based on the parishes drawn up by the Church between the tenth and twelfth centuries. Communal perimeters were redrawn during the French Revolution, but they usually respected the older parish boundaries. Although the size and character of communes vary enormously, each disposes of the same legal rights and obligations. This creates major difficulties, given that the policy problems faced by municipal authorities in large French cities have little in common with those of rural hamlets. Apart from the special exceptions of Paris, Lyons and Marseilles, the same municipal laws have traditionally regulated local government in large cities as well in small rural communes. Until 1977, Paris did not have a mayor, but a prefect and a prefect of police named by the central government. In 1977 the first direct election of the mayor of Paris transformed the office into a major national political prize. No government can henceforth ignore the Paris town hall, the powerbase from 1977–95 of President Chirac. Special regimes were also introduced for Lyons and Marseilles in 1982.

Most French citizens identify with their commune, and express confidence in their mayor. Attempts to reform local government by regrouping communes into larger units have usually been met by hostility. The commune is a symbol of civic identification; the next echelon, the canton, is a far more artificial institution, which often regroups communes with diverging interests and different socio-economic compositions. Because of their diverse situations, it is difficult to make too many generalisations concerning France's 36,500 communes. The size and geographical location of a particular commune is more indicative of its nature than the mere fact of its being a commune. We must distinguish between small and medium-sized communes (up to 20,000 inhabitants), which generally exist in a dependent relationship with, and look for protection from, higher placed local, regional and state authorities (especially the ninety-six departments); and larger urban communes, which adopt characteristics of city governments. The preoccupations facing the two types of authority are completely different. Small rural communes usually have to combine forces to provide even such basic services as water provision and waste disposal. Large urban communes are genuine city governments with large budgets, often employing thousands of local authority employees and providing a wide range of social, economic and cultural services.

Communes are distinguished from other layers of French subnational government by their proximity to local citizens. The demands placed on municipal governments far outweigh their legal responsibilities. Their core service delivery responsibilities involve primary education, water, fire prevention, land use, streetlighting, sewerage and waste disposal. Ambitious communes provide a range of additional services in areas such as cultural and economic development. Aside from their role as service providers, municipal governments are the focal point of France's thousands of local communities. They are also the site for the playing out of local political rivalries and personal ambitions. The communes remain the foci of local identities. As Nemery (2003) argues, all reform projects that have been based purely on technical/economical imperatives have failed. Thus the 1971 law allowing for the merging of communes had a very weak impact, and the 1982 Defferre law ignored fusing communes altogether.

The key resource that all communes share (and jealously guard for themselves) is that they control the development of the land over which their jurisdiction is based. This comprises a total of 90 per cent of national territory. Within the confines of the Urban Code, communes can grant or withhold planning permission for public or private sector developments. Such a resource is becoming increasingly important as the demand for development land intensifies. Environmental critics complain that weak planning controls – and the general lack of a Green Belt policy – have led to uncontrolled expansion initiated by irresponsible local authorities. Urban expansion has occurred in part because communes compete with each other in order to attract business and consumer investment into their areas.

The central figure in French small-town and rural society is the mayor, who performs the combined roles of locally elected politician and servant of the state. The contrast between the mayor of a small town of between 1–10,000 inhabitants and the mayor of a large metropolitan city is striking. Whereas the former personally or indirectly knows most of the town's citizens, the relationship between the big city mayor and his electors is based on more indirect channels of communication. The big city mayor is usually a national political figure as well, with severe constraints on his or her time. In small communes the mayor is usually the only person who can coordinate the activities of the different administrative agencies. In the large cities, mayors will use their national influence to ensure – as far as possible – that the decisions taken by local administrative agencies do not discriminate against their interests. In both types of commune, mayors attempt to consolidate their local influence by sponsoring a range of local associations. The delivery of local services can create faithful clients anxious for the survival of the municipal team in place. A successful mayor attempts to maintain good relations with the principal interests of her commune, including the main local associations and charities, local businesses, representatives of the state (prefectoral and ministerial field services) and political interests (especially the local party and local electors).

In the main cities, French mayors have performed a prominent role in promoting local economic networks to attract funds and investment into their localities in an era of increasing municipal competition (Le Galès, 1993, 1995). The mayor-entrepreneur metaphor should not be over-stressed, however. Mayors must interest themselves in everything that goes on in their cities, including in the insalubrious poorer quarters: efforts to improve living standards in visibly deprived areas are probably more important for their survival than high level prestige projects, especially in a climate of municipal corruption. If French mayors have forged closer links with business interests since the early 1980s, these are not exclusive; close links with networks of non-economic associations have proved essential for their survival. The decentralisation process has also strengthened the role of the mayor's fellow executive officers (*adjoints*), sometimes capable of building their own powerful networks independently of their mayor.

On paper, the communes gained least from the 1982–3 decentralisation. Municipal governments already had an elected executive. The mayor has always had responsibility for drawing up the commune's budget and executing the decisions of the municipal council, although traditionally this power depended upon creating a *modus vivendi* with the prefect (or subprefect for mayors of smaller communes). Active municipal councils in the major French cities were already pursuing ambitious programmes of urban renovation in the 1960s and 1970s (Cole and John, 2001). Since the 1982–3 legislation, the prefect can no longer veto the mayor's decisions, which must be implemented if they respect the law. The prefect retains the right to challenge their legality or financial probity in the administrative courts or regional Courts of Accounts, but this control is exercised a posteriori. These powers are used sparingly. The mayor's powers have undoubtedly been reinforced in numerous spheres: for example over town planning, municipal housing, employment and local economic policy.

As measured in terms of budgets and staff, the communes remain by far the most important local authorities in France, but their situation varies dramatically. The ability to exercise an influence beyond their traditional duties depends upon the financial and logistical resources that communes have at their disposal. Small communes continue to depend upon outside advice and assistance in order to carry out their legal functions. The mayors of small communes used to depend upon the prefect or subprefect for advice; they now seek protection from elected representatives of the departmental councils. The smallest communes are often incapable of deciding upon the merits of planning applications, for example. Preceding decentralisation, small communes called upon the field services of the Equipment Ministry (DDE) to examine applications for building permits. Since 1983, they have as often called upon the technical services of the Departmental Council, but they continue to call for outside assistance. The mayors of large cities fared better from decentralisation. Only large cities are in a position to create extensive bureaucracies. Urban planning agencies have expanded in the main French cities, testament to the determination of local authorities to plan their local environment. Dynamic entrepreneurial mayors have succeeded in launching major local renovation projects in large metropolitan centres, such as Grenoble, Toulouse or Lille.

The system of local government taxation traditionally increased such competition between communes. Though councils are recipients of four separate taxes, most local taxation is raised by the *taxe professionelle*, a business tax levied on local businesses. The business tax produces obvious territorial inequalities. Richer communes with fewer social problems are attractive to business and hence raise more money from taxation, while poorer communes, less attractive to business investment, have the greatest social needs. In the absence on an overarching system of fiscal transfers (*péréquation*) communes compete with each other for business location decisions. Many of the most obvious inequalities occur within cities, where richer communes are often resolutely hostile to sharing the fiscal resource with their less endowed neighbours. A law of 12 July 1999 greatly reduced the fiscal autonomy of urban communes by its provisions for a single rate of business tax throughout the new city-wide communities (see next section).

The large number of French communes remains a source of weakness. Even large communes have not fully developed their technical, informational and bureaucratic resources. They are often forced to turn to private sector operators to provide services such as sewerage, heating and incineration. Moreover, parochial, political and fiscal rivalries will often resist inter-communal collaboration unless it is imposed from the exterior.

Inter-communality

However deeply embedded in French political culture, the commune is rather ineffective in terms of delivering services. The extreme fragmentation of French communes requires cooperation between them to provide basic services. At its most elementary level, single function (SIVU) or multiple function (SIVOM) inter-communal syndicates ensure such cooperation between communes. Rural communes rely on such arrangements to carry out their basic duties in areas like transport, road maintenance and waste disposal. Large cities face different types of problems. While large cities typically contain thirty to eighty communes, public policy problems do not respect such small communal boundaries. City centre authorities are usually associated with outlying communes in order to provide services such as housing, fire prevention and urban planning. There has been a growing impetus behind the development of city-wide local government structures as a tool for tackling problems of urban governance. The most complex of these city-wide inter-communal structures are the urban communities, which have taken over many of the traditional communal functions in France's largest cities, such as Lyons, Marseilles and Lille. Created by central government in 1968, the urban communities have gradually become key players in the governance of the larger French cities, though their development has been hampered by their indirect method of election and their narrow fiscal base.

The 1990s witnessed a major legislative effort to strengthen further inter-communal structures, particularly through developing the inter-communal public corporations (*Établissements publics de co-operation intercommunal* – EPCI). In French public law, the EPCI has the statute of a public corporation. It is not a fully constituted local authority – such as a commune, department or region – but it has an independent executive and certain tax-raising powers. The principal EPCI are the urban communities, urban districts and the new city-wide communities (*communuatés d'agglomeration*). Moves to strengthen the EPCI were driven by the desire to discourage local tax competition, to ensure a more equitable distribution of resources and to promote appropriate structures for tackling organisational weakness.

In the morass of laws and regulations addressing issues of subnational governance in the 1990s (including the Pasqua Law of 1995 and Voynet Law of 1999 which dealt with rural areas), two important laws explicitly addressed the combined problems of inter-communal cooperation and local government finance. The Joxe Law of 1992 gave the urban districts, urban communities and the new 'communities of towns' and 'communities of communes' the possibility of implementing fiscal transfers from richer to poorer communes by levying the business tax on a city-wide basis. The Chevènement Law of 12 July 1999 went much further, by creating new city-wide communities, wherein the business tax would be levied and distributed at a supra-communal level. For the first time, recalcitrant communes could be forced to join these communities. In a move interpreted by many as a return of the state, the prefect could insist that individual communes form part of a city wide community. Close observers considered the Chevènement Law to be a major success. In the first three years of its existence 120 *communautés d'agglomeration* came into existence. By the end of 2002, the number of EPCI had risen to 2174, from 466 in 1993.

Henceforth, three-quarters of French communes form part of larger inter-communal public corporations, which cover 45,000,000 French citizens (INSEE, 2003). The EPCI are gradually replacing the older functional syndicates (SIVU and SIVOM) as the principal agencies of inter-communal collaboration, not only within the main cities (urban communities) but across medium-sized

Table 7.1 Subnational authorities in mainland France

Type	Number	Functions
Communes	36,500	Varying services, including local plans (POS), building permits, building and maintainance of primary schools, waste disposal, some welfare services
Voluntary Intercommunal syndicates*	not available	Groups of communes with a single function (SIVU), or delivering multiple services (SIVOM)
Tax-raising intercommunal public corporations (EPCI)* Includes: urban communities; city-wide communities and communities of communes	2174	Permanent organisations in charge of inter-communal services such as firefighting, waste disposal, transport, economic development, housing
Departmental Councils	96	Social affairs, some secondary education (*collèges*), road building and maintenance
Regional Councils	22	Economic development, transport, infrastructure, state-region plans, some secondary education (*lycées*)

* These organisations are legally considered as local public establishments, rather than fully fledged local authorities

towns as well (city-wide communities) and to a lesser extent within rural areas (communities of communes). The spread of inter-communality has led to powerful demands for direct democratic elections to these powerful new structures, which, thus far, have not been implemented.

The departmental councils

The decentralisation reforms of the early 1980s set 'departmentalists' against 'regionalists'. While the former wanted to concentrate most decentralised activities in the ninety-six General Councils, the latter advocated recognising a leadership role (amongst the subnational authorities) for the Regional Councils. In most respects, the 'departmentalists' won this particular battle. The departments emerged as the clear victors, invested with larger budgets, more staff and more service-delivery responsibilities than the regions. Powerful entrenched interests already operated through the departments, while the regions were untried and untested. Central government preferred to deal with the relatively subservient departments, rather than strong regions which might contest its authority. Decentralisation conferred new functions on the departments, but these were not new institutions. Departments are composed of cantons, of which there are some 2000, generally concentrated in rural and small town areas. Along with the commune, the canton has subsisted since the French Revolution. The original justification for the department was to enable any inhabitant to travel on horse to the prefecture and back in one day; this makes no sense in the age of the fast-speed train, the TGV. Due to population movements and demographic changes, the boundaries of France's 2000 cantons are heavily over-representative of rural areas.

With the 1982 decentralisation, the Departmental Councils gained a new democratic legitimacy, in addition to increased staffs and budgets. The presidency of the Departmental Council has become one of the coveted positions in French local government. Since 1982 the president of the Departmental Council has been legally recognised as the fount of executive power within the department, replacing the centrally-nominated prefect. In the opinion of one interviewee: 'the change at the level of the departments was enormous, far more significant than for the communes'. The president of the Departmental Council has inherited certain functions of the prefect, notably that of advising and coordinating the activities of small communes. For this reason, the presidency of the Departmental Council has been a favoured resting place for ex-ministers.

The Departmental Councils possess important financial, bureaucratic and legal resources. The financial resources of the departments are significant: benefiting from the transfer of state funds (in the form of specific grants-in-aid and a general block grant), the departments also have the right to raise local taxation and to charge for services. The departmental president is responsible for preparing the council's budget, previously drawn up by the prefect's services. Departmental budgets can be considerable: that of the Nord department in 1995 was twice the amount of the Nord/Pas-de-Calais regional council's budget, although the region catered for 4,000,000 inhabitants, as against 2,500,000 for the department. The imbalance between departments and regions has become less marked since 1995, but remains consequential. In the Brittany region in 2002, for example, the Regional Council and the Departmental Council of Finistère (one of four departments within Brittany) had approximately the same budget.

The key advantage held by the departments over other territorial authorities stems from their powerful bureaucratic means: with decentralisation, the departments took in charge many of the civil servants previously attached to the prefectures. In certain rare cases, the Departmental Councils have also taken direct control of the personnel of the field services of government ministries, notably the DDE. The departments were able to rely upon a tested bureaucratic personnel, while the regions had to experiment and innovate.

These inequalities reflect the differing services that are delivered by the two types of authority. The services that the Departmental Councils are legally obliged to deliver include social services, some healthcare, post-primary education and departmental road-building programmes. Defenders of the departments point out that these basic services rarely occupy the limelight, but involve an extremely sophisticated financial and organisational infrastructure. The cost of social service provision has escalated dramatically, plunging several Departmental Councils into a severe financial crisis. Departments have also taken over responsibility for services they did not ask for: this is notably the case for the minimum income, created by the Rocard government in 1988.

Apart from their statutory obligations, Departmental Councils can engage in policies in other areas, except where they are specifically forbidden to do so. The Departmental Councils compete with the regions and the communes in the economic development sphere, adopting their own policies usually concerned with safeguarding non-urban interests. As for big city mayors, the launching of major infrastructure projects can be a matter of prestige; each departmental President wants to associate his name with a major project.

The constraints weighing upon France's ninety-six Departmental Councils are multiple. Many Departmental Councils have fallen seriously into debt in carrying out their new responsibilities (INSEE, 2003). In spite of their powerful organisation, and financial resources, the departments are felt to lack political legitimacy. Departmental councillors are renewed by halves every three years. They represent individual cantons, rather than places on a party list. Unlike the mayor, the departmental president is not directly elected as head of a party list, but represents an individual constituency (or canton). Her status is that of *primus inter pares*, rather than that of executive mayor. Presidents must strike bargains to rally support from other councillors, who are often *notables* in their own right. This electoralism militates against the promotion of coherent long-term policies. Departmental presidents might be *notables*, but they have to deal equally with other *notables*, especially the mayors of large cities. They must also cooperate with powerful deputies or senators, and party chiefs. Departmental Councils must also cope with the competition of other layers of subnational government, namely the regions and the cities. Relations between the Departmental Council and the department's leading city are often acrimonious, on account of the over-representation of rural and small-town areas in most Departmental Councils. The political affinities of the large cities and the countryside are frequently opposed, with the left strongly represented in urban areas and the right in the departments. The Departmental Council feels more at ease with the small and medium-sized communes, for whom it performs a role of adviser and benefactor. Insofar as they are capable of performing such a role, the departments attempt to act as arbiters between the traditional ethos of the French countryside and the dynamic, growth-oriented towns.

The regions

Regionalisation in France dates back to the late 1950s but reached its high point in the period 1982–6 with the setting up of elected regional councils as part of a wider programme of decentralisation (Cole and John, 2001; Loughlin and Mazey, 1995). The regional institution in France is the result of a long process of what might be called 'creeping institutionalisation' as it was gradually (and grudgingly) granted a position in the politico-administrative system alongside the departments and the communes. The regional institution was established while retaining the longer established and, in many ways, more powerful departments. Consistent with the territorial management policies of the post-war French state, French administrative regions were first established in the 1950s as technocratic advisory bodies to assist in strategic functions of economic development, transport and territorial planning. They have been fully operational subnational authorities only since 1982, with their main (limited) responsibilities in economic development, transport, education, training and culture.

The innovation of the 1982–3 decentralisation legislation lay in the provision that the regions should be directly elected. To the extent that the regions owe their existence as full authorities to the 1982–3 decentralisation legislation, they can also claim to be victors of the decentralisation process. They benefited indirectly from the removal of prefectoral control, and from the creation of a directly elected executive. This gave them an authority they had never possessed before. Most experts today consider that France's system of subnational government has 'one layer too many'. While the department has its defenders, for many the region would appear as a more logical structure, especially in the context of European Union regional policy, which only recognises states and regions as possible recipients of EU aid.

As argued above, the 'regionalists' lost out in the debates surrounding the decentralisation legislation. Relations between the departments and the regions are often acerbic. At their inception, the regions had neither the organisational past, nor the bureaucratic resources available to the Departmental Councils. Unlike the departments, they were unable to rely on the transfer of state personnel, although many state civil servants opted for the challenge of serving the new regions. In contrast with the sizeable bureaucracies serving the large cities, and the departments, the organisational resources available to the regions are minimal: there are fewer than 100 salaried staff in most regions. Moreover, as untested institutions, existing *notables* preferred not to invest their time in adding regional posts to their existing offices. Most regional presidents were initially second-rank politicians, placed in position by departmental elites who were anxious to ensure that the regions did not discover a real existence. A few powerful regional presidents emerged, but their power had been established prior to acceding to the regional presidency. Examples included Olivier Guichard in Pays de la Loire, Michel d'Ornano in Basse-Normandie, or Jacques Chaban-Delmas in Aquitaine. Except in these isolated cases, regional political leadership was no real match for that of the large cities or departments. This situation has changed gradually, but there remains a penchant for other elective offices before those of the region.

The president of the Regional Council is elected by her peers at the first council meeting; this usually involves horsetrading between several parties and subtle coalition arrangements which vary from one region to another. The regions have suffered from the electoral system used for the six-yearly elections to the regional assemblies. The use of a highly proportional version of proportional representation for elections to the regional assemblies has produced numerous hung councils since 1986, which have proved incapable of imposing a clear political direction. The electoral system used for regional elections from 1986 to 1998 did little to enhance a sense of regional identity. In 1986, 1992 and 1998, Regional Councils were elected on the basis of departmental lists, with the departmental party organisations determining positions on the list. In 2004, a two-round proportional system was introduced, with a high threshold to representation (10 per cent) and an advantage to the leading list. The new electoral system, it was hoped, would prevent the fragmentation of party support and limit the influence of the extreme right that had made the effective functioning of Regional Councils so difficult after previous elections, that of 1998 in particular. Under Jospin, the proposed electoral reform would have used the regions as single constituencies. In the event, the Raffarin government tinkered with the old system, leaving the departments as the base units for selecting candidates and calculating votes. The precise operation of this system was not known at the time of writing. The contrast offered with the Departmental Councils, where the use of the majority two-ballot system in cantonal elections has encouraged single party majorities, or at least coherent coalitions, was one consideration in changing the electoral system in 2004.

The regions have neither the organisational heritage, nor the political or bureaucratic resources available to the Departmental Councils. But the Regional Councils do have precise legal responsibilities in economic development, secondary education, training, transport and several other fields. They have used their powers ambitiously and are actively seeking and obtaining new powers. The Vaillant Law of 2002, though falling well below regionalist expectations, transferred new responsibilities to the regions (in regional transport and adult training) and granted a right to regional 'experimentation' in certain prescribed areas (for instance culture). The Raffarin reform of 2003–4 strengthened further the regions in ways we describe below.

The real problem with the French regions is that they are institutions without a clear link to territory. The process of regionalisation in France bears the hallmarks of the centralising French republican tradition. Regions were created in a standardised form throughout the French territory, including in areas where no regional tradition existed. Regional boundaries do not usually respect the informal boundaries of France's historic regions. The Region of the Centre thus enjoys exactly the same prerogatives as Brittany. To institutionalise France's historic regions would be tantamount to admitting the posthumous existence of a union state of the UK variety, rather than the French unitary version. This highlights the technocratic nature of French decentralisation; proximity would produce more effective decision-making, but was not intended to give rise to 'communautarian' or regionalist identities. Decentralisation was intended to promote local democracy and administrative efficiency, not to challenge the underlying principles of the French unitary state, although some of the older regionalist demands (the Corsican *Statut Particulier*) were taken on board while others (the unified Basque department) were quietly dropped. We can draw no easy conclusions as regards the efficiency of the regional councils. Some regional councils such as Rhône-Alpes have succeeded in carving out a niche for themselves as 'strong' regions, despite their artificial character and lack of regional identity. Others, such as Languedoc-Roussillon, have manifestly failed to develop an identity (Keating, Loughlin and Deshower, 2003).

The regions possess two powerful resources: they are the natural negotiating partners of the state, through the mechanism of the State-Region Contracts, and the regional level is that favoured by European Union regional development policies. This brings them into permanent contact with the regional field services of the French state, especially those involved with European policy. As their authority has become established, there is some evidence that the regions have acted as the intermediaries between the state and other local authorities and that they are acquiring new policy responsibilities. On occasion, they have been invested with authority to negotiate in the name of the other local authorities. These factors promise a brighter role for the regions in the future, but for the moment they remain the newcomers in the French system of local governance.

7.5	The French prefect and the decentralised state

Local policy implementation, coordination and arbitration were classically the domain of the French prefect, the official representative of the centralised post-Napoleonic state in the French departments. Directly appointed by the Interior Minister, until 1982 the prefect was able to exercise a considerable degree of supervisory control – *la tutelle* – over local authorities. As representative of the central state, the prefect retained formal hierarchical control over local authority budgets and policy implementation, leaving locally elected authorities in a clearly subordinate position. The reality was more complex than this formal hierarchical model suggests. The exercise of the prefect's influence depended not only upon support from Paris, but also on striking compromises with mayors, departmental presidents and other local *notables*. For the successful prefect was both a central agent in relation to the local political community, and a firm advocate of the department's cause in Paris. The extent of any prefect's influence depended traditionally as much upon the position he occupied within a local political community, as upon the formal powers invested in him by the state. Even before the 1982 decentralisation reforms, the mayors of large French cities were able to override departmental prefects on account of their national standing and their access to government departments (Crozier and Thoenig, 1975). The prefect's influence was more obvious in small communes (where he acted as adviser and occasional provider of funds for investment projects), than in large cities.

The prefect undoubtedly lost prestige during the early stages of the decentralisation process, symbolised by the material fact of losing many staff. But there is a case that the prefect has gained more influence as the recognised coordinator of the state at the level of the department than he lost as the *tutelle* authority. The traditional prefectoral control role has weakened. True, the prefect retains two principal formal powers in relation to local authorities. The prefect can refer all local decrees to regional administrative tribunals to ensure their legality. This power is used sparingly, but its tempo does vary according to political circumstances. The threat of decrees being referred to administrative tribunals is usually sufficient to ensure that municipal acts are rigorously in accordance with the law. The prefect also has the right to refer local authority budgets to the regional Courts of Accounts. A posteriori control over local decisions has been used extremely sparingly, and usually on minor issues. Prefects continue to act as advisers to mayors of smaller communes, but the latter turn increasingly to departmental councillors and officials instead. Prefects have recognised their diminished status; a considerable number have gone 'on sabbatical' in order to take up positions as Chief of Staff under the presidents of Regional or Departmental Councils. The prefect retains his traditional control over law and order.

In theory, the post-decentralisation period has witnessed a return of the prefect as arbiter and coordinator of the local state. As the chief representative of the state, the prefect formally exercises authority over the ministerial field services (Alliné and Carrier, 2002). In the 1992 Deconcentration Charter, the prefect was recognised as the sole coordinator of the government's activities. The impact of the 'deconcentration' measures of the 1980s was rather paradoxical and uneven across the different ministries concerned. As a general rule, deconcentration combined more autonomous decision-making powers (or at least discretion) for the ministerial field services, with a reinforced coordinating role for the prefect. These two principles are not necessarily compatible. Tensions are apparent when considering the relations between the prefect and officials from the ministerial field services. The extent of the prefect's control over the field services of the Parisian ministries varies considerably according to locality, as well as the nature of the government department involved. In one study (Im, 1993), three distinct types of relationship were described: those where the field services were placed under the direct control of the prefect (Employment, Youth and Sports); those ministries where field services enjoyed a good deal of autonomy, but where the prefect could prevail if necessary (Equipment, Agriculture); those ministries which fiercely resisted any prefectoral oversight (Finance, Justice, Education).

In practice, the central divisions of Paris-based ministries often insist on transmitting orders directly to their field services, openly bypassing the prefect's coordinating role. The prefect has few resources at his disposal to prevent this. The official means by which the prefect ensures coordination is via the interministerial mail service (*service du courrier*): all correspondence and government circulars must first be addressed to the departmental prefecture, before being distributed to the relevant agencies. But, as one General Secretary admitted, there was nothing to stop Parisian civil servants from sending faxes to their field services. More official coordination occurs via the Regional Administrative Conference: this monthly meeting brings together the departmental prefects of a region, along with key representatives of the ministerial field services, in an attempt to coordinate government policy. A participant of these meetings was of the opinion that they tended to ratify agreements reached informally elsewhere.

The various field services receive their budgets directly from their department's expenditure total. They do not depend upon the prefecture for their resources. Financial and accounting controls are carried out by the *Trésorier-Payeur Général* (TPG). This departmental representative of the finance ministry is completely independent of the prefecture. An agent of the Finance Ministry is attached to each field service, ensuring that decentralised budgets are spent in accordance with Finance Ministry rules (Jones 2003). The real coordination of the state's activity at local, departmental and regional level is achieved more effectively by the Finance Ministry than by the prefectures.

7.6 Revisiting decentralisation: the 2003–4 reforms

On 17 March 2003, the Congress (the special convening of both houses of the French parliament) met at Versailles and agreed to a constitutional reform that gave formal constitutional recognition to the regions for the first time. General De Gaulle had planned to refer to regions in the 1958 Constitution, but was dissuaded from doing so by his first Prime Minister Debré. De Gaulle subsequently lost the 1969 referendum in part on the issue of regionalism. The defeated 1969 proposal would have created strong regions, affirmed their superiority over the *départements* and given a special statute to Corsica. Recalling the legacy of the General, candidate Chirac publicly committed himself to a 'new stage' in decentralisation in a speech in Rouen on 10 April 2002.

There are three main principles to the constitutional reform. First, it embeds the regions in the Constitution and refers to the decentralised organisation of the Republic. The original version, proposed by premier Raffarin, had proclaimed that 'France is an undivided, lay, democratic, social and decentralised Republic'. On the insistence of President Chirac, the new Article 1 of the Constitution now reads: 'France is an undivided, lay, democratic, and social Republic. Its organisation is decentralised'. This weaker formulation does not challenge the hierarchical control of the state over its constituent regions and France remains very much a unitary state. Explicitly rejecting federalism (though in Article 72 referring to the principle of subsidiarity), the Constitution reaffirms that all territories must be treated according to the principle of equality. The French Constitution now recognises four levels of local authority within the constitution: the commune, the *département*, the region (new) and those with a 'special statute'.

The 'special statute' clause covers the various inter-communal bodies we referred to above (such as the *communautés d'agglomeration*). It also refers to the eventual merging of existing subnational authorities into larger units, potentially a radical break with the past. In July 2003, a referendum was held in Corsica to determine whether a single regional authority should replace the Haut-Corse and Corse-Sud departments. The Corsican voters narrowly rejected the proposition, stopping in its tracks one of the more innovative developments promised by the 2003 reform. In December 2003, voters in Martinique (narrowly) and Guadeloupe (overwhelmingly) also rejected proposals to merge the Departmental Councils into single regional authorities.

Second, the constitutional reform introduces the possibility for the experimental transfer of functions to subnational authorities. Any subnational authority – a region, but also a department, an inter-communal structure or a commune – can bid to exercise a range of responsibilities – such as training, roads, airports – that were previously in the policy domain of the central state or other public authorities such as the chambers of commerce. The initial expectation was that the regions would impose a form of leadership over other authorities, as these strategic responsibilities are best exercised at a regional level. But the weight of the pro-department and pro-communal lobbies ensured that these other layers of authority could also bid to run services. As in 1982–3, the competition between regionalists and departmentalists has prevented a genuine clarification. A strong rearguard action in the Senate (where most senators favour departments over regions) has ensured that responsibilities will continue to be blurred. The idea of the lead authority (*chef de file*) notably, was abandoned after objections from the Council of State. There remains enormous confusion about who does what.

The spirit of uniformity remains more pervasive than that of local or regional differentiation. Though any subnational authority can bid to run services on an experimental basis, this decision will need to be approved by parliament. Moreover, after a five-year period, the French parliament will then have to decide whether the transfer of functions should be made permanent. If so, the new policy responsibility will be transferred to all cognate subnational authorities throughout France, thereby ensuring equal treatment. The proposals for experimentation were watered down in the course of the bill's passage through parliament, particularly after the serious doubts expressed by the Council of State.

An internal note circulating within the French Prime Minister's office, dated 2 December 2002, defined the likely future transfers as well as the areas of experimental transfer. The regions were the most likely to benefit from the experimental transfer of functions. The bolder French regions have made ambitious demands, including education (Île-de-France), transport, health services (Nord/Pas-de-Calais), universities, ports and airports (Brittany). Most regional presidents, however, argued they needed more time and resources to deal with the responsibilities they already had, such as economic development, training, European funds, planning and tourism. In two areas, the government backed down faced with the opposition of the trade unions: the building and maintenance of hospitals and the management of technical and administrative staff in higher education. The most significant permanent transfer to the regions is likely to be complete control over European structural funds.

At the time of writing the precise contours of the reforms are unclear. But experimentation already exists and it is likely to be strengthened by the 2003–4 reform. It already exists, for example, in the operation of the inter-communal authorities, which exercise widely varying functions. The creation after 1999 of powerful inter-communal authorities (EPCI) in France's large cities (the city wide authorities notably) and in small towns and rural areas (the *pays*) has increased the diversity of local practices beyond that previously ensured by the principle of 'free administration'. Within limits, the EPCI are free to negotiate which policy responsibilities are transferred up to the supra-communal body and which remain with individual communes. The *pays* are potentially even more innovative. These inter-communal bodies introduced by the Jospin government are based on specific local projects, which, by definition, involve experimental transfers of authority. Indeed, the *pays* can span across departmental boundaries, thereby challenging traditional administrative divisions. Insofar as they rely on the approval of the regional council, the *pays* strengthen a pattern of regional governance. These inter-communal structures testify to the reality of experimental outcomes and variable configurations.

Third, there were rather conflicting provisions for local government finances. On the one hand, there is now a constitutional provision for the redistribution of resources between rich and poor regions. On the other hand, the constitutional reform embeds the principle of the financial autonomy of local authorities. Local and regional authorities are to be given far greater tax-raising powers, able to vary, within limits, local taxation. Financial transfers from central government will be reduced accordingly. This provision raised much opposition on behalf of local and regional politicians themselves. The tax-raising power, welcome in principle, would force local politicians to raise local taxes in order to run unpopular services.

7.7   Decentralisation in France: concluding remarks

The decentralisation reforms have had a major impact upon French centre–periphery relations, but the consequences of the decentralisation reforms were not those initially predicted. The most obvious impact has been in relation to new financial commitments, partnerships, municipal corruption and the increased complexity of subnational decision-making.

The problem of local and regional debt emerged as one of the principal challenges during the first decade after the 1982–3 laws. State financial transfers form an important part of the budgets of Communal, Departmental and Regional Councils. In addition to a general central government block grant (*dotation globale de fonctionnement*), regional and local authorities receive financial support from the decentralisation grant (*dotation générale de la décentralisation –* DGD), a fund specifically designed to compensate for new policy responsibilities under decentralisation. The regions and the departments also benefit from specific grants-in-aid in order to fulfil their responsibilities in education and to cover investment items. The proportion of state transfers as a proportion of local government revenues has diminished progressively since 1982, with around 50 per cent of income derived from local taxation in 2002 (INSEE, 2003). With diminishing real central government income for local authorities, ambitious economic development or cultural projects in the 1980s and early 1990s had to be financed through borrowing, raising local taxes, or investment from the private sector. By the early 1990s, a large and increasing proportion of local government revenue was spent on servicing debt. The options open to mayors and other local players were limited: revenue raising by increasing local taxes hits companies who are relied upon to provide local employment. The financial situation of local and regional authorities has improved markedly since the mid–1990s, as large capital investment projects have been implemented (especially in education). In 2002, local and regional authorities carried out over 70 per cent of all public investment, a proportion likely to increase as the 2003–4 decentralisation reforms are implemented.

Partly as a consequence of their financial straits, decentralisation increased the number and variety of partnerships with which local and regional authorities are involved. Certain public sector partnerships are virtually imposed by the central state: the quinquennial State-Region Contracts, for instance, determine the rights, responsibilities and financial contributions of the various public sector partners called upon to participate in mainly centrally-defined programmes. Though these five-year plans are aimed mainly at the regions, departments and large cities can also sign up to all or part of the plan. In a context where responsibilities are blurred, major infrastructure projects require cooperation between several actors. Other forms of partnership encouraged by decentralisation have included joint venture projects between local authorities and private sector capital (the Mixed Economy Societies), and the more systematic tendering out of municipal services (such as waste disposal and heating) to the private sector.

The granting of control over new resources to local politicians coincided with a spate of local corruption scandals. These practices were not necessarily new, but became more visible with decentralisation. In several cities (for instance Grenoble), the role of mayors in determining public works contracts, or in granting land use permission for development were exposed as powerful incentives for corruption. While there is evidence of local corruption, those involved in municipal politics often suspected the anti-corruption campaign of being coordinated by Parisian *grands corps*, determined to recover their lost influence. The technical *corps* – notably the Mining and Bridges and Highways *corps* – experienced the whole decentralisation process as an affront to their own legitimacy and prestige. These *corps* sought to recover power, especially since the bureaucratic services of the regions and cities escaped from their influence. The enhanced role of cities in urban development has occurred at the expense of central planners and engineers, whose role has undoubtedly diminished.

On a positive reading, decentralisation has improved local democracy, reduced the tutelage of the central state and strengthened the checks and balances within the French political system. A less positive interpretation might point to a confusion of service delivery responsibilities, and an absence of genuine political accountability. There is certainly much confusion about the division of policy-making and administration. There are now as many as seven layers of public administration between the French citizen and Europe (commune, inter-communal structure, *pays*, department, region, nation-state and European Union). Everybody admits there are too many layers of subnational administration in France, but it has proved much more difficult to reform the complex and confusing structure. Each reform adds a new layer, but is incapable of dispensing with the old. Recent reforms – the Voynet and Chevènement Laws of 1999 and the Raffarin reform of 2002–3 – have been consistent to form. They have introduced new structures (communities of communes, urban communities) without fundamentally overhauling the existing pattern of territorial administration. No French government has genuinely confronted the problem of the articulation between the ninety-six Departmental and twenty-two Regional Councils, let alone the various inter-communal and *ad hoc* structures that exist. Central governments are loath to challenge the role of the departments, because the organisation of the state's own field services – especially the prefectures – remain based upon the departments. There is, in many respects, an objective alliance of the Departmental Councils, the prefectures and the central ministries, whose field services operate generally at a departmental, not at a regional level. The state can rely on the departments to be relatively compliant with its own interests – unlike some regions and the communes in larger cities. The departments remain a force of conservation, institutionally, if not always politically. The Raffarin reforms of 2003–4 were true to form, in that the conservative administration shied away from choosing between the twenty-two regions and the ninety-six Departmental Councils. The embedded interests entrenched in the departments once again proved their resilience.

If certain segments of the state have suffered from the effects of decentralisation, it would be unwise to conclude that there has been a general weakening of the state. The French state retains enormous regulatory and fiscal powers and remains deeply involved in local affairs. The state acts as an arbiter between the conflicting claims of different local authorities. The state defines the conditions under which decentralised units function. It retains control over most local government finance. It continues to determine apportionment criteria for grants to subnational units. The taxation instruments available to local councils are crude and they are not at liberty to avail themselves of new instruments. Finally, more than any other western European state, France remains a unitary system of government, whose elites are imbued with a belief in the wisdom and equity of central state guidance.

Political forces and representation

8 The French party system: change and understanding change*

8.1 Introduction

Contemporary France is a democratic polity within which political parties perform such essential functions as political mobilisation, the aggregation of interests, organising political competition, feedback, public management and political recruitment. In comparative terms, however, the French polity is usually perceived to perform these essential functions rather poorly. The portrayals of French political culture we encountered in Chapter 3 pointed to *incivisme*, individualism and a distrust of organisations as important features of French society. Though these portrayals are overly impressionistic, French citizens do appear more reluctant to join party organisations than their northern European counterparts. Mass membership parties of the German or Scandanavian variety are rare; only the Gaullists and Communists have presented examples of mass parties. Of most significance, a powerful strand of the French republican tradition has denigrated political parties as divisive, fractious organisations, whose existence is barely tolerated, and this on condition that they do not threaten the superior interests of the Republic. This distrust is best exemplified by the classic Gaullist tradition, within which the political movement facilitates a direct relationship between the providential leader and the nation, but does not presume to intervene in this privileged relationship (Knapp, 2003). The distrust of parties is deeply embedded in the ideology of the republican state itself, where the state represents the general will, superior to the particularistic interests represented by parties, groups and regions. There is no natural sympathy for doctrines such as pluralism which emphasise the importance of the *corps intermediaires* between the citizen and the state.

8.2 The French party system before 1981

The history of French parties prior to 1940 was one of fragmentation, regional specialisation and ideological posturing. On the centre and right of the political

* An earlier version of this chapter was published with the title, 'Stress, strain and stability in the French party system'. In J. Evans (Ed.) (2004) *The French Party System*. Manchester: Manchester University Press, pp. 11–26. Alistair Cole is grateful to MUP and to Jocelyn Evans for allowing a modified version of this chapter to be reprinted here.

spectrum, party labels either did not exist, or signified different political realities in different parts of the country. Centralised, coherent and disciplined parties did not emerge until 1945, with the creation of the Christian Democratic MRP. The situation was clearer on the left, where there existed two well-organised rival parties after the Tours split in 1920: the Socialist SFIO (PS after 1969) and the Communist PCF. These fraternal enemies of the left have experienced a relationship based on mutual distrust. Long periods of conflict and rivalry have been punctuated by much shorter episodes of left unity (the tripartite government of 1944–7, the Union of the Left of 1972–7, the Mauroy government from 1981–4, the plural left government from 1997–2002).

During the Third and Fourth Republics, the fragmented structure of the party system, along with the parliamentary basis of political power, had a direct and divisive impact upon governmental stability. No single party, or coalition of parties could normally gather a lasting majority of support either within the country, or within parliament to sustain majoritarian governments. Cabinets lasted an average of twelve months in the Third and seven months in the Fourth Republics (Williams, 1964). This pattern changed abruptly with the creation of the Fifth Republic. After an initial period of confusion from 1958–62 linked to the consolidation of de Gaulle's leadership, the party system was simplified throughout the 1960s, 1970s and early 1980s on account of the process known as bipolarisation. By bipolarisation, we mean the streamlining of parties into two rival coalitions of the left and of the right. Beginning in earnest in 1962, the height of bipolarisation occurred in the 1978 parliamentary election. The structure of the party system in 1978 was that of a bipolar quadrille (*quadrille bipolaire*). Four parties of roughly equal political strength divided voter preferences evenly between left (PCF-PS) and right (RPR-UDF) coalitions. These parties were the PCF and the PS on the left, the neo-Gaullist RPR and the liberal conservative UDF on the right. There were several explanations for this process of electoral rationalisation.

The first series of explanations relate to the institutional rules of the game (Bartolini, 1984). The enhanced prestige of the presidency as modelled by de Gaulle between 1958–69; the bipolarising pressures of the direct election of the president after 1962 (only two candidates go through to the decisive second ballot), and the strengthening of executive government in the constitution of

Table 8.1 Major French political parties: origins and evolution

Party	Initial creation	Current initial	Past initials
Communist	1920	PCF	PCF
Socialist	1905	PS	SFIO, FGDS
Radical	1900	Radical/Radical party	MRG, Radical
Centre	1945	UDF	MRP, CD, CDP, CDS, FD
Gaullist	1947	(in UMP)	RPF, UNR, UDR, RPR
Union for a Popular Majority	2002	UMP	UMP
Conservative		CNI	CNIP
Republican	1962	(in UMP)	RI, PR, DL
National Front	1972	FN	FN

the Fifth Republic all favoured a rationalised party system. Even in the 2002 electoral series, the argument remained valid that the institutional architecture of the Fifth Republic and the rules of the game favoured a bipolarised party system. In historical terms, these institutional factors were even more important. With the emergence of strong, stable governments encouraged by the 1958 Constitution, parties were deprived of their former capacity for Byzantine political manoeuvre in an Assembly-dominated regime.

A separate, related institutional argument highlighted the role of the second ballot electoral system in parliamentary elections. By its discriminatory effects against smaller parties, the second-ballot electoral system forced the centre parties to choose between the Gaullist-led majority or the left, in order to survive. The second-ballot system also provides powerful incentives for ideologically neighbouring parties – such as PCF and PS – to form alliances, and it has squeezed out minor parties (such as the Greens or the FN) at important stages of their development. While the discriminating effects of the majoritarian system are obvious, the electoral system has not in itself prevented the emergence of new parties – as we shall see below.

The essence of the institutional argument relates to the emergence of the presidency as the linchpin of the political system from 1958–86 (Bell, 2000). With the development of the presidency as the most powerful institution, the key contenders for office refocused their attentions upon the presidential election: to exercise influence, parties had to form part of rival presidential coalitions – a lesson learnt even by the PCF. The existence of disciplined, pro-presidential coalitions controlling the National Assembly for most of the period since 1958 contrasted with the instability of the Fourth Republic, where governments were short-lived and multifarious, usually based on unstable coalitions and shifting party alliances. In short, until 1986 parliamentary majorities were elected to support the President.

Institutional explanations were necessary, but insufficient. Any analysis of the evolution of the party system needs to include more specifically political explanations: notably the political leadership of de Gaulle, the historic impact of Gaullism and its role as a federating force of the centre and right; the survival instinct of the left-wing parties; the rejuvenation of the French PS and the rebalancing of the French left in the 1970s; the talented mobilisation of prejudice by Le Pen during the 1980s and 1990s.

Analysis of the evolution of the party system must also incorporate – a third series – explanations based on social change: these varied from neo-Marxist arguments relating to the emergence of the social class as the salient electoral cleavage, giving a sociological underpinning to left-right bipolarisation to sociological analysis pinpointing the emergence of the 'new middle classes' as the central groups in post-war French society, favouring the emergence of broad-based parties such as the PS (Mendras, 1989).

The process of bipolarisation resulted from a combination of institutional, political and social pressures, though the precise alchemy between these different elements is rather more difficult to measure. Gathering pace from 1962 onwards, this process of electoral bipolarisation between left and right reached its height in the 1978 National Assembly election. At this election, the four leading parties (PCF, PS, RPR and UDF) obtained over 90 per cent of the vote, with each party polling between 20–25 per cent. By 1978, the independent centre had been completely subsumed by the rival coalitions, mainly aligning itself with the Gaullist-conservative camp.

Since the mid-1980s, the structure of the French party system has become far less neatly balanced. The neat symmetry of the party system in 1978 has given way to a more complex pattern of uncertain and changing contours. There has been an increase in the number and a change in the nature of parties and the issues processed through the political system. The bipolar contours of the French party system have also been challenged by the emergence of new political issues, such as those of immigration, security and the environment. The rise of the Front national from 1982 onwards was both cause and effect of a changed political agenda that the mainstream parties were unable to filter. Likewise, the fluctuating fortunes of the Green parties have proved a test case of the disruptive force of new political issues and the difficulties experienced by the mainstream parties in articulating new political demands, notably those concerning the environment and post-materialist values. The five main developments in the past two and a half decades have been:

■ the decline of the PCF and the emergence of the PS as the main party of the left;

■ the breakthrough, persistence, strengthening and division of the FN;

■ the emergence of minor, but significant parties such as Greens, MPF (Mouvement pour la France), LO (Lutte ouvrière) and LCR (Ligue Communiste révolutionnaire);

■ a pattern of increased electoral volatility, with each election since 1978 going against the incumbent government;

■ a certain disaffection towards traditional politics, as demonstrated in higher abstention rates and the weakening of the parties of the 1978 bipolar quadrille.

While PCF, PS, UDF and RPR obtained over 90 per cent of the vote in 1978, in 1997 these parties scraped 67 per cent. In part, the weakening of left-right bipolarisation stems from features peculiar to each party. The decline of the PCF is clearly a central theme (Santamaria, 1999; Courtois and Lazar, 1995). Any attempt to chart this decline must combine appraisal of the mistakes committed by the Communist Party leadership, with longer-term sociological and ideological trends, and the impact of the new post-Communist world order. Likewise, the breakthrough of the Front national is equally, if not more, important (Mayer and Perrineau, 1989; Mayer, 1999). A comprehensive overview would require a similar approach to be applied to each single party, a task beyond the confines of this chapter. We now describe the main features of party system change in the turbulent decades since 1981.

8.3 The changing French party system

When observing the French party system in 2004, one is struck by the opposition between a formal, bipolar and structured party system, as represented in national political institutions (the presidency, the National Assembly, municipal government) and an unofficial multipolar, fragmented and *contestataire* pattern of party support. While there are many enduring features of party system stability, which we will explore in the final section, we are primarily concerned in the subsequent section to identify stresses and strains and to map out the important changes that occurred in the 1980s and 1990s.

The challenge of new parties

The emergence of new parties (or the breakthrough of previously marginal parties) and the reaction of pre-existing players to these party newcomers is the most obvious development. The most significant of these parties are the Greens and Lutte Ouvrière (LO) on the left; and the Front national (FN) on the right (Evans, 2003). There has been a plethora of more temporary and marginal forces that have had a lesser, but real, impact upon specific elections, or across particular issues. Such ephemeral or marginal forces as La Droite of Charles Millon, the Rassemblement pour la France (RPF) of Charles Pasqua and Philippe de Villiers, the Mouvement d'Ecologie Indépendent (MEI) of Antoine Waechter, and Saint-Josse's Chasse Pêche Nature Tradition (CPNT) fit this category. These movements testify to the importance of 'flexible specialisation' (Kitschelt, 1997) as issue-specific parties rise and fall to exploit the contradictions of broader-based structures. These marginal parties invariably define themselves as being against the parties of the political establishment and perform better in 'second-order' elections fought under proportional representation (regional elections, European elections) than in the decisive parliamentary or presidential elections. In the 2002 National Assembly election, a total of 8455 candidates presented themselves in 577 constituencies, an average of 14.65 per seat, the highest ever.

By far the most significant of these parties is the FN. With around 15 per cent in the presidential (1995), parliamentary (1997) and regional (1998) elections, the FN could already claim to be the second formation of the French right. On the first round of the 2002 presidential election Le Pen and Megret, the two candidates of the far-right, polled almost 20 per cent between them (16.86 per cent for Le Pen, 2.34 per cent for Megret) outpolling the combined Socialist-Communist total in mainland France.

In party system terms, the success of the FN above all harmed the mainstream right, or, at least, it did until 2002. For almost two decades, the FN damaged the cohesion of the parties of the right by posing highly divisive dilemmas of alliance strategy, organisational discipline, political philosophy and policy adaptation. We can illustrate the damaging corrosive effects of the far-right by comparing the 1997 and the 2002 National Assembly elections. In 1997, consistent with Le Pen's desire to defeat the Juppé government by fair means or foul, the FN maintained its candidates wherever it could on the second ballot. There were seventy-six left-right-FN triangular contests; the left won forty-seven, the right twenty-nine. Given the closeness of the result, the FN's tactics undoubtedly facilitated the arrival in power of the Jospin government. In the changed political circumstances of the 2002 National Assembly elections, the far-right parties were less able to influence the outcome of the mainly bipolar left-right second round contests (Cole, 2002). With a reduced first-ballot score in 2002 (11.33 per cent for the FN, 1.10 per cent for the MNR), the FN was less able to provoke the three-way contests that had been particularly damaging for the parties of the mainstream right in 1997. In 2002 there were only nine three-way fights, down from seventy-six in 1997. There were twenty-eight duels between FN and UMP (from fifty-six in 1997) and only eight duels between the left and the FN (from twenty-five in 1997). The right won back forty-three of the seats it had lost as a result of three-way contests in 1997. The main difference between the two elections related to the level of FN support, as well as the degree of unity of the mainstream right parties (low in 1997, high in 2002), a theme to which we shall return.

The real impact of the FN lay in its agenda setting role. The FN has forced issues such as immigration and security on to the political agenda and ensured that they remained there. If primarily detrimental to the mainstream right in party system terms, the FN has had a corrosive impact on all existing parties, especially insofar as it skilfully exploited the theme of the political corruption of the pro-system parties, the RPR, UDF and PS.

From faction to party

One of the most striking developments of the 1980s and 1990s was the rise of internal factionalism in almost all major political formations. There is nothing new about party factionalism. Divisions within parties were inherent in the parliamentary organisation of the Third and Fourth Republics. In the Fifth Republic, the modern PS was reconstructed after 1971 as an explicitly factional party, with the right to free expression of factions (*courants*) guaranteed within the party's constitution. Initially the preserve of the PS, in the 1990s party factionalism became as characteristic of the RPR and UDF, not to say the PCF and the FN.

The most intractable factional conflicts arise in relation to personal rivalries, political strategy and policy differences. Personal rivalries testify in part to the normal contradictions of human agency. They also respond to precise institutional incentives in the Fifth Republic, to the pivotal role of the presidential election and, recently, to the organisational incentives for ambitious politicians to stand as a candidate for the presidency. Even more than personal rivalries, however, during the 1990s the main parties (especially the RPR and UDF) were divided on the question of alliance strategy and in relation to specific policy issues (such as Europe and immigration). Though there has been a narrowing of distinctive economic policy positions between the main parties, issues such as European integration and immigration have divided existing parties and cut across traditional lines of political cleavage. The neo-Gaullist RPR was divided over European integration; the UDF was split wide open by the question of immigration and alliances with the FN.

If the first twenty years of the Fifth Republic were characterised by a tendency for the emergence of broad-based coalitions, the last decade of the twentieth century sorely tested the capacity for *rassemblement* of the main political formations. Each of the main party families experienced a schism within its midst, as there was a general move from faction to party. This move occurred within the PS (the creation by Jean-Pierre Chevènement of the MDC), the RPR (the creation of the RPF by Pasqua) the UDF (the breakaway of Alain Madelin and Démocratie libérale) and even the FN (the split of December 1998 and the creation of the Megret's MNR). Paradoxically, the pitiful performance of all of these factions-cum-parties reinforced the centrality of the party and of the main political families. While factions can often exercise influence within a party, once outside the party fold their influence is either negative and short-lived (as in the case of Chevènement in the 2002 presidential election) or non-existent.

The diminishing legitimacy of party politics?

Various converging forces allow us to pose the diminishing legitimacy of party politics as a central research question. However we interpret the success of the FN – as a modern variant of fascism or as something else – the persistence at a high level of support for two decades of a populist far-right party reveals an ambivalent attitude towards existing political supply (and indirectly towards liberal democracy) on behalf of a significant minority of voters. The inadequacy of political supply can be measured in other ways, most notably by the diminishing support for representatives of the two main political families, PS and RPR, and by growing rates of abstention. In the 1994 European election the two leading lists were reduced to a combined total of 40 per cent; in 1999 this figure was even lower. On the first round of the 1995 presidential election the two leading candidates (Jospin and Chirac) polled just over 40 per cent of the vote, a far weaker proportion than in any other presidential election (Cole, 1995). In 2002, the two leading candidates (Chirac and Le Pen) did even worse: with 36.74 per cent of voters and barely over a quarter of registered electors (Cole, 2002).

France's historic political families were each challenged on the first round of the 2002 presidential election, at which Jean-Marie Le Pen won through to the second ballot run-off against Jacques Chirac. Communists, Socialists, Gaullists, Liberals, Christian Democrats, even Greens performed under par. None of these candidates did as well as they might have expected and many electors were dissatisfied with all of them. The strong performance of the far left and far right candidates, the high abstention rate (at 28.30 per cent a record in any presidential election) and the general dispersion of votes to candidates not generally considered to be genuine presidential contenders (such as St Josse, Chevènement and others) were all part of this trend. Chirac and Jospin, the announced second round contenders, obtained only just over one-third of votes and one-quarter of registered electors between them.

The corollary of this is the development of parties and movements which have defined themselves against the existing political elites, such as the FN, but also Lutte Ouvrière (LO) and the Ligue Communiste Révolutionnaire (LCR). While these forces are marginal in the bipolar party system, they demonstrate the survival of a tradition of radical politics on the far left and extreme right, potently recalled on the first-round of the 2002 presidential election when the far-left (10.44 per cent) and extreme-right (19.20 per cent) captured almost one-third of votes between them. The persistence and strengthening of the parties of the far-left and (especially) extreme-right articulates a profound disillusion towards the 'parties of government' of all complexions on behalf of a popular (working and lower-middle class) electorate. More than ever, the Le Pen electorate in 2002 was over-representative of those suffering from the most acute sentiments of economic and physical insecurity. According to the Louis Harris post-election poll published in *Libération* (23 April 2002) Le Pen was the favoured choice of the lower middle classes (31.9 per cent) and of workers (26.1 per cent), far outdistancing both the Socialist Jospin and the Communist Hue in working class support. The French electorate's vote on 21 April 2002 suggested an unresolved tension between French identity, the implicit promises of French citizenship (including the economic promises) and the uncertainty provoked by Europeanisation, globalisation and an unpredictable future.

A more general cause of fragility lies in the pessimism of public opinion, which has lacked faith in political parties (defined broadly) to resolve intractable policy problems. This has tormented each government since 1981. After the economic miracle of *les trente glorieuses* (1945–74), political parties in government have proved incapable of dealing with the perception of prolonged economic crisis. In comparative European perspective, the reality of the French crisis is debatable, but the perception of economic malaise has had a destabilising effect on all incumbent governments since 1974. The problem of unemployment has proved to be particularly intractable – the real yardstick against which governments have been measured. Since 1981, every single decisive election (presidential or parliamentary) has gone against the incumbent government, in a manner that suggests the electorate's dissatisfaction with the performance of successive governments.

This lesson was repeated in 2002, when the Prime Minister of the outgoing plural left government failed even to reach the second round of the presidential election. In a very real sense, the 2002 campaign was fought as a single-issue campaign, but this time over the issue of insecurity rather than unemployment. Events and campaign strategies converged to define the agenda. A concatenation of events – the middle–east crisis, the aftermath of September 11, and above all a set of particularly shocking murders and violent disorders in France itself – set the agenda for the two months of the 2002 campaign proper. In all other recent election campaigns, the theme of unemployment has emerged as the principal preoccupation of voters. Not so in 2002. SOFRES polls demonstrated that from January 2000 insecurity had replaced unemployment as the principal subject of concern of French voters. To some extent, outgoing premier Jospin was a victim of his own success in bringing down unemployment rates. The unemployment problem was perceived as less acute than in the past, surpassed in importance by the ubiquitous theme of insecurity, much less favourable political terrain for a centre-left candidate.

Political variables are equally pertinent in explaining dissatisfaction with existing political supply. For over two decades, the problem of corruption has been at the top of the political agenda. There is some evidence of endemic political corruption, and much media speculation around the subject. Political corruption has centred on the operation of local and regional government, the imperatives of party finance and organisation, the attribution of public markets and personal enrichment. In the classic schema, political parties received occult commissions for attributing public markets; any firm had to factor the party commission into its bid. Cases of personal enrichment are rarer, but there are several celebrated examples to demonstrate the enduring appeal of avarice (Evans, 2002). The problem of corruption is a complex one. Most corruption cases have involved raising finance to fight prohibitively expensive election campaigns. While corruption has probably always existed, new incentives have been provided by the decentralisation laws, which leave important powers of planning and the attribution of public markets in the hands of mayors and their *adjoints*. More cases of corruption have been uncovered as a result of the increased activism of the investigating magistrates (*juges d'instruction*). The negative political fallout of any hint of corruption is such that incumbent ministers (such as Strauss-Kahn in November 1999) invariably resign if they are investigated by the *juge d'instruction*, even before any formal allegations have been made.

The French party system was shaken to its core by problems of political, institutional and ideological coherence throughout the 1980s and 1990s. Party fragility was real, but there were also countervailing forces in play. In the ensuing section, we identify three underlying causes of party continuity: institutional incentives, flexible and adaptable party organisations and the absorptive capacity of the main French political traditions.

8.4 Underlying continuities in the French party system

The prestige of the presidency and the majoritarian effects of the second-ballot electoral system are potent institutional variables. In a formal sense, at least, the bipolar party system remains a structural variant of the rules of political competition in the Fifth Republic, though we observe an ever increasing gap between formal bipolarity, on the one hand, and the underlying fragmentation of electoral choice on the other.

The electoral series of 2002 defied many basic bipolar rules of the Fifth Republic. The first round of the presidential election did not produce a run-off between left and right. The second round was a quasi-referendum for democracy that produced the largest victory for any candidate in any free election in recent memory. The changing role of the presidential election points to the danger of attributing eternal features to the operation of particular political institutions. Rather than supporting from the first round the candidate they ideally want to see elected President (as in the traditional slogan 'choose on the first-round, eliminate on the second'), electors have begun treating the first round of the presidential election as a 'second-order' election, expressing a preference in the same way they would in a regional or European election. That the 2002 campaign was closed rather than open encouraged such a fragmentation of support. The belief that the first round did not count encouraged electors to support minor or extreme candidates, either through obstinacy or as a way of influencing the agenda of the candidate eventually elected President. There was certainly a lot of choice. With sixteen candidates in competition in 2002, the first round played the role of a non-decisive proportional election, with the bulk of electors firmly believing in a Chirac–Jospin run-off. That this outcome did not materialise deprived the second round of its usual left-right configuration.

On 9 June and 16 June 2002, the French party system returned to something resembling its normal bipolar state. Two parties – the UMP on the right and the PS on the left – occupied almost 90 per cent of parliamentary seats, a far greater measure of bipartisanship than in recent elections. The hegemony of the UMP on the right was matched by a domination of the Socialists on the left, in votes as well as in seats. The far-left parties (2.83 per cent) were squeezed by the movement to use usefully for the Socialists, as was the Republican pole (Chevènement's supporters) with just over 1 per cent, and, to a lesser extent, the Greens (4.5 per cent) and the Communists (4.8 per cent). The far-right lost one-third of its electorate by comparison to 21 April (11.33 per cent for the FN, 1.10 per cent for the MNR) and was unable to repeat its spoiling tactics of 1997, when it had helped the left win the election. In elections fought under the single-member constituency second-ballot system, the four parties of the 1978 bipolar quadrille (PCF, PS, RPR and UDF) have continued to dominate parliamentary representation. Only one deputy (out of 577) was elected in 1997 from outside the rival electoral coalitions and none in 2002. Because the vast bulk of parliamentary seats are confined to members of the left- or right-electoral coalitions, the ability to form alliances is crucial. Its isolation has deprived the FN of major national parliamentary representation except from 1986–8.

On a formal institutional level, the 2002 electoral series ended with a return to (bipolar) politics as normal, powerfully assisted by the second-ballot electoral system which, deprived of FN-provoked primaries, operated in a classic majoritarian manner. The PS was more than ever the dominant party of the left, the FN did not elect a single deputy, minor parties of all hues who had performed well on 21 April 2002 were not confirmed in subsequent contests, the RPR re-established its traditional domination within the French right and the President recaptured control of his presidential majority in the Assembly.

In addition to the institutional underpinnings of the Fifth Republic, the cohesion of the French party system also rests upon the bedrock of municipal office (as witnessed by the longevity of the generation of mayors first elected in 1977) which has itself been transformed into an arena of (mainly) bipolar political competition. The bipolar basis of political competition in the Fifth Republic has spilled over into local government (municipal and cantonal) elections fought under the second-ballot system. Since 1977, municipal elections in the large cities have by and large been contested by rival left and right lists, a pattern confirmed in 2001.

Structural explanations, then, are important in identifying how the institutional rules of the game have shaped important aspects of party competition in the Fifth Republic. But they do not tell the whole story. They have difficulty in distinguishing between different types of party supply and they underplay the dynamic and unpredictable qualities of the party system, as demonstrated by the breakthrough of new parties and the adaptation of older ones.

The underlying stability of the French party system also rests upon flexible and adaptable party organisations. This is a double-edged sword. On the one hand, French citizens appear more reluctant to join party organisations than their northern European counterparts. But this relative weakness of party organisation *stricto sensu* has certain advantages. The weakness of organic links with the trade unions or business, for example, has allowed French parties to reposition themselves more convincingly than their counterparts in certain other European countries. More generally, flexible organisational forms are well adapted to the particular structure of incentives in the French polity, focused on the exercise of power in municipal government as well as on the conquest of decisive (presidential and parliamentary) elections. Here we would again emphasise the importance of municipal government. For certain parties (PS, UDF) municipal government has served as a long-term substitute for a powerful party organisation; for others (PCF, RPR) municipal government has under-pinned the illusion of a genuine party organisation. Once the municipal support is removed, the organisational chimera is laid bare. Even 'strong' parties, such as the PCF and RPR, have relied more on the logistical infrastructure provided by municipal government than on their formal party organisations. This has been demonstrated in numerous former Communist municipalities (such as Le Havre) where the PCF organisation has been severely damaged following the loss of the municipal council.

The weakness of party organisation is not necessarily synonymous with a lack of organisational efficiency. The renewal of the French Socialist Party in the 1970s was predicated upon an open dialogue with voluntary associations much more than upon a revival in party membership. Their cross-cutting membership served the interests both of the party and supportive voluntary associations, facilitating the exchange of policy ideas and personnel. In their own very different ways, the Greens and the FN learnt a similar lesson in the 1990s. The organisa-tional capacity of the French Greens has been strengthened by the strong links maintained with voluntary associations (not just environmental groups). In the case of the FN in Orange and Toulon, the far-right municipalities created a net-work of parallel associations under the tutelage of the townhall (McAna, 2003), somewhat along the lines of traditional Communist-run municipalities. These practices have positive and negative characteristics. They can be interpreted as embodying new forms of political participation. They can also contribute to a lack of transparent governance – municipally financed associations are some-times little more than vehicles for the exercise of informal partisan influence.

Lastly, the robust character of the main political traditions principally underpins the stability of the French party system: French-style communism, socialism, liberal conservatism, Gaullism, Christian Democracy and national populism. They can each trace their lineage back to the Second World War or much earlier, and have each demonstrated the capacity to reinvent themselves to cope with changing circumstances and political incentives. Even when threatened by the rise of new parties and by the manifestations of disaffection with existing political supply, over time the French party system has proved its absorptive capacity. The 'absorptive capacity' (Hanley, 1999, 2002) of the French party system is particularly marked on the left. This is demonstrated by the ability of the PS to transcend internal divisions and changing ideological fashions, and retain its dominant position on the left. The emergence of the Greens as a post-materialist, new politics party forces us to modify this appreciation, but only partially: the three Green deputies are entirely dependent on alliances with the PS.

It is rather more difficult to apply the thesis of the absorptive capacity of the party system to the French right. The French right has been hampered by its divisions ever since the decline of historic Gaullism and the creation of the RPR (1976) and UDF (1978) in the 1970s. In addition, the rise of the FN from 1983 onwards has posed acute dilemmas of alliance strategy and political positioning for the parties of the mainstream right. The FN was a problem because the right was divided, hence too weak to ignore the far-right movement. The failure of the RPR to stamp its authority on the French right during the 1990s was all the more damaging in that a Gaullist President occupied the Elysée palace from 1995 onwards.

In one important respect, the 2002 electoral series represented a return to the sources of the Fifth Republic. Once re-elected President, Chirac imposed the creation of the Union for the Presidential Majority (UMP) as a presidential platform to which all existing parties (RPR, UDF, DL and so on) would have to subscribe. UMP candidates had to accept sitting in the same parliamentary group in the National Assembly, to support the President and to participate in the creation of a vast new party of the French right in autumn 2002. A committee containing representatives of the three main pro-Chirac parties (RPR, DL, part of the UDF) distributed UMP candidacies in the parliamentary contest. François Bayrou led the resistance of a centrist rump, retaining the title UDF and pledging critical support for Jacques Chirac. The presidential party strategy worked exactly to plan. This strategy involved not just providing a majority for the President, but also engineering a realignment within the right in favour of the RPR, to sweeten the pill of the dissolution of the Gaullist movement into a much broader conservative party.

The 2002 elections represented the first time since 1973 that there had not been at least two major parties on the French right. Right-wing unity paid off handsomely. The UMP won an overall majority (399 seats out of 577), only the third time in the history of the Fifth Republic that a single political formation has held an overall majority (the Gaullists from 1968 to 1973 and the Socialists from 1981 to 1986 being the other examples). In 2002, the UMP formula masked a new domination of the RPR. With the election of an overall majority for a single formation of the mainstream right, the French party system again resembled in part that of the 1960s, when a dominant presidential rally was flanked by a small centre party, a 'reservist' force of the right whose existence was barely tolerated.

The capacity for absorption is limited to the formal party system, as measured in decisive elections fought under the second ballot system. It can account neither for fragmentation of party support in second order elections, or for the evidence of dissatisfaction with political supply and demand that we uncovered in the previous section.

One explanation of party persistence might be that parties give expression to deeply embedded cleavages. Joachim Schild (2000) summarises the principal cleavages in French politics as being positional (left versus right), existential (religious versus lay), ideological (cultural liberalism against authoritarianism), socio-economic (class conflict) and issue-based. These *variables lourdes* have lessened in significance since the early 1980s. The left/right cleavage remains pertinent in certain respects, but its mobilising force has been diminished as a result of the Mitterrand presidency and the decline of the PCF. The religious/lay cleavage retains the capacity to mobilise opinion on specific issues such as the defence of, or opposition to *écoles libres*, but the relation of cause and effect is uncertain. We demonstrated above that ideological cleavages can cut across party lines, as can those based on issues. Voting patterns corresponded far less neatly to social class identities in 2002 than they did in 1978 (Capdeveille, 1981; Perrineau and Ysmal, 1998, 2002). The electoral volatility of the new middle classes and the strengthening of the FN amongst the working and lower middle class electorate explain these cross-cutting pressures. Moreover, as the issue of European integration demonstrates, party structures do not always correspond neatly to divisions over issues or ideologies. Traditional cleavages have clearly lessened in importance, as France has undergone multiple internal and external changes, but they remain as cognitive maps within the collective memory. While there is no easy relationship between political attitudes and behaviour, partisan lenses can provide one way of comprehending and reinterpreting a changing environment.

8.5 Concluding remarks

The decline of parties is not terminal. It is contingent on underlying political and economic circumstances. We can draw three main conclusions from the partially contradictory evidence presented in this chapter. Party system change is the first one. That the French party system has undergone change is obvious. The challenge of new parties, the decline of certain older parties (notably the PCF) and the limited capacity of existing parties to articulate new political issues have impacted upon the number and the nature of parties. The issues processed by the party system reflect a changing policy agenda. On the one hand, new political issues such as the environment and immigration have forced their way on to the agenda. On the other, governmental realism and the end of 'lyrical illusions' associated with the abandoning of a certain type of left project under Mitterrand have refocused elite attention on public policies, rather than competing visions of society. Partisan discourses have not proceeded apace. The resulting distance between political discourse and policy achievement has created disillusion and demobilisation amongst many French electors. This is one of the most convincing explanations of the public disaffection with political parties during the 1980s and 1990s. This aspect of the crisis of party politics is more apparent in France than in comparable countries. Because partisan discourses are deeply embedded in French republican political culture, public expectations have been higher and the electoral retribution for failure has been harsher. This is the specifically French dimension of a broader pan-European phenomenon, whereby established party families have had to adapt to a series of internal and external shocks over the past two decades, cognisance of which has preconditioned their ability to survive and prosper.

Indeed, this absorptive capacity of the main political families modifies the first conclusion. While the traditional parties were at times unnerved by the new issue politics, the resulting new parties such as the Greens and the FN failed to replace the existing players. The Greens owe their political survival to the PS. Over a long period, the FN has articulated a powerful strand within French public opinion and indirectly influenced the political agenda. Without allies, however, it has failed to translate its electoral potential into full political capital and has lacked second round credibility, both in the 2002 presidential contest (where Le Pen polled 17.85 per cent against 82.15 per cent for Chirac) and in parliamentary elections, where the Front usually fails to hold on to its first round vote in those rare constituencies where it can fight the second.

The existing parties absorbed the fluid centre of gravity of French politics. They occupied a strategically and organisationally privileged position to adapt to and interpret a changing internal and external political agenda. The same process transformed the leading parties (especially PS and RPR) in important respects both by the exercise of domestic power and by the changing European and international policy agenda.

We conclude thereby in the persistence of a rather artificial bipolar multipartism, the left and right coalitions functioning most effectively when one party assumes a dominant role – the Gaullists from 1962 to 1974, and the PS from 1981 onwards. This leads naturally to our third and final conclusion. To the extent that two blocs provide the mainstay of political competition across most European countries, French party competition has moved closer to the mainstream European model. As in most West European democracies, the mainstay of political competition is between left of centre and right of centre parties and their respective political allies. The pattern of party fragility in the 1980s and 1990s was not specific to France but in many respects formed part of a pan-European adjustment to the end of post-war prosperity. The form such fragility took in France – the rise of the extreme right, increased abstentions, a weakening of party identity – was nationally specific, but similar phenomena could be observed in comparable countries such as Italy (where the entire post-war party system collapsed under the weight of political corruption), Germany (where the 'new politics' prospered on the failure of traditional social democracy) and Britain (where the electoral swing of 1997 broke all post-war records).

To achieve a just measure of the balance between party stress and party stability, we can learn from longitudinal historical and cross-national comparison. Longitudinal comparison suggests that there is no real equivalent to the party system stress of the Fourth Republic in the late 1940s, when the PCF and RPF – forces openly antagonistic to the regime – obtained the support of half of the voters. We must not lose a sense of perspective. From a cross-national perspective, while allowing for nationally tinted referential frames and for the discursive traditions of the main political traditions, we observe that the pressures on the French party system are broadly consistent with those observed elsewhere.

9 French parties today

9.1 Introduction

In Chapter 9 we consider France's major and minor parties. We provide a brief summary of the most important features of each of the main parties. Because these are different types of party, with varying historical, organisational and ideological traditions, the traits highlighted for each party are not necessarily the same. As a general guide, a brief history of each party will be followed by an overview of its beliefs, political appeal, organisation and leadership.

9.2 The Gaullists

History

The Gaullist movement derived its initial legitimacy from General de Gaulle's proclamation in favour of a Free France in 1940. The first organised Gaullist movement – the Rassemblement du peuple francais (RPF) – was created by de Gaulle in 1947. It became a powerful mass movement, deriving its identity from a combination of vigorous anti-Communism, nationalism, hostility to the parliamentary regime of the Fourth Republic and personal attachment to de Gaulle (Charlot, 1983). One of the principal movements of the late 1940s, by 1953 de Gaulle had dissociated himself from the RPF, a movement hijacked by conservative *notables* in quest of a bandwagon.

Gaullism as a political movement was resurrected by the events of May–June 1958. When De Gaulle returned in 1958, his followers formed themselves into the Union for the New Republic (Union pour la Republique nouvelle – UNR). Emerging as a major political force almost overnight in 1958, the UNR became the pivot of de Gaulle's Fifth Republic (Charlot, 1970). In keeping with his suspicions of political parties, de Gaulle did not openly acknowledge any link with the UNR, but he 'never denied that the UNR provided his most solid basis of support' (Duverger, 1977). The UNR was the first *de facto* presidential party. De Gaulle's Prime Ministers Debré (1958–62) and Pompidou (1962–68) called upon the Gaullists to imitate what was perceived to be the practice of the British Conservatives and the German Christian Democrats: to provide unflinching public loyalty, and to keep criticisms away from the public eye. Debré set the tone from 1958 onwards. The UNR was expected to be a subordinate institution, with no formal (or informal) influence over presidential decision-making. In return for supporting the President, the party benefited from de Gaulle's unprecedented popularity and from public approval of the new regime to strengthen its position. In June 1968, taking advantage of the fears raised by the May '68 events, the Gaullists won an absolute majority of seats.

After de Gaulle left the political scene, the Gaullists lacked a definite sense of purpose and ideological cohesion. There is a strong case that historic Gaullism died with de Gaulle. The UDR's difficulty in existing after 1969 testified to the personal rally facet of the Gaullist movement, a personalism that undermined the party after de Gaulle's departure. In the 1974 presidential election, former premier Chaban-Delmas, the official Gaullist candidate, obtained only 15.1 per cent, as against 32.6 per cent for Valéry Giscard d'Estaing, an independent conservative candidate. Giscard d'Estaing won the presidency in 1974 in part because the Gaullist Interior Minister Chirac led a powerful revolt of forty-three Gaullist deputies in his favour. Shortly after his appointment as premier in 1974, Chirac took over control of what remained of the Gaullist party. President Giscard d'Estaing's acquiescence was bought in the belief that the Gaullist movement would be delivered to the new President. Chirac intended otherwise. Control over the UDR was a means of reviving Gaullism from its electoral abyss, if necessary at the expense of President Giscard d'Estaing's own supporters. Conflict between Giscard d'Estaing and Chirac was thenceforth probable. Chirac's resignation as Prime Minister in August 1976 accelerated this movement. In December 1976, Chirac transformed the old party into a dynamic new organisation, renamed the Rally for the Republic (Rassemblement pour la République – RPR), bearing a close resemblance to De Gaulle's RPF of the Fourth Republic. Although membership figures are notoriously unreliable, the RPR claimed to have an effective campaigning party organisation, along with the PCF and the FN (Knapp, 1996, 2003).

The RPR officially ceased to exist in 2002, with the creation of the UMP. Any evaluation of the RPR must be mixed. All in all, the RPR occupied some sort of governmental office in only eleven out of the twenty-five years. Jacques Chirac was unsuccessful in presidential elections on two occasions – in 1981 and 1988 – but victorious on two others – 1995 and 2002. Even in 1995 and 2002, however, the electoral totals available to the RPR candidate bore little in common with the previous feats of de Gaulle in 1965 or Pompidou in 1969. Chirac's first round total in 1995 (20.8 per cent) was by far the weakest of any successful presidential candidate in the Fifth Republic, a weakness surpassed only in 2002, when the outgoing President polled 19.88 per cent on the first round.

As a general rule, the strengths of the RPR lay in those areas of weakness for the early Gaullist movements: especially municipal government, and party organisation. The failure of past Gaullist movements (especially the UNR) to secure a solid base in local government was a key source of weakness (Williams and Harrison, 1965). The powerbase of the RPR was its control over Paris, presided by Chirac from 1977–95, and by Jean Tiberi from 1995–2001. The patronage and political prestige of the Paris town hall made up for the fact that the RPR continued to trail the centre-right UDF in terms of overall presence in local government (the ninety-six departmental councils, 36,518 communes, and the twenty-two regions). The loss of the Paris town hall to the Socialist Bertrand Delanöe in 2001 proved a bitter blow from which the RPR never really recovered.

Beliefs and political appeal

The RPR differed in key respects from the historic Gaullism of the 1960s. The UNR was both a personalist rally behind a charismatic leader and a vehicle for mobilising support for the Fifth Republic. It was a movement with a broader sociological base than that typical of French right-wing parties. It obtained support from across the social spectrum, with a strong undercurrent of working-class Gaullism essential for its success (Charlot, 1970). The beliefs propounded by de Gaulle's UNR also set the movement apart from traditional conservative movements. Strongly influenced by de Gaulle's brand of nationalism, the UNR advocated national independence, social and economic interventionism, popular participation, support for a charismatic leader and loyalty to the institutions of the Fifth Republic. This alchemy of nationalism and populism set the Gaullists apart from mainstream European conservative or Christian Democratic traditions, which were more integrationist and Atlanticist. Under President Pompidou (1969–74), the UNR became a more recognisably conservative movement, both in terms of the sociological composition of its electorate, and in its beliefs and policies.

In its twenty-five years of existence, the RPR oscillated between portraying itself as a French Labour party (1976), a tough anti-Communist movement in the style of de Gaulle's RPF (1979), as a 'catch-all' party and a classic right-wing conservative party. Its message varied according to climate and clientele. At various times it stressed national populism (Chirac's 1979 Cochin appeal), at others European integration (the 1992 referendum). In the economic sphere, at times it appeared to favour economic neo-liberalism (1986–8), at others it advocated interventionist policies aimed at combating unemployment (Chirac's 1995 campaign). On the specifics of policy, the Gaullist movement was frequently divided. The cleavage over Europe was probably the most significant in this respect. During the Maastricht referendum campaign of 1992, the RPR was openly divided between opponents of the treaty (Séguin and Pasqua) and supporters (notably Juppé). Gaullist deputies were also divided on issues of constitutional reform, economic policy and popular participation.

This flexibility was an important part of the RPR, a movement that placed greater emphasis on leadership, patriotism, and the tradition of volontarisme in domestic and foreign policy than on the specific content of policies. There were multiple strands to Gaullism, corresponding in part to specific generations, in part to the demands of different historical situations. Chirac's 1995 campaign against the 'technostructure' and in favour of direct contact between the President and the people responded to one powerful strand of popular Gaullism, one rather distrustful of representative democracy and in favour of a direct contact between the leader and the people. In spite of itself, the RPR was a recognisably conservative party, the key party of the French right. Chirac's first round electorate in 1995 demonstrated this sociological conservatism (and that of 2002 even more so). In 1995, strong support for Chirac came from the youngest age cohorts and from students, but he also enjoyed a firm showing amongst more traditionally conservative categories such as business, the liberal professions and the farmers. In contrast, Chirac's working-class support (15 per cent) trailed that of Jospin (21 per cent) and Le Pen (27 per cent). In 2002, the youth vote deserted the incumbent President. Chirac's 2002 electorate was a classic conservative one, dominated by older age groups, small businesses and the retired. Chirac performed best in traditional conservative (but not tradition-ally Gaullist) areas in the western and central areas of France, but was much weaker in the northern and eastern half of France and along the Mediterranean (Cole, 1995, 2002).

Organisation and leadership

More than any other presidential party, leadership has always played a con-sciously important role in the Gaullist movement. The style and dimensions of such political leadership have varied over time. De Gaulle's authority over the Gaullist party was immense; to label the UNR as a personalist movement accurately captures at least part of its essence. De Gaulle's authority did vary somewhat according to different generations. The wartime *compagnons* were entirely devoted to de Gaulle, and accepted his decisions even when they dis-agreed with them (as leading Gaullists such as Michel Debré did over Algeria). But the younger Gaullist generation, first elected as UNR deputies in 1958 or 1962, was less inherently deferential towards de Gaulle, more concerned with its own career advancement. The quality of the UDR as a presidential rally diminished greatly during Pompidou's presidency: from being in part a person-alist movement dedicated to serving de Gaulle, the Gaullist party became less unconditionally devoted to its presidential leader, more a network for the dis-semination of patronage.

The historical filiation of Chirac's RPR with Gaullism was undeniable, but Chirac's political leadership was markedly different from that of either de Gaulle or Pompidou. It was based on different criteria: that of a party leader in all but name. Chirac's stewardship of the RPR from 1976–95 was often criti-cised, including from within the ranks of the RPR itself. Internal dissent developed in several directions after the 1988 presidential election defeat. That Chirac managed to survive the outbreak of factionalism within the RPR after the presidential defeat of 1988 confirmed the strength of his leadership. That he managed the retain the support of most RPR deputies, and the bulk of party members when premier Balladur appeared best placed to carry the 1995 pres-idential election provided additional proof of the loyalty Chirac had built up over a twenty-year period. In 1995, the support of a powerful political party was an important ingredient of presidential success, one commonly overlooked in an age of modern political communication. Chirac's election as President in

1995 changed the nature of his relationship with the political movement he had created in 1976. The divisive circumstances of his 1995 election left a bitter taste. After his defeat in the 1997 National Assembly election, President Chirac lost direct control over the RPR, which fell first to his historic rival Seguin (1997–9), who in turn lost control of the ailing movement in 1999. The last leader of the RPR, Michèle Alliot-Marie (1999–2002), was not regarded as a Chirac loyalist and was elected against the President's preferred choice Delevoye (Knapp, 2003). In a remarkable turn around of fortunes following his re-election in 2002, Chirac was able to impose the creation of the UMP, first as a platform for the 2002 parliamentary elections, then as an old-style party to support the President.

9.3 The Union for French Democracy (UDF)

History

The Union for French Democracy (Union pour la démocratie française – UDF) was formed in 1978 as a confederation of parties supporting President Giscard d'Estaing. It provided a fairly loose structure that housed the two main non-Gaullist movements of the centre and right: the non-Gaullist conservatives in the Republican Party (PR) and Centrist Christian Democrats (CDS). The other three component elements of the UDF were the Radical Party, which could trace its origins back to 1901; Perspectives et realités (a small party dedicated to former President Giscard d'Estaing) and the UDFs 'direct' members. Rather than being a party in the conventional sense, the UDF was a confederation of separate political parties, each anxious to preserve its identity and positions of political strength. Only the few direct members gave the UDF any genuine existence as a federation.

The UDF was created just weeks before the 1978 parliamentary elections. The President's various parliamentary supporters (conservatives, Christian Democrats, Radicals) were forced to agree an electoral pact in order to stand a chance against rival RPR candidates. Each party agreed in advance which constituencies would be contested. The second-ballot electoral system for parliamentary elections (which usually discriminates against small or divided parties) and the prevailing atmosphere of conflict between Giscard d'Estaing and Chirac combined to promote the creation of the UDF as a matter of electoral necessity. In 1978 UDF candidates faced first round competition from RPR candidates, but in subsequent elections, the UDF and RPR agreed single candidates in most constituencies before the first ballot. The UDF lasted in its original form until 1998 (Sauger, 2003). The 'UDF' label continues to survive today, but most of the electoral and organisational resources of the old confederation are now housed within the UMP. When we refer to the UDF in this section, we signify the 1978–98 organisation. When we talk of the 'UDF' we refer to its rump successor led by François Bayrou. Individual components of the UDF are referred to by their titles in 1978.

The UDF was a limited success as an electoral cartel, but a failure as a presidential party – or as any sort of party come to that. The UDF was most effective as a loose structure allowing the non-Gaullist parties of the centre-right to cooperate in their mutual interest and to bargain with the RPR. In 1978, the UDF comfortably outscored its RPR rival in terms of votes cast (though not deputies). In the 1981 presidential election, Giscard d'Estaing saw off the challenge of rival Chirac, only to lose to Mitterrand on the run-off. In 1988, for the first time, the UDF became the larger of the two right-wing formations in terms of deputies, a position it held until the 1993 election. The UDF and its allies consistently outpolled the RPR in local elections. Former UDF notables controlled a larger number of departmental councils (*conseils généraux*) than any other party, as well as several leading French cities (notably Lyons (until 2001) Marseilles, and Toulouse). The UDF has always had more of a presence in the French Senate than the Gaullists.

Giscard d'Estaing had hoped that the UDF would be the basis for the emergence of a great centre-right party, a dominant presidential party to replace the Gaullists. But the UDF was a failed presidential party. Even while Giscard d'Estaing remained at the Elysée, the UDF lacked an effective organisational basis upon which to mobilise support. Once Giscard d'Estaing had lost the presidency, the UDF became little more than an electoral cartel. The UDF was weak and fairly undisciplined as a parliamentary party. From 1988–93, the CDS formed its own autonomous group, before returning to the UDF fold in 1993. In the European parliament, UDF deputies formed part of various separate parliamentary groups. As a presidential party, it is doubtful whether the UDF as such ever existed. In the 1981 election, Giscard d'Estaing completely ignored the UDF, as did Barre in 1988. In 1995, the UDF was hopelessly split between those advocating support for Balladur, those demanding a UDF candidate, and those backing Chirac. That the UDF refrained from running a candidate in 1995 seriously called into question its status as a party. The UDF finally split in 1998 over the issue of whether or not to accept support from the FN in order to run a number of regional councils. UDF regional politicians accepted such support in four regions, provoking their exclusion and a formal split. In May 1998, Démocratie Libérale (the successor to the Republican Party) withdrew from the UDF. In November 1998, the 'UDF' reconstituted itself as a single party under François Bayrou's leadership, essentially as the latest emanation of the French centrist and Christian democratic tradition. The new 'UDF' was determined to reject any compromise with the FN or its offshoots. Under Bayrou's leadership, the 'UDF' also fought hard to prevent first Chirac's RPR, then the unified UMP from completely dominating the political space on the centre and right of French politics. Bayrou's creditable performance in the 2002 presidential election (6.88 per cent) gave the 'UDF' a new lease of life.

Beliefs and political appeal

The history of the UDF is also the history of its component parties and the trajectories of a number of key individuals (such as former President Giscard d'Estaing, and former premier Barre).

The largest party in the UDF was the Republican Party (1977–98). Its precursor, the Independent Republicans (1962–77), was created by Giscard d'Estaing in 1962 in order to rally those old-style conservatives who wanted to support de Gaulle over Algerian independence and over the direct election of the President. Most Fourth Republic conservatives opposed de Gaulle on these issues, but Giscard d'Estaing's pro-Fifth Republic movement progressively supplanted them. The Independent Republicans represented the bulk of the non-Gaullist fraction of the presidential majority, providing critical support for the Fifth Republic, for de Gaulle and later for Pompidou. The alliance between Giscard d'Estaing's Independent Republicans and the Gaullist Party provided the core of the presidential majority during the De Gaulle and Pompidou presidencies. The Independent Republicans were replaced in 1977 by the Republican Party, ostensibly as a disciplined party capable of standing up to the RPR. In practice, the Republican Party was very similar to the older formation it replaced. It had a weak central organisation and was dominated by conservative *notables*, with their independent bases of political power, usually in local government. The Republicans were the inheritors of the independent conservative traditions of the Third and Fourth Republic. Their loose style of organisation reflected their origins as provincial notables with a strong sense of independence, of innate superiority and of hostility to the organisational constraints of belonging to a political party. In 1998, the Republican Party transformed itself into Démocratie libérale, a more explicitly economically liberal and socially conservative party inspired by Alain Madelin. The poor performance of Madelin in the 2002 presidential election (3.91 per cent) suggested there is little demand for explicit neo-liberalism in France. Démocratie libérale in turn joined the UMP in October 2002.

The other principal party within the UDF was the CDS (Force démocrate from 1996 to 1998, 'UDF' after 1998). In terms of its organisational filiation, broad philosophical outlook, and geographical implantation, the CDS was the inheritor party of the MRP, the important Christian Democratic party of the Fourth Republic. The CDS could probably lay the strongest claim to representing a 'centre' party in French politics. The CDS was the inheritor of the social Catholicism of the old MRP. Its political identity was consistently Catholic, social and European. It was less inclined to accept an unregulated free market than the 'neo-liberals' of the Republican Party. There was a good measure of geographical complementarity between the CDS and the Republicans. The Republicans were strongest along the Mediterranean coast, and in the Rhône-Alpes area, where there is no strong Catholic tradition. The CDS electorate was a (rural) conservative electorate, with a geographical preponderance in western and eastern France. As with the Republicans, the real strength of the CDS lay in its fortresses in local and regional government, and its strong parliamentary representation. Its influence was also manifested through a range of associations promoting semi-Catholic causes.

The reformed 'UDF' represents the latest attempt to build an autonomous party of the centre. The 'UDF' was created as a single party (rather than a confederation) in 1998, by and large out of Force démocrate. In 2002, the UDF had a group of 30 deputies. Its leader, François Bayrou, performed honourably (6.88%) in the 2002 presidential contest. Most sitting UDF deputies, however, deserted to the new pro-Chirac platform, the Union for a Presidential Majority (UMP) even before the 2002 parliamentary election. The 'UDF' faces difficulties analogous to those of earlier attempts to build a centre party. Openly centrist parties or presidential candidates have not performed particularly well in the Fifth Republic. Due to the constraints of the second-ballot electoral system, self-identified centre deputies in the Fifth Republic have generally owed their election to conservative electorates and to alliances with parties of the mainstream right. This was notably the case for most 'opposition' centrists from 1962–73. In 2002, the 'UDF' returned thirty deputies, but only six of these were elected against UMP opposition on the first round (the other twenty-four relying on the UMP not presenting a candidate). In presidential elections, self-proclaimed centre candidates (such as Barre in 1988, Balladur in 1995 and Bayrou in 2002) have lacked credibility. The bipolarising pressures of the Fifth Republic have thus made life difficult, if not impossible, for a centre party that is genuinely independent from the parties of the left and right.

Leadership and organisation

Throughout its existence, the UDF remained a loose confederation without a mass membership or a structured party organisation. The UDF provided a loose structure to regroup the non-Gaullist elements of the right-wing coalition, and to allow for the survival of distinct political and geographical traditions resistant to Chirac's brand of Gaullism. These specific traditions included those of social catholicism, independent-minded conservatism, and the vestiges of peasant anti-clericalism. In the terms of Duverger's (1964) classic formulation, the UDF was composed of a loose collection of cadre parties forced to cohabit by the exigencies of the Fifth Republican political system. It was neither a presidential rally of the Gaullist type, or a well structured party such as the Socialists. With its solid base in local government, and in the context of the French practice of multiple office holding (*cumul des mandats*), power within the UDF lay less with a designated leadership than with powerful regional barons, who combined strong positions in subnational government with leading roles on the national level.

9.4   The Socialist Party

History

The first unified Socialist Party in France, created in 1905, carried the curious title of the French Section of the Workers' International (Section Française de l'Internationale Ouvrière – SFIO) in deference to its formation on the orders of the Second International. It brought together a total of six small Socialist parties, an early pointer to the divided nature of the French left. Each of these pre-parties represented different traditions, ranging from anarchism, to French

Marxism, to reformist socialism. Throughout its existence (1905–20), the first (and only) unified Socialist Party was racked by conflict between orthodox Marxism and evolutionary, gradual Socialism. This conflict has remained present within the French left ever since. At the congress of Tours in 1920, the SFIO split into two parties in response to the challenge posed by the Bolshevik Revolution of October 1917. A majority (around two-thirds) of delegates voted to accept Lenin's twenty-one conditions and created the PCF. A minority of delegates retained the title SFIO. This fundamental division of the French left into Communists and Socialists has never been overcome. The history of the French left since this date has been one of long periods of fratricidal strife interrupted by short-lived spells of alliance, themselves a prelude to renewed inter-party conflict.

The Socialist minority at Tours retained the party's initial title SFIO, in order to demonstrate its organisational continuity with native French Marxism. The SFIO vehemently rejected the Bolshevik model and declared itself committed to working within existing parliamentary and republican institutions. Although the Communists were the larger element in 1920, by 1932 the Socialists had come to dominate the French left, with the PCF reduced to being an isolated minority. In the 1936 election, a left-wing alliance of Communists, Socialists and Radicals won the first ever real left-wing majority in France's history. Following the Popular Front election victory, the Socialist leader Léon Blum formed a Socialist-Radical coalition government. The PCF, arguing that it was a revolutionary party, refused to join. Despite a series of important symbolic social reforms being enacted (paid holidays, the 40-hour week), the left-wing government rapidly ran into serious economic and political problems. It survived barely one year, collapsing when the Radicals withdrew from Blum's government.

During the period 1945–69, the history of the French Socialist Party was one of almost uninterrupted decline. From a post-war high of 21 per cent in 1945, the SFIO had declined to 12.5 per cent in 1962, before sinking to 5.1 per cent in the 1969 presidential election. The Socialist Party experienced the first decade of the Fifth Republic as a stagnating party with few new ideas, an ageing political personnel, and an outdated political strategy. The Algerian crisis (and the role performed therein by the former SFIO premier Guy Mollet) produced a formal split within the SFIO in 1958, with the creation of the Autonomous Socialist Party (PSA) in 1958, becoming the Unified Socialist Party (PSU) in 1960. From the early 1960s onwards, key initiatives came from outside of the SFIO, from several left-wing political clubs and from the PSU. Most future Socialist personalities began their careers either in the clubs or the PSU. Few began their careers in the SFIO. François Mitterrand took control of the party in 1971 at the congress of Epinay, at the head of a heterogeneous alliance principally directed against the former SFIO leader Mollet. As so many others in the new PS, Mitterrand came from outside the SFIO, the powerbase of the future President being a movement of left-wing political clubs known as the Convention of Republican Institutions (CIR).

The rise of the Socialists was the major political occurrence of the 1970s. Political strategy, sociological change, ideological evolution, and Mitterrand's political leadership were all important in explaining the success of the PS (Cole, 1994). During the 1970s Mitterrand's PS was a party well-attuned to the institutional, social and political imperatives of the Fifth Republic and the social structures of French society. Unlike a classic social democratic party, there was never any organic link with organised labour, arguably an advantage for a broad-based party. As in Italy, however, for many years the PS had to adapt its strategy to cope with the leadership (until 1974) of the Communist Party (PCF) on the left. Only upon victory in 1981 were the Socialists finally liberated from the overbearing ideological presence of the Communists, a legacy that still influences the party's verbal radicalism today. Unlike the PCF, the PS was a party which, on an institutional level, could credibly contend to win the presidency, the supreme political prize of the Fifth Republic. Mitterrand understood that there was no future for a party, such as the old SFIO, which refused to respect the new political rules of the Fifth Republic, centred upon victory in the presidential election. Mitterrand finally achieved such a victory on his third attempt in 1981. After the decade of revival (1971–81), the French Socialists experienced a decade of being the presidential party (1981–93), before being brutally rejected by the French electorate in 1993, unexpectedly returning to office in 1997 and losing again in 2002.

Beliefs and political appeal

Mitterrand's Socialist Party came to articulate the demands of many new social movements arising in the 1960s and 1970s. New social movement activists figured prominently amongst the influx of new party members, which by 1975 had transformed the old SFIO into a recognisably new party. On a sociological level, the French Socialist Party (in 1981 and 1988 especially) appeared to be a genuinely interclass party, repeating a feat achieved previously only by the Gaullists in the 1960s. At its best, the French Socialist Party managed an original synthesis between being a catch-all party, appealing to the traditional left-wing electorate attracted by orthodox Marxism (the culture represented by the French Communist party) and articulating the concerns of new social movements and themes given expression in May '68.

The electoral coalitions built by Mitterrand in 1981 and 1988 were not sufficiently robust to guarantee against a downturn in party fortunes after the inevitable compromises made in office. In 1993, the PS lost almost half of its 1988 electorate, and, though the decline from the 1997 election was less marked in 2002, the direction was the same. In 1993 and 2002, the popular electorate appeared to have lost faith in the Socialists after long periods in office. In 1993, the party was reduced to under 20 per cent of the electorate. While PS support held up amongst its new middle class voters, the party's popular vote collapsed. The Socialist Party paid the electoral price in 1993 for a decade of economic austerity and rising unemployment, which hit the party's traditional electorate with particular intensity. Apart from narrow economic issues, the Socialists also suffered from their perceived inability to provide responses for 'new' issues such as immigration or the environment, and from the highly damaging impression that, with so many of its politicians involved in corruption scandals, the PS had lost its claim to occupy the moral high ground in French politics.

The plural left's electoral victory in June 1997 brought the Socialists back to power rather earlier than most observers expected, as the key player in the plural left government. Jospin's government delivered a distinctive political programme that bore some similarities with the 1981–3 period. As the French Socialist Party returned to office shortly after the election of the Blair government in the UK, the comparisons were inevitable. Consistent with its own traditions of discursive radicalism and the enduring influence of French Marxism, the French Socialists rejected most of the precepts of New Labour. In response to Blair's 'third way' between the old left and the new right, Jospin pointedly refused to define a new orientation between social democracy and liberalism, preferring the former to the latter. While Blair advocated reforming the policy environment to adapt to globalisation, Jospin stressed the importance of EU and state-level public policy intervention to control globalisation. While Blair assiduously courted business during the first term, the landmark reforms of the Jospin premiership, and especially the 35-hour week, were implemented in the face of fierce business opposition. Consistent with the ingrained traditions of the French left, the discursive basis of Jospin's method was that politics matters. There was a strong faith in state action to fight un-employment, promote growth and reform society.

In spite of the reputation of the plural left as a bold reforming government, the Socialist Party suffered major setbacks in the 2002 presidential and parliamentary elections. In the presidential contest, Jospin failed to make the second round, trailed the FN leader Le Pen and promptly resigned on the evening of 21 April 2002. In the ensuing parliamentary elections, the PS lost half its parliamentary seats, though its vote held up well. A post-election survey by AOL-Louis Harris highlighted the gulf separating the Socialist candidate from the popular electorate on the first round of the 2002 presidential election (Cole, 2002). Jospin obtained his best votes amongst the highest socio-economic categories, especially in the public sector and the best educated. Jospin polled more support than any other candidate in two categories: managers and higher intellectual professions (23.8 per cent) and intermediary professionals (21.1 per cent). But the Socialist candidate was deserted by industrial workers, with only 12 per cent, trailing far behind Le Pen (26.1 per cent) and even Chirac (13.6 per cent). The aversion of the industrial working classes and lower clerical workers to the Socialists in 1993 and 2002 was striking. The PS culture of discursive radicalism counted for little when the party was being judged upon its record in office.

Leadership and organisation

The post-1971 Socialist Party (PS) represented, amongst other things, an uneasy compromise between a Gaullien-style presidential rally (inspired by Mitterrand's leadership after 1971), and a strong tradition of party organisation and self-sufficiency (as embodied in the old SFIO). The tension between traditions of party patriotism and the exigencies of presidentialism (notably Mitterrand's self-elevation above the party) was a constant feature of internal PS dynamics during its decade of renewal (1971–81). The post-1971 party laid great stress on its quality as a democratic party, as an aspiring mass party, even as a *parti auto-gestionnaire* inspired by the ideals of May 1968. Of equal importance was its character as a factionalised party: the resurrection of the PS during the 1970s was linked to the fusion of a variety of pre-existing political groups into a single party (Clift, 2003). The PS is the most openly factionalised of French political parties, to the extent of career advancement depending upon belonging to one of the party's key factions. Factions are officially represented on the party's governing organs. As a general rule, in the 1970s factionalism could be portrayed as synonymous with internal party democracy (hence positive). In the early 1990s or since 2002, factionalism carried more negative connotations, synonymous with patronage, policy division and power politics. The structures of power within the Socialist Party continue to be determined by factional allegiances. At the Dijon congress in 2003, First Secretary François Hollande (originally a Jospin supporter) headed a composite motion including a finely balanced representation of most of the leading factions (Fabius, Rocard, Mauroy, supporters of Jospin) flanked by two traditional left-wing texts and a motion presented by the rebellious head of one of the party's largest federations (Nord). The leading factions each represent specific political traditions, as well as strongholds within the party itself (such as local government, think-tanks and structures of expertise, the interests of the parliamentary party or principled opposition to the leadership).

9.5 The Communist Party

History

The creation of the French Communist Party (PCF) at the congress of Tours in 1920 was one of the key developments in the history of the French party system. The consequences of the Tours split were long lasting. It gave the PCF a revolutionary identity, a belief in its destiny as the future harbinger of Socialist revolution. It also ensured that the PCF accepted the leading role of the Soviet Union in world affairs. During the inter-war period, the PCF was gradually transformed away from being an ill-organised collection of romantic revolutionaries into becoming a tough Bolshevik organisation, dedicated to furthering the aims of the USSR, and tightly organised along democratic centralist lines (Tiersky, 1974). The shift from a 'class against class' isolationist strategy between 1928–32 to a popular front option in 1936 depended far more upon Stalin's evaluation of the dangers of fascism than any indigenous political reasoning on behalf of the Communist Party leadership. By lessening its isolation, however, the 1936 election proved that left-wing unity benefited the PCF even more than the SFIO. The PCF leapt overnight from 8 to 15.7 per cent of the voters, including for the first time majorities in many of the working-class suburbs surrounding Paris. The wartime Resistance movement transformed the PCF into the major political force of the left, a status it occupied until the mid-1970s. In 1944 the Communists joined with Socialists and the Christian Democratic MRP in a post-war resistance coalition, which collapsed under the impact of the Cold War in May 1947, with the Socialists and the MRP combining to expel the Communists from government.

The party's weakest performance in the Fourth Republic (25.8 per cent in 1956) comfortably surpassed its best showing in the Fifth Republic (22.5 per cent in 1967). Throughout the Fourth Republic, the PCF acted as a counter community, in opposition to the rest of French society, in some senses a mirror image of the Catholic Church (Kriegel, 1985). The party was a highly organised community, which offered its members the emotional satisfaction of belonging to a cohesive, well-organised counter-society. The PCF was by far the best-organised French party, the only one with an activist mass membership. The PCF's obsession with workerism (*ouvrièrisme*) reflected its own position within the political system, as the bulk of the party's electoral support came from industrial workers. In 1947, the PCF captured control of the CGT, the largest trade union, and it exploited its control of the union to further the party's political aims. With its conquest of the CGT, the PCF was the only party that could lay a genuine claim to be able to organise the working class politically. Communist party cells proliferated in factories throughout France, especially in the larger industrial concerns. Inspired organisationally by Marxism-Leninism, the PCF also inherited older French anarcho-syndicalist traditions, which stressed the autonomy and self-sufficiency of the working class (Ridley, 1970; Lorwin, 1972).

The PCF leadership pledged absolute loyalty to the USSR. During this period, the PCF was the most Stalinised party in western Europe, although national revolutionary symbols also played their part in the construction of PCF identity. Loyalty to the USSR was an article of faith. How can we explain this? The PCF had been moulded into an effective pro-Soviet party during the inter-war period, whereas the other important west European Communist parties – in Italy and Germany notably – had been crushed under fascism and had been reconstructed as new parties during the wartime resistance to fascism. PCF leaders felt they owed a great debt of loyalty to the USSR, and to Stalin in particular. In contrast with the Italian party notably, the PCF had retained its organisational continuity throughout and had never lost its faith in the revolutionary leadership of the USSR.

The PCF in the Fifth Republic: decline and resistance

The creation of the Fifth Republic marked a fundamental watershed for the PCF. The party opposed the return of de Gaulle and paid a heavy price for it. In 1958, the PCF lost one-quarter of its electorate, most of the lost voters being working-class people attracted by de Gaulle's blend of nationalism, charismatic leadership and promise of strong government. From being France's largest party in 1946, with over 28 per cent of the vote, the PCF candidate Hue polled just 3.37 per cent in the 2002 presidential election. How can we explain this? Alongside purely institutional explanations (such as the operation of the electoral system or the role of the presidency), the PCF's decline can be related to the process of social and ideological change, the collapse of communism and repeated mistakes made by the Communist Party leadership.

Social change

The PCF always relied disproportionately on the industrial working class for its electoral support. The party's traditional strongholds were in the industrial conurbations of the Paris region, the North and the Mediterranean around Marseilles. In the Fifth Republic, it has rarely been able attract much support outside of these areas, except in certain rural strongholds where the party led the French Resistance movement. The PCF was a victim of the modernisation of French society and the economy. Not only has the industrial working class has been rapidly declining in France, but the party's hold over its working-class constituency has weakened to the point of extinction. From the mid-70s onwards, the PCF faced fierce competition for working-class votes, first from Mitterrand's PS in the 1970s, latterly from Le Pen and the Front national. Since 1981, the PS has attracted substantially more electoral support amongst workers than the PCF, as a more credible party of the left. And since 1988, the Front national has also consistently outpolled the PCF amongst industrial workers, as, in 2002, did the far-left Lutte ouvrière.

Strategic inconsistencies

The French Communist Party has been damaged by repeated changes of strategy, oscillating between unity with the Socialists and hard-line anti-Socialism. After the debacle of the 1958 election (18.9 per cent, ten seats), the PCF adopted a renewed popular front strategy of alliance with the Socialists. The PCF argued strongly in favour of a Common Programme with the Socialists from 1962 onwards. Such a programme – the Common Programme of the Left – was eventually signed with the Socialists in 1972. As the alliance appeared to work in favour of the Socialists, the PCF abandoned the Common Programme in 1977. The left parties subsequently lost the National Assembly election of 1978 which they had been expected to win.

In 1981, Mitterrand invited the Communists to join Mauroy's government. From 1981–4, the PCF had its second experience in government. This was largely an unhappy affair. There were only four Communist ministers out of a total of forty-four, and they had little impact on government policy. The PCF finally quit the government in 1984 after its humiliating reversal in the 1984 European election (11.2 per cent). The ensuing decade witnessed a return to harsh anti-Socialist rhetoric, suspended only to enable the PCF to conclude electoral pacts with the Socialists in 1988 and 1993. In 1997, the PCF joined the government again as part of the plural left administration. Though the PCF was the favoured coalition partner of premier Jospin and exercised an important influence on policy, the PCF candidate Hue was humiliated in the 2002 presidential election. This latest version of the PCF acting as a governing party posed once again the unanswerable question of what the party is for.

The collapse of communism

The PCF was the most Stalinised party in western Europe. By the time it attempted to liberalise its doctrines in the mid-1970s – on account of the alliance with the PS – it was probably too late. Mitterrand's Socialist Party had already succeeded in attracting the support of those who might have been tempted by a reformed Communist Party along the lines of the Italian example. After the break with the Socialists in 1977, the PCF reverted to its former deference to the USSR. For as long as it survived, the PCF was never really able to distance itself sufficiently from the USSR and the Soviet model of Communism. With the collapse of the Soviet Union, the PCF lost its most consistent model of reference. It has proved unable, or unwilling, of replacing it with anything else. The survival of the PCF is a more open question than ever. The party underwent historic losses in the 1995 and 2001 municipal elections, losing most of the large cities it controlled (with serious consequences for the party's organisational survival). The main trade union, the CGT, has completely liberated itself from PCF control. After the 2002 National Assembly election, the PCF managed (just) to hold on to its parliamentary group, 4.8 per cent of the vote and twenty-one deputies. Even its claim to articulate the radical tradition in French politics rings hollow faced with the rise of the far-left parties.

9.6 The National Front

History and electoral evolution

The National Front (FN) was born in 1972 as the 'latest attempt at regrouping the forces of the extreme-right' (Shields in Cole, 1990). The FN's electoral audience was initially limited. In 1978, the FN obtained 0.4 per cent. In the 1981 presidential election, Le Pen failed to obtained the 500 signatures necessary to stand as a candidate. The FN's electoral breakthrough first became apparent in 1983: scattered successes in the municipal elections were followed by good performances in by-elections towards the end of the year (at Dreux and Aulnay-sous-Bois). The first national breakthrough occurred in the European election of 1984: 10.95 per cent. In subsequent elections during the 1980s, the Front polled an average of 10–12 per cent. During the 1990s, this figure was closer to 15 per cent. With around 15 per cent in the presidential (1995), parliamentary (1997) and regional (1998) elections, the FN could claim to be the second formation of the French right until fractured by the Le Pen-Mégret split of

December 1998 and the subsequent electoral collapse of June 1999 (5.1 per cent for the FN, 3.3 per cent for the splinter party, the National Republican Movement (MNR)). Even during the abyss of 1999, however, the combined FN and MNR vote was around 10 per cent in local elections. The earthquake of 21 April 2002, when Le Pen broke through to the second round, saw the combined FN and MNR electorate fall just short of 20 per cent (19.2 per cent). The overwhelming rejection of Le Pen on 5 May 2002 (81.25 per cent) also demonstrated limits of FN electoral support.

Interpretations vary as to why the FN was able to achieve a major breakthrough. At least five important explanations relating to the Front's initial successes appear credible, though none is satisfactory on its own.

1 The breakthrough of the FN was an ultra-Conservative reaction to the radicalisation of politics in the aftermath of Mitterrand's victory in May 1981. For the most hardline faction of the right-wing electorate, the parties of the mainstream right appeared lacklustre in their opposition to the Socialists' radical reform programme of 1981–3. The Front offered uncompromising opposition to the Socialist-Communist government. The 1984 FN electorate was bourgeois in its socio-professional profile (Mayer and Perrineau, 1989). Early support for Le Pen came from the most hardline faction of the traditional right-wing electorate and the popular classes only joined the Le Pen bandwagon later on.

2 The breakthrough of the FN was facilitated by the existing political parties, insofar as these parties attempted to exploit concern over immigration to score political points off their rivals. The PCF was the first party openly to exploit the theme of rising immigration for its own political purposes (Schain, 1987). The RPR-UDF opposition used immigration as a stick with which to beat the Socialists during the 1983 municipal elections. The Socialists themselves retained an ambiguous attitude towards the FN, whose survival would weaken the parties of the mainstream right. Mitterrand's introduction of proportional representation for the 1986 National Assembly election was inspired in part by the calculation that a parliamentary presence for the FN might prevent the RPR/UDF coalition from obtaining an overall majority.

3 The breakthrough of the FN was tied to economic crisis. Neither left nor right had been able to come to terms with the post-1973 economic crisis. The assimilation of unemployment with immigration was a central feature of Le Pen's initial political message. Simplistic solutions to the problem of unemployment were attractive to a proportion of the electorate alienated by the broken promises of left and right. As it became an established political force, the FN picked up substantial support in the deprived outskirts of leading French cities, where high levels of unemployment and crime coexisted with large numbers of 'immigrants'. Although detailed studies repeatedly demonstrated that there was no easy correlation between FN support and the concentration of immigrants (Fysh and Wolfreys, 1992) post-electoral surveys also consistently portrayed FN voters as those for whom immigration and security were the principal political issues.

4 The breakthrough of the FN was a manifestation of discontent with the political system. Popular distaste for mainstream politicians was increased by the spate of corruption scandals that occurred throughout the 1980s. The FN appealed for support on the theme of 'clean hands' (borrowed from its Italian sister party). Le Pen skilfully exploited an antipolitical strand within French political culture. As a new party, the FN was not tainted with the failings of the existing parties, partly because it did not hold many positions of elected responsibility. It was a virgin party that stood outside the existing 'corrupt' political system. Le Pen's attacks against the 'gang of four' should be understood in this sense.

5 As a practitioner of demogogic political leadership, Le Pen has not been surpassed. He has astutely manipulated the personalisation inherent in the Fifth Republic's presidential system, and has exploited the mass media in order to spread his message. The simplistic solutions advocated by Le Pen make it difficult for mainstream politicians to compete on grounds the FN leader himself has defined. Le Pen's personal leadership skills contrasted with the determinedly uncharismatic Megret after the split within the FN in 1998/9.

No single explanation will suffice to demonstrate the National Front's break-through. Each contains partial truths, but also its own internal weaknesses. Explanations based on the resurgence of a national populist strand of political culture do not account for the fact that the FN emerged at a particular point in time. The personal leadership explanation underplays the social forces under-pinning the FN's emergence. The initial political explanation (the idea that the FN was a radical reaction to the left in power) cannot account for the fact that the FN initially performed better under the right from 1986–8 and 1993–5 than it had done under left-wing governments. The economic crisis interpretation can not account for the fact that the crisis had persisted since 1973–4 without political extremism. All of these ingredients are necessary to explain Le Pen's breakthrough.

Despite predictions of its imminent demise and a formal split in 1998/9 (when former General Secretary Bruno Mégret was expelled from the FN and promptly created a carbon copy, the MNR), the FN has proved its capacity to resist in each type of election the regime has to offer, whatever the electoral system used. This sets it apart from past far-right movements, such as Poujadism of the Fourth Republic. It has performed well in elections fought under proportional representation (European and regional elections), but it has stood up well in other contests as well (cantonal, municipal and legislative elections). Its most spectacular performances have been in presidential elec-tions. The 'earthquake' represented by Le Pen's performance in the first ballot of the 1988 presidential election (14.4 per cent) was surpassed by his 1995 score (15 per cent), which in turn trailed his exceptional performance in 2002 (16.86 per cent on the first round, 17.85 per cent on the run-off).

The Front has occupied few positions of direct influence within the French political system. It has no deputies (despite polling 13.6 per cent in 2002), although it had a group of thirty-five after the proportional representation elec-tion of 1986. The second-ballot electoral system used for National Assembly, cantonal and municipal elections penalises parties, such as the FN, which are unable to make alliances with other parties. With 13.6 per cent in the 2002 National Assembly election, the FN elected no deputies. In contrast, the PCF obtained 4.8 per cent but returned twenty-one deputies. Whereas the PCF could count upon electoral alliances with the Socialists on the second round, no one would ally with the FN. In 2001, it had only five members of the European parliament. Its largest influence is within the twenty-two Regional Councils, where it elected hundreds of councillors in 1992 and 1998. In four regions, centre-right (UDF) politicians accepted FN support to win the regional presidencies. In seven other regions elected in 1998, where there was no overall majority, FN support was refused.

Until 1995, it ran no large councils. The capture of three major councils in the 1995 municipal election (Marignane, Orange, and Toulon, to which Vitrolles was added shortly afterwards) was an important breakthrough. For the first time, the FN had access to the various resources provided by control over municipal government (such as land use, housing, culture and some municipal employment). A major study concludes that two of these four municipalities (Toulon and Orange) were run in very different ways (McAna, 2003). In the large city of Toulon (over 100,000 inhabitants), the FN council was unable to implement much of its electoral programme, hedged in by legal constraints, opposition from state officials (in the prefecture) and internal divisions. The municipal majority disintegrated with the split in 1998 and the FN was severely defeated in the 2001 election. In the smaller town of Orange, the popular mayor Bompard acted as any other Mediterranean notable would, exercising a form of personal, clientelistic leadership that allowed him to bargain local support for his policies. Mayor Bompard was triumphantly re-elected in 2001, standing on a ticket that no longer explicitly referred to the FN. In no case was the central party leadership able to exercise a tight control over the activities of the FN-run councils. In Vitrolles and Marignane, the municipal councils rallied to Megret's National Republican Movement (MNR), the splinter party created in 1999. On balance, the experience of the FN in municipal power demonstrated the absorptive capacity of French municipal government. Though each was different, the four councils each adapted to local political circumstances and learned (or not) to cope with local civil society. Though the FN will never be a 'party like the others', municipal councils did not provide the laboratories for the policies of 'national preference' that the FN leadership had hoped.

Interpretations of the character and appeal of the FN vary and the movement itself has evolved during its existence. How best can we understand the political appeal of Front national?

A protest movement?

The FN is a party that is used as a protest vehicle for a variety of different discontents with the existing political parties and political system and French society in general. The political message of the FN is best understood as a form of national populism, which is flexible enough to respond to changing public anxieties. The search for historical predecessors is probably necessary, but certainly insufficient in order to understand the FN. It bears certain similarities to the short-lived Poujadist movement of the 1950s. The latter – which polled some 12.5 per cent in the 1956 election – often evokes comparisons, but they are somewhat misleading. The Poujadist movement was an anti-tax, anti-modernism movement of shopkeepers, traders and small businessmen (Williams, 1964), whereas Le Pen recruits from a far broader social spectrum. While Le Pen obtains his highest support in large cities, the 1956 Poujadist movement fared best in the rural areas and small towns of west and south-west of France.

Le Pen's politics are the politics of fear. The FN has proved capable of mobilising popular fears across a range of apparently unconnected themes: such as immigration, anti-Semitism, AIDS and European integration. Each appeared to threaten an idealised national identity. The politics of fear has paid dividends, because France is a society in the throes of an ideological vacuum, after the perceived failure of the right- and left-wing alternatives. Above all, the threat to national identity is the linchpin of Le Pen's mobilising appeal.

A fascist party?

In its capacity as a rally of the far-right, the FN has attracted (and continues to attract) a rag-tag of marginal groups committed to various lost causes: monarchists, Vichyites, former Poujadists, *pieds noirs* (former Algerian settlers), integrist Catholics, anti-Communists, anti-abortion activists, self-proclaimed fascists.

Fysh and Wolfreys (1992) conclude their study with the assertion that the FN is a 'fascist' party. Two principal objections might be levelled against such a conclusion. First, it might be objected that fascism refers to a specific movement associated with unprecedented problems of dislocation and defeat in inter-war Europe. Second, it is debateable whether 'mass unemployment, a social crisis and bankrupt politics' accurately describes the state of contemporary French politics and society. Such appraisals can be historically misleading. It is unlikely that the FN would enjoy the level of support it currently does if its political message was limited to expounding the themes of the French or European extreme-right. On the other hand, a threatened sense of national identity, a feeling of anomie, and menacing representations of the adversary all recall certain features of fascism, as well as the more obvious reference to the cult of the leader.

A single issue movement?

The FN has been portrayed as a single-issue movement, rallying support around the theme of immigration-invasion (Mitra, 1988). While not exactly a single-issue party, Le Pen made his political reputation by stressing one issue above all others. This might be summarised as 'France for the French'. Immigration and security are consistently cited as the essential policy issues by FN voters (Mayer, 1999; Mayer and Perrineau, 1989). France has always been a country of immigration. But whereas past immigrants were Catholic Europeans (in the twentieth century Italians, Portuguese and Spanish), post-war immigrants were mainly of North African origin, with their own well-developed culture and religion, which many feel to be antagonistic to mainstream French culture. The arrival of second-generation immigrants on to the French labour market, and manifestations of cultural difference have reinforced the problem of the integration of ethnic communities into mainstream French culture.

A populist movement?

The social bases of the FN are different from those of the classic right-wing parties. The FNs electorate is more masculine and popular than those of the traditional right-wing parties. In the 1995 presidential election Le Pen out-polled any other candidate amongst industrial workers (27 per cent). In 2002, Le Pen was the favoured choice of the lower middle classes (31.9 per cent) and of workers (26.1 per cent), far outdistancing both the socialist Jospin and the communist Hue in working class support (Cole, 1995, 2002). In 2002, the Le Pen electorate was also the least well-educated electorate of the three main candidates. All electoral surveys since 1986 converge in their main findings. As time has progressed, the FN electorate has become more popular and less bourgeois. The centre of gravity of Le Pen's electorate has shifted. In 1984, the FN was supported primarily by traditional right-wing voters radicalised by the presence of the left in power, and their dissatisfaction with the divisions of the main right-wing parties. By 1986 (and in subsequent elections) these electors had returned to their traditional conservative base. A more popular electorate has replaced them. The Front has traditionally obtained good scores in the eastern half of France, especially in the large cities, where there are large concentrations of immigrants, combined with situations of urban deprivation. The strongest concentration of support is along the Mediterranean coast: in Marseilles, Nice and Toulon. In these cities urban tensions are complicated by the presence of large numbers of *pieds noirs*, white Algerian settlers forced to return to the mainland after Algerian independence. The breakthrough of the FN is symptomatic of urban anomie, and of a measure of social and political disintegration. Polls show that FN voters are unlikely to trust anyone outside of family and a small circle of friends; outsiders are distrusted or despised (Mayer and Perrineau, 1989). The notion of crisis also explains why the FN performs well in localities where local political elites are in crisis. By contrast, where local political elites are well implanted and respected, the FN has made less impact.

9.7	The Greens

Before 1989 the new wave of Green party politics which had influenced most of western Europe appeared to have by-passed France (Villalba and Vielliard-Coffre, 2003; Sainteny, 2000; Faucher, 1999). Since the creation of Les Verts in

1974, the French Greens had experienced only intermittent minor successes, such as the 3.8 per cent vote for Antoine Waechter in the 1988 presidential election. Environmental concerns had been placed on the political agenda by the May '68 movement and resurged periodically throughout the 1970s, usually in the form of anti-nuclear protest. But aspirations of social change (including ecological change) rested firmly upon the mainstream left-wing parties, especially the Socialist party. The ecological constituency was also represented by well-organised pressure groups, such as Friends of the Earth (Les Amis de la Terre). The breakthrough of the French Green parties in the early 1990s represented part of a European-wide movement, based on the new saliency of the environment as a political issue. Within the context of the French party system, the success of the Greens was suggestive of the difficulties faced by the mainstream parties in articulating new political demands, in particular those associated with the environment.

The breakthrough for political ecology occurred between 1989 and 1992. In 1989, the French Greens – with 10.53 per cent – first broke through into the European parliament. In the 1992 regional election the two rival Green lists polled almost 14 per cent between them (7.1 per cent for Génération ecologie; 6.8 per cent for Les Verts). 1992 was the year that saw the entry en masse of Greens into France's regional assemblies, where they participated in several regional executives. The failure to achieve heady expectations in the 1993 National Assembly election (a total of 7.6 per cent for the two Green parties) sparked off a spiral of internal recriminations and divisions, which grew in intensity as the Greens' opinion poll fortunes diminished. By the 1994 European election, the French Greens (2.84 per cent) had squandered the electoral capital carefully acquired in the course of the past ten years. The Greens have since then recovered, and established a lasting presence, whether in presidential contests (3.3 per cent for Voynet in 1995, 5.25 per cent for Mamère in 2002), parliamentary elections (6.86 per cent and eight deputies in 1997, 4.5 per cent and three deputies in 2002) or as part of the left-wing alliances that govern several of France's main cities, including Paris.

Organisation and leadership

Under the informal leadership of Antoine Waechter from 1986–93, the Greens stuck rigorously to a strict autonomy line, known as 'neither left, nor right' whereby the party refused to consider alliances with any other political parties. At the 1993 General Assembly, Waechter was ousted by a heterogeneous coalition of factions spanning the extreme-left to centre of Les Verts. Dominique Voynet embodied this new orientation. Under Voynet's informal leadership from 1993–2002, the French Greens situated themselves resolutely in the tradition of the alternative left. Those Green deputies elected in 1997 and 2002 depended for their success on support from Socialist voters, and the prior standing down of PS candidates. In the 2004 regional elections, the Greens and the PS concluded electoral pacts in several regions. The Greens performed an important role in the 1997–2002 plural left government, within which Voynet occupied the Environment brief. Though part of the five-party plural left coalition, the Greens adopted an increasingly critical stance towards the Jospin government as time wore on, especially after the 2001 municipal elections.

Unlike for most French parties, the official organisation of the Green party is highly indicative of its genuine character. The central organisation of Les Verts is extremely weak, with only minimal control over local and regional organisations. The internal decision-making processes are based mainly on direct democracy, with the party's sovereign annual Assembly remaining open to all members: around 600–700 members usually attend out of a total membership of some 5,000. Rather than nominating an official leader, Les Verts designate four national spokespersons. Alone amongst French parties, the party's activists exercise considerable control over the strategic choices made by the party leadership. As in other Green parties, there is no unified leadership in Les Verts, rather, fluid factions representing different sides in internal conflicts have risen and fallen. This informal type of party organisation has bred organisational chaos. At the Toulouse congress of 2000, for example, six separate tendencies vied for control. There has, moreover, been a marked tendency for former leading personalities to quit the party once their influence has diminished: after Lalonde's desertion in 1990, former leader Waechter left Les Verts in 1994 in order to create his own minuscule movement (Mouvement de l'écologie indépendent). Taking these factors together, the French Greens appear increasingly as a modern version of the old Unified Socialist Party (PSU), a movement bursting with ideas, but hopelessly divided and with a limited electoral clientele.

It would be misleading to judge the Greens merely by weighing their electoral performance. As harbingers of political ecology, the French Greens have contributed to placing new issues on the political agenda which mainstream parties have been forced to address. The influence exercised by environmental issues remains strong within French public opinion. As the German example reveals, the electoral fortunes of Green parties ebb and flow rather more than those of older established European parties. This is partly incumbent upon their representing a particular type of party. Rather than a party, in the classic sense of the term, the French Greens appeared to many as a single-issue movement, notwithstanding their efforts to produce coherent policies across the whole range of issues. There has never been a consensus that a political party is the most appropriate means of promoting Green issues: social movements such as Greenpeace and Amis de la Terre have in the past been critical of any attempts to organise ecologists into a political party. As their counterparts elsewhere, the French Greens appear as a radical middle class new social movement. The social characteristics of party activists in Les Verts are consistent with the young, highly educated and new middle class profile of activists in other Green parties.

9.8   The minor parties

Ever since its origins, the French party system has spawned a rich progeny of minor parties and personalities. To retrace the history of France's minor parties, political clubs and extra-parliamentary groups lies outside of this chapter, but a brief attempt will be made to classify different types of party. Four main types of minor party might be identified:

- Former party factions have transformed themselves into independent political parties. One of the best examples is that of the Mouvement des citoyens (MdC) a party created in 1990 out of the former CERES faction within the Socialist party. The MdC retains certain pockets of support where the CERES faction was formerly strong, notably in Paris and in the Territoire de Belfort department, which leader (and former Interior Minister) Chevènement represented as deputy until 2002. The MDC and the 'Republican Pole' failed to build upon Chevènement's creditable performance in the 2002 presidential election (5.33 per cent) in the ensuing parliamentary contest (1.1 per cent, no deputies). This failure demonstrated party factions' difficulties in surviving on their own outside their former parties.

- Since the inception of the Fifth Republic, political clubs have performed a major role, both in transforming parties from within, and challenging them from outside. During the 1960s, left-wing clubs were instrumental in renovating the structures of the non-Communist left outside the SFIO. Since the 1980s, most club activity has occurred on the right, with certain clubs – such as GRECE – acting as bridges between the far-right and mainstream conservative politicians. Some of these clubs are genuine think-tanks; others are mini-political parties, or else operate as factions within or across parties.

- Certain parties form around particular individuals in dispute with their original party formations. The best recent example is that of Philippe de Villiers and the Mouvement pour la France (MPF). In opposition with the UDF over the Maastricht Treaty, and representative of an ultra-conservative strand of public opinion, de Villiers ran an independent list in the 1994 European election, which polled over 10 per cent, a freak performance de Villiers was unable to repeat in the 1995 presidential election (4.80 per cent)

- Since May 1968, various small but significant anti-system left-wing parties have provided real competition for the Communist Party in its control over the far-left electorate. Those have included Trotskyites, Maoistes and *gauchistes* of various guises. The most enduring (and endearing) is Lutte ouvrière, a Trotskyite party which can trace its geneology to the inter-war period. One of the principal surprises of the 1995 presidential campaign was the 5.37 per cent polled by LO candidate Arlette Laguiller in her fourth presidential campaign. In the 2002 presidential election, the three extreme left candidates (Laguiller for LO, Besancenot for the LCR and Gluckstein for the PT) obtained 10.64 per cent, a remarkable performance that demonstrated the persistence of a vibrant and rebellious political tradition to the left of the Communist Party.

9.9 Concluding remarks

The existence of such a broad range of anti-establishment and minor parties acts as a counterweight to the centripetal tendencies of the French party system analysed in Chapter 8. It helps explain the continuing fragmentation of the party system, especially in non-decisive elections, such as European and regional elections and the first round of the presidential election. In the 1994 European election the two leading lists were reduced to a combined total of 40 per cent. On the first round of the 1995 presidential election the two leading candidates polled just over 40 per cent of the vote, a far weaker proportion than in any other presidential election. In 2002, the two leading candidates polled barely over one-third of votes cast (36.74 per cent) between them. Even more than in 1995, the 2002 presidential election also witnessed an usually strong showing of anti-system candidates, with the combined totals of far-left (10 per cent) and far-right candidates (20 per cent) approaching one-third of the voters, in addition to a higher than average abstention rate and number of spoilt votes (Cole, 1995, 2002).

The sudden emergence of the Greens in 1989, through their peak in 1992–3 and their subsequent virtual collapse illustrated that the party system had to be analysed in terms of being an active evolving structure, rather than a static range of pre-established political positions. The party system appeared more fragmented in 2004 than in the early 1980s. The decline of Communist Party in particular has accentuated the imbalance between the left and the right, while liberating the Socialists from an encumbering presence to their left. In spite of the rich variety of anti-system parties (especially the FN) , the French party system has become rather more like those of its European neighbours in one important respect. The mainstay of political competition is provided by a social-reformist inclined PS, and the conservative RPR-UDF coalition, now renamed UMP. The major developments outlined in this chapter – the decline of the Communist Party, the breakthrough of the extreme-right and the varying fortunes of political ecology – reflect broader European trends observable in countries such as Italy, Austria or Belgium. The major political blocs in France – conservative, and social democratic – are broadly comparable to those present in comparable European countries. As in certain other European countries, however, the real dangers lie in the extent to which these blocs are challenged by political forces ambivalent towards liberal democracy. In terms of the operation of the French party system, the image of French exceptionalism no longer comes from a strong Communist Party, but from assertive and visible far-right and far-left movements. The ability to manage these movements poses a new test both for the integrative capacity of the French Fifth Republic, and for the welfare of liberal democratic values in French society.

10 The representation of interests

10.1 Introduction

In Chapter 10, we discuss group activity in France at some length. We begin by offering several definitions and exploring the various types of group activity. We describe in some detail the main economic interests. We investigate the mechanisms by which groups exert pressure and study the relations between groups, the state and the European Union. In a final section, we examine alternative explanations for understanding group activity, arguing that the French case can be fitted easily neither into the traditional pluralist nor corporatist models of state–group relations.

10.2 The context of group activity

Modern post-revolutionary France has been built upon a strong normative belief in the superiority of the central state, representing the general will, over intermediary interests, be they localities, political parties or organised groups. Organised group activity was forbidden during the French Revolution. Only in 1884, with the repeal of the *Loi le Chapelier*, were professional groups allowed to organise, but they remained weak (Guilani, 1991). The 1901 law fully legalised associations. From the outset, there was a bias in favour of 'good associations' which were inclined to work with the state in the pursuit of the general interest (Barthélemy, 2000). State recognition of 'representative' groups and its *de facto* accreditation of certain associations (at the expense of others) represents a strongly corporatist feature of modern French politics.

The existence of a powerful central bureaucracy, imbued with the ideology of the higher interests of the state, contributed to the comparatively weak role of organised interest groups in policy-making. At the same time, powerful vested interests did manifest themselves within what remained until 1939 an overwhelmingly rural, agricultural-based society. The influence exercised by interests such as wine growers or North African settlers during the Third and Fourth Republics was well documented by Philip Williams (1964) in *Crisis and Compromise*. During the parliamentary-centred Third Republic, interests focused their attention on key parliamentary committees with power to distribute resources. The capture of deputies, even parliamentary committees by specific interests counterbalanced the official discourse valorising the higher role of the neutral state. In the course of the Fourth Republic, agencies of the state themselves operated openly as powerful interests, weakening the myth of the unity and indivisibility of the French state. The French military in particular progressively detached itself from the tutelage of the republican state. The constitution of the Fifth Republic refers to the indivisibility of the French state, but it recognises that political parties and interest groups have a legitimate right to exist.

Various attempts have been made to explain the apparent weakness of French associational life, notably by referring to traits embedded in French political culture. Michel Crozier's 'stalled society' embodied this tendency; the French have a fear of face-to-face contact, and are incapable of operating a normal model of political bargaining (Crozier, 1963). As a nation of individualists, the French are reluctant to join groups. Those that do belong to groups distrust the state, as well as each other, and are disinclined to enter into a political bargaining process. For its part, the French state continually contests the representative character of groups. The state occupies a powerful position because it is able to decide which groups are 'representative' of a particular sector. These arrangements benefit the group concerned in relation to its rivals. More than in most nations, the state thus arbitrates between which groups are 'good', and which are narrow and self-serving.

It is useful to draw distinctions between different types of organised group activity in France. We use pressure group as a generic term to describe all types of groups that seek to engage pressure to modify outcomes. This very general label covers a vast variety of specific groups. Some political scientists have preferred the term 'cause' group to designate those groups that advocate specific causes. The term interest group usually refers to professional groups, such as trade unions, or employers' associations. In the French context, sociologists often refer to social movements, rather than groups (Neveu, 2002). For Alain Touraine, social movements are structures between the individual and the state that seek to change society. The labour movement is the original social movement and most associations during the early twentieth century were created as part of this broader class-based movement. New social movements are broadly 'post-modern' in character. They mobilise opinion to defend causes – such as the environment or feminism – that are not purely economic in character. All associations are a means of linking the individual and society. Even when they are completely apolitical, associations provide a form of social counterbalance to state control.

According to French law, voluntary associations or clubs must be registered under a law dating from 1901 as 'non profit-making' associations if they are to be assured legal protection. '1901 Associations' are required to adopt certain organisational characteristics (such as having written statutes, and a management board) and are obliged to register their existence with the prefecture. In return, these 1901 Associations can expect to receive public subsidies. This enables a fairly precise representation of the extent of civic participation in voluntary associations. In its declaration of general policy in May 1995, the

Juppé government estimated that 20,000,000 French people were active in associations of one form or another. In their loosest definition as associations, groups in France have proliferated during the post-war period. The legendary French reluctance to join groups has been contradicted by a explosion of voluntary associations at all levels of society (especially locally).

Whether these groups can be described as pressure groups, in the sense defined above, is debatable. Pressure groups are groups that seek to exercise pressure in order to secure their objectives; they are not simply groups of citizens coming together in pursuit of common interests. The format of the 1901 Association covers an infinite range of activities. The types of voluntary group activity have changed. Traditionally the 1901 Association represented benevolent activity on behalf of charitable groups, such as Catholic Aid organisations. Some argue that the 1901 format has become a cover to enable public funds to be directed to organisations serving private interests. The distinction between genuinely private groups, and those depending on public, or semi-public authorities has become blurred. The boundaries between 1901 Associations and private companies are not always clear and certain organisations benefit from both statutes. The main economic interest groups – such as the MEDEF or the CGT – have created pseudo '1901' organisations, in order to receive public subsidies. Under the Jospin government, the 1901 Association statute also allowed organisations to recruit heavily subsidised young workers (*emplois-jeunes*), a source of labour considered vital for the survival of many of these organisations (interviews). Even government departments have on occasion created '1901 Associations' in order to overcome particular legal restrictions on their activity as public sector authorities. The most widespread distortion of the 1901 format is that instigated by municipal governments (see below). The 1901 Associations have become one of the most prosperous – and least understood – areas of French democracy.

10.3 Economic interest groups

One of the main puzzles of contemporary France is that of occupational interest groups. Weak in terms of their own organised structures and membership, they can exercise a strong influence in key sectors of the economy. In vital policy sectors such as agriculture or education, well-organised professional interest groups can enjoy a neo-corporatist-style relationship with the ranking state ministry, involving groups in the formulation and implementation of policy. The role performed by the farmers union, the FNSEA, has been extensively researched in this sphere (Keeler, 1987; Culpepper, 1993). The weight of certain professional orders – notably amongst doctors, lawyers, architects – also lends itself to a corporatist-style analysis. The most tightly organised French interest groups are the corporate professional orders, membership of which is compulsory for the professions concerned. The Ordre des Médecins is the most notorious. A number of French professional groups receive substantial financial contributions from the state, in return for performing a series of semi-official public functions. The system of the corps strengthens the professional bodies in determining conditions for new entrants (Guilani, 1991).

In other sectors, contact between the state and organised interests ranges from sporadic to non-existent. This is partly because of the reluctance of the state to share policy-making responsibility with private interests; partly because groups are too weak, and partly because the state itself is divided. In an attempt to link French experience with those of comparable liberal democracies, certain French public policy specialists have diagnosed a 'French' model of corporatism, based on the role of public sector professionals and the *grands corps*. We consider these arguments below.

Business interests

Business represents the key cluster of interests in capitalist liberal democracies, both in the form of employers' associations and the activity of individual firms. Employers' associations vary in their structure from one country to another. Employers in France are represented in different organisations according to their size: large firms are represented in the MEDEF (MEDEF); small and medium-sized enterprises in the *Confédération générale des petites et moyennes entreprises* (CGPME), or the *Union des patrons artisanaux* (UPA). The most important of these organisations is the MEDEF. The MEDEF is composed of representatives of the professional branches (e.g. the metallurgy industry, the building federation, the textile employers' federation), as well as members of the 'interprofessional' local, departmental and regional unions. The MEDEF and its member unions perform a range of functions: these include social and legal assistance, as well as more classic lobbying activities. Much of the energy of the MEDEF and of its local and regional federations is spent in providing representatives to sit on the tripartite committees that govern the social security and unemployment regimes, as well as the labour disputes courts.

As a confederation, the MEDEF has a relatively weak control over the economic interests it represents. Though it has changed its name (from CNPF to MEDEF in 1995), the main employers' federation is still organised as first created in 1946. The main professional branches within the MEDEF are those of the 'old' economy: iron and steel, engineering, chemicals, the building trade, agri-business and so on. Most professional federations represent trades or professions that have evolved beyond recognition since the late 1940s when CNPF statutes were drawn up. The MEDEF is rather unrepresentative of the new economy and the service sector. The MEDEF is also frequently divided, especially between its largest member – the UIMM – and other branches, and between the branches and interprofessional unions at the local and regional level. Leading companies represented within the MEDEF will more often than not operate as economic actors in their own right, weakening the effectiveness of collective employers' action. The MEDEF commands respect, however, on account of the vital importance of the interests it represents. Its pressure has been efficient under governments of different political persuasions, though it complained bitterly of being excluded from the main decisions taken by the Jospin government of 1997–2002 (especially the 35-hour week). Its lobbying activities are concentrated upon Paris and Brussels (where it forms an active member of UNICE, the European Employers' federation).

The MEDEF mainly represents big business. It is often at odds with the CGPME, representing small- and medium-sized employers. Unlike the MEDEF, the CGPME or the UPA (representing lone traders) will rarely, if ever, be drawn into the government's policy orbit.

Alongside employer's federations, the Chambers of Commerce, of Agriculture and of Trade perform an important role in representing industrial and commercial interests in the localities and regions, as well as performing a number of quasi-administrative functions. The Chambers of Commerce are the most important. They are semi-public organisations: in the words of one General Secretary interviewed, the Chambers have 'one foot in the public, one in the private'. They perform three essential functions. They represent the interests of local firms (industrial and commercial), both in terms of lobbying and of providing firms with business advice. They are themselves important local economic interests (the Chambers have traditionally run most of France's ports and airports, as well as many commercial and industrial zones). They carry out important administrative and regulatory functions as local agencies of the Ministry of Industry and Commerce. Relations between the Chambers of Commerce and the local employers' federations are often tense. The Chambers enjoy compulsory membership from all firms registered in their localities, giving them substantial financial resources, since each firm has to pay 1 per cent of its turnover to the Chamber.

Although French employers seek to present a united front, there are many sources of internal pressure: between small and big businesses, between industrial and commercial interests, between competitive and closed sectors, between export-driven and neo-protectionist sectors, between conservative and liberal employers. The vital economic role performed by the larger companies places them in a strong bargaining position with the government, especially as the government will identify its aims with its industrial 'national champions'. Private companies such as PSA, TOTAL and Rhône-Poulenc occupy a powerful bargaining position. In the industrial sphere, French traditions of powerful state interventionism have limited somewhat the freedom of manoeuvre of large indigenous firms although this pattern is changing under the impact of privatisation and globalisation (see Chapter 12). The French state has less freedom in relation to multinational companies. The delocalisation of Hoover from Reims to Scotland in 1993, for example, revealed the impotence of the French government to control the flow of industry in the open European market.

Trade unions

Trade unions constitute the second most powerful cluster of interests in the capitalist democracies. But they are generally more divided even than employers' associations, and have suffered since the early 1980s from a steadily less favourable policy climate. European Social Democratic governments have generally maintained closer relationships with trade unions than conservative governments, but this neo-corporatist model has been in decline across Europe. Although the 'social partnership' model is important in some respects in France (especially in relation to training and labour disputes) economic interests are somewhat less integrated into the decision-making machinery in France than in Germany or the Scandanavian countries. As with the MEDEF and its member unions, the main trade union federations serve on the tripartite boards administering the social security and unemployment systems, and the labour disputes boards. Elections to these boards enable the strength of the various trade union federations to be gauged on an annual basis.

French trade unions are amongst the weakest in EU nations, as measured in narrow organisational terms of membership (Parsons, 2004; Andolfatto and Labbé, 2000). A combination of France's late industrialisation, the difficulties of legal existence and political divisions meant that trade unions were never as firmly rooted in France as they were in Britain, Germany or the Scandinavian countries. The early history of the trade union movement was one of a struggle between anarcho-syndicalist traditions of the craft unions, and the collective proletarian ethos of later industrial unions (Lorwin, 1972). From the anarcho-syndicalist heritage emerged a deeply imbued sense of workerism (*ouvrièrisme*) and working-class self-sufficiency; this was later articulated by the *Confédération générale du travail* (CGT) and the PCF. The capture of the CGT by the Communist Party in 1947 aggravated political divisions between French trade unions, to the detriment of collective unified action. The division into five national trade union 'peak' federations, split along lines primarily of political affiliation rather than occupational status, proved a major weakness for French trade unions, which found it as difficult to speak to each other as to engage in a dialogue with employers or the state.

At their height, French trade unions occupied powerful positions of strategic importance within French industry: in traditional heavy industries (mining, shipbuilding, automobile construction) the rate of unionisation was upwards of 50 per cent, with certain sectors (dockers, printers) operating an effective closed shop. Certain of these heavily unionised industries (mining) suffered an irreversible decline in the course of the 1980s, whereas others (automobiles) adopted new working practices less conducive to traditional union influence. Industrial rationalisation in the 1980s had a detrimental effect on union strength, as did the rise in unemployment. Alongside the decline in traditional heavy manufacturing industries, unionisation is virtually absent in newer industries, as well as in small-scale firms with less than fifty employees.

Trade union representatives perform an important role in the administration of the social security system; in the works councils that have a statutory existence in all companies employing over fifty employees; on labour disputes boards, and in various local, regional and national consultative committees. But, even in elections for these boards, the largest union is that of non-union members. The crisis of French trade unionism forms part of a wider post-industrial movement. All trade union federations, whatever their ideological leanings, have

Table 10.1 French economic interest groups

Type	Organisation	Influence	Weaknesses
Business groups			
MEDEF (Mouvement des Enterprises de France)	Confederal. National Council unites representatives of sectoral branches (e.g. textiles, metallurgy, construction)	Lead employers' organisation. Representative of big business. Chief negotiator with government in most sectors. Helps run social security system with unions and state	Large firms often act alone. Serious internal divisions
CGPME (Conseil général des petites et moyennes entreprises)	Confederal	Strength amongst small and medium-sized businesses	Not an insider. Distrusted by governments
Labour unions			
CGT (Confédération générale du travail)	Confederal. CGT was for long the largest French trade union, both in terms of votes cast in works councils' elections and membership	Traditionally strong in ports, mines, shipbuilding, iron and steel and other heavy industry. Steep decline in works councils' elections (from a highpoint of 45% in 1967 to under 25%)	The CGT has lost influence with industrial decline. Haemorrhage of members (from over 3,000,000 in 1978 to under 1,000,000 in 2003)
CFDT (Confédération française démocratique du travail)	Confederal. The CFDT was created in 1964 out of the older CFTC. Traditionally Socialist inclining but suspicious of the PS, the CFDT was influenced by the strong ideological currents of May '68. In maturity it has become the 'responsible' voice of French trade unionism	Traditionally poor sister to the CGT, the CFDT overtook the former in workplace elections in 1995. 5–600,000 members. Its zones of strength are less tied to heavy industrial plant than the CGT	Certain branches traditionally opposed to leadership. Leadership contested since 1995. Split in 2003
FO (*Force ouvrière*)	Born out of a split with the CGT in 1947, FO is France's third most significant union. Marked by a tradition of anti-communism	Strong in certain white-collar professions, and in the civil service	Serious internal divisions from Trokskyite factions. Marc Blondell's leadership contested. 300,000 members
Other economic interests			
Fédération syndicale unifiée (FSU) Fédération de l'Education nationale (FEN)	Born in 1994 after a split with the FEN, the FSU has 11 member unions, the most important being the secondary school teachers' union (SNES)	FSU less prone to cooperation, or co-decision-making than the FEN. Favours street demonstrations over negotiations	The formal split within the FEN has weakened the weight of one of the strongest sectoral unions that France has ever known
FNSEA (Fédération nationale des syndicats des exploitants agricoles)	Represents all interests in the agricultural sector. Shares features in common with labour and employers' unions	Close contacts maintained between FNSEA officials and government ministers	FNSEA increasingly contested by rural 'coordinations'
'Coordinations'	'Spontaneous' groups arising in wildcat strikes with increasing frequency. Testament to the weakness of traditional unions	Coordinations have appeared amongst nurses, health workers, railwaymen, farmers	They are single-issue groups, which often disappear once a strike is over
Others	A spate of single sector unions since the mid-1990s, of which SUD is the most important		

suffered from the impact of the economic crisis, the effect of new technologies, declining working-class consciousness and the rise of individualism. In France, trade union decline has been superimposed upon a weak initial base of union membership: never more than 15–20 per cent of the overall workforce were unionised, a proportion well under 10 per cent today. Employers' associations and public policy-makers are often inclined to the view that French trade unions are too weak; there are scarcely enough activists to serve as union representatives on the social security committees, or to engage in collective bargaining negotiations with employers. Many labour disputes that have broken out since the early 1980s have been provoked by spontaneous strike committees ('coordinations'), completely outside the control of the official unions. Such strikes are more difficult to control in the absence of recognisable bargaining partners. The activities of militant grass-roots activists have provoked the unions into pre-emptive radicalisation in an attempt to control the labour movement. Since the anti-Juppé strikes of 1995, in particular, trade unions have been engaged in a rearguard action to defend working conditions against the perceived threats of unbridled liberalism, invisible globalisation and individualisation. The mass strikes against Raffarin's pension reforms in Spring 2003 demonstrated that the unions still had the capacity to mobilise employees for strike action.

The public sector unions: resisting reform

At the forefront of the 2003 strikes were the public sector workers, including those working for state firms (EDF-GDF or SNCF) that were not even concerned by the reform proposals. The level of union membership in the French public sector is much higher than in the private sector, well over 20 per cent in education and public finance and higher still in the electricity industries and the railways. The influence of the trade unions extends well beyond their formal membership. Public sector unions are institutionalised as 'ideological veto players' (Chevallier, 1996), often able to block reforms they fear will alter their terms and conditions. We observed in Chapter 7 that a large proportion of public sector workers enjoys the status of civil servants and is protected by the 1946 civil service statute, or by the specific statutes that govern particular corps. Chevallier (1996) points out that the 1946 civil service code does not generally enter into negotiations on reform of the state.

In the French civil service, trade unions are viewed as social partners and participate in joint committees (*Commissions mixtes paritaires*) that deal with all aspects of employment, training, work organisation and productivity. Ministers involve the unions closely. *Force Ouvrière* is the most traditional of all trade unions, the most reluctant to accept any changes in working practices. Since the strike movement of November–December 1995, the activity of the public sector unions has become almost entirely defensive, namely to resist any changes in codes, rules or working practices, and to defend the corporate ethos against any attempt to introduce individual incentives or more flexible working practices. The activity of the tax officials working in the Finance Ministry in resisting the attempt to reform the system of tax collection provides an excellent example (see Chapter 7).

In other parts of the public sector, trade unions exercise a strong influence, especially in the state-owned and 'public interest' firms, such as the gas and electricity conglomerate, EDF-GDF and the national railways, the SNCF. More than any other group of public sector workers, the teaching profession has arguably proved the most effective in defending terms and conditions and resisting reform. The civil servants of the main divisions within the Education Ministry and the powerful teaching unions act as the gatekeepers of professionalisation at a national level. So characteristic were professional influences on French education policy-making that the sector was described as neo-corporatist by Ambler (1985). Ambler diagnosed three neo-corporatist features to French educational management: a mass membership trade union movement (then the FEN, now the SNES); a centralised form of bargaining and access to central policy-makers; extensive delegated administrative powers. As civil servants themselves, secondary schoolteachers are the self-appointed high priests of a national system of professional regulation. They are organised into powerful trade unions which co-manage issues of salaries, pay and promotions with Education Ministry officials. As their support is essential for individual teacher mobility, the unions have a captive constituency amongst secondary school teachers. This bureaucratic-professional coalition has a strong normative attachment to centralisation as the only means of preserving public service, equality of opportunity and national standards. The opposition of the teaching unions (by and large supported by public opinion) has been instrumental in forcing a series of ambitious Education Ministers to water down their projects. In 2000, Claude Allègre was forced to resign after incurring the wrath of the teaching unions by proposing more autonomy for schools and changes in working practices. In 2003, Premier Raffarin had to postpone plans to decentralise the management of school auxiliary workers, when faced once again with the opposition of the main teaching unions.

The farming unions

Farmers unions display characteristics that are reminiscent of both trade unions and employers' associations. Despite the demographic decline of agriculture, these organisations continue to wield considerable influence in France, as well as in a number of other European countries. The political pressure brought to bear by farmers stems in part from the unity of the agricultural sector: employers and employees tend to make common cause in defence of agriculture, in a manner rare in the secondary and tertiary sectors. The near-monopoly of representation by the leading French farmers' organisation – the *Fédération nationale des syndicats des exploitants agricoles* (FNSEA) – has traditionally acted as a resource unavailable to labour unions, as have the close contacts maintained between FNSEA officials and government ministers. The modest economic weight of agriculture (Chapter 12) is counterbalanced by the fact that French farmers generally have political support, and employ pressure tactics to marshal this support to maximum effect. French farmers are stoutly defended by conservative-inclining parties since they are perceived to symbolise essential features of national identity in a period of rapid social and economic change. The efficacy of the agricultural lobby has been demonstrated in successive rounds of GATT/WTO talks since the early 1990s, in which French governments have sought to protect French farmers from the full effects of international competition.

There is undoubtedly a deep cultural sympathy felt for the plight of small farmers in France, a nation with a profound rural heritage (Boussard, 1990). Like some other groups, the farmers have repeatedly demonstrated their willingness to resort to methods of direct action. The French farmers' unions have learnt lessons from early syndicalist movements. Their violence is in proportion to their desperate plight and the uneconomic foundation of their livelihoods, especially after reforms to the EU's Common Agricultural Policy (Tacet, 1992). As with the trade unions, the position of the main farmers' union (FNSEA) has been undermined by the rise of rural 'coordinations', and by the emergence of the Peasant's Confederation of José Bové as a serious contender for influence.

10.4 Groups and the French political system

Groups apply pressure wherever power is held by the state, or by public authorities. They attempt to concentrate their activity in the arena where the state (or state-like polity, in the case of the European Union) is at its most powerful. The highly centralised political executive of the Fifth Republic acts as an incentive for interest groups to 'network' with central state decision makers. Interest groups will often employ full-time lobbyists to present their organisations' case. These figures are increasingly deployed in Brussels as well. There are, however, several points of access open to groups, with much French activity concentrated at the micro-level.

The legislature

Classically, parliament was the central focus for pressure in the French republican tradition. Power appeared to reside in parliament, and deputies were far more accessible than remote civil servants. In the Third and Fourth French Republics, individual deputies were often totally beholden to the pressures of particular vested interests, who provided financial support in return for supporting their cause. The case of the alcohol distillers (*bouilleurs de cru*) in the Third Republic was a celebrated one. With the general weakening of parliament in the Fifth Republic, the emasculation of the committee system, and stringent conditions for the introduction of private members' bills, such pressure tactics have proved less effective. Those groups that are forced to lobby deputies to support their causes are usually those without direct access to government departments.

The executive

The political executive and the bureaucracy are nearly everywhere primary targets of interest groups. The capacity of a group to maintain a network of national contacts within government departments is testament to its influence, or to its 'insider' status. Serious negotiations between government departments and large firms, to take one example, take place behind closed doors, in a myriad of formal committees and informal meetings. Large French firms – such as Total – are received as partners by the ministers or civil servants concerned. The input of groups depends somewhat upon the characteristics of the policy sector. Certain interests impose themselves as major players because of their powerful strategic position. The main economic interests, notably large multi-national firms that occupy specific market positions, are a case in point. Governments will often rely on large firms for detailed information concerning exports, markets and technologies. Such a specialised source of information can be beyond the capacity of the state itself. In those issue-areas where social partnership is strong (labour regulation, training, the management of the welfare state), social partners are deeply involved in the formulation and imple-mentation of public policy. In some issue-areas – agriculture and education especially – the prevailing image is one of the 'bureaucratic capture' of the governmental machinery by organised interests, although this impression is not really accurate. In other sectors, groups are largely disconnected from the executive agencies. In still others, there is a cooperative mode of collaboration between the French state and economic interests deemed of vital importance for the country. To this extent, the description by Knapp and Wright (2001) of state–group relations representing an 'untidy reality' is accurate.

A government in power is, *a priori*, more likely to be sympathetic to groups with which it feels ideologically akin. Knapp and Wright (2001) point out how successive Education Ministers in the 1970s and 1980s attempted to push through university reforms by relying upon the sympathetic teaching unions, at the expense of their rivals. More recently, the MEDEF complained bitterly through-out the Jospin government that it was excluded from any influence over policy. After the return of the right, Premier Raffarin made a point of personally attending the MEDEF conference in 2003 to signify the changed circumstances.

We referred above to a cooperative mode of collaboration between the French state and powerful economic interests. As we demonstrate in Chapter 12, relations between the state and the business community have evolved subtly in the course of the past two decades. It remains the case that there is close collaboration between the French state and well-identified economic interests. Fairbrass (2002) draws a very interesting contrast in this respect between France (where governments actively support the interests of French firms in lobbying Brussels) and the United Kingdom (which adopts a more hands-off approach). The principal economic interest groups – employers fed-erations, trade unions – aspire to influence national (or Europeanised) policy processes as a priority, in the belief that decisions taken nationally will filter down to regional and local levels. Lobbying in Paris or Brussels bears more weight than regional or local lobbying.

Direct action

In most European democracies, groups that resort to street demonstrations will generally tend to exercise the least pressure, except where demonstrations are massive, and highly symbolic of widespread support. In France, however, such methods have a long history. Direct action tactics have become a regular feature of group activity, superimposed upon a distant memory of a revolutionary tradition. French farmers, fisherman and lorry drivers have perfected strategies designed to cause maximum possible disruption to the normal functioning of French life. The apparent success of such procedures has encouraged further their protagonists. For groups such as farmers, direct action tactics go alongside behind closed door negotiations between interest group representatives and state officials. A more serious problem revealed during the 1990s has been the inability of interest group representatives to conclude deals that are acceptable to their members, a phenomenon afflicting such venerable institutions as the FNSEA, the FSU and the main students' unions. The rallying of public opinion to a particular cause provides a political resource that can radically enhance a group's bargaining position. Overwhelming public support for the cause of the nurses and health workers in 1989, for instance, forced Rocard's government into making concessions it had not initially envisaged.

Subnational government

The strengthening of local and regional levels of subnational government has created new arenas for group influence and activity. Most voluntary associations exist at a local, or subnational level. The interpenetration between municipal governments and voluntary associations reveals the dependency that exists between the two types of organisation. Many 1901 Associations are created on the initiative of local authorities themselves: municipally inspired sports clubs, social or cultural associations provide examples. Such groups can in practice be difficult to distinguish from agencies of local government. The system of local authorities' providing financial support for local voluntary associations means that even groups bitterly opposed to the local authority often depend upon grants for their continued existence. Most French associations are usually in a weak position with regard both to elected authorities and governmental agencies. They depend upon the latter both for financial support and for information. The relationship between local associations and the town hall in particular is a complex one; the mayor claims to personify the general interest, whereas local associations can only claim to represent one fraction of the population. To implement policy effectively, however, the town hall needs a network of associations in all different spheres of local society. These reinforcing pressures usually create a *modus vivendum* between the municipal government, and the principal local associations. In practice, funded associations are *de facto* implementing agencies for public policies across a very wide range of areas. That so many French voluntary associations depend for their survival upon grants from local government limits their autonomy and weakens their bargaining stance.

The European Union

It lies beyond the scope of this book to present a detailed account of French lobbying in the European Union (Grossman and Saurugger, 2004; Saurugger, 2003; Fairbrass, 2003). Suffice it to say that French lobbying tactics are increasingly directed towards the institutions and actors of the European Union. Sites of pressure vary: they include the Commission (especially), the European Parliament (increasingly), the European Court of Justice (sometimes) and the summits of European leaders (for symbolic purposes). Types of pressure also vary. They include:

- direct action tactics adopted by French farmers and workers in Brussels;
- transnational cooperation between employers and trades unions;
- lobbying on behalf of French cities (usually in European networks of similar cities);
- lobbying by industrialists representing particular sectors (such as the Steel industry);
- Targeting particular officials working in Commission directorates to further group aims.

Such forms of lobbying have developed exponentially in recent years, as groups attempt to reverse unfavourable arbitrations at the national level.

10.5   Social movements old and new

Economic interests form only one type of group activity. Most groups are concerned with non-economic, voluntary or promotional activities. Pressure groups might include associations dedicated to the defence of the environment, feminist movements, regionalist movements, anti-nuclear movements, groups espousing specific moral causes, cultural movements, neighbourhood defence groups and so on. Certain associations might pursue overtly political objectives; others might be essentially non-political, becoming involved in politics only when government proposes to enact policy that affects its interests. The evidence presented in this chapter suggests that there has been an increase of participation in group activity in the French case, throwing into relief the traditional stereotype of the French as a nation of uncivic individualists. There has been a growth of groups as the state has increased the scope of its intervention. In any area of policy, groups tend to crystallise on either side of the argument: for instance, pro- and anti-abortion associations; pro- and anti-hunting lobbies. This can be seen in relation to the environment, a relatively new area of political interest. Environmental groups sprung up in France in the 1970s, initially in an attempt to halt the construction of nuclear power plants. In response to environmental pressures, the French nuclear industry then organised itself as a highly effective lobby against Green movements. As with the environmental groups, the pro-hunting lobby provides another example of the difficulties of maintaining a strict distinction between political parties and pressure groups. In the 1994 European election, the pro-hunting lobby ran its own list, *Chasse, nature, pêche et tradition*, which received 4 per cent, comfortably surpassing that polled by Les verts. In subsequent elections, the hunters and fishers have proved their ability to cause electoral upsets.

In the course of the 1970s, the development of new social movements, such as environmental, feminist, and regionalist movements, appeared less in evidence in France than in Britain or Germany. The French party system long remained impermeable to the disruptions of the new social movement politics of the 1970s and early 1980s, whereas these single-issue movements wreaked havoc in Britain and Germany. As argued in Chapter 2, the legacy of May '68 expressed itself within existing political parties. Until 1981, aspirations of social change rested firmly upon the mainstream left-wing parties, especially the Socialist Party, which partly resurrected itself in the 1970s by articulating the demands of a variety of new social movements. These new social movements were so disappointed with the Mitterrand presidency (1981–95) that many turned to more independent forms of activity. As the example of the Greens illustrated, however, these movements were too heterogeneous to articulate a coherent political message. The demands articulated by new social movements in the 1970s have either been incorporated by mainstream political parties, or else (as with the nuclear issue) represented only a small minority of public opinion.

The number of associations created in France doubled between 1975 and 1990. Waters (2003) refers to the emergence of a new citizenship to describe the growth in associations since the 1980s. The new associations that have emerged, she argues, are explicitly focussed on issues of citizenship, democracy and participation. These associations are suspicious of the state and of traditional political parties. New social movement activity since the 1980s has centred on anti-racism (SOS-Racisme, SCALP, Ras l'Front), human rights (Amnesty International, Ligue des droits de l'homme . . .), defending the unemployed (Agir chomage), the rights of immigrants (Les sans papiers) and the rights of gays (Act-up). Broadly speaking, there are two types of group amongst the new social movements: those focused on gaining access to French society on behalf of previously excluded groups (such as the 'sans papiers', or SOS-Racisme); and those contesting the underlying foundations of global capitalist society as it currently functions. New social movements often present themselves as rivals to political parties, though a number of these social movements have strong links with the resurgent far-left (for example Agir chomage with the LCR) (Wolfreys, 2003). The division between new social movements and the mainstream left has been deepened by the success of the antiglobalisation ('alter-mondialiste') movement. Some of the most prominent new social movements have been closely associated with the pan-global, antiglobalisation protests that have gathered pace since the failure of the Seattle round of trade talks in 1999. They have crystallised around the charismatic figure of figure of Jose Bové, and are much closer to the Ligue communiste révolutionnaire than to traditional left parties such as the PCF or PS. These antiglobalisation groups have undoubtedly influenced the climate within which French politics is carried out and have created a major headache for the main left-wing party, the Socialist Party, seen as the natural home of new social movements in the 1970s.

10.6 Concluding remarks: a 'French-style corporatism'?

In the Anglo-Saxon tradition, most democratic theorists regard the freedom to organise interests into groups as a fundamental prerequisite for the operation of liberal democracy. For sound historical reasons, prevailing French theoretical frameworks – equating democracy with a Rousseauan general will – have been less inclined to accept groups as a legitimate expression of the democratic process. The French state has historically been less tolerant towards autonomous groups than in comparable countries. In the French republican tradition, the state is held to be superior to the total of competing interests; groups exist in a sub-ordinate relationship with the state. This order of priorities was written into the 1958 Constitution, and is constantly reiterated in the discourse of politicians and civil servants. In the US, by contrast, a system of freely competing interest groups is held to be synonymous with democracy itself: the state prefers to see itself as a referee between the key interests in society. The French and American examples provide two differing views of liberal democracy: in the first the people's representatives (and the state) express the general will; in the second, the popular will emerges as the result of the confrontation of conflicting private interests. These historical, cultural and political traditions affect the role of groups and patterns of group–state relations in both countries.

Two ideal-type models of state–group relations (and their adjectival extensions) have prevailed in the academic literature on interest groups. The pluralist model portrays democracy in terms of the free interplay of competing groups, with the state reduced to an arbitral role. The corporatist model describes a pattern of state–group relations within which groups are fully integrated into the machinery of the state and where relations between groups are largely non-competitive. Neither is entirely applicable in the French context. Pluralism is alien to the institutional and philosophical framework of the French polity. The pluralist portrayal of politics in terms of a system of groups competing on a relatively level-playing field underestimates the role of the state in arbitrating between groups, and deciding which ones are legitimate. This is particularly important in France. Pluralism appears particularly ill-adapted to explain the French traditions of a strong, directive state defining the parameters of group activity, and a relatively weak system of national bargaining.

The corporatist model, as defined by Schmitter and Lehmbruch, appears more appropriate (though still inadequate) when considering French state–group relations. Schmitter and Lehmbruch (1979) defined neo-corporatism in terms of a number of principles: non-competition between groups, recognition of groups by the state, representational monopoly of the single group, and compulsory membership of professional groups. In the corporatist schema, groups do not compete with each other, as much as cooperate closely in their mutual interest. This is typified notably by national collective wage agreements negotiated between the state, employers and the unions; by the representation of capital and labour on key policy-making committees; by the existence of single powerful labour and employers' federations; and by the existence of closed shops and compulsory membership.

We can recognise several of these features in the French experience. In certain of the policy sectors we surveyed above – such as agriculture or education – the neo-corporatist model fits quite well, in others much less so. The role of 'social partners' highlights the paradox of the French model of state–group relations. French trade unions occupy a paradoxical position. They are undermined by weak organisation, low membership, and internal divisions, but they occupy strong institutional positions. The power of employers and trades unions lies in their co-management of the social security and labour disputes machinery. The social partners make decisions that affect almost all French citizens (in health, for example) and manage colossal budgets that have a direct impact on people's lives. Though the French state has exercised a closer supervision of over health expenditure since the Juppé plan, the 'social partners' remain key institutional players. In addition, trade unions are involved in a range of statutory consultation processes that can produce substantive, as well as procedural results. The importance of agreement with the trade unions for firm-level training plans, for example, gives organised labour a measurable impact. The strong legal tradition that we discussed in Chapter 7, combined with the institutionalisation of group relations, produces a heavily regulated labour market where unions are the gatekeepers of professionalisation and working conditions. Collective bargaining must be understood within the context of this strong legal tradition. Collective agreements (usually national, branch specific agreements) are signed by employers and at least one accredited 'social partner' (usually the CFDT or the CGC, rather than FO or the CGT). The ability of the state to determine which partners are representative is a strongly corporatist feature of the French model. But, unlike in pure corporatist countries, the representative basis for trade union agreement for collective conventions is often weak. Making agreements stick can be difficult, as the professional groups are too divided to articulate a single voice.

There is a strong argument that a French-style corporatism best captures the French situation (Jobert and Muller, 1987; Mény and Thoenig, 1989). While recognising that aspects of neo-corporatism are inappropriate in the French context, these observers maintain that the French case is characterised by certain corporatist features, notably the institutional incorporation of the main social partners (employers and trade unions) into the state, via the tripartite system. The specific character of the French model relates to its strong public sector corporatism and its pattern of representing interests within the state. The French system of the *corps* gives French corporatism a stato-centrist coloration absent in other European nations. The role of *grands corps* (especially the mining, bridges and highways, and rural engineering corps) surfaces in numerous public policy studies. Separate studies have highlighted the importance of engineers from the bridges and highways corps in urban policy in the 1960s and 1970s (Thoenig, 1973); that of mining engineers in energy policy (Cohen, 1988), and that of arms engineers in civil aviation (Muller, 1989). The advantage of such studies is that they highlight the role of powerful actors within the state, as much as the incorporation of outside interests into the decision-making machinery. Even so, not all French observers are convinced of the wisdom of adapting a foreign concept such as corporatism to fit the murky reality of the French situation. Fontaine (1996) points to the forces challenging the French model of public sector corporatism, namely the evolution of the state faced with pressures of European integration and decentralisation and the changing role of the *grands corps*.

It is difficult to fit the French case into either of these models – or their variants – which appear designed to depict different social and political realities. The above analysis would suggest that state–group relations are one sphere in which a distinctive French model persists, though in a much weaker form than previously. In part, this is the inescapable heritage of France's past historical development, which has ensured that trade unions perform a subaltern role, that direct action tactics can pay dividends, that technical state *corps* have great prestige, or that the state exercises an essential role in defining the parameters of legitimate group activity. This conclusion needs to be modified in certain respects, however. First, state interests (such as the technical *grands corps*) have been weakened, and new public and private actors have emerged to contest their role. Second, French groups have discovered new arenas for their activity, at the European and subnational levels especially. Finally, though measurement tools are crude, the number of new associations created annually suggests that French citizens participate more actively than ever before in groups, at least some of which have an incidence on public policy.

Part 4

Reshaping modern France

11 Society, citizenship and identity

11.1 Introduction

Neither the political institutions appraised in Part 2, nor the representative forces analysed in part three of this book can be dissociated from their surrounding social and economic environments. We address several interlocking questions in this chapter. Has the evolution of French society in the post-war period been conflict-ridden or consensual? How resilient is the republican model of citizenship? How is identity construction experienced amongst minority 'ethnic' groups? Why are lesser used languages seen as a threat to the French Republic ? What evidence is there of multiple and overlapping identities in contemporary France? We seek answers to these essential questions, each of which inform debates about the future direction of French politics and society.

11.2 The evolution of French society: social consensus or social fracture?

Table 11.1 portrays the changing French class structure during the post-war period. Even a cursory glance reveals that the old French class configuration has been greatly modified. The peasantry and the traditional bourgeoisie have virtually disappeared. The popular classes (industrial workers, low-status clerical workers, shop assistants) have declined. There has been a marked expansion of the new middle classes (higher-status clerical workers, managers and related workers in the public and private sectors). If French observers broadly agree on the contours of the evolution of French society, however, they disagree firmly upon the interpretation that should accompany this evolution.

The optimistic school argue that France, like many other advanced industrialised states, has moved towards a happy state of social harmony and prosperity, with the growth of an affluent middle class. They celebrate the emergence of a new national consensus, based on an end of ideology, an enhanced material well-being and a virtual eradication of class conflict. Imitating Daniel Bell in the US, they refer to the new middle classes as the purveyors of a new focal culture disseminated to the rest of French society. Not only have the middle classes expanded in number, but members of the older social classes, such as

Table 11.1 Social change and the evolution of the French workforce (excluding retired and non-active)

	1954	1962	1975	1982	1990	1999
Farmers	21	15.5	7.5	6.5	4	2.5
Artisans, small business, shopkeepers	13	10.5	8	8	7	6.5
Higher management, intellectual and liberal professions	3	4.5	7	8	11	12
Intermediary professions (teachers, social workers, middle management, civil servants, etc.)	9	11.5	17	18	19	22
Non-managerial clerical workers (*employés*)	17	18.5	24	26.5	28	30
Industrial workers	37	39.5	36.5	33	31	27

Source: INSEE, *Tableaux de l'économie française*, 2003–2004 (1999 and 1990 figures); INSEE censuses and employment surveys, 1954–82 figures. Cited in Dirn (1990) *La Société française en tendances*, p. 160.

farmers or industrial workers, have come increasingly to imitate the middle class in their lifestyles, so much so that they have lost many of the specific traits associated with their class of origin. The boundaries between different social classes have become blurred. This extolling of the beneficial effects of social change was pushed furthest by Mendras (1989) who discerned a Second French Revolution. Mendras argued that the structure of French society had been overhauled during the post-war period in a manner just as radical as that following the 1789 French Revolution. There were seven principal characteristics of this Second French Revolution:

■ An unprecedented demographic and economic expansion during the first thirty years of the post-war period, labelled by Jean Fourastié as *les trente glorieuses*. After a century of demographic stagnation (1840–1940) France's population rose dramatically after the war, from 42,000,000 to 55,000,000 within one generation. Economic production multiplied five-fold within several decades; national wealth increased in an unprecedented manner; the structure of the French economy was radically altered.

■ Economic take-off caused the expansion of tertiary sector employment, radically changing the nation's social class structure. The two dominant social classes produced by the French Revolution, the peasantry and the bourgeoisie, have disappeared, replaced by a new dominant middle class.

■ Despite the post-war economic boom, industry and the industrial working class are in decline, leading to a weakening of subcultural resistance to national integration.

■ The spread of urbanisation has weakened the traditional opposition between the town and the countryside; an urban lifestyle now prevails everywhere.

■ The great national institutions such as the army, the Church and the Republic, are no longer challenged in principle by particular sections of French society. They have lost their symbolic importance and ideological character.

- The uniformity promoted by the French education system and the post-war development of the mass media have contributed to the sense of a unified national community.

- Individualism has made such progress that it is no longer considered as an ideology, but merely as a manner of living shared by everybody.

Such optimism is challenged by other sociologists and social historians. Emmanuel Todd (1988, 1995), for instance, directly challenged the thesis of the end of ideology, and insurged against the conformity (*la pensée unique*) that this notion implies. Todd diagnosed a 'social fracture' based on the division of French society into two antagonistic camps of approximately the same numerical weight: the middle classes (*classes moyennes*), and the popular classes (*classes populaires*). The former had benefited from the process of European integration, industrial modernisation and tertiary sector expansion. The latter had been sacrificed, especially during the 1980s, to the exigencies of economic austerity and capitalist rationalisation. The popular classes were alienated from the more privileged section of French society. Although the middle classes had increased in numbers, the popular classes continued to represent a small majority of the population (Todd, 1995). Rather than a broad social consensus, a social fracture had come into existence, with whole swathes of French society being abandoned as victims of the process of social and economic modernisation. The divorce of the popular classes from the socialist left was particularly marked, since their conditions of existence had worsened during the socialist decade of the 1980s. The fears of the disadvantaged half of the French population were expressed in the emergence of a new cleavage: one based around national identity and a rejection of cosmopolitanism. This was articulated with particular clarity during the referendum on the Maastricht Treaty in 1992. Traditional left-wing areas were in their majority opposed to ratification of the Maastricht Treaty, and amongst the popular electorate, opposition to the ratification of Maastricht reached two-thirds of those voting.

These two portrayals of the evolution of French society contain alternative visions of social reality, but both would concur that the post-war period has witnessed the development of new social groups of a composite range and nature. As in other European countries, the emergence of new social groups (especially managers and clerical workers) was related to the social and economic transformation of French society during the post-war boom, and to the expansion and democratisation of the education system. France's industrial take-off during the 1950s led to changing demands being placed upon the workforce: more technical and managerial staff were needed to run new industries and services, at the expense firstly of farmers, latterly of manual workers. The result of these developments was that France became far less of a rigidly class-bound society than it had been in the 1930s. Social mobility has increased and class has become less of a structuring element in most people's daily lives; this does not signify that social class has disappeared altogether. The new middle classes are themselves fragmented, especially in relation to whether they work in the public or private sector, but also with regard to their political beliefs, their socio-economic status, and their cultural preferences. Amongst the new middle classes, there is considerable diversity in terms of occupation, lifestyle, income and education. The rise of the new middle classes is in marked contrast with the virtual disappearance of the peasantry, and the fragmentation of the industrial working class.

The end of the peasantry?

At the height of the crisis in Franco-American relations occasioned by the GATT agreement in 1993, the French daily *Libération* rebaptised the French revolutionary slogan to read *Liberté – egalité – fraternité – ruralité* (freedom, equality, brotherhood, rusticity). Images of France as a traditional rural society continue to permeate the perceptions of the country held by French people and foreign observers alike. As illustrated in Chapter 11, the success of French farmers in imposing their corporatist demands represents one of the constant features of French politics. It is a testament to the historical conscience of a nation whose identity was forged on the land. France of the nineteenth century was often portrayed as an inward-looking autarky, a rural, believing society, pervaded by an all-encompassing distrust of Paris and the outsider. Outside the handful of cities, the lives of most French people were confined to their immediate locality and kinship networks. During the nineteenth century, the occupational background of most working Frenchmen was linked to the land: France was still overwhelmingly a rural society at the turn of the twentieth century (Tacet, 1992).

At the end of the Second World War, France was the most rural of all Western nations: 45 per cent of the population lived in rural communes and one-quarter of the labour force worked in agriculture. As Williams put it: 'Agriculture was far more important than in Britain: in 1946, France still had one industrial worker for every agricultural worker, while Britain had nine'. (Williams, 1964) Fifty years later France had become a heavily urbanised nation, in which agriculture directly employed under five per cent of the working population. There were as many as six million agricultural workers in 1946, but only just over one million in 1986, with five times fewer workers producing twice as much as forty years previously. Throughout the course of the twentieth century, France became an industrialised nation comparable with other European industrialised nations. It is today a post-industrial nation comparable with the others. Notwithstanding this evolution, the nation's rural conscience has remained intact. The rural myth is one that continues to motivate political action and to have a major impact upon political choices. The farming lobby has attracted considerable support from *citadins* in part because of the sentiment that the splendid French countryside must be managed, rather than left to decay. The process of rural desertification is considered as part of a broader social problem. Protection of farming communities not only protects an endangered economic activity, but helps to preserve the nation's rural patrimony as well.

Working class radicalism

The structure of protest politics in France is another feature setting the French apart from their North European neighbours. Traditions of direct action stem in part from the consequences of France's late industrialisation. By the end of the nineteenth century, France was barely industrialised, outside a number of geographically specific areas. Throughout the nineteenth century French industry remained essentially small scale and rural, concentrated in small companies employing less than 100 workers. By the end of the nineteenth century, only iron, steel and mining were beginning to take the shape of modern heavy industries. The great working-class strikes at the beginning of the twentieth century were as much the product of pre-industrial workers, such as winegrowers, shoemakers and woodcutters, as they were of genuine industrial workers (Ridley, 1970).

By comparison with the United Kingdom, or Germany, France industrialised in a late and imperfect manner. The early decades of the twentieth century witnessed the growth of a heavily concentrated urban working class, with a strong sense of its own identity. Industrial workers were geographically separated from the rest of French society. They lived in tightly knit communities, where proletarian consciousness was high. Such proletarian communities existed, for instance, in the mining areas of the Nord/Pas-de-Calais, in the Paris industrial suburbs and in the large Mediterranean cities such as Marseilles. Unlike the peasantry, whose ancestry was ancient, the lineage of the French industrial working class was far more recent. Indeed, the survival of a large peasantry retarded the development of an industrial working class in France. France's industrial take-off began in earnest from 1900 onwards and continued uninterrupted, despite the war, until 1930. The birth of heavy industry in urban conurbations brought about the creation of the modern working class and the beginnings of a new feeling of class consciousness. The older artisanal pre-industrial working class, which had prevailed until the turn of the century, had prided itself upon its trade consciousness, based on the exercise of skilled occupations which gave it professional autonomy and self-confidence. The new industrial working class of the early twentieth century adopted a more genuine proletarian consciousness based upon poverty, deprivation and the performance of menial, unskilled tasks. Both these rival forms of class consciousness became part of the modern working-class mentality in France. At its height, the French Communist Party (PCF) was the only party capable of expressing these two different forms of working-class consciousness. The working class could in some senses be considered as a subculture, with a high sense of class consciousness, and belief in its destiny as the harbingers of socialism. Its grandiose demands were in part an extension of its minority status and its besieged mentality. More than most of their European counterparts, French workers believed in the Marxist-inspired myth that the working class was the class of the future and that it was destined to play a central role in the creation of a socialist society.

Divisions produced by France's late industrial revolution of the twentieth century continue to manifest themselves in a variety of forms. The bitter class against class confrontation of the 1930s–50s has given way to a less structured urban anomie, where a new type of urban poverty sets immigrants and paupers against the traditional proletariat. Unemployment and the shift to a post-industrial society have decimated the ranks of the traditional industrial working class. The structure of the industrial working class has altered as well. It is no longer a male bastion, since 40 per cent of workers are women, often part-time workers. France's large immigrant community is also concentrated within the working class, and performs most of those menial tasks that native French workers now refuse to do. In political terms, the weakening solidity of the industrial proletariat has accentuated the decline of the French Communist Party. The breakdown of traditional working class subcultures has also facilitated the emergence of the FN as a new movement of urban protest of a rather different type.

The competing visions of French society as social fracture and social consensus both correspond to a genuine perception of reality. Without accepting all the tenets of the optimistic school, social change has tended to enhance the sense of national community – up to a point. As old cleavages based on class and sub-cultural identity have diminished, however, new ones have emerged, notably those tied with the advent of a post-industrial, multi-cultural society. We now consider how the republican model of citizenship has coped with these countervailing pressures.

11.3 The republican model of citizenship and its limits

In the opinion of one Breton autonomist interviewed in the summer of 2001, the French nation-state had been imposed by 'blood, sweat and tears'. Through a gradual and uneven process of territorial aggrandisement and military conquest, France was constructed as a state-nation, before becoming a nation-state, with a determined central authority relentlessly imposing a single national identity upon the various territorial, linguistic and religious identities of the peoples that came together to form France. This process began during the *ancien régime*, advanced during the French Revolution and Napoleonic periods, and consolidated itself in stages thereafter. French nationhood was imposed upon mainly unwilling provinces (such as Normandy, Brittany, Aquitaine, Burgundy, Provence) by a succession of French kings, and later by the Revolution.

The French revolution gave rise to a universalist concept of citizenship and nationhood, postulating equal rights and duties for all French citizens. The 1789 Charter of the Rights of Man and Citizen guaranteed a number of fundamental rights and granted citizens equal treatment under the law. For the period, ascribing rights and duties was indeed revolutionary, laying the foundations for the development of the French model of the nation-state. The classic republican tradition modeled France as a nation which is one and indivisible, made up of a politically homogeneous citizenry. As the Republic was for long a fragile edifice, menaced by counter-revolution and clerical reaction, universalism developed a defensive character. Equality was interpreted as uniformity, to be safeguarded by an interventionist state that had the duty to enforce written rules. As it emerged historically – and as certain politicians would like to restore it today – the French republican tradition did not easily accommodate difference.

Equality is a formal requirement of the French republican tradition, rather than a substantive outcome. Specific identities are considered a threat to the direct relationship between citizens and the nation, an idea that unites republicans from the left and the right. Even today the most ardent republicans are intensely suspicious of any deviation from the ideal of equality and the centralisation and conformity that this imposes. This belief – almost an official doctrine – has militated against the development of particular identity-based social movements. Such groups – the gay movement, the women's movement, even environmental groups – find it more difficult to operate in France than elsewhere (Duyvendak, 1995). This universalist concept of citizenship also explains the desire by French elites to assimilate minority ethnic groups into mainstream French culture.

The 'right to difference' was a rallying slogan in May '68. The growth of voluntary associations and New Social Movements during the 1970s underpinned the revival and eventual victory of the French Socialists. Ideas of social experimentation, decentralisation, the right to difference, regionalism and an acceptance of the legitimacy of identity-based social movements were characteristic of the French Socialists during the 1970s, and to some extent in power in the 1980s and 1990s. However, some of the most ardent defenders of central standards are also to be found amongst those proclaiming the lay tradition within the Socialist Party. The question of contemporary French identity is one that cuts across France's political parties, as it does public opinion. In the ensuing sections, we investigate at some length how minority 'ethnic' groups experience identity construction, why regional languages have to struggle to survive and how people in the Brittany region reconcile their multiple and overlapping identities.

11.4	Immigration, integration, assimilation and ethnicity: conceptual problems and the Jacobin state

France can lay a plausible claim to be the 'crossroads of Europe'. It shares a land border with six European countries (Belgium, Germany, Switzerland, Luxembourg, Italy and Spain), and is connected to England by underground tunnel. Its proximity to former colonies, especially in the Maghreb, makes it an attractive destination for would-be immigrants. Its population has consistently been the most cosmopolitan of any European nation. Since 1945, most immigrants have been of North African Arab origin. According to the 1999 census the total immigrant population presently stands at 4,310,000 million, or 7.4 per cent of the entire French population (INSEE, 2003). Over three-quarters of these belong to seven main nationalities. Portuguese are the largest single group, closely followed by Algerians and Moroccans. Initially immigrants into France came from neighbouring European countries such as Belgium, Italy, Poland and Spain. However, since 1945 there has been a marked shift away from countries bordering

France to those on the extremes of the Mediterranean basin (the countries comprising the Maghreb in particular) and further afield in central Africa and more recently South East Asia.

At the end of World War Two, for a combination of demographic and economic reasons, France needed to supplement its existing workforce. Immigration was one of the easiest ways to achieve this and thus a policy of recruiting migrant workers was begun. The policy laid down that immigrants would work and reside in France for a fixed period of time, contributing to economic development, at the end of which they would return to their country of origin. In order to achieve this end, a strictly controlled policy of entries and departures was to be put in place. This included the establishing of an official body regulating migratory flows, the Office national d'immigration (ONI) and the prioritising of single male migrants who would be housed separately from French nationals in foyers. The sheer volume of immigrants overwhelmed the ONI and in practice it proved impossible to halt the flow of illegal immigrants, much sought after by employers since they did not have to pay the former the same wages as indigenous French workers. French governments were able to exert relatively little control over the number of foreign nationals entering France. Since 1974, several types of policy response have been adopted to deal with the complex phenomena of immigration, cultural assimilation and ethnicity. Giscard d'Estaing was elected President at a time of major economic and social instability. The effects of the economic crisis, set off by the oil embargo in 1973, began to be felt and in July 1974 France decided to suspend all further immigration. The Chirac and Barre governments embarked upon a series of repressive reforms aimed at reducing the presence of foreigners in French society. The measures included forbidding the reuniting of immigrant families (*le regroupement familial*). They were designed to reinforce the perception that immigration was a short-term phenomenon and to encourage migrant groups to return to their country of origin. In 1980 the Bonnet law enabled procedures to be put in place for the immediate expulsion of immigrants, reinforcing the existing control that the state exerted over foreign nationals.

The Socialist candidate Mitterrand fought his 1981 campaign on a manifesto that explicitly opposed the measures initiated by Giscard d'Estaing. Upon entering office, Mitterrand immediately cancelled the previous laws of the right and introduced a series of new measures. Three in particular are noteworthy. Firstly, those foreign nationals without official documentation could 'regularise' their status. Secondly, the policy of family reuniting was re-established. However, perhaps the most innovative new measure was repealing the 1939 law with regard to foreign associations. Henceforth foreign nationals would no longer require prior government authorisation in order to create their own associations. This measure provided a useful framework within which youths, particularly of Maghrebian origin, were able to gain associational experience and resulted in a considerable increase in new associations being created. Two of these, SOS-Racisme and France-Plus would gain national notoriety.

Public opinion in France remained sensitive to the permanent settlement of immigrants in French society. This sensitivity was displayed with regard to the question of foreign nationals being able to vote in local elections, a cause that

Mitterrand had publicly endorsed. Public opinion polls were repeatedly hostile to the idea and as a result government relegated the subject to one of secondary importance. In 1983 the FN made its first inroads into the political arena. The traditional political parties were taken aback by the rise of the extreme right and were immediately forced on to the defensive. For the Socialists in power this meant rethinking and changing policy to take account of public dissatisfaction. As a result some of the policies that the Socialists had criticised during the Giscard d'Estaing presidency were reintroduced under a different guise. These included the former measure of *'aide au retour'*, renamed *'aide publique à la réinsertion'*; new restrictions on family unification; an intensification of the battle against illegal immigration and the suppression of the Secretary of State for Immigrants. There was a more aggressive tone adopted with regard to migrant groups. In 1991 Prime Minister Cresson talked openly of using aeroplane charters to send back illegal immigrants and backed this up in practice by returning a number of Malians to their home country. Even Mitterrand himself stressed the limits of French willingness to accept the presence of foreign nationals, by evoking the notion of the 'threshold of tolerance' to justify limitations.

All subsequent governments have been torn between projecting an outwardly tough stance on immigration, and facilitating the settlement and 'integration' of migrant groups into French society. With the recognition of the long-term settlement of migrant groups in western industrialised nations, emphasis has shifted from the reasons for their emigrating from the country of origin to the nature of their permanent installation in the country of immigration. Crucial to an understanding of the debate, it is therefore important to understand the gradual distinction between the term immigration and those of integration and assimilation. Immigration can be defined in a straightforward manner as referring to migratory movements from one country to another. Integration, assimilation and ethnicity are more problematic.

Until recently assimilation, with a stronger meaning than integration, has been the preferred term in France since historically it has been allied with the Jacobin concept of the 'one and indivisible' Republic. According to this immigrants became part of French society by adhering to its values, rules and institutions on an individual basis. In this sense assimilation refers to a *rapprochement* between French nationals and immigrants, but with the latter eventually adopting the identity of the former. This ideology was initially used to deal with regionalist/autonomist movements who wished to differentiate themselves from the rest of France. It was then adapted to the context of immigrant communities. With the first wave of immigrants entering France predominantly from neighbouring countries and often with shared cultural characteristics (i.e. religion or ethnic origin), there was a conscious attempt by some to conceal any differences. Thus foreign-sounding names were frenchified (Ivo Livi becoming Yves Montand is but one example). One of the most often cited ways of assimilating into French society was by adhering to French social movements, notably trade unions. In so doing immigrants from Belgium, Italy, Poland and Spain were able to become an integral feature of one France by combatting another (Jazouli, 1986).

While questions of immigration and integration have become the focus of national debate in France over the last decade, the notion of ethnicity has been noticeably absent from discourse, giving rise to the opinion that it remains a taboo subject. Until recently its usage in France was confined to studies of anthropology and ethnology, but never included in any general political debate. We shall therefore adhere to the following definition according to Isajiw (1974) and argue that ethnicity refers to: 'An involuntary group of people who share the same culture or to descendants of such people who identify themselves and/or are identified by others as belonging to the same involuntary group'.

In France the media, politicians and social scientists have all been wary about discussing ethnicity. There has been a reluctance in many cases even to acknowledge its existence, this despite the fact that groups such as Maghrebians in practice are distinguished from the white French population on ethnic grounds. The reluctance and even refusal to acknowledge the existence of the notion of ethnicity in France can be attributed not simply to historical reasons, but crucially to those of an ideological nature. Let us examine the former. Distinguishing citizens on the basis of ethnic criteria is not a phenomenon new to France. It was in fact an integral feature of government policy during the Vichy period when French citizens of the Jewish faith were discriminated against. In the minds of many academics and politicians, reintroducing the concept would be tantamount to conjuring up the divisive nature of the Vichy period once again. Consequently the study of ethnicity has, to a great extent, been discredited and the parallel with discrimination against Jews by a French administration has not been lost upon French academics. In the Jacobin tradition, the concept of ethnicity evokes images of a segregated society, with parallels with the Unites States often being cited (Schnapper, 1994). Traditionally influenced by republican ideals, social scientists in France are almost unanimous in their rejection of and opposition to the emergence of potentially divisive 'community' or – worse – 'communitarian' mentalities in their own country.

Relatively little attention has been paid to the status of minority groups within French society. Equality is a formal requirement, rather than a substantive outcome. Before the parity reforms of the Jospin government, there had been no explicit commitment to equal opportunity policies, ideologically suspect as running against universalist values. There is no equivalent body in France to the British Commission for Racial Equality, with responsibility for ethnic monitoring of job applications. This throws up broader questions of citizenship and in particular of the participation of migrant groups in the political process.

The headscarf affairs and the place of Muslims in French society

The notion of the Jacobin state and its continued relevance to French society was, perhaps, never more clearly illustrated than during the repeated headscarf affairs, which arose in 1989 and have resurfaced regularly since (most recently in 2003). We focus here mainly on the 1989 affair. On the surface it may have appeared to be a somewhat banal refusal by two French school girls of the Muslim faith to remove the *foulard* or veil while at school. However, underlying the whole debate were two diametrically opposing views of French society. On the one hand there were those who championed the Jacobin notion of the one and indivisible Republic and the concept of secularity. The principle of secularity is in fact one traditionally espoused by the left and this dates back to the Third Republic when, as a result of the laws of 1881 and 1882, national unity in France was cemented by a system of secular schools. The separation of Church and state became law in 1905.

According to the partisans of this vision of society, the Muslim girls wearing the veil at school were in fact negating Republican values since they were visibly differentiating themselves from other pupils and in so doing drawing attention to their religion. The secular school should permit no distinctive sign indicating the religious denomination of the pupil. Instead the defenders of the Jacobin vision argued that Islam and indeed any religion should be practised in private, and that preferably Muslims should be persuaded to endorse secular values. The supporters of the notion of secularity included Socialist MPs and intellectuals of the left such as Elisabeth Badinter. In the opposing camp were those who had forged close links with minority groups in French society, or who believed that the Jacobin vision no longer corresponded to the realities of life in contemporary French society and most certainly did not reflect the diversity of its population. According to the proponents of this vision, Islam was not considered incompatible with the rules, institutions and values of French society. The Education Minister Jospin, appeared at first sight to be an ally of the second school of thought. He stressed the importance of dialogue with the Muslim girls, arguing that French society was pluralistic and that secularity no longer needed to be of an antagonistic nature. French Muslims were, to a large extent, excluded from the debate that ensued. When the views of Muslims were sought, invariably they tended to be those of individuals or groups on the extremes who were not necessarily representative of the views of French Muslims in general.

What does the whole issue tell us about how Muslims are perceived in French society? The debate on secularity intruded upon the question of the presence of ethnic minority groups in French society. The two issues were confused. They resulted in the misleading image that to be Muslim implicitly inferred that one could not be French. This was clearly an erroneous image given that Muslims in France had in their overwhelming majority settled permanently in France and, on the whole, abided by the laws and rules of that society. Nonetheless the image undoubtedly persists. It is a view cultivated by the Iranian revolution in 1979 and the fundamentalist image projected and, more recently, by the activities of certain Muslims in the 11 September outrage. The increasing visibility of Maghrebians in French society has compounded this representation, illustrated by the emergence of the so-called 'second' generation of youths largely born and bred in France. Consequently a feeling of wariness and even hostility has greeted the recognition that Maghrebians would henceforth be a definitive feature of French society.

In practice, the headscarf affairs revealed that different standards were seen to apply depending upon one's religion. This was particularly the case for children of the Jewish faith, who had not been prevented from wearing the kippa at school, and those of the Catholic faith, who were allowed to wear crucifixes. This was the source of a great deal of bitterness and frustration among Muslims. The headscarf affair was a litmus test of the acceptance or not of a diversity of cultures in French society. The vociferous defence of the Jacobin concept suggested, perhaps, that large sections of the French public were not yet prepared to accept the reality of a permanent Muslim presence and that the latter continued to be regarded as illegitimate actors by French society. Others, particularly those in positions of authority, were prepared to give at best a begrudging acceptance.

Assimilationist patterns have proved stronger in France than in most other European countries. This is tied up with a particular conception of Frenchness, predicated upon a long experience of assimilating different regions and peoples into a single entity, and the persistence of a Jacobin tradition distrustful of distinct cultural identities. Assimilation proved successful in relation to the pre-1940 European immigrant communities, who shared common religious and political beliefs. Arab immigrants have been less easy to assimilate. Increasingly, government efforts to promote the assimilation of Arab communities into mainstream French culture have coexisted alongside an acceptance of the cultural specificity of France's Muslim population. French Muslims have been forced to question their own place within French society. In the case of the headscarf affairs, the most fundamental question of all was being posed. Can one be both Muslim and French?

In fact, there has been a renegotiation of the specific place of Muslims in French society. This has taken the form neither of outright assimilation, as was the case for previous waves of immigrants, nor an acceptance of pluralism where diverse cultural systems are able to co-exist (Hargreaves, 1995; Kiwan, 2003). Instead there has been a policy of co-option where differences have been tolerated, but where the government has sought to limit divergent behavioural patterns in order that they are compatible with the cultural norms of the dominant society. This is, perhaps, best exemplified by the manner in which French governments, most recently the Interior Minister Sarkozy (2003), strove to provide an organisational framework for Islam in France, similar to that of the Judeo-Christian religions. By creating organisational structures, and by supporting mosque building programmes, governments have aspired to prevent external forces from exerting influence over the French Maghrebian community. They have also attempted to exert a greater degree of control over this community themselves.

11.5 Language and identity in contemporary France: the case of minority languages

Language is another highly sensitive issue. The relationship between a state and its constituent language groups is indicative of the nature of the state itself. In bilingual societies, there is often a tension between, on the one hand, an official administrative language, and, on the other, a plurality of spoken languages. There are powerful pressures pushing for unilinguism: state policies, economic globalisation, bureaucratic necessity all drive in the same direction. Linguistic uniformity often assumes political overtones because the consolidation of the dominant language is associated with the victory of one ethnic group over another. In the case of France, the official language is recognised as such in the written constitution, and given pre-eminence over other languages. Even where there is no constitutionally based recognition of linguistic uniformity, most nation-states are predicated upon a single administrative language.

There has been an explicit French language policy since at least the sixteenth century. The French language was one of the weapons of the state in building modern French identity and in imposing cohesion upon a divided society. Whether by accident or design, regional languages were a major causality of the process of nation-building. The Catholic Church, deeply rooted in areas such as Brittany where regional languages prospered, opposed the spread of French throughout the nineteenth century (Poignant, 1998). Once the Republicans won back control of the (Third) Republic in the late 1870s, they were determined to break the power of the Catholic Church. The Ferry laws of 1881 and 1882 created a system of universal, lay primary education that was primarily aimed to promote national unity and combat obscurantism, but which also had a devastating effect on regional languages. The Unity of the Republic passed by the political pre-eminence of Paris and, secondarily, the linguistic domination of French. The weakening of regional languages such as Breton can also be traced to economic change in the nineteenth and early twentieth centuries and to the impact of the First World War that forged a unified French national consciousness (Le Coadic, 1998; Hoare, 2000). In spite of centralising tendencies, the French nation remained extremely diverse prior to the Second World War and French remained a minority language in some regions until the twentieth century.

Whether through design or accident, the Republic actively suppressed regional languages, a number of which have disappeared completely. The zealous activities of republicans often had no legal basis. On the ground, the most ardent persecutors of regional languages were not national politicians, but middle-ranking state officials. Primary schoolteachers, serving their communities, practised regional languages themselves, but they were brutally called to order by the state officials (the Academic Inspectors) who were the real agents of centralisation and French language monopoly.

There are a number of regional languages in France today and a larger number of dialects. The main regional languages are: Alsacien, Basque, Breton, Catalan, Corsican, Occitan and Creole. There are many dialects, and several linguistic registers between dialects and languages. Certain languages have disappeared, or survive only as dialects. This is the case, for example, for the dialects of the *langue d'oïl*: gallo, picard, poitevin, saintongeais, normand and morvandiau. The main languages that survive are those which enjoy geographical density. Breton is spoken in the west part of Brittany. It is also taught in several cities outside the Brittany region, such as Nantes and Paris. The various languages that are taught in French schools are Alsacien and Breton (both of which now have publicly funded teacher training programmes), Basque, Catalan, Creole, Flamand and Corsican. Each language has specific characteristics and a different relationship to French. A number of these are 'border languages'; this is the case for Alsacien (close to German), Flemish (spoken across the border in Belgium), Catalan (vigorously supported by the Catalan provincial government in Spain). Others – such as Corsican and Creole – are island languages. Breton falls into none of these categories; it is a romano-celtic language that is separated from the British Isles from which it originated.

The regulatory framework of language governance in France is hardly propitious to the diffusion of regional languages. As France has become ever more deeply embedded in multilateral and international structures, French state actors and politicians have sought to defend what they deem to be the core of French sovereignty: namely the French language. There was an explicit linkage between identity and language in the Maastricht referendum of 1992, where France simultaneously committed herself to an enhanced degree of European integration and the codification of French as the official language of the Republic. The proclamation in 1992 of French as the official language of the Republic was purportedly as a means of defending French as an international language against English. In practice, Article 2 has mainly been used to stifle the development of regional languages. Almost all regulations and directives dealing with regional language issues have been confined to the sphere of education; any proposition deemed to threaten the official unilingual policy have been declared as unconstitutional by the Constitutional Council or the Council of State.

The Maastricht referendum provides the backdrop for France's continuing inability to ratify the European Charter of Lesser Used Languages. The Charter was adopted by the Council of Europe in 1992. Though France initially abstained, the Jospin government rallied to the Charter in 1997. Article 7 of the Charter set out several general principles to which France's state-centric institutions could take offence, most notably the public use of another language apart from French. The Council of State ruled in 1996 that France could not ratify the Charter. There was no problem with provisions for teaching regional languages in schools, as long as there was no element of compulsion. But the Council of State challenged Articles 9 and 10 of the European Charter: the right to use a lesser used language in dealing with administrative and judicial authorities was deemed unconstitutional in the light of Article 2 ('the language of the republic is French'). On 15 June 1999, the Constitutional Council also declared the European Charter of Regional Languages to be contrary to the French Constitution. The Council justified its decision by the preface, which guarantees the right to use a minority language in public as well as in private. The Constitutional Council also pointed other articles of the Charter as being against the Constitution, notably those bestowing specific rights on regional groups, interpreted as going against the principle of the 'indivisibility of the French people'. But the inside view was that the public use of another language apart from French was what really worried the Council.

The French language itself might have an interest in supporting regional languages. As a world language French is suffering. Though it is deeply rooted in France and the African subcontinent, elsewhere it is in decline. The French ought perhaps to have a better comprehension of the fate of regional languages now that the future of the French language is in some doubt.

11.6 Multiple identities in contemporary France: a case study from Brittany

The problem of political and national identity is revealed as an essential problem throughout most of French history. Identity is a compound, not to say a nebulous concept. Identity can be personal, social, or collective. Political identity can be understood as 'common purpose', something that persists through time. It consists of a combination of myths, symbols, rituals and ideology. In the French case, several centuries of political engineering were required to create the myths, symbols, rituals and ideologies that underpin contemporary French identity. In this section, we present some empirical evidence about multiple identities in a historic French region. The data presented are drawn from a mass survey and interviews carried out in the French region of Brittany in 2001 and 2002.

One of the most distinctive regions of France, Brittany has a strong sense of its specific position within French society. Formerly an independent Duchy (from 818 to 1532), then a French province with special prerogatives (1532–1789), reduced for long to being a collection of disparate departments before becoming an administrative then political region, modern Brittany is a French region with a difference. Unlike many other French regions, it can look to its past existence as an independent political entity, with its own founding myths and political institutions. Though the symbols of statehood have long been repressed, the region retains many distinctive characteristics. The Breton language is the European continent's only Celtic language. The enduring symbolic importance of the Catholic religion is ever present physically in the architecture of Breton villages, as well in higher than average rates of religious practice. The spectacular growth of Breton cultural movements (dance, theatre, costume and music) is a testament to a revival of Breton values and self-consciousness.

Brittany is sometimes taken as a litmus test for the health of regional identity within France. In post-war Brittany, there has been a strong political consensus among the regional elites in favour of enhanced regionalisation. From 1950 onwards, Breton actors of all political persuasions cooperated closely in the CELIB – Comité de d'étude et de liaison des intérêts bretons – the archetype of a post-war regional advocacy coalition. Under the impetus of CELIB, Brittany was the first French region to publish a regional plan (in 1953), calling for industrialisation and improved transport facilities. The CELIB served as a model for post-war French planning. The activities of CELIB inspired the state to launch its first regional plan in 1956. The lobbying activity was crowned with success, as the French state poured massive resources into Brittany in the 1950s and 1960s. The CELIB could certainly claim the credit for many of the improvements in transport infrastructure consented to the Brittany region in the 1960s and 1970s and remains a powerful reference point today.

There is, in Brittany, a tradition of cross-partisan regional advocacy that sometimes assumes political overtones. From the state's point of view, the logic of massively investing in Brittany was an instrumental one: to bring a backward region into national productivity. For the most regionally minded politicians, entering into a dialogue with the French state was the only way forward after the bitter divisions of the inter-war and wartime period. Breton-style identity politics were discredited by the collaborationist activities of a minority of Breton activists during the war. The prevailing post-war model of political activism has been one of territorial solidarity aimed at procuring material advantages for Brittany, namely through raising living standards in what had been France's poorest region in 1945.

Interviews with surviving actors and published historical accounts demonstrate that instrumentalist ends coexisted within the CELIB with a high degree of regional consciousness and a desire for powerful regional political institutions. Whether or not to affirm Breton identity continues to be a source of division within Brittany. The mainstream view has been to lobby for increased state and EU resources to rescue Brittany from its isolated geographical position and to assure its integration with the rest of France (and Europe). Looking to the state, whether for industrial investment or for support to a fledgling intensive agriculture, has been a favoured position. This integrationist position has always been contested by the autonomist minority, more concerned to safeguard and strengthen Breton identity rather than assure its integration within the French nation. This dichotomy was illustrated in interviews by the case of the fast-speed train (TGV): while most interlocutors favoured extending the fast-speed train to Brest, in the far-west of Brittany, a minority of cultural activists was opposed in the name of defending Breton identity.

The dominant political culture is one of political accommodation. Breton politicians of all parties, however divided they are internally, will tend to close ranks against threats from the outside. Despite a strong regional identity, however, Brittany has not produced significant regionalist parties, or at least parties that have been capable of winning seats in departmental, regional or national elections. Only one left-wing regionalist party, the Union démocratique bretonne (UDB) has managed some victories at the municipal level and then usually in collaboration with the PS. This apparent paradox might be explained by the predominance of the consensual political traditions mentioned above. Le Coadic (1998) interprets this phenomenon as a consequence of the deeply rooted legitimist strand within Breton public opinion. Imbued by a Catholic, conformist ethic, the Breton public is not prepared to support pro-independence or pro-autonomist parties. This conformist sentiment is reflected in the modest scores obtained in elections by the UDB and the smaller Breton regional or autonomist parties. We should note that the mainstream political parties in Brittany, especially the PS but also the UDF and UMP, have adopted regionalist themes and are more 'regionalist' than their national counterparts. Although Breton regionalism has, at times, been violent, this never reached the levels experienced in Corsica, the Spanish Basque country or Northern Ireland.

Table 11.2 Multiple identities in Brittany

Q: 'Do you feel yourself to be . . .	%
Breton, not French	2
More Breton than French	15
Equally Breton and French	57
More French than Breton	17
French, not Breton	8
Don't know/Other	1

Source: Mass survey carried out by the polling organisation Efficience 3 in Brittany in June and July 2001, with a representative sample of 1007 individuals.

Does identity matter? We carried out a mass survey with a representative sample of Breton public opinion in June 2001. We asked respondents in the survey to state whether they considered themselves to be Breton, not French, more Breton than French, equally Breton and French, more French than Breton, or French, not Breton. The results are presented in Table 11.2. The table is highly revealing. In Brittany, the sense of regional identity is strong, but this is not considered as being in opposition to an overarching French nationhood (Cole and Loughlin, 2003). Regional identity is not a surrogate nationality. Interestingly, these findings were backed up by interviews and by a question-naire we distributed to members of the Breton policy community. Our findings highlighted the paradoxes and limitations of the Breton autonomist cause. Even those working for greater Breton autonomy (the case for many of our sample) felt a deep sense of their French identity and declared themselves proud to be French. The French state building enterprise has been thorough.

Around three-quarters of Bretons feel a sense of regional identity that is at least as powerful as their pride in being French. Our survey findings suggest, however, that there is a comfortable linkage between regional identity and regional and national political institutions in the case of Brittany, testament in the long run to the efficacy of the French state project.

11.7 Concluding remarks

What does French identity mean today? Identities based on class and religion have diminished in significance during the post-war period. With the decline of class and religion, there has been a weakening of old-style identity politics, as manifested in the Communist and Catholic subcultures. The nation remains a strong reference. French elites – and more generally public opinion – continue to regard their nation as the best defender of European civilisation and culture against Anglo-Saxon imperialism. These attitudes were overwhelmingly sup-ported by public opinion (and cleverly articulated by President Chirac) during the 2003 Gulf War. A sense of a mission in the world sets France apart from most other European nations, with only Britain equal in pretension. The symbols of the French revolution – the Rights of Man and Citizen; liberty, equality, fraternity; even the republican tradition – are more widespread, less controversial and less meaningful than ever before. One might observe that as the French Revolution has finally passed into collective French identity, it has lost its obsessional, divisive quality in the process. Even Le Pen declares himself a republican. One reading of contemporary France is that the underlying political consensus is stronger than at any stage since the French Revolution. The republican form of government is no longer seriously challenged by anybody. The Fifth Republic has survived by combining stability and flexibility. Past cleavages – those based on class and religion – have declined in intensity, or disappeared completely. French civil society appears less differentiated than at any stage in the past; the rise of the new middle classes and the advent of mass society in the post-war period have in general reduced differences based on locality, social class, and workplace.

The argument is counterbalanced by the persistent difficulties of France's democracy in embracing the diversity of French society. The evidence we presented in our public opinion survey was eloquent on this point. Though Bretons are supportive of a more thoroughgoing regionalisation, this choice in no sense limits their attachment to the broader French nation. As there is little or no conflict between local, regional and national identities (with the exception of Corsica), the French government ought to be able to devolve more responsibilities to localities and regions with a clear conscience. The same conclusion holds true for regional languages. If the survival of endangered regional languages is a threat to the Republic, this invites reflection on the solidity of the republican edifice. France's legalistic culture is best demonstrated in the case of *laïcité* and the veil. For two decades, there was a legalistic void, following a Council of State ruling that fudged the issue. In late 2003 the Raffarin government announced that a law would be drafted to forbid wearing any religiously ostentatious symbols. For the first time, the veil, the kippa and the cross would be treated as the same. Turning to the law allowed the republican forms to be respected, while postponing decisions of how to accommodate diversity in contemporary French society.

The area of 'community' identities provides a good example of the French Republic's propensity to insist upon rules, but to accept exceptions to rules. As long as rules are observed in the abstract, the precise responses to pressing policy problems can be pragmatic. There is an essential duality in French discourse. In practice, French governments adopt more pragmatic responses than they profess in public. This duality plays itself out in each of the case studies we have presented. Though French politicians used the language of assimilation, in practice successive Interior Ministers sought to come to an accommodation with organised Islam and, if not to convert it, at least to minimise the threat it represented to the Republic. In the case of lesser used languages, at least some French politicians were anxious to recognise the country's rich linguistic patrimony and to take steps to guard this. Though restating that French is the language of the Republic, French governments have financed regional language schools, such as DIWAN in Brittany. The tendency to repeat rules and negotiate exceptions to rules also reveals rival legitimacies at the heart of the French state. While politicians are willing to negotiate 'exceptions' to republican norms of integration, the institutions best representing the French state tradition have much greater difficulty in accepting this. The Council of State and the Constitutional Council both appear determined to preserve a stato-centrist interpretation of Frenchness. To provide one example of many, French politicians signed the Charter of Lesser Used Languages, but the Council of State and later the Constitutional Council were determined that the higher interests of republican conformity should prevail.

What conclusions can we draw from this? France in the third millennium is a pluralistic society that contains a broad range of political orientations and cultural practices within its midst. Social and political change has been pronounced throughout the post-war period. With the weakening of traditional structures of power, there has been a move towards a greater autonomy in all strata of society, a move facilitated by the weakening of the influence of traditional institutions such as the Church, the state, political parties, the military and the extended family. These social changes have produced a weakening of traditional myths, symbols and beliefs of French identity. But, while many older references appear archaic, it is not clear what has replaced them. French-style republicanism appears stubbornly resistant to ideological change and to theorising the diversity that is a fundamental trait of complex, post-modern societies. Consequently, though the traditional French model is unfolding, France's leaders are not quite sure what to put in its place.

12 The economy and economic governance

12.1 Introduction

The French model of economic and industrial management has long fascinated foreign observers (Zysman, 1977; Hall, 1986, 1989, 1993, 2001; Schmidt, 1996; Hayward, 1986, 1997). We set out in the main body of this chapter to provide a general overview of processes of economic governance in contemporary France. After a brief presentation of the structure of the French economy, we consider the legacy of *dirigisme*, the core feature of the orthodox French model. We then move on to to describe the change in economic direction of the 1980s and 1990s. After undertaking a case study of privatisation, we conclude the chapter by highlighting underlying continuities in the practice of French economic management.

12.2 The French economy

French Presidents love to boast of the French economy being the fourth largest in the world, though this status is now disputed by the United Kingdom (and soon will be China). Thirty years of spectacular economic growth from 1945–74 – *les trente glorieuses* – placed France second in the ranking of European nations, trailing only the Federal Republic of Germany. The French economy was transformed during this period from 'a partly agricultural to a service economy, with the relative weight of industry (broadly defined) remaining constant' (Flockton and Kofman, 1989). The French economy has performed particularly well in the agricultural and service sectors, with a more mixed manufacturing performance (Bensahel, 1998; INSEE, 2003).

Its record in the agricultural sector has been the most spectacular. Buoyed by exceptional increases in agricultural productivity, and supported by the incentive structure of the common agricultural policy (CAP) France has become the world's second largest food exporter, behind the United States. The inbuilt French surplus in agricultural products is of great benefit for the French balance of trade account, counterbalancing the nation's energy deficit. Alongside its mixed record of success in the high technology activities such as information technology, computers, and consumer electronics, the French economy has

Table 12.1 France in the European Union: some comparative data

Country	Date of entry into EU	Population 2002 (millions)	GDP (standard purchasing power)	Inflation 2002	Unemployed 2002
Austria	1995	8.1	26,450	1.7	4.9
Belgium	1958	10.3	25,950	1.3	6.9
Denmark	1973	5.4	27,340	2.6	4.3
Finland	1995	5.2	24,810	1.7	10.4
France	1958	61.1	24,660	2.2	8.7
Germany	1958 (1990 ex-GDR)	82.4	24,630	1.1	8.5
Greece	1981	11.0	15,810	3.5	9.6
Ireland	1973	3.8	29,850	4.6	4.3
Italy	1958	58.1	24,570	3.0	9.2
Luxembourg	1958	0.5	45,380	2.8	2.6
Netherlands	1958	16.1	27,010	3.5	2.6
Portugal	1986	10.4	16,490	4.0	4.5
Spain	1986	41.3	20,210	4.0	11.1
Sweden	1995	8.9	24,520	1.7	5.0
United Kingdom	1973	60.2	24,780	1.7	5.0
USA		287.4	33,010	2.4	5.8
Japan		127.4	24,440	−0.3	5.4

Source: INSEE, *Tableaux de l'Économie Française*, 2003–4, p. 6.

performed well in intermediate branches such as car manufacturing, glass, rubber and chemicals. These are sectors where long-term state investments facilitated economies of scale. As in Germany and other EU nations, a decline in the traditional manufacturing sector (textiles, steel, mining, shipbuilding) has occurred in France, but French performance in the service sector has more than compensated for its mixed industrial performance. France is one of the world's largest exporter of services, with particular strengths in tourism, retailing, transport, banking and insurance. With agricultural and industrial employment in permanent decline, tertiary sector employment is the source of most new job creation. Service sector growth has proved sluggish since the early 1980s, however, reflecting lower growth rates throughout the French economy.

The 'thirty glorious years' from 1945 were followed by thirty rather uncomfortable ones, three decades of painful adjustment to depressed conditions in the world economy. The oil crises of 1973 and 1979, the processes of economic globalisation and the march of European integration during the 1980s and 1990s all highlighted the importance of the external constraints weighing upon the French economy, and the limited margins of manoeuvre of its governments in inventing new economic policies. The pressures facing French economic policy-makers at the beginning of the third millennium are rather similar to those facing policy-makers in other developed European countries: namely, how to promote economic growth and stimulate employment while retaining a tight control over inflation and limiting budget deficits. These economic priorities have – in theory at least – become institutionally embedded in the architecture of Economic and Monetary Union.

12.3	'Dirigisme' and its limits

France, Germany, Britain, Italy and many other European countries were devastated by the effects of the Second World War. Throughout western Europe, there emerged a broad consensus in favour of adopting new policy instruments to tackle the challenges of post-war reconstruction. The post-war consensus involved a new form of settlement between politics and markets. It implied an acceptance of a higher degree of state interventionism in economic management (especially through the budget), the public ownership or regulation of certain key industries, Keynesian demand management in macro-economic policies, universal social security provision and high taxation. What set French post-war capitalism apart from experiences elsewhere was that it was state-driven rather than being managed through social partnership (as in the corporatist Scandinavian states, as well as Austria and Germany) or on a market basis.

State interventionism (*dirigisme*) in economic policy-making formed the core of the French economic model. We can identify five characteristic features of *dirigisme* as it operated during the *trente glorieuses années*: indicative planning, administered financing, the state as entrepreneur, a skewed pattern of government–industry relations and an active industrial policy.

Planning

From 1947 onwards, the French state introduced a series of five-year plans, drawn up in the main by ambitious civil servants. Schmidt (1996) points to the 'independent administrative bureaucracy' as an important actor in driving economic modernisation. For Hayward (1986) state interventionism was able to flourish within the French economy because of a combination of active techno-bureaucratic leadership and passive democratic support. These plans fixed goals for particular industrial sectors, and singled out priorities for economic development. Heavy state investment in industrial plant helped French industry recover during the early years after the war. In the words of Schmidt (1996: 78) 'Planning was an unquestioned success between 1946 and 1963 when it had a clear set of goals and a limited set of programs focused on restoring health to a small number of industries'. But, as Hall (1986: 147) puts it, 'as the plans became more grandiose, they became more fragile'.

Most observers now agree that, except in the period of immediate post-war reconstruction, the importance of state planning should not be exaggerated. Over time the *dirigiste* element of state planning decreased significantly. In 1947 the state budget was directly responsible for 50 per cent of all investment, yet by 1958 this figure had fallen to 22 per cent (Bauchet, 1986). Hall (1986) has claimed that, by the sixth plan, the French government had lost much of its independence from the social groups that the state was supposed to steer. Only the first plan (1947–52) was of a command nature. Unlike the Soviet plans, which set compulsory targets for industrial sectors, the French plans were indicative: they attempted to influence private investment decisions and to mobilise social actors in favour of economic growth. There was little relationship between the sectoral priorities outlined in French plans and public finance. The French state spent far more on housing, infrastructure and agriculture than it did on industry. The plans were unable to dictate investment decisions even on public sector industries. Of the greatest importance, the Finance Ministry was not required to take into account the objectives outlined in the five-year plans, which singularly limited their effectiveness (Flockton and Kofman, 1989).

An economy of administered financing

A related feature evoked by Schmidt (1996) is that of a 'strict and detailed supervision of credit by the state', what Cohen (1995) refers to as 'capitalism without capital'. The French model looked to the state as the main investor in firms, rather than the Paris Stock Exchange, or the international financial markets (Cohen, 1995; Kassim, 1997). There was a common consensus in the post-war period, shared by the state and social partners, that socio-economic change could be induced through the use of state control. As the private sector depended – by and large – upon the state for capital, governments had the upper hand in their relationships with French firms (Hayward, 1997). With control over the Bank of France and the banking and insurance systems, the state controlled the flow of credit. This account of the dependency of French firms is questioned in some more recent accounts (Howarth, 2001).

The state as entrepreneur

In the words of Zysman (1977: 51), writing in the 1970s, 'the anti-market tradition in France has its origins in the very process of industrialisation, which was initiated by a strong and centralised state . . . Closed borders, active entrepreneurial intervention by the state, and negotiation rather than competition between businesses within France have all served to insulate the economy from the market'. *Dirigisme* refers both to direct state management of important industrial sectors and indirect state involvement with the decisions taken by private companies. This interventionism was decidedly a post-war phenomenon. From the perspective of the left, nationalisation was ideologically suspect in the inter-war period. During the popular front government (1936–7) no major nationalisations were programmed, except in the specific cases of the arms industry and the Bank of France. State economic ownership was feared as a tool of fascist governments. State ownership was given a massive boost, however, in the changed climate of the immediate post-war period. The nationalisation programme of 1946 created large state firms in key sectors such as energy (GDF, EDF, CEA, CDF), transport (Air France) industry (Renault), banking and insurance. Through its control of the banking system and the distribution of credit, the French state occupied a powerful position to influence the investment choices of French firms. The state was thus simultaneously a gatekeeper, a mobiliser and an agent of economic development.

The Bourse: the Paris Stock Exchange, symbol of France's economic liberalisation

At its height, the French state justified its economic activism with the argument that it intervened directly in areas where private capital was absent, and where the national interest was at stake. Gaullist policy-makers in the 1960s interpreted the national interest in terms of giving France a lead in the most technologically advanced industrial sectors. Likewise, Socialist ministers justified nationalisation in 1982 as a means of giving the state a lead in major infrastructure projects unattractive to private capital. The success of state investment depended upon the sector involved: massive financial investment gave France a technological edge in sectors such as aerospace, nuclear energy, and transport but it had less impact elsewhere (as with the steel plans of the 1970s, or the failed biotechnology, satellite or cable plans). The competitiveness of industry was severely diminished under Giscard d'Estaing, whose policy of rescuing companies on the verge on bankruptcy essentially substituted a policy of support for 'lame ducks' for de Gaulle's 'national champions'.

In addition to the extension of direct state ownership in 1946, the Socialist government's 1982 Nationalisation Act took into public ownership all large private banks, several of France's largest industrial groups, and a number of smaller concerns. The result was that the public sector increased from around 8 per cent to around a quarter of French industrial capacity and 50 per cent of industrial investment, while the nationalisation of the main banks left the state in control of virtually all credit. The Socialist nationalisation programme represented the apogee of French economic interventionism. Direct state involvement in economic development has subsequently diminished. The retreat of the state has occurred partly as a result of budgetary constraints, but also because of European policy fashions, promoting greater marketisation and privatisation. Whatever its industrial logic, nationalisation proved expensive. Within two years of their 1982 Act, the French Socialist government began backtracking. In 1984 state firms were allowed to issue 'investment certificates' to private sector investors, in an attempt to raise capital. This preceded the large-scale privatisation programme of the Chirac 1986–8 government, which was resumed with a new vigour in 1993 by the Balladur government and continued in the Juppé administration of 1995 (Bauer, 1988; Dumez and Jeunemaitre, 1993; McClean, 1997). We examine the specific case of the Jospin government (1997–2002) in some detail below.

An active industrial policy

French industrial policy was traditionally built upon the belief in the failure of perfect competition and the right to protect industries. In a *dirigiste* sense, governments should be able to direct market competition. Governments should protect their industries against disloyal competition and social dumping, and engineer industrial change in the long-term national strategic interest. Here we should sound a note a caution. The original features of French postwar economic management (such as planning) had faded in importance long before French governments attempted to harmonise economic policy with European Union partners in the 1980s and 1990s (Cohen, 1996). On the other hand, within the limits of European Union competition policy (see Chapter 13) the French economic model still looks to an active industrial policy. State activism is directed to encouraging and financing extensive research and training, bringing under-performing regions into national productivity (*aménagement du territoire*), promoting collaboration (rather than competition) between leading French firms, pursuing prestige projects (*grands projets*) and building essential economic infrastructure.

During the *dirigiste* phase, various types of instrument were used to attempt to promote French industry. These involved first and foremost the promotion of state-led prestige projects (*grands projets*) in sectors considered vital for national independence such as nuclear power, space exploration, the railways, the defence industry, aerospace and telecommunications. The *grands projets* were/are multibillion euro investment projects, designed to channel funds into the industries of the future. Many of these had politico-military origins (in aerospace, or atomic energy, for example). They were often state-driven conglomerates designed to retain and develop French scientific expertise. Public ownership was not a condition for state involvement. Private sector actors (for example the aerospace firm Dassault or the conglomerate Alcatel-Alsthom) could also benefit from state aid, notably by indirect protectionist forms of assistance in the form of state procurement policies, low-interest credits, tax-breaks and export credits. In all cases, there was a strong desire that French firms avoid foreign influence (making them more dependent upon the French state).

Under governments of the Gaullist right, as well as of the Socialist left from 1981–3, the official aim of industrial policy was to promote national champions in technically advanced sectors, especially in the sphere of transport and energy. The policy of creating national champions depended upon fulfilling certain criteria that assumed a strong (if flexible) state and a high degree of national economic sovereignty. According to Cohen (1995) the preconditions were offensive protectionism, technical innovation, public procurement policies, direct state aid and long-term political support (but weak political interference). Single national champions were created in the public sector. The private sector also depended upon the state for capital – giving governments the upper hand (Hayward, 1997). Apart from the *grands projets*, industrial policy also involved direct government grants to industrial sectors in difficulty, such as coal, textiles, machine tools, and shipbuilding. Such state grants and sectoral plans have become more difficult since the Single European Act.

A skewed pattern of government-industry relations

During the *dirigiste* phase, there was a widespread belief that the market needed to be regulated by a central state vested with an unchallenged political legitimacy. The state represented the general will of the people, over and above the particularistic interests of business, unions and voluntary groups. Moreover, in the economic sphere the state was vested with the duty of public service. The public sector was responsible for providing essential services (and ensuring essential investment) that private capital interests were unwilling (or incapable) of assuming. This produced a pattern of close interlocking relationships between the civil service, political elites and the boards of the leading French firms, which depended to some extent on public procurement policies.

Government–industry relations were complex. While state planners could orientate the activities of private sector firms in sensitive industrial spheres, there was evidence that large private firms were able to 'exert subtle influence over the government machinery' in order to promote their objectives (Cohen, 1995). Once established in the international market place, the most successful French firms demanded greater autonomy from the state, including in their detailed investment decisions, whether they were owned by the public or the private sector. In the course of the late 1980s and 1990s, the French state acceded to these demands, in order to assist the transformation of French firms into global players.

Though largely state-driven, this interventionist model came to be appropriated by social partners. The 1936 Matignon Agreements established a tradition of centralised bargaining that remains, in many senses, applicable today. Trade unions (especially) and the main employers' association (CNPF) looked in the main to the state to arbitrate a top-down style of industrial relations, where the state pointed the direction to the employers and the trade unions, a form of dependency upon the central state that would be alien to today's leaders of the MEDEF. In November 1968, the president of CNPF (Conseil national du patronat français – the leading French business organisation) claimed that, far from the growth in foreign competition necessitating a withdrawal of governmental support, this should serve as a further justification for continued state assistance (Hayward, 1986: 21).

The high economic growth rates of *les trente glorieuses* facilitated the type of interventionist policies adopted by French governments. In her major study of

French economic management, Schmidt (1996) refers to the 'inflationist social compromise' as one of the underpinnings of the post-war French economic model. Under the guise of social partnership, there was a convergence between the state, the trade unions and the employers not to control nominal changes in income. The model relied upon inflation to finance growth, an option that became untenable from the late 1970s onwards.

The orthodox model was challenged on all fronts from the mid- to late-1970s. The 'inflationist social compromise' led to the franc being devalued on several occasions. The massive French firms created by industrial engineering were ill-adapted to the changing international environment. Firms needed to become less dependent on the state, more on the markets. Forged during the prolonged post-war period of growth and prosperity (1950–74) Keynesian demand management policies proved incapable of addressing the crises of the early 1970s (namely, the ending of the Bretton Woods fixed parities system in 1971, and the OPEC oil price rises of 1973–4). The basic assumption of Keynesianism was that an interventionist state could control the economic cycle through the use of demand-management techniques. With the move to global recession after 1973–4, Keynesian policies, where applied, increased public expenditure and aggravated inflation. Growth management faltered under the accumulated pressures of stagflation, unemployment, balance of trade crises and state debt. These pressures proved at least as challenging to France as to any other advanced economy.

12.4 From inflation to European integration

With the onset of world economic crisis in 1973, the margins of manoeuvre open to governments have been limited, as have their policy responses. From 1976 onwards, the anti-inflation strategy has (for most of the time) officially been at the centrepiece of French macro-economic policy. The attempt by the conservative premier Barre to rein in public expenditure and to master inflation in 1976–81 floundered in part because of the belief that there was an alternative economic strategy, a belief not confined to the ranks of the left-wing opposition. The failure of the Socialist government's attempt at reinvigorated Keynesianism from 1981–2 revealed that this was not the case. Let us consider, briefly, the case of the French Socialists in office.

The Mauroy government (1981–4) began life by enthusiastically adopting classic social democratic remedies while these were being progressively jettisoned elsewhere. The Socialist-led government implemented Keynesian demand management policies to stimulate growth and combat unemployment. In the early 1980s, with the US and western Europe in the midst of recession, the French socialist government's counter-cyclical economic policy contrasted starkly with the macroeconomic policies being pursued by France's principal trading partners. Its audacious industrial policies (the 1982 nationalisation of thirty-six banks and five major industrial groups) also ran directly counter to the incipient privatisation trends elsewhere. Its social generosity (as measured by increases in pensions, the minimum wage, and family allowances) contributed to the goal of economic relaunch and fiscal redistribution (consolidated by the wealth tax), but created intolerable economic strains. The French economy simply could not absorb the pressure imposed by spiralling trade and budget deficits. The left's economic U-turn, which took place in two stages in June 1982 and in March 1983, demonstrated for most observers France's economic vulnerability: unilateral Keynesian reflationary policies were no longer possible for a medium-sized nation such as France in an interdependent world economy.

The economic U-turn of 1983 destroyed the French Socialists' illusions of economic independence and shook their faith in nationally distinctive paths to socialism. The failure of Socialist reflation from 1981–3 revealed the pressures for convergence between French economic policies and those of its main competitors, especially Germany. The belief in the virtues of mirroring the powerful German economy became an article of faith from the mid-1980s onwards. The devaluation of the franc on three occasions from 1981–3 highlighted the fallacies of a belief in national economic sovereignty and unilateral neo-Keynesian relaunch (Cameron, 1996). Tying the franc to the Deutschmark through the exchange rate mechanism of the European Monetary System, on the other hand, produced substantial economic benefits. It allowed inflation to be mastered, the productivity gap with Germany to be narrowed, and even an improved commercial balance with Germany. Hence the importance of the strong franc policy engaged with vigour from 1984 onwards and only loosened under Jospin once France had qualified for single currency membership (Aeschimann and Riché, 1996; Clift, 2002). The perceived downside was one of persistently high unemployment (over 10 per cent for most of the 1990s). As the price to pay for German unification from 1990 onwards, moreover, the German Bundesbank imposed punitively high interest rates on Germany's partners.

The French government – along with others – drew the lesson that sovereignty could best be recovered by the solution of Europeanisation. Since monetary sovereignty had already disappeared, a single currency would allow the French and others to recover elements of national sovereignty by participating in decisions concerning monetary policy. The Maastricht Treaty of 1992, with its core single currency decision, represented a victory for French President Mitterrand (Cole, 1997). At the same time, Maastricht posed new challenges to the traditional French economic policy paradigms valued by many Socialists (such as the political direction of economic policy and governmental control over monetary policy instruments).

There are several good accounts explaining why French governments pushed so hard for EMU in the late 1980s and early 1990s (Dyson and Featherstone, 1999; Howarth, 2001). EMU had long been a French policy demand. French economic conservatives in the Treasury division (Trésor) of the Finance Ministry had advocated it since the late 1960s. EMU would tie-in the Germans to the European economy and harness German economic strength to European objectives. It would impose internal discipline on France and encourage long overdue structural reforms. It would allow France more influence into the definitions of economic policy priorities – largely dependent on the Bundesbank since the late 1960s. French leaders also favoured EMU as a means of increasing

European autonomy from the United States. There was, in addition, a clear economic case for monetary union. EMU should lower production costs, thereby helping France to recover its share of the world market. Growth would create jobs. EMU would allow for lower interest rates. The principal political motivation, however, was that France would recover influence with EMU; it would be present in those institutions making monetary policy decisions. From the perspective of French policy-makers, monetary union was a means of diluting German economy hegemony, while tying Germany into the European economy for the benefit of its main trading partners (especially France) and reducing transaction costs for everybody.

The discipline of French governments from 1983 to 1999 (the date of the introduction of the single currency) brought definite economic rewards. In the course of the 1980s and 1990s, the French disease of high inflation and regular trade deficits gave way to low inflation and trade surpluses. This occurred at the expense of sluggish growth rates (by French standards) and an exponential rise in unemployment, a major political issue in the 1995 presidential campaign. There were some negative by-products of this policy, especially a stubbornly high unemployment rate. A powerful theme of Chirac's presidential campaign in 1995 was his refusal of *la pensée unique*, the notion that there was only one economic path (the strong franc policy) if France was to meet the convergence criteria for participating in a single European currency. This populist (and popular) position suggested that high unemployment would tempt governments to relax their strict codes of economic management at some date in the future. The cue was taken by the Jospin government (1997–2002) which used the resources of economic growth to further pump-prime the economy and bring down unemployment, rather than reducing deficits as suggested by the European Commission.

There is a strong argument that, once the decision on parity rates had been taken in 1998 and the single currency introduced in 1999, the French government did everything in its power to renationalise economic policy, faced with the costs of full European economic integration. The crisis in the Stability Pact in 2003 (when France and Germany announced their inability to bring down their budget deficits in 2004 to under 3 per cent of GNP for the third year running) was the logical outcome of national policy choices remaining central to French government thinking. The 2003 crisis highlighted the ingrained tensions between French national traditions of economic management and the institutional design of the European single currency. Put simply, French national traditions involve asserting the primacy of 'politics' over 'economics'. Ever since Maastricht, French governments have argued in favour of 'economic government', of allowing politicians ultimate control of the governance of the single currency. Under the influence of German Chancellor Kohl, the institutional design of the single currency could not easily accommodate the French vision. Once the single currency decision had been imposed upon Kohl at Maastricht, the practical details of EMU bore the imprint of German rigour at every stage of policy implementation: from the location of the European central bank in Frankfurt, to the name of the currency (the euro, rather than the ECU favoured by France), to the 'stability pact' accompanying its implementation. Above all, Germany was able to insist on tough convergence criteria accompanying the implementation of the single currency. The criteria outlined in the Maastricht Treaty included precise objectives for inflation (within 1.5 per cent of the best performing state), budget deficits (no more than 3 per cent of GDP) and public sector borrowing (below 60 per cent of GDP). They also required central bank independence and the complete mobility of capital. The Stability Pact was the final piece in the institutional jigsaw, insisted upon later (in 1995) by German Chancellor Kohl to ensure lasting economic convergence once the currency was in place.

If Germany imposed the basic institutional design of the new monetary institutions, the end game of monetary union revealed itself to be a process with unintended consequences. At the Amsterdam summit of 1997, the Jospin government secured the creation of a committee of euro-zone Finance Ministers (later known as the Euro-Group) to monitor the work of the European central bank. The Jospin government's view of the Euro-Group was not far removed from the traditional French preference for an economic government wherein politicians would determine economic priorities to be implemented by the system of central banks. This view was strongly contested by the Kohl administration in Germany, as it had been throughout the Maastricht negotiations (Dyson and Featherstone, 1999). In 1998, at the Dublin summit, there was open conflict between President Chirac and Chancellor Kohl, about the role and status of the Stability Pact. The change of government in Germany in 1998 moved the Euro-Group closer to French conceptions. German Finance Minister Oskar Lafontaine was convinced of the need for greater political direction to the single currency project. The formal launch of the euro in January 1999 coincided with a strong push from EU Finance Ministers for more political oversight over the central bank. French Ministers have continued to advocate developing the Euro-Group as an embryonic 'economic government', an idea (if not a terminology) that has gradually gained political credibility.

The Stability and Growth Pact empowered the Council of Ministers (ECOFIN) to determine whether or not any sanctions should be taken against member-states that have transgressed the Maastricht criteria. On 25 November 2003, a blocking minority (France, Germany, Italy and Portugal) of the twelve euro states prevented France and Germany from having to pay stiff fines for failing to control their budget deficits. The paradox of Germany, in particular, falling foul of the rules it had imposed was not lost on anybody. The unwillingness of the two largest euro-zone states to play by the rules of the game was, understandably, resented by smaller members of the euro-zone – such as Ireland, Spain or Finland – which had made efforts to respect the rules of the pact. From the perspective of French economic policy-making, the episode demonstrated the extent of economic interdependence within the euro-zone (at the same meeting, France and Germany pledged to bring their budgets under control by 2005). It suggested above all, however, that French politicians of left and right have great difficulties in accepting that the 'gnomes of Brussels' have any right to interfere in their sovereign control over economic policy-making. Such fundamental ambivalence reflects a preference for overarching national discursive frames. This is also apparent when considering the case of privatisations.

Changing policy fashions: the case of industrial privatisations

The French model of politics and policy presupposed a rather different equilibrium between state and market than its neighbours. There was more *dirigisme*. But there have always been two faces to French state activity. On the one hand, an interventionist state that actively promoted national champions and engaged in neo-protectionist practices. On the other, French governments in the Fifth Republic pursued a liberal macroeconomic policy based on sound money policies and international competitiveness (Dyson and Featherstone, 1999; Howarth, 2001). The French economy thus developed under the dual impetus of state capitalism and classical liberalism.

As we demonstrated above, state capitalism took the form of an interventionist industrial policy. After 1945, the French state became a first rank economic actor in its own right. The expansion of public services during the post-war period was built on the perceived incapacity of the private sphere to spearhead investment and reconstruction. After the 1946 nationalisation programme, the French state owned large tracts of French industry, notably in the sectors of transport, automobile, steel, and energy. With the nationalisations of 1946, the national public monopolies spearheaded the efforts of national reconstruction. The Socialists' nationalisation programme of 1981–2 added a number of leading industrial groups, and the bulk of the banking and financial sector to the state's portfolio.

Since 1986, French governments – albeit intermittently – have been busy privatising not only those firms nationalised in 1982, but also those in public ownership since 1946. The privatisation programme began during the Chirac 1986–8 government. After a five-year pause ('ni-ni') during Mitterrand's second term, privatisation was resumed with a new vigour in 1993 by the Balladur government and continued in the Juppé administration of 1995. In terms of receipts from sales, however, the Jospin government of 1997 surpassed all its predecessors. More than any other, the Jospin government also illustrated how French governments seek to reconcile inevitable privatisation with the pursuit of an active industrial policy. For France remains committed to a larger measure of state economic interventionism than Anglo-Saxon or Germanic economic liberals consider appropriate. The nature of the French privatisation programme in 1986–8 illustrated this. The French state preserved a powerful oversight role for itself, through the policy of creating a 'hard core' of institutional shareholders close to the state's economic interests (Dumez and Jeunemaitre, 1993; Maclean, 1997). This consistency with national traditions is demonstrated most convincingly when considering the record of the Jospin government (1997–2002).

In a rather paradoxical manner, the Jospin government reinvented privatisation as a tool of industrial policy. The left for long resisted privatisation in any form. Even after accepting the economic 'conversion' in March 1983, the left had insisted upon a strong role for the French state: as provider of welfare, as economic regulator, as guarantor of employment. During the 1988–93 administration, the Socialist government's position had been determined by

Mitterrand's 'ni-ni' policy. In his 1988 letter to the French people, Mitterrand promised 'neither nationalisation, nor privatisation'. This commitment led to a policy position based upon inertia. Consistent with their own partisan and statist traditions, in their 1997 manifesto *Changeons d'avenir* the French Socialists categorically pledged to 'stop' the privatisations commenced under the Balladur and Juppé administrations. Once in power, the Jospin government was less categorical. Its responses attempted to marry strategic interest and ideological preference. Campaign promises notwithstanding, in July 1997 Jospin declared 'pragmatism' to be the guiding principle in its attitude towards privatisations: everything would depend upon the interests of the firm concerned, and the finances of the state. There was a clear industrial strategy underpinning Jospin's 'privatisations'. In one or two instances, 'privatisation' was forced upon the French government by past commitments or by EU competition policy adjudication, as in the case of GAN-CIC and Crédit Lyonnais. These cases were relatively rare. Most 'privatisations' were undertaken with a view to strengthening the strategic role of the state in an age of economic interdependence and globalisation. There were three main types of instrument under Jospin: partial privatisations, designed to prepare state firms for competition; majority sell-offs, where the state retained an important blocking influence; and sell-offs strengthening the cooperative sector.

Semi-privatisations as a tool of industrial policy

The main justification for semi, or partial privatisations was the pursuit of an active industrial policy during a period of economic interdependency. Partial privatisation refers to the French state selling off minority shareholdings, but retaining overall control over key national firms. The principal justification for this policy was that reducing the share of state capital would allow leading French firms to build international alliances by facilitating cross-shareholdings. The state floated shares in France Télécom in 1997 in the expectation that it would build a strategic alliance with the German firm Deutsche Telekom. In the event, the Germans preferred an alliance with the Italians, and gave the French government a harsh lesson in the realities of international political economy. The opening up of 20 per cent of the capital of France Télécom in 1997 would encourage international alliances, assist the telecommunications giant to become a global player and facilitate raising finance on the international money markets. But there was no question of outright privatisation. The public service mission of France Télécom was to remain. Moreover, the main institutional shareholders in France Télécom were traditionally close to the French government: Bouygues, and Compagnie générale des eaux were two of the most important. A similar procedure was adopted for Air France in February 1999.

The defence sector provided specific challenges. The case of Thomson was another example of a controlled, or *dirigiste* partial privatisation. A running saga since November 1996, the privatisation of Thomson was unfinished business from the previous government. Initially opposed to any privatisation, Jospin was persuaded that the status quo was not an option in the rapidly evolving defence world. There were too many medium-sized defence firms, not only in France, but in Europe as a whole. Rationalisation of this sector was essential, if the European defence industry was to survive the American challenge. While the Juppé government had favoured a strategic alliance between Thomson and the missile constructor Matra (itself in alliance with the German DASA and British Aerospace), Jospin arbitrated in favour of the rival firm Alcatel, in alliance with Aerospatiale and Dassault. Later on, in 1999, the Jospin government engineered the fusion between Aerospatiale and Matra. Given their dependence upon public procurement policies, even private defence firms could not resist the will of the French government in this sphere. The 'privatisation' of Thomson-CSF in reality involved the French state dictating an industrial alliance (cemented by cross-shareholdings) between Thomson-CSF, Alcatel-Alsthom, Dassault and Aerospatiale, as a prelude to a larger European-wide rationalisation.

The advantages of semi-privatisations were numerous. Partially private companies could raise money on the financial markets, while retaining state majority control. Workers could be associated with the company by becoming shareholders. In exchange, salary cuts could be demanded (as in the case of Air France, when floated on the Paris stock exchange). Finally opening up capital allowed French firms to seek new industrial partners, while attempting to forestall hostile takeovers.

Covert control through cross-shareholdings

Even when the state lost a majority shareholding, it was often able to retain control. The *gré-à-gré* procedure (which allows the French government to choose shareholders, without necessarily floating shares on the Paris Bourse) was vital in this respect. The influence of the government in drawing up the stable shareholding at the moment of privatisation was essential. Thus, in Thomson CSF, the state's shareholding declined from 58 per cent to 43 per cent. But the other groups represented on the board (Alcatel, Dassault, Aerospatiale) were all close to the French state. Past experiences (such as that of the French insurer AGF, taken over by the German Allianz) demonstrated that such interventionist attempts to create stable shareholdings did not always work.

Financial privatisations in favour of the mixed economy

Wherever possible, the Jospin government attempted to make the associative and cooperative financial institutions the chief beneficiaries of privatisations in the financial sector. Thus, the CIC bank was ceded to Crédit Mutuel. Likewise, GAN was sold to Groupama. In both cases, the French state used to *gré à gré* procedure and favoured mutual banks over French and foreign commercial rivals. By ceding state financial groups to mutual banks, the government was strengthening the mixed sector of the economy. In French law, the cooperative sector was vested with a public service mission, thereby subject to administrative law. The Finance Ministry had the right to block any decision taken by the cooperative sector that it considered against its interests. By giving this sector a public service mission, France hoped to escape from EU oversight. In a rather paradox manner, in the banking sector privatisation strengthened the public service.

These examples demonstrate that innate resistance to forms of privatisation has faded in the face of changing global policy norms, ideological fashions and budgetary realism. But, under the Socialists at least, the state used all the tools at its disposal to attempt to shape the direction of industrial policy change. For Jospin, privatisations were a new tool of industrial policy. Partial privatisation allowed strategic alliances to be formed and capital to be raised on the financial markets. Reinventing industrial policy compatible with globalisation lay at the heart of the Jospin government's strategy. The opening up of European and world markets was the driving force behind privatisation. In Peter Hall's language, there was an underlying continuity of policy goals (French national champions), though the instruments used to achieve these goals were flexibly administered.

12.6 Concluding remarks

There is a vast literature on economic policy and policy-making in France, some references to which have been provided in this chapter. Probably the most influential study in the past two decades has been that of Peter Hall (1986), which did much to contribute to refining the new institutionalist approach to the study of public policy. There are three central themes in Hall's approach: institutions matter in explaining stability and change; the social power of ideas is maximised when they are embedded in institutions; policy goals remain relatively stable over time, though instruments may vary. Hall (1986, 1989) uses institutions and ideas almost interchangeably to explain economic policy governance in post-war France. The tradition of the strong state in France first legitimised the activist role of planners, who came to the fore in the wartime period and during the immediate post-war reconstruction. Planners had a firm institutional base in the Planning Commissariat especially. The ideas they disseminated rapidly gained currency as the predominant policy paradigm. Ideas of active state interventionism remained potent until the late 1970s and early 1980s, when planners themselves began to question the assumptions of the previous framework. Institutions not only provided stability for three decades, but also drove change once elite-level ideas about policy instruments began to shift. In the Hall schema, institutions were the critical drivers of change. French society accepted the leadership of the state, because the French public has traditionally accorded a degree of legitimacy to the state and state intervention.

The second major contribution of the Hall approach is that ideas are embedded in institutions. State interventionism and *dirigisme* were most important at the level of ideas, or policy prisms. The idea of state interventionism was as important as the precise mechanics through which this idea was implemented. The success of state interventionism came through its adoption as a legitimate policy paradigm. However, the tensions caused following economic downturn and stagflation in the 1970s forced the government to rethink its economic policy and, gradually, a paradigm shift ensued. Third, and most interestingly, Hall's analysis focuses attention on levels of policy change. For Hall (1993) there are three central variables to policy-making. First, there are the overarching goals that guide policy in a particular field. Second, there are the techniques or policy instruments used to attain goals. Finally, there is the precise setting of these instruments. Alteration of the settings (first level change) or an alteration of the instruments (second level change) could be seen as normal policy-making. A third level change, an alteration of the goals would be a discontinuity. Economic policy-making during the post-war period has changed its policy instruments and settings, but the overarching goal – maintaining France's international standing and economic modernisation – has remained fairly stable over time (Hall, 1993, 2001).

Hall's study usefully emphasises the continuities underpinning economic policy-making in post-war France. As surveyed throughout this chapter, there have also been important changes to processes of economic governance. Though changes were externally driven, they became internally institutionalised, especially during the 1990s. Moreover, as the works of Dyson and Featherstone (1999), or Howarth (2001) show, there has always been a plurality of viewpoints about the appropriate relationship between state and market in France. The role of economic conservatives in the Treasury division of the Finance Ministry has been identified in terms of providing a domestic tradition conducive to the sound money policies of the 1980s and 1990s. In relation to economic and industrial policy, on balance France has been forced to succumb to changing policy fashions, rather than initiate them. The combined impact of globalisation and European integration has been to lessen the possibilities open to the French state to engage in a 'heroic' policy style, a style traditionally more visible in industrial policy than anywhere else.

If French governments have had to face similar social and economic challenges to their European counterparts, these are usually interpreted in accordance with established discursive registers (of which state interventionism and economic liberalism provide two alternatives). Traditions of state economic intervention are deeply rooted in France. The public sector remains stronger in France than elsewhere, as does the weight of the state in the French economic management. The French notion of public service remains distinct from that of other European nations. The French model has undoubtedly been weakened during the period since 1983. But old habits die hard.

13   Europe and Europeanisation

13.1   Introduction

That European integration has called into question prominent features of the French model has been a cross-cutting theme of many of the preceding chapters. In the 2000s, European integration weighs heavily on the conduct of domestic French politics. In this penultimate chapter, we investigate the paradoxical nature of France's relationship to the European Union, a body which appears simultaneously as a powerful constraint on domestic public policy and a source of unrivalled opportunity for contemporary French governments to exercise influence on a wider world stage. In section 13.2, we provide a historical overview of France's relationship with the European Union, as informed primarily by the experience of the five Presidents of the Fifth Republic. In section 13.3, we take stock of France's relationship with the European Union in the early 2000s by focussing on a number of key themes. In section 13.4, we address the theme of the Europeanisation of the French polity.

13.2   France and the European Union

French statesmen were in the forefront of the process leading to the EEC with the Treaty of Rome in 1957. In the opinion of Hilary Winchester (1993): 'Much of the credit for the organisations of European unity must go to France; not only were individuals, such as Jean Monnet, influential in setting up the early European structures, but France as a whole adopted an expansive view of European unity, in which a strong Europe was viewed as an extension of French national interests'. This was vital. Underlying its supranational discourse, the European Union (EU) has always been regarded as a means of enhancing French national prestige. To this extent, Europe was a French invention, and served French interests as much as those of any other nation.

As surveyed briefly in Chapter 1, the principal moves towards closer European cooperation in the 1950s were of French, or Franco-German inspiration: the European Coal and Steel Community of 1951, the abortive European Army of 1954, the Treaty of Rome of 1957. The reasons underpinning moves towards closer European integration were multiple. Foremost was the need to end the ruinous European civil war that had plagued Europe for the past century, and to make future wars impossible. The genuine federalist idealism of the founding-fathers coexisted alongside harsh calculations of national self-interest. European integration rested upon a reconciliation of France and Germany; cooperation between these hereditary enemies underpins the history of the European Union (Cole, 2001a). In effect, as the Community progressed, what amounted to a bargain was struck between the two countries: France would offer political leadership, while recognising Germany's economic primacy. The Treaty of Rome signed in 1957, which created the European Economic Community (EEC) was 'essentially a compromise between German interest in market liberalisation, and French interest in support for agriculture' (Pedersen, 1998: 80).

French Presidents and Europe in the Fifth Republic

Since the inception of the Fifth Republic, Europe has formed part of the presidential sphere of interest. Though the governance of European issues is far more complex than this simple assertion implies, the 'history-making' decisions of French European policy have, by and large, resulted from the personal priorities of successive Presidents, and their evaluation of whether the European balance of power would permit specific policy initiatives (Moravscik, 1991; Dyson and Featherstone, 1999). In the ensuing section, we consider briefly the evolution of French European policy since 1958 from the perspective of five French Presidents.

More than any other French President, de Gaulle (1958–69) personified one of two recognisable tendencies in French European politics: that which stressed the value of cooperation between nation-states, rather than the vision of a federal United States of Europe, as espoused by the European visionaries Jean Monnet and Robert Schuman. De Gaulle's preferences were far removed from the avowed federalism of Europe's founders. To an ever-closer union, de Gaulle preferred a Europe of the nation-states. This might be summarised as a strong Europe with weak institutions under French leadership, a conception considered in some detail below. A strong Europe was essential, in order to counter American cultural and economic hegemony, and to defend western security interests against an aggressive USSR. French leadership was a *sine qua non* for such a Europe; Germany remained a semi-sovereign state; Britain was too close to the Americans. France aspired to a leadership role at the head of a confederation of nation-states. The nation-state – with its contradictions, symbols, identities – would remain the focus of political organisation. Nation-states provided a stable bearing in the rough sea of international anarchy. It was through the nation-state that order and prosperity could be organised.

Cooperation between nation states would enhance French influence within Europe. As President of the Fifth Republic after 1958, de Gaulle first proposed a Franco-British-American 'directorate' over the affairs of the West. Faced with Anglo-Saxon indifference, de Gaulle then advanced a Franco-German partnership, aimed at weaning Germany away from NATO, and proposing a dual leadership of a Europe which was neither Atlanticist, nor *communautaire*. The opening to Germany bore fruit in the signing of the Franco-German friendship treaty of 1963 (Cole, 2001a). This assertion of Franco-German friendship accurately reflected the Gaullist vision of European priorities. De Gaulle attempted to force Germany to choose between France and the US in international forums such as NATO. This was too provocative for the West German lower chamber, the Bundestag, which insisted on adding a preamble reaffirming in strongly pro-Atlanticist terms Germany's participation in GATT and NATO. In spite of their official friendship, during the long Gaullist interlude, in many respects the two countries held conflicting political visions. These divergences became clearer once Adenauer had left office in 1963. They centred on the role of supranational institutions, the importance of the Atlantic Alliance and the role of the US in Europe.

De Gaulle's preference for a Europe of the nation-states contrasted with the federalism of Europe's early visionaries. In terms of the EC's institutional structures, this meant that de Gaulle preferred an intergovernmental organisation to a supranational one. It was the duty of national leaders to preside and decide. De Gaulle's empty chair policy of 1965 testified to his determination to preserve French national interests. In conflict with her European neighbours over extending the use of majority voting for EC decisions, France refused to attend meetings of Community institutions for a six-month period. France would not be bound by decisions with which it did not agree. This stalemate was ended by the 1966 Luxembourg compromise, which gave any member state a right of veto over EC policies that it considered harmful to its vital national interests. The Luxembourg compromise represented a victory for the French government against the federalist enthusiasm of the smaller European nations. De Gaulle's intergovernmental conception of the EC was not seriously challenged again until the mid-1980s.

The prevailing judgement is that de Gaulle was the least pro-European of all French Presidents, with each of his successors becoming progressively more pro-European, at least until the election of President Chirac in 1995. In certain respects, this judgement is rather superficial. De Gaulle certainly regarded himself as pro-European; indeed he did not separate European and French national interests. Europe was to be led to independence from American hegemony under France's enlightened military and political leadership. Only France, the lone continental European nuclear power, was strong enough to provide an alternative to American leadership. Thus, de Gaulle's decision to withdraw from NATO in 1965 was justified by the imperative of French military independence (although the General was careful not to discard the safety of the US military umbrella). Other European nations (especially Germany) were dubious of the French alternative, and remained committed to NATO. De Gaulle's repeated vetoes of British entry to the EC, in 1963 and 1967, stemmed from the belief that the UK was an American Trojan horse within Europe, and that British influence would be to the detriment of French influence. In this way, a 'French' Europe was juxtaposed to an Anglo-Saxon non-Europe. De Gaulle was above all a French patriot, one for whom European identity was important as a means of enhancing the continent's independence from the superpowers. De Gaulle's Europe was predicated upon a dominant Franco-German axis, upon French leadership within that axis, and upon a distrust of Anglo-Saxon influence. These themes represented the core of the Gaullist heritage that his successors had to take on board.

President Pompidou (1969–74) accepted the main traits of the Gaullist heritage, while demonstrating more flexibility in relations with the United States and Britain. The second President of the Fifth Republic was less averse to the accession of the United Kingdom to the EC, with British entry finally accomplished in 1973. In the early 1970s, British entry favoured French interests, for it was felt to counterbalance a reviving Germany. British entry into the EC was only agreed once the Common Agricultural Policy was firmly in place. Apart from the question of British entry, there was much continuity in the transition from de Gaulle to Pompidou. Both were determined to preserve French political pre-eminence within the Community, to favour common policies that were in French interests, and to resist federalist developments. With respect to relations with Germany, President Pompidou lessened, but did not fundamentally alter the Franco-German basis of the European community, though President Pompidou and Chancellor Schmidt did not enjoy a warm personal relationship.

As his predecessors, President Giscard d'Estaing (1974–81) regarded the European option as the best means of strengthening French influence. Tight Franco-German cooperation was again the driving force of European integration. Two decisions in particular helped to revive the process of European integration. In 1974, President Giscard d'Estaing and German Chancellor Schmidt agreed to create an institutional basis for the regular summit meetings that took place between the heads of EC member states. Henceforth, summits were to take place at least once every six months, with these meetings known as the European Council. The creation of the European Council relaunched the process of European integration on an intergovernmental basis. Major EC policies would be decided in these six-monthly meetings between the heads of government. The Gaullist lineage was evident; heads of government, rather than supranational commissioners, would make the essential decisions. Summit agreements lay behind major EC initiatives, such as the enlargement negotiations, leading to the accession of Spain and Portugal in 1986; the intergovernmental conference in 1985, which resulted in the Single European Act and the intergovernmental conference of 1991 that produced the Maastricht Treaty. The second principal policy based on a Franco-German initiative was the creation of the European Monetary System (EMS) in 1978. As with his predecessors, President Giscard d'Estaing promoted closer European cooperation as an alternative to economic domination by the United States. The creation of the EMS (which tied leading European currencies to narrow exchange rate variations) was crucial in this respect, since it laid the bases for future moves towards a single European currency.

His European mission gave a sense of direction to President Mitterrand's long presidential term-in-office (1981–95). In European policy, in symbolic and substantive terms, Mitterrand's Europe was far more integrationist than that espoused by de Gaulle. Initially preoccupied by domestic politics, Mitterrand left his personal mark on French European policy, arguably more so than any President since de Gaulle. President Mitterrand could claim a major input into the two principal European decisions of the period 1981–93: the launching of the process leading to the Single European Act of 1986, and the Maastricht Treaty of 1992 (Cole, 1994; Friend, 1998). There was much continuity in European policy between Mitterrand and his predecessors. Mitterrand preferred a compact, cohesive Community, based on a Franco-German directorate, rather than a broader nebulous of less cohesive nations. This explained his initial reluctance to envisage the enlargement of the Community to include Spain and Portugal, as well as his later resistance to closer ties with the new democracies of eastern Europe. Both stances were later reversed, in order to placate Mitterrand's chief European ally, Chancellor Kohl of Germany. As with previous French Presidents, Mitterrand's Europe was conceived of as an intergovernmental rather than a federal entity: the same suspicion of the European parliament, and of the Commission (even when led by Frenchman Delors after 1985) surfaced on many occasions. But, in the broader interests of European integration, Mitterrand proved more willing to sacrifice elements of national sovereignty than any of his precursors had been. In the Single European Act of 1986, the French President accepted that majority voting should become the norm for EC decisions, although the Luxembourg compromise (right of national veto) formally remained intact. Since the passage of the Single European Act, the Luxembourg compromise has virtually fallen into disuse. Not even over GATT in 1993 did the French government feel confident enough to use its veto. In the Maastricht Treaty, further provisions for majority voting were enacted, along with some strengthening of the powers of the European parliament and the European Commission, traditionally anathema to French Presidents.

From 1984 onwards, Mitterrand concentrated upon portraying himself as a great European statesman, with a coherent vision of Europe's future. Mitterrand's close cooperation with Chancellor Kohl, and Commission President Delors after 1985 produced a powerful coalition in favour of a more cohesive European Community. As with past French Presidents, Mitterrand juxtaposed French European culture and Anglo-Saxon non-European culture. Mitterrand's preferred European Community was one strong enough to survive in an increasingly interdependent age. This implied a commitment to common policies to enable Europe to exist as a political, social, economic and military entity. Mitterrand was a firm supporter of Economic and Monetary Union, a cause the French President promoted with insistence at Maastricht. Mitterrand's conversion to EMU reflected French fiscal and monetary rectitude during the 1980s; it also revealed a determination on behalf of the French President to exercise more control over European monetary policy (see Chapter 12).

The style adopted by President Chirac (1995–) was in stark contrast to that of Mitterrand. This became clear at the Cannes summit of June 1995, which terminated France's presidency of the European Union. In a language unusual for diplomatic gatherings, Chirac publicly accused the Italian premier Dini of engineering a competitive devaluation of the lire in order to harm French agriculture and clashed with the Dutch premier over the Netherlands' policy on drugs. This was followed by criticism of the Greeks for indulgence towards the Bosnian Serbs. These early skirmishes faded in significance beside the uproar caused by Chirac's decision of July 1995 to resume French nuclear testing in the South Pacific. This decision, taken without any negotiation with France's European partners, was condemned virtually unanimously by other nations, including most of France's European allies. Though relations with France's allies have improved (especially Germany), President Chirac still arouses deep suspicions amongst France's partners. There are numerous examples of Chirac fighting hard to defend the French national interest: over the Growth and Stability Pact in 1996; during the 'Trichet affair' in 1998; over the reform of the Common Agricultural Policy in 1999; during the negotiations leading to the Treaty of Nice in 2000, over Iraq in 2003. On occasion, Chirac's style has appeared anachronistic, the arch-defender of the grander and least sustainable aspects of French exceptionalism. At other times, however, Chirac has caught the European mood, as in his sustained opposition to the prospect, then occurrence of war in Iraq in 2003.

In his 1995 presidential election campaign, Chirac delivered an ambiguous message in relation to European integration, criticising the widespread belief that the strong franc policy was the indispensable corollary of closer European integration. Although Chirac had supported the Maastricht referendum of 1992, two-thirds of RPR supporters voted against the ratification of the Maastricht Treaty. Torn between a sceptical electorate, and the need to reassure financial markets and prevent a run on the franc, President Chirac maintained an ambiguous attitude towards European integration for the first six months of his presidential term. Any lingering doubts over France's commitment to the Maastricht Treaty were forcibly dispelled in a press conference in October 1995. President Chirac affirmed that the primary economic goal of the French government was to cut public sector deficits, in order to meet the convergence criteria to enable France to participate in the single European currency (see Chapter 12 for more detail).

More than any of his predecessors, the influence exercised by President Chirac over European policy has varied according to the prevailing political climate. With the advent of the third cohabitation in 1997, President Chirac lost uncontested control in the sphere of European policy. In the field of European policy, the third cohabitation imposed a form of co-management of EU affairs. The President retained an essential role on account of his treaty-signing power, his function as chair of the Council of Ministers, and his status as elected head of state, guaranteeing his presence in European and international summits. But the French presidency remained a fairly light infrastructure, and the government controlled the essential levers of EU management. Specifically, the French Prime Minister controls the General Secretariat of the Interministerial Committee (SGCI) an interministerial bureaucratic agency charged with coordinating French governmental responses to the European Union.

During the 1997–2002 cohabitation, both branches of the French executive accepted the new rules of the game, in the overriding national interest. French Foreign Minister Védrine publicly stated in December 1997 that, where European policy was concerned, he took responsibility, acting on Prime Minister Jospin's authority, with the assistance of Pierre Moscovici (the Minister delegate for European Affairs), and with President Chirac's agreement. President Chirac reciprocated the confidence in April 1998 by affirming that there was a 'common understanding' on European affairs within cohabitation. There was, moreover, a degree of policy based convergence between the two heads of the French executive; neither Chirac, nor Jospin favoured the flights of rhetorical Euro-fantasy of Mitterrand. Both men were resolute in defence of vital French interests, as over CAP reform (1999), the Seattle World Trade Organisation (1999) talks, British beef (1999) or the Nice Summit (2000). In foreign policy-making, the need to present a united front in defence of prevalent national interests ensured coordinated policy-making between the two branches of the French executive. In the specific case of the Kosovo War, there was a markedly high degree of inner executive coordination, with daily contact between Elysée and Matignon advisers and military chiefs.

What overarching themes can we identify in French European policy from this overview of the past fifty years?

13.3   *Quelle finalité européenne?* The French vision of Europe

French approaches to European integration have combined an astute mix of visionary discourse and instrumental policy position-taking that has proved very effective in defending French national interests over time. France has always believed in a European finality, though there have been many contradictions in the French vision of Europe. In the ensuing section, we identify some of the main themes associated with the traditional French discourse on European integration. Through concentrating on themes, rather than periods, we might imply staticity, but this is not our intention. French attitudes to Europe are continually evolving as domestic and external circumstances change and, not least, as the EU develops itself as a polity-like regime. The salient themes we identify as the 'constants' of French approaches to European integration are: neo-realism and national purpose; the cultural attachment to European values and civilisation; the Franco-German relationship; suspicion towards an enlarged Europe and the preference for a strong Europe with weak institutions.

Neo-realism and national purpose

Though its political discourse has been visionary, supranational and integrationist, the realist presupposition of Europe as an extension of French influence has been embraced more overtly than in any other European country. French governments in the Fifth Republic for long accepted the canons of classical Gaullism unquestioningly. The Gaullist paradigm that prevailed until the mid-1980s – and remains influential today – might be summarised in terms of six principal features: a cultural attachment to European values and civilisation, notably as embodied by France; a Europe prepared to protect its industry and agriculture; the promotion of common European policies where these do not endanger French interests; a marked anti-Americanism and advocacy of a more independent security and defence identity; a tight Community based on a Franco-German directorate, rather than a looser more nebulous grouping of nations; and a preference for intergovernmental over supranational institutions. There were many contradictions in this (Gaullist) French vision of Europe. France wanted a strong Europe with weak institutions (Le Gloannec and Hassner, 1996). There was a supranational discourse stressing the primacy of politics, but a fear of a genuinely supranational entity that might challenge the (self-appointed) role of French political leadership of the European integration project. In essence, France wanted to retain its role as a great power and to harness the resources of the Community to this effect. The EC was explicitly framed in national (and European) terms, as a means whereby France could escape dependency, recover sovereignty and export its policy models to the supranational institutional arena.

A cultural attachment to European values and civilisation

French governments continue to lobby hard in favour of an understanding of the European Union that goes beyond the Union as an 'extended free trade zone'. They have been strong advocates of a cultural attachment to European values and civilization, especially (but not uniquely) as personified by France. This has often manifested itself by a declared anti-Americanism. During the GATT negotiations of 1993–4, for example, the French Gaullist government of Balladur (supported by the Socialist President Mitterrand) held out for protectionist measures in favour of defending French cinema, a move justified by the need to support European civilization against Anglo-Saxon encroachment.

This European patriotism is invoked in favour of affirmative policy stances. Shared European values and interests are juxtaposed to those defended by America (and sometimes Britain). All Presidents have criticised unbridled economic liberalism, in a manner which sets France at odds with partners such as Britain (and to some extent Germany). The French have traditionally advocated a Europe prepared to protect its industry and (especially) agriculture. The French have been adept at suggesting common European policies, especially when these benefit French interests. The CAP is the classic example. Other examples include the creation of the European Monetary System in 1978, which aligned the franc against the German mark; EUREKA (the European space programme), and other related industrial projects with beneficial spin-offs for French industry. France has been in the forefront of suggesting these policies, aimed at creating a European Community capable of competing with other trading blocks, notably the US and Japan. Defending European values requires a strong single currency, for example, that can displace the dollar on international currency markets; or an active European security policy that can defend European interests independently of the Americans.

A Franco-German directorate?

Franco-German reconciliation underpins the history of the European Union. Even during their numerous episodes of mutual misunderstanding, French and German leaders have repeatedly expressed their belief in continuing European unification, and in the decisive role that the German Chancellor and the French President must perform in this process. Disagreement over specific policies, and even over more fundamental aspects of the European integration process (such as the finer details of monetary and political union, or foreign policy) can not detract from this belief that Franco-German cooperation is critical to the future of Europe. Personal relations between French and German leaders have always been important. The Franco-German relationship works best as an informal, often invisible compact, driven by networks of officials sharing common understandings and engaged in inter-elite bargaining and policy learning (Webber, 1999). French and German leaders have figured prominently as the driving force of the Franco-German relationship. There is an understanding that French and German leaders will attempt to reach agreement where possible, even against their initial preferences.

Ever since 1963, it has become commonplace to refer to the Franco-German 'couple' as an axis upon which closer European integration turns, or as the 'motor' providing leadership of the European integration project. At times, the Franco-German relationship has seemed to be a powerful axis, with which all other European powers must compose. In the 1980s (Single European Act) and 1990s (Maastricht Treaty), moves towards closer European political integration and cooperation were dependent upon Franco-German agreement. Metaphors of the Franco-German motor or axis are, however, partially misleading as they are ahistorical. We need a full historical appreciation of the role of the Franco-German relationship, how its internal functioning has varied over time and the extent to which it has able to offer leadership of the European integration project. From 1992–2002, for instance, France and Germany started from opposing positions on many of the issues facing Europe. These included, *inter alia*, the GATT/WTO negociations (in 1993 and 1999), CAP reform (in 1993 and 1999), the Atlantic Alliance, Yugoslavia, Bosnia, enlargement, financing the EU and the weight of the respective countries within the EU institutions (at the Nice summit in 2000). Chirac's re-election as President in 2002, followed shortly after by Schröder's surprise victory in Germany appeared to breathe new life into a relationship that looked moribund at the Nice Summit in December 2000. And yet, faced with stiff resistance from Spain and Poland, France and Germany were unable to impose agreement on the new European Constitution at the Brussels summit of December 2003.

The case for Franco-German leadership is strong, but should not go unanswered. The governance of the EU is inherently complicated and militates against the emergence of clear leadership structures such as an overarching Franco-German alliance. The metaphor of the Franco-German motor underplays the complexities of European integration. There are too many other bilateral and multilateral relationships. The Franco-German relationship can perform a powerful agenda-setting role in the right circumstances. Its leadership is most effective when it is encouraged by other states to be proactive. We note, finally, that for most of the time, French leaders have been more insistent about the need for joint Franco-German leadership of the European integration project than their German counterparts, for whom alternative coalitions are available.

A multi-speed, rather than an enlarged Europe

France has always been suspicious of EU enlargement. This has manifested itself at each widening of the Community to include new members (1973, 1981, 1986, 1995, 2004). For France, 'widening' the Community is usually felt to be incompatible with its 'deepening' and its construction as an entity capable of imposing common policies. French leaders have also believed that widening dilutes French authority within the institutions of the European Union and its influence within and beyond Europe. France's main partner Germany has supported both widening and deepening. However, France has been powerless to prevent successive widenings of the European Union, most notably that of 1995, which introduced Sweden, Austria and Finland to the European club, and that of 2004, which added a further ten members (mainly from the former Communist states of central and eastern Europe). Faced with the inability to control the evolution of the European Union, French leaders have called for 'enhanced cooperation' in the sphere of monetary policy, foreign and security policy, defence, and home affairs. Faced with the failure to adopt the European Constitution at the Brussels summit in December 2003, President Chirac called publicly for 'pioneer groups' to be formed amongst the most advanced states to push ahead with integration. This call was not echoed by Germany.

A strong Europe with weak institutions?

There is an inherent tension between substantive and procedural views of Europe. In substantive terms, France has always wanted a strong Europe. A strong Europe signifies a cultural attachment to European values, the advocacy of a Europe prepared to protect its industry and agriculture, to engage in ambitious common European policies and – under progressive French leadership – to recover international prestige. In procedural terms, there has often been a gulf between the European policy ambition of French governments and the supranational institutional adaptation of the EC/EU called for by countries such as Germany (Cole, 2001a). Though French governments have accepted – some would say instigated – major shifts to a more integrated European polity, the dominant representation of European integration in France has been largely synonymous with a state-centric notion of a strong Europe, with power channelled through national institutions and delegated, where appropriate, to weak European institutions. This elucidates the intellectual tradition of the Fifth Republic which, applied to Europe, has been based on the primacy of national sovereignty in opposition to doctrines of federalism. French politicians for long resisted any strengthening of the European Union's supranational institutions –

the European Commission and the European Parliament – and there remains deep unease with the 'foreign' concept of federalism which runs against the grain of French republican traditions.

In spite of the federalist rhetoric of men such as Jacques Delors, French politicians initially displayed limited enthusiasm in relation to extending the powers of the European Union's supranational institutions, the European Commission and the European Parliament. French Presidents have traditionally preferred an intergovernmental institutional approach, which preserves their own decision-making power in relation to European policy. But they have also espoused common interventionist European policies when these have favoured French interests, and have to some extent accepted supranational extensions of the EUs authority in the broader interests of European union (as in the Single European Act, the Maastricht Treaty (1992), the Amsterdam Treaty (1997) and the Nice Treaty (2001)). French approaches are more flexible than they often appear. The French vision of grandeur – Europe as an extension of France – would be meaningless without a stronger European Union, if necessary one in which the French could occasionally be placed in a minority. France needs the EU to develop or face the consequences of a loss of international influence.

Though the legacy of Gaullism remains highly influential, the debate has moved on since the paradigmatic shift of the mid-1980s. By the end of the century the mainstays of traditional French understandings in Europe had been challenged in several important respects. The most important of these were: German unification and its aftermath, which altered the internal equilibrium within the Franco-German alliance; the widening of the EU and the corresponding challenge to French policies such as CAP; the activism of individual policy entrepreneurs in areas of sensitive domestic concern (such as competition policy and public services) and an emerging referential paradigm which challenged many French conceptions about the role and nature of the European Union. Let us now consider how Europeanisation has had an impact upon domestic French politics.

13.4 France and Europeanisation

There is common agreement that European integration has called into question many features associated with the traditional model of French politics and policies (Gueldry, 2001; Cole and Drake, 2000; Ladrech, 1994). This process has not been limited to France, but is driving change across European countries. It is difficult, however, to disentangle the impact of European integration from other causes of policy change, such as economic globalisation, changing policy fashions and endogenous political reforms.

What is Europeanisation?

The best working definition of Europeanisation remains that offered by Ladrech (1994: 70), namely: 'Europeanization is an incremental process reorienting the direction and shape of politics to the degree that EC political and economic dynamics become part of the organizational logic of national politics and policy-making'. Elsewhere, I have identified three main uses of Europeanisation: as an independent variable driving policy and institutional change, as a form of emulative policy transfer, and as a smokescreen for domestic reform (Cole and Drake, 2000; Cole, 2001b).

As an independent variable, Europeanisation drives policy and institutional change. Identifying the impact of European integration is relatively easy. In Chapter 5, we ascribed the increased judicialisation of French politics in part to the importance of a supranational legal order represented by the European Union and other international organisations. As an independent variable, it can be demonstrated that the European Union has produced policy change in specific policy sectors. This is the case in the examples of industrial policy and public services that are considered below. The regulatory policy style of the European Union can conflict with the policy norms prevalent in member states. The role of individual commissioners as policy entrepreneurs, such as Leon Brittan or Karel van Miert in the sphere of competition policy, has highlighted the tension between EU regulatory norms and national political traditions. We saw in Chapter 12 how the institutional architecture of EMU runs against the grain of French traditions of 'economic government'. Such a process might be described as 'EUisation', insofar as it refers to the impact of the institutions, actors and policies of the European Union on its member states.

At a rather more subtle level, Europeanisation can be used to signify lesson-drawing and benchmarking. In the mid-1990s, when France was making determined efforts to meet the convergence criteria for participation in the single currency, the London *Economist* ventured the belief that 'the secret to understanding French politics in the 1990s lies across the Rhine'. French economic policy had been driven since 1983 by a determined effort to match Germany in terms of economic performance, a precondition for preserving French rank as a pre-eminent European power. As we saw in Chapter 12, the French model – based on centralism, state intervention in economic management, high inflation, and growth – had given ground to a German model, with its insistence on low inflation, high productivity, central bank independence and a strong currency.

As a form of emulative policy transfer, Europeanisation is perhaps a misnomer. The process whereby member states are influenced by strong national models within their midst is demonstrated clearly in the monetary sphere, with the German model of monetary policy management acting as a benchmark for others. Best practice and a desire to imitate the most successful can produce a type of institutional isomorphism (Radaelli, 1997). Insofar as this involves importing models from a non-native political culture, this can also be considered as a form of Europeanisation. In a more indirect sense, the European perspective has affected cognitive assumptions about national and European models. French public policy has become less self-sufficient, far more embedded in interdependent structures, and French elites have been more willing to engage in policy learning and to experiment with new discursive forms.

Europeanisation has also been used as a smokescreen for domestic political strategies. Dyson and Featherstone (1999) demonstrate very convincingly how an advocacy coalition of conservative economic liberals in the French Trésor and central bank officials promoted economic and monetary union in the 1980s as a means of pursuing an orthodox liberal economic policy and modernising the French economy. Others have established how the European 'constraint' made it easier to implement difficult domestic reforms. Administrative modernisers in France, Italy and elsewhere used Europe as a powerful domestic political resource for driving through change (Lequesne, 1993, 1996; Radaelli, 1997). Conforming with the Maastricht convergence critieria provided an opportunity to cut public expenditure and raise taxes; the Italian case was exemplary in this respect. Overdue reforms could be laid at the door of the European Union.

Armed with our fairly straightforward definition, how best can we understand Europeanisation in contemporary France? We now consider the impact of Europeanisation upon French institutions and actors, public policies and public opinion.

Europeanisation, institutions and actors

The development of the European Union has challenged the policy style and political capacity of existing institutional actors. French European policy has become less obviously the domain of the French presidency than traditionally described. In domestic politics, presidential pre-eminence in European affairs was so pronounced that Europe was considered to form part of a 'reserved sector', and the main European decisions have been taken by French Presidents. Thus, President de Gaulle launched the Fouchet plan, decreed the 'empty chair' policy and negotiated the Luxembourg compromise. President Pompidou agreed to the accession of Britain, Ireland and Demark to the Community. President Giscard d'Estaing accepted direct elections to the European Parliament and the creation of the European Council. President Mitterrand agreed the reduced British budgetary contribution, and played a major role in negotiating the Single European Act and the Maastricht Treaty. The EMU decision was brought about as a result of strong political leadership on behalf of President Mitterrand (Dyson, 1997), while President Chirac ensured that France signed the Amsterdam Treaty in 1997 and (with premier Jospin) the Nice Treaty in 2000. Presidential pre-eminence, however, does not imply that French Presidents determine French policy towards Europe in isolation from other French political actors and institutions. The President of the Republic might be the most important actor, but others are also influential: the Prime Minister, individual ministers, high-ranking civil servants, representatives of French companies. Always overstated, moroever, the hyper-presidentialist thesis has become less tenable with the changing political environment since the 1980s (the push to more supranational forms of decision-making and closer integration), the inherent fragmentation of the EU policy process, and repeated instances of 'cohabitation'.

French European policy is officially managed by the body known as the General Secretariat of the Interministerial Committee (SGCI), an interministerial bureaucratic agency charged with coordinating French governmental responses to the European Union, and formally attached to the Prime Minister's office (Lequesne, 1993, 1996; Harmsen, 1999). There have been determined attempts to centralise the coordination of French policy on EU-related matters through the SGCI. Indeed, the SCGI provides a model of strong, centralised EU coordination rivalled only by the British and the Danish (Wright, 1996). It attempts to anticipate EU policy initiatives, to coordinate interministerial responses, and to formulate common policy positions and influence the EU policy agenda. But even in the French case, efforts at central coordination have run up against the inherent fragmentation of the EU policy-making process. Conflicts of interest can occur between the SGCI – imbued with an administrative coordinating logic – and the French Permanent Representation in Brussels, demanding more flexibility to adapt to a rapidly changing policy environment. Moreover, national ministries (and even more presidential advisers) are often reluctant to submit to an interministerial structure such as the SGCI. Direct relationships between ministerial and Commission officials can hamper efforts at central coordination; as can deeply ingrained rivalries within the French administration, and even direct relationships between Commission officials and subnational actors (such as regional prefects, representatives of the regional councils, and local politicians). Finally, the SGCI does not substitute itself for political decisions. The principal policy decisions of the Mitterrand presidency, for instance, were taken by Mitterrand himself, rather than by advisers or officials. The SGCI was not obviously involved at any stage of the EMU decision, though others were (in the Trésor and central bank notably) (Dyson and Featherstone, 1999).

The Maastricht Treaty (1992) represented an important staging post of Europeanisation in several respects. The idea of a European citizenship enshrined in the Maastricht Treaty broke the organic link between the nation and legal citizenship in the French Jacobin tradition (Ladrech, 1994). The Maastricht Treaty also made timid moves towards redressing the 'democratic deficit' at both French and EU levels. At the EU level, the powers of the European parliament were strengthened in important respects. In the case of France, the constitutional amendment of 1992 allowed the National Assembly and the Senate to vote 'resolutions' on European laws, rather than merely expressing 'opinions', although the French Constitutional Council subsequently adjudged that parliament could not undermine the government's prerogatives in negotiating European laws. These parliamentary provisions were strengthened during the prolonged parliamentary debates on the Amsterdam Treaty, finally ratified (after constitutional amendment) in March 1999.

Europeanisation has had a major impact upon the role and perspectives of the French higher civil service and the system of *grands corps* (Thoenig, 1996). Europeanisation has proved a major challenge for the *corps* across three separate dimensions: those of cognitive assumptions, policy styles, and patterns of interest intermediation. The cognitive world of the French higher civil service was classically one of centralised elitism and organisational self-sufficiency;

members of the *grands corps* could not admit any external authority that could challenge the principles of the French state. There was a close relationship between conceptions of sovereignty, the unified and indivisible state, a narrowly recruited politico-administrative elite and a bureaucratic model of policy-making, in which the *grands corps* dominated. The economic U-turn of 1983, followed by the Single European Act (1986) and the Maastricht Treaty (1992) had a salutary effect on French civil servants (Lequesne, 1996). The extent of France's economic and institutional interdependence was fully driven home by the integrationist agenda of the 1980s and early 1990s, when Europeanisation came to be regarded by economic and administrative modernisers as an opportunity to help modernise an ossified French administration, an over-protected economy and a conservative society. In 1989 even the Council of State – the most prestigious of the *grands corps* – finally gave up its resistance to the primacy of EU law.

The French system of 'sectoral corporatism' has also been weakened (Fontaine, 1996). The centrality of the *grands corps* in the French pattern of interest intermediation has been undermined from above (notably with the emergence of new interlocutors in the European Commission, and the European Parliament) and from below (where, as a result of the decentralisation reforms of the 1980s, professional interests have improved access to sub-national actors). The preparations for economic and monetary union, moreover, introduced new policy actors into the fray, most notably the French central bank. The independence of the French central bank after 1993 (and the European central bank since 1999) removed executive control over instruments of monetary policy such as interest rates. Central bank independence appeared to have strengthened the role of monetary policy technocrats at the expense both of the Finance Ministry, and of the traditional political leadership (Guyomarch, 1998).

We referred in Chapter 5 to the enhanced judicialisation of French politics. This is derived in part from the ongoing consequences of France's membership of the European Union. As Europeanisation has deepened, France's legal obligations have extended into new policy areas. New institutions have come to the forefront of domestic French politics, and older institutions have been forced to re-evaluate their role.

The most important 'new' institution is the European Court of Justice (ECJ), created by the Treaty of Rome in 1957. The ECJ is the highest legal body in the EU. It has responsibility in three main areas. It can hear actions against member states brought by the Commission and/or other member states (the Commission against France over British beef, for example). It can review the actions of EU institutions. Member states can ask the ECJ to make rulings on aspects of EU law. Within France, the ECJ has a two-fold domestic importance. It can decide for itself whether French law is compatible with EU law (auto-saisine) and it sets judicial standards for the courts in France. The ECJ can (and does) strike down national decisions that are in conflict with EU law. French courts have used the ECJ in two distinct ways. The Courts have asked the ECJ to make rulings about the applicability of EU law in France. There were twelve such occasions in 2000 (from the regional courts of appeal, the Council of State and the Court of Cassation). The Courts have also used ECJ rulings to make case law (Elgie, 2003).

The ECJ has been a powerful force promoting 'spillover' (Costa, 2001). The Court has tended to give a generous interpretation to EU powers in the treaties. The ECJ affirmed the character of the EU as a legal order in a judgement as early as 1964 (Knapp and Wright, 2001). Its rulings in the area of competition policy have proved especially uncomfortable for France.

Europeanisation has also forced older institutions to re-evaluate their role. The Council of State ignored the principle of the supremacy of EU law for many years after signing the Treaty of Rome. According to Drake (2004), there were two consequences of this: France's elite legal establishment has had a poor training in EU law, and France's poor record of transposition of European directives took root. This position changed in a series of judgements in the late 1980s and early 1990s (the 1989 Nicolo judgment in particular). The supremacy of EU law was finally given a constitutional basis as a result of the Maastricht Treaty. In its judgement on the Maastricht Treaty, the Constitutional Council accepted that France can accept transfers of competencies to permanent international organisations. Since 1992, European Union decisions are enforceable directly through the French courts.

National state traditions are inevitably weakened in the melting-pot of the EU policy process. European integration has recast state administrations, introduced new spheres of EU policy intervention, and created new opportunities for variable coalitions of subnational, national and EU actors. Even more than the role of particular political institutions, a certain idea of the state and a certain policy style have been called into question by the process of European integration. This can be demonstrated by considering the impact of European integration on specific French public policies.

Europeanisation and French public policies

Changes in EU laws and treaties have modified national traditions of policy-making, and the freedom of manoeuvre of national decision makers. This is most obviously the case in two primordial policy areas brought into focus by the Single European Act and the Maastricht Treaty: EU competition policy in the former case; the implementation and management of the single currency in the latter. We considered briefly the case of the single currency in Chapter 12. The challenges posed by the evolving European policy process to traditional French policy paradigms can be demonstrated in a more direct sense in the sphere of monopoly public services and industrial policy, which we now consider.

The French notion of public service (*service public*) has traditionally gone well beyond that of universalistic welfare to include a high degree of interventionism in the industrial sphere, and the defense of monopoly utility providers such as the gas and electricity conglomerate EDF-GDF. The process of European integration directly challenges this aspect of the French state tradition, which includes a widespread positive connotation of the state as an instrument of public service, as an agent of economic development and as a guarantor of equality between French citizens. Traditional French conceptions of public service were based on the delivery of essential services by public sector monopolies (gas, electricity, rail, postal and telecommunication services, air transport), which benefited from protection against domestic or foreign competition, and which were recognised with a public service mission in French administrative law (Gugliemi, 1994). The CGT, the Communist-dominated trade union federation, occupied a strong position within many of these public sector firms (EDF-GDF, SNCF).

The implementation of EU competition policy posed a stark challenge to traditional paradigms. As it evolved during the 1980s, this model of delivering public services ran against the grain of EU competition policy. The legal basis of the European treaties is against state aids, public monopolies, and assisted sectors. In practice, however, until the mid-1980s, the Commission intervened very rarely in national practices of industrial management. This changed with the Single European Act (SEA). Strengthened by the tough competition regulations of the SEA, the Commission developed several mechanisms to break-up monopolies, based on the model of US anti-trust legislation, backed up by independent regulators. Favoured measures included privatisation, the strict regulation of state subsidies, the opening up of specific industrial sectors to competition and the creation of independent competition agencies (Thatcher, 1997, 1999). There was a strong belief that this emerging EU regulatory model was incompatible with the French public service mission. Even determined French pressure was unable to prevent the liberalisation of the telecommunications and air transport markets, traditionally the bastions of French state 'national-champions'. At best, France was able to delay opening up the energy and postal sectors to competition. Though French governments could claim some negotiating successes in the details of implementation, the direction of change was clear. At the Barcelona summit in 2002, the French agreed to open up the private domestic energy market by 2007 (the 400 largest energy consumers have been able to choose since 2001). With the return of the right to power in 2002, moreover, plans were rapidly drawn up to part-privatise EDF and GDF.

Competition policy had a spillover effect in the sphere of industrial policy. A belief in the need for an interventionist industrial policy was widely shared for much of the post-war period (see Chapter 12). The Socialist nationalisation programme of 1982 left the French public sector in control of the commanding heights of the French economy. The left government's (1981–6) policy of creating national champions assumed a strong state and a high degree of national economic sovereignty. There were obvious tensions between this model and the emergence of the EC as a regulatory arena from the mid-1980s onwards. The post-1986 EC regulatory framework challenged the traditional French industrial model in important respects. According to Cohen (1996) offensive protectionism, technical innovation, public procurement policies, direct state aid and long-term political support underpinned traditional French industrial policy. Most of these characteristics would have been in breach of EC competition law.

The causality of policy change is less obvious here than in the case of public service reform. Where the interventionist French state has ceded ground, this is only in part due to European regulation (for example, the privatisation of the Crédit Lyonnais bank on the orders of the European Commission). The original features of French post-war economic management (such as planning) had faded in importance long before the implementation of the Single European Act. If we except the brief 1981–3 interlude, French economic policy has been driven since the mid-1970s by an underlying European-wide convergence of macro-economic policy trends and objectives. The increasing weight of intra-EC trade has incited France to align its economic policies closely with those of its main trading partners, notably those of Germany. The about-turn of Mitterrand's Socialist government in 1982–3 should be signalled for particular attention in this respect. Though Mitterrand's governments always resisted industrial and financial privatisations, the French state began divesting itself of expensively acquired industries from 1986 onwards, first under Gaullist-led administrations (1986–8; 1993–7) and most recently under the Jospin government (1997–). Privatisation occurred as a result of the combined pressures of budgetary retrenchment, changing policy fashions and the need to build transnational industrial alliances, and only marginally as a consequence of direct EU intervention.

But the new regulatory climate nonetheless posed an ongoing challenge. French governments have repeatedly clashed with the European Commission over direct state grants to industry and on the preservation of state-owned industrial monopolies. Moreover, a limited number of privatisations were directly forced upon the French government by EU competition policy adjudication (as in the case of GAN-CIC and Crédit Lyonnais). Most important, perhaps, French advocacy of EU-wide industrial policies generally fell on deaf ears.

Public service reform illustrated the complex interplay between the persistence of ingrained national traditions, and the strains produced by exogenous policy changes. While macroeconomic and monetary policy represent a plausible case of emulative policy transfer (with France formally aligning itself with the German model) this is less the case in public services, or in related areas such as employment policy, where the French social model is perceived to be under attack (Cole, 2001b).

Europe, public opinion and political parties

The European debate has polarised French public opinion. In a referendum to approve or reject the Maastricht Treaty in September 1992, only a narrow majority of French voters (51/49) were in favour. It might be surmised that this total would have been higher had the referendum not widely been seen as a manoeuvre by Mitterrand to restore his flagging popularity. However we interpret the result, the 1992 referendum illustrated a degree of polarisation over the issue of further European integration which belied official discourse. Detailed analysis revealed that a majority of industrial workers, low status clerical workers and farmers opposed the Maastricht Treaty. These were the losers – or feared losers – of the modernisation process associated with further European integration. This explained why traditionally left-inclining industrial areas – such as the Nord/Pas-de-Calais – voted against the treaty. To some extent, and in different circumstances, this social division recalled Hoffmann's appreciation of a dynamic France and a static France in the Third Republic. The strongest supporters of the treaty were amongst the professional middle classes, especially in heavily urbanised areas. The regions with the strongest Yes votes were those which had most obviously benefited from closer European integration, but which maintained a distinctive identity within the French nation, such as Alsace and Brittany.

Notwithstanding the close vote in 1992, the Eurobarometer polls have generally portrayed French citizens as being amongst the most enthusiastic Europeans. In a major survey carried out in 1997, Euro-sceptical responses were in a small minority on each of the nine relevant questions, with strong majorities favouring continuing membership of the European Union, supporting the euro and advocating strengthening the powers of the European Union in relation to its member states (Cautrès and Dennis, 2002).

During the course of the 1990s, Europe emerged as an issue that cut across traditional party lines. Each of the main parties was divided on the issue, some more than others. The PCF came out strongly against the Maastricht Treaty, as creating a Europe of central bankers and capitalists; the PCF was one of the least divided parties on this issue. The PS contains the full range of policy positions on the issue of Europe and further European integration (Cole, 2001b). Since Jospin's defeat in the 2002 presidential election, factional infighting has broken out within the PS on the issue of European integration. In 2003, the two minority left-wing factions came out in opposition to the party supporting the proposed European Constitution produced by Giscard d'Estaing's Convention. The majority UMP also revealed its divisions over whether France should have abandoned the Growth and Stability Pact in November 2003. In its time, the Gaullist RPR had been the most divided of all parties, with two-thirds of RPR deputies coming out against ratification of the Maastricht Treaty in 1992. For its part, the old UDF always contained fervent pro-Europeans within its ranks, notably amongst the inheritors to the Christian Democratic tradition. Alongside a Christian Democratic vision of Europe, however, the UDF also contained economic liberals in favour of a *laissez-faire* agenda, and against a single currency, as well as ultra-conservatives such as de Villiers. The reformed 'UDF' led by Bayrou has staked out a claim to be the most pro-European party. Finally, while the FN was predictably against the Maastricht Treaty, with its challenge to national sovereignty, Le Pen claimed to be pro-European, insofar as European culture needed to be defended against the threat of invasion from non-European peoples.

| 13.5 | Concluding remarks |

The public policies, political agendas and governing styles of French political actors have all been modified by the processes of Europeanisation. We have seen that, in so far as Europeanisation is a definable process with tangible consequences, neither its pace nor its direction is entirely predictable. We can understand Europeanisation in the top-down sense of being an external constraint imposing policy change. In the policy areas surveyed, this usage of Europeanisation appeared quite convincing to explain public service reform and competition policy; but rather less cogent with respect to EMU (best understood as a nested bargain linked to German unification) or industrial policy, areas we surveyed in Chapter 12. In the sphere of public service reform and competition policy, as well as in relation to important aspects of French macro-economic management, 'Europeanisation' appears to go against the grain of a traditional French model of politics and policies. All French governments have to live with the consequences – unintended or otherwise – of the agenda-shaping decisions of the mid-1980s and early 1990s taken by President Mitterrand.

We can also understood Europeanisation in a bottom-up sense, as an extension of the domestic political project. The European level has traditionally been valued as a site for the export of French ideas, policies and personnel. Traditionally expansive French views of Europe depended upon a vision of Europe as an extension of France; hence the emphasis placed on exporting features of the French model for the benefit of others (Harmsen, 1999). Strengthening the European arena as a level of concerted public policy action was an important aspect of the Jospin government's official European policy, in part because it implied the coherence of the domestic political message and its propensity for export. The results of this attempt to export the French model have been limited, however. In the policy areas we have surveyed, we find relatively little evidence of French ideas driving change at the European level. The powerful alliance of France and Germany remains a formidable force, but even the Franco-German juggernaut was unable to force Spain and Poland to accept the European Constitution at the Brussels summit of December 2003.

The process of European integration has posed other dilemmas as well. The successive enlargements of the European Union have increased speculation over a two- or more speed Europe. The idea of a Europe of variable geometry has been proposed on and off by French politicians for over two decades. President Mitterrand made several oblique references to the possibility in the 1980s. Mitterrand's proposed European confederation of 1990 was in some senses consistent with this idea, whereby a hard core of closely integrated nations (France, Germany, Benelux, perhaps others), would be surrounded by a looser periphery. In 1994, German Chancellor Kohl's party, the CDU, argued that Europe should be composed of a 'core' of five member states (the original six minus Italy), the minimum number feasible for the introduction of a single European currency. For his part, President Chirac referred to the need to create pioneer groups in 2000 and again in 2003. Herewith lies a central dilemma for French policy-makers. It is inconceivable that France could be excluded from an inner core of nations, including by the Germans themselves. In a narrow first division of European nations, however, France runs the danger of being submerged in a Germanic sphere of influence.

These challenges of Europe and Europeanisation are amongst the most difficult that face French policy-makers at the beginning of the twenty-first century.

14 Reinventing French politics and society

14.1 Introduction

As investigated during this book, the French polity has slowly mutated under the combined impact of internal and external pressures for change. Long a country which exported its model to others – within and beyond Europe – French elites have had to integrate new ideas and practices into their patterns of domestic government. In this final chapter, we provide a series of concluding judgements about continuity and change in contemporary France. The position is a complex one, since there are countervailing pressures at work. The French political system retains features setting it apart from other European nation-states, but also faces a number of common difficulties and challenges which have brought it closer to its European neighbours.

14.2 *Exemplarité* and exceptionalism

Most specialists agree that France is a country of paradoxes. It was for long considered an exception to the norm of established western European democracies such as Britain or Germany, with their stable political systems, and their regular alternations-in-power. A great deal has been written about French exceptionalism, including in the first edition of this book (Hewlitt, 1998; Cole, 1998; Lovecy, 2000; Collard, 2002). Lovecy (2000) and Collard (2002) in particular have each undertaken detailed investigations into the geneology, uses and abuses of the concept. For Lovecy (2000), we must distinguish between two faces or readings of French exceptionalism, involving two alternative normative discourses, centred around change and resistance to change. The first school talked of the end of the French exception and looked to an optimistic future whereby peaceful and gradual internal change would fundamentally modify the conflict-ridden society inherited from the French revolution. Mendras (1989) referred to a Second French Revolution, an endogenous process that had overhauled the norms of French society and reshaped French institutions (the family, the army, the church, even the Communist Party). Furet, Juillard and Rosanvallon (1988), associated with a particular group within the Socialist Party, proclaimed the advent of the Republic of the Centre, signifying the end of ideological politics, changing political discourses (less rooted in traditional ideological referents) and the acceptance of new paradigms of economic competitiveness and social modernisation.

The message of these revisionist political sociologists was echoed in rather different terms by legal constitutionalists, who pointed to the triumph of the rule of law and the institutional embedding of legal norms in bodies such as the Constitutional Council (Cohen-Tangui, 1990). France was moving closer to other democracies – European and American – insofar as it had accepted the rise of constitutionalism as a governing ethic and embedded it within its own institutional practices. As similar processes were going on at the EU level, there was a goodness of fit between France and the emerging European polity. These writers were innovative, in that they established a revisionist critique of the French revolution itself and cast French *exemplarité* as a flawed model.

The debate on the end of French exceptionalism soon produced a vigorous reaction on the part of those who sought to defend the French model, endlessly reinvented for political or intellectual purposes. There were, broadly speaking, three assaults on the 'end of the French exception' thesis. The first was intellectual. It found its resonance in the writings of those such as Todd (1995) who argued that a deep social fracture had opened up in French society as a result of social and economic modernisation and the imposition of 'external constraints' on French society. Deepening European integration, in particular, had created a new cleavage within French society that separated the haves from the have-nots. At a more scientific level, academic experts pointed to the persistence of specific national traits, especially in relation to French capitalism (Cohen, 1996). Studies inspired broadly by historical institutionalist approaches found in France an ideal terrain to discover path dependent processes and to refute arguments based on convergence (Thatcher, 1999). At a more explicitly political level, politicians from across the political spectrum welcomed the calling into question of the 'external constraints' that had justified every government activity during late Mitterrandism. Whether from the left (Chevènement) or the right (Chirac) a strongly defensive political appeal was made in favour of the French model, phrased in terms of defending national capitalism, protecting the social welfare model under attack from invisible forces and supporting the integrative model of citizenship.

The third assault against the 'end of the French exception' thesis came from within academia, to some extent setting essentialists against comparativists. For comparativists, the claim of French exceptionalism is tautological. Each country can lay a claim to its own form of national distinctiveness. In the 1980s, Italy was 'a difficult democracy'; in the ensuing decade, it became even more difficult, as the Italian Republic collapsed amidst popular revolt against generalised corruption and political instability that far surpassed anything witnessed in France. For British premier Thatcher (1979–90), the whole of the European continent appeared out of step; the powerful coalition of heads of the major European states against the Iron Lady suggested that the UK was really the exceptional power. Similar judgements could be reached at with respect to other European nations. Germany, for instance, proved exceptional in a rather different sense, insofar as the German model became (for a while) a benchmark for other countries of the Union, particularly in monetary and economic terms. If each country is distinctive, logically none is exceptional.

This third criticism is well founded, though much of the writing on French exceptionalism was implicitly comparative. The 'French exception' has had the merit of stimulating a debate about the nature of the French polity and society and has phrased this in implicitly comparative terms. We must acknowledge the descriptive utility offered by the French exception. Notions of the French exception have a useful heuristic value, insofar as they describe an assortment of features – some contradictory within their own terms of reference – commonly associated with a traditional model of French politics and policy. They also elucidate a particular type of political discourse that remains deeply embedded within French discursive and ideological frames. The rather paradoxical alchemy of exceptionalism (France as unique) and universality (France embodying human values applicable everywhere) describes the perception that many French institutions and actors have of their role. Though the 'end of French exceptionalism' debate was excessively normative, we need some frame against which to measure continuity and change within contemporary France.

Using an inductive rather than a deductive approach, in the previous thirteen chapters we have described an orthodox French model of politics and policy-making and set out the principal challenges to this model. The orthodox model of French politics and policies was an ideal type and has been subjected to many pressures for change since the late 1970s. For the purposes of clarity, we identified the following core features of the orthodox model:

- a powerful (though fragmented) central state, a legacy of the process of nation-building;

- a belief in the general will and a strict separation between the public and private spheres, producing a distrust of intermediary institutions and a suspicion of civil society;

- a model of top-down territorial administration based on the uniformity of rules, though in practice accepting exceptions to rules;

- an incestuous and relatively homogeneous political, administrative and economic elite;

- a tradition of state intervention (*dirigisme*) in the economic and industrial sphere;

- an ideologically charged political discourse, the legacy of France's past revolutionary tradition and late industrialisation;

- the existence of powerful anti-system movements challenging the regime such as the French Communist Party;

- an unwillingness of groups to engage in face to face contact, hence the weakness of a bargaining culture;

- a model of republican citizenship based on formal (rather than substantive) equality, a valorisation of society, but a rejection of community;

■ an awkward posture within the European Community, aimed at claiming a leadership role for France within Europe.

The themes we have studied throughout the past thirteen chapters are each revealing of countervailing pressures. We conclude *French Politics and Society* by presenting the case for continuity, the case for change and our preferred position which combines elements of both.

14.3	French national distinctiveness

A belief in national distinctiveness is inherent in the notion of the *sui generis* French exception (Lovecy, 2000). It is also present in some new institutionalist writing and underpins the notion of historical path dependency. Societies and their political systems evolve according to nationally distinctive patterns. Specific political cultures, different state traditions and complex popular beliefs and symbols that only have meaning within the confines of the nation-state shape them. Change occurs, but it can only be comprehended by reference to established institutional rules, procedures and patterns of belief (March and Olsen, 1989; Hall, 1986; Thatcher, 1999; Pierson, 1996). These forms of argument based on national distinctiveness are those which sit the most easily with French exceptionalism. They do not even require a comparative dimension. They emphasise the persistence of state structures and relationships in spite of the changing external and internal environment.

In the case of France, national distinctiveness appears especially pertinent in relation to models of citizenship, ideas about the state and public service, the separation of public and private spheres, the difficulties of dealing with minorities, the refusal of cultural differentiation, the suspicion of regional languages and territorial identities. The republican model is defective in important senses, but it provides a framework for making sense of a complex modern society when other frameworks (for example Anglo-Saxon economic liberalism or 'communitarianism') run against the grain of domestic political traditions. Reinventing and modernising an existing model is a more feasible enterprise than abandoning it and importing new frameworks.

At times in the book, we have observed a powerful coalition of French institutions, ideas and interests all reinforcing each other and resisting change. National, path dependent processes are important for understanding many endogenous traits. The orthodox French model appears alive and well in relation to the defence of French language, and in the universalist message of French culture, for example. The French model of citizenship is one based on integration, or assimilation, rather than recognition of cultural diversity. These attitudes are determined by past experiences of nation, state and Republic building, and by the defence of established institutions and interests. Consistent with the weight of legal traditions, French governments have tended to look to the law to provide solutions for societal problems. The 2004 law forbidding pupils from wearing 'ostentatious' religious symbols in school (the veil, the kippa, the cross) was a perfect example of this tendency to look to rules to solve the contradictions of a multicultural society. For foreign observers, France seemed to be forever playing out the French Revolution or the Church and state conflicts of the eighteenth and nineteenth centuries. The principal challenge for French decision-makers in the twenty-first century is to adapt a republican model constructed in the very different circumstances of the nineteenth century to the new age. The underlying elements of continuity are often framed in defensive terms, timeless qualities (such as *laicité*) to be enforced by the law, rather than embraced by popular assent.

Continuity is also ensured by deeper underlying structures that are not specifically linked to a particular political regime, but in some cases predate the modern republican form of government. Political and ideological beliefs can span several political generations, or even regimes. In relation to institutions, we must distinguish between the Fifth Republic as a political system and deeper institutions that are not specific to a particular regime. As far as the Fifth Republic is concerned, the converging of the presidential and parliamentary majorities in the 2002 elections and the subordinate relationship of the latter to the former would appear to signal a return to a pre-eminently presidential practice. The underlying legitimacy of the system is shaped by the choices made by all key actors in favour of the presidential election as the decisive election in the Fifth Republic. The case for continuity is strengthened once we move from the formal institutional superstructure to regarding deeper institutions, those which go to the heart of the state and which defend the French state tradition. We identify the civil service (*fonction publique*) and the Council of State as two such forces. As developed in Chapters 6 and 7, these institutions are inclined to resist changes that challenge a rather conservative republican uniformity. The most powerful institutions at the heart of the French state have clung on to symbols of sovereignty, wherever possible. When so much policy-making escapes the control of national governors, those areas that remain within the preserve of the nation-state are jealously guarded. While the state has lost some functions, it has also developed more efficient ways of central steering. One interpretation of decentralisation is that the state has divested itself of difficult, politically unrewarding policy areas (such as social policy) in order better to concentrate on its core tasks. The French state tradition remains vigorous, demonstrated by the continuing control of the *grands corps* over much public policy and the pattern of recruitment of political, administrative and economic elites.

Existing institutions are defended by sets of interests that occupy powerful positions within the French state (and which rely on the state to promote their interests in Brussels and elsewhere). The role of the farm lobby, for instance, is very well documented in shaping the position adopted by French governments of all persuasions in international arenas, whether the European Union, the World Trade Organisation or elsewhere. The teachers are another body that can be relied upon to resist change. Underpinning institutions and interests are a set of well-defined ideas, about the appropriate relationships between politics and economics, about the role of the individual and the society, about the need for equal treatment to which political discourse needs to appeal. These ideas generally consolidate existing preferences and practices. Ideas – such as the general will, equal treatment, solidarity – support the concatenation of interests and institutions that promote stability, to the extent that sectional groups seek to capture these ideas in order to defend their own causes. The equality and neutrality of the state in particular forms an important part of the French republican tradition.

From the perspective of these embedded endogenous traits, French distinctiveness appears alive and well. The continuity of the French model is provided by an interconnecting set of institutions, interests and ideas that provide long-term cohesion and allow internal and external changes to be interpreted in manners that are comprehensible to the French.

14.4 Political and policy change

However much the French Council of State might regret diminishing state sovereignty, it cannot by itself reverse this process. Even the powerful French state no longer controls its own destiny in an increasingly interdependent world. In the 2000s, there are comparable forces provoking change in most European countries. These include global economic change, the impact of European integration, pressures for economic convergence, a calling into question of certain types of political institution and the changing role of the state. As a leading European nation with a particular state tradition and historical legacy, these pressures have produced at least as many tensions in France as in any other European state.

Both European integration and globalisation have called into question many features associated with the traditional model of French politics and policies. As we saw in Chapter 13, Europeanisation imposes change even in spheres once considered as core areas of state sovereignty, such as public services and monopoly capitalism. As the process of European integration has gathered pace, the role of the French state in economic management has diminished. In the sphere of industrial policy, the interventionist state has ceded ground under the pressure of European regulation. Even here, there are countervailing pressures: we saw in Chapter 12 how, under the Jospin government, privatisation programmes were formulated in terms of adapting (rather than abandoning) state industrial policy. On balance, the French state has had to cede ground to the supranational appetites of the European Union in a range of policy sectors, where it is no longer able to act alone.

The ground is familiar and we discussed Europeanisation is some detail in the previous chapter. We will focus here on the complex and paradoxical relationship with globalisation (Brender, 2002; Gordon and Meunier, 2002; McClean and Milner, 2001). There is a mainstream ideological reluctance in France to accept the ascendancy of 'neo-liberalism': that is, economic liberalism and unregulated international free markets. One of the few social movements to have experienced real growth in the past few years is the antiglobalisation movement, symbolised by ATTAC and by Jose Bové, each interpreted as a defence of a particular vision of the French model. Globalisation challenges the traditional French model in several ways. The global – American – model poses an obvious threat to a French culture that has always proclaimed itself universalistic, quite apart from the menace caused to the French language by a rampant American English. In the economic arena, global capitalism lessens the reliance of French business on the French state and increases the importance of international capital flows, cross-shareholdings and the international strategies of French groups (themselves very proficient at playing the global card). Inward investment decisions taken by foreign companies can have a major impact on French employment levels, but foreign companies are not usually willing to channel their investment in accordance with French regional policy objectives. Globalisation also threatens well-entrenched domestic interests, especially in two very influential areas: culture and agriculture. In culture, French governments fought long and hard to obtain a 'cultural exception' in the 1993 GATT round and are resisting attempts to dilute this in the current round of World Trade Organisation (WTO) talks. In agriculture, French governments of all persuasions have fought a rearguard action in the EU and the WTO to defend the interests of domestic farmers through export credits and production subsidies. In short, globalisation not only lessens the capacity of the state to act in a voluntaristic manner, but also its ability to protect its key client groups.

Rather than specific policies, however, Europeanisation and globalisation can both appear to go against the grain of *une certaine idée de la France*. The belief in the universal mission of French civilisation is menaced by European integration and by globalisation once the European construction is a melting pot of European cultural influences, rather than a mirror to reflect French grandeur or a policy space to regulate world capitalism.

Change is by no means limited to 'external' factors impacting upon domestic politics. There has been some degree of reflexivity upon past practice and a gradual shift in domestic frames of reference. One fundamental change relates to the diminishing – though by no means vanquished – power of ideology to mobilise political action. Despite the plurality within both left and right, until (and including) 1981 each political camp was able to mobilise by referring to distinctive sets of values. Whichever side one was on, the sense of identity and of belonging to one camp or another was strong. Since the Socialist experience in office (1981–6, 1988–93, 1997–2002), and especially since the end of the Cold War, the ideological bearings of left and right have become far more confused. Put simply, the left/right cleavage is of less significance in French politics today than it was in 1980. The general ideological climate has changed, both in France and elsewhere, as have perceptions of the possibilities of governmental action. Marxism in particular has lost its attraction for the French left, as have May '68-inspired ideas of 'autogestion'. Values have tended to become more instrumental, elections more prone to the exigencies of political marketing and the circumstances of particular elections.

There are limits to this weakening capacity of ideology to drive action. There persists a vibrant far-left, revolutionary tradition that now seeks expression in the antiglobalisation movement, the LCR or LO, rather than the Communist Party. In comparative terms, the discursive register of politics in France remains more ideologically structured than in the United Kingdom or Germany. There are important areas of non decision-making, where no government dares venture until forced to by impending crisis (the case of pensions or public sector reform, for instance). In comparison to earlier periods of French history, however, the capacity of ideas to drive politics has diminished.

The 2002 electoral series posed starkly the issue of political legitimacy (Perrineau and Ysmal, 2002). Let us recall some simple facts. Chirac and Jospin, the announced second-round contenders, obtained only just over one-third of votes and one-quarter of registered electors between them. France's historic political families were each challenged on 21 April: Communists, Socialists, Gaullists, Liberals, Christian Democrats, even Greens. None of these candidates performed as well as they might have expected and many electors were dissatisfied with all of them. The strong performance of the far left and far right candidates, the high abstention rate (at 28.30 per cent a record in any presidential election) and the general dispersion of votes to candidates not generally considered to be genuine presidential contenders (such as St Josse, Chevènement and others) were all part of this trend. Once again, the election went against the incumbent government, as has every decisive election since 1978 (except where, as in 1981, 1988 and 2002, parliamentary elections have followed shortly after the presidential contest). The exceptional nature of Chirac's second-round victory on 5 May 2002 could not conceal his poor performance of 21 April (19.1 per cent) and this provided a narrow basis for holding all the key offices of the Republic. While clarifying institutional practice in a pro-presidential sense, the electoral series of 2002 left many questions unanswered, the most important of which was whether France's new rulers would be able to build bridges with that sizeable proportion of the French electorate that appears alienated from political processes and takes refuge in support for extremes.

14.5 Reinventing modern France

As a general, though not absolute, rule, external factors drive changes that are initially resisted by variable internal constellations of institutions, interests and ideas. External changes need to be domesticated before they enter into the domestic *acquis*. Even radical changes can be accepted, as long as they are justified in terms of reference that are comprehensible and acceptable to French society. Thus, two decades ago, the Mauroy and Fabuis governments justified the economic U-turn by appealing to social solidarity and the necessary modernisation of France, both themes that are broadly acceptable in terms of domestic reference frames (Gaffney, 1989). European directives that French governments disprove of, but feel necessary to implement are justified in terms of the European general interest, a familiar discursive register. Europeanisation can also be used as a means of blame avoidance, an unwelcome constraint that ties domestic hands (Dyson and Featherstone, 1999). As French governments usually seek to present Europe in a positive light, they will, by and large, embrace Europeanisation as a positive signal to accept change (even when they have fiercely resisted change behind closed doors). French governments will make the necessary discursive gymnastic effort for Europeanisation, but not for globalisation, which is represented in terms of the new external adversary. Europeanisation is the recipient of French traditions of affirmative public action, even though the French view is often not that which guides decision making within the EU (Cole, 2001b).

There is some evidence of lesson-drawing from past experience (reflexivity) and some frame reflection, but an external shock is usually needed to drive changes, which rarely manifest themselves spontaneously. Whether or not we are witnessing the end of the French exception, the political and policy space has become more complicated, in France as elsewhere. There are a number of common pressures impacting upon European nations. Each European nation has interpreted pressures in accordance with its own traditions, but these traditions have gradually been reinterpreted to take account of new realities. In the case of France, the distance travelled is far, especially in the case of macro-economic policy. The highly distinctive nature of the original model has made the ideological effort of legitimisation more difficult. As Schmidt (1999) argues, there has been a failure to develop an accompanying discourse to legitimise changes. French governors have been forced to rely on discursive tools developed at various pivotal points in French history (equality and the general will from the French revolution; *laïcité* from the clerical-republican conflicts of the nineteenth century, modernisation from the period of post-war social and economic reconstruction). None of these has equipped French governments particularly well to respond to the challenges of the third millennium. The one exception is that provided by Europeanisation, which is even more useful in domestic politics than it is as an instrument of foreign policy. There is, by and large, a goodness of fit between the prominent images of Europeanisation and the expectations and representations of the French population towards Europe and domestic politics.

National context must not be confused with a static version of national purpose. Arguments based solely on national, institutional or cultural distinctiveness – such as that of the French exception – cannot cope with policy change. French responses to change are embedded in precise contexts, but they are not literally pre-shaped. The above comments emphasise our preferred 'constructivist' position. Countries faced with comparable pressures might adopt dissimilar responses consistent with their own political traditions. The institutions, ideas and interests to which common pressures give rise can be nationally specific. This is one area of empirical investigation. Most importantly, external changes need to be legitimised by reference frames shaped according to dominant domestic discursive traditions. Change might in some respects reinforce national policy styles. Social constructivist approaches facilitate an understanding of how the craftsmanship of discourse operates in these precise circumstances. Change in French politics and policy-making is processed in accordance with recognised codes and by identifiable institutions and interests.

Change itself has gradually reshaped the nature of these codes and the policy province of these established institutions and interests. The effort to legitimise change has lagged the process of change itself.

There is a close interplay between, on the one hand, the strains produced by endogenous and exogenous policy change and, on the other, the persistence of ingrained national traditions. Equally interesting as the fact of change is the manner in which French governments have attempted to recodify change in accordance with French reference frames. The really interesting question is not the balance between continuity and change, but whether change reinforces national contextual traditions, or goes against the grain of them. To some extent, this is sector-specific. In the case of economic policy, there is a strong argument that global economic change has forced a radical rethink of the French model of macroeconomic management. In the case of education, on the other hand, there is a fairly strong argument that policy changes are path dependent; they are interpreted and managed in ways that are entirely consistent with national traditions.

As the French model becomes challenged from several directions, potential losers have rallied to its defence. Defence of the French model is most obvious in terms of public service and the public sector. In November–December 1995, a major social movement appeared to emerge out of nothing in reaction to premier Juppé's proposed reform of the social security system. As is often the case in these circumstances, the strikers articulated a range of contradictory, sectoral demands. The common plea appeared be a defensive one: to preserve features of the French model under threat from a variety of external forces. The policy responses adopted by French governments will continue to combine particular patterns of governing inherited from French history, with necessarily flexible responses to the changing circumstances of policy-making in the twenty-first century.

Bibilography

Aeschimann, E. & Riché, P. (1996). *La Guerre de sept ans – histoire secrète du franc fort*. Paris: Calmann-Lévy.

Alliné, J.-P. & Carrier, R. (Eds) (2002). *Le Préfet et le développement local*. Paris: Dalloz.

Allison, M. & Heathcote, O. (Eds) (1999). *Forty Years of the Fifth Republic. Actions, Dialogues and Discourses*. Bern: Peter Lang.

Almond, G. & Verba, N. (1963). *The Civic Culture: Attitudes and Democracy in Five Nations*. Princeton: Princeton University Press.

Ambler, J. (1985). Neo-Corporatism and the politics of French education. *West European Politics*, **8** (3).

Ameller, M. (1994). *L'Assemblée nationale*. Paris: PUF.

Andersen, R. & Evans, J. (2003). Values, cleavages and party choice in France, 1988–1995. *French Politics*, **1** (1).

Anderson, R.D. (1977). *France 1870–1914*. London: Routledge and Kegan Paul.

Andolfatto, D. & Labbé, D. (2000). *Sociologie des syndicats*. Paris: La Découverte.

Andrews, W. & Hoffmann, S. (Eds) (1981). *The Fifth Republic at Twenty*. Albany, New York: State University of New York Press.

Appleton, A. (2000). The new social movement phenomenon: placing France in comparative perspective. In R. Elgie (Ed) *The Changing French Political System*, 57–75, London: Frank Cass.

Archambault, E. (1997). *The Non-profit Sector in France*. Manchester: Manchester University Press.

Ashford, D. (1982). *British Dogmatism and French Pragmatism: central-local policy making in the welfare state*. London: Allen and Unwin.

Avril, P. (1992). *Le Conseil constitutionnel*. Paris: Montchrestien.

Baguenard, J. (1996). *Le Sénat*. Paris: PUF.

Balme, R. (1999). *Les Politiques de néo-régionalisme*. Paris: Economica.

Balme, R., Faure, A. & Mabileau, A. (Eds) (1999). *Les Nouvelles politiques locales: dynamiques de l'action publique*. Paris: Presses de Science Po.

Banchoff, T. (1999). National identity and EU legitimacy in France and Germany. In T. Banchoff & M.P. Smith (Eds) (1999). *Legitimacy and the European Union. The contested polity*. London: Routledge.

Barthélemy, M. (2000). *Associations: un nouvel âge de participation*. Paris: Presses de Sciences Po.

Bartolini, S. (1984). Institutional constraints and party competition in the French party system. *West European Politics*, **7** (4).

Basso, J. (1983). *Les Groupes de pression*. Paris: PUF.

Bauchard, P. (1986). *La Guerre des deux roses*. Paris: Grasset.

Bauchet, P. (1986). *Le Plan dans l'économie française*. Paris: Economica.

Bauer, M. (1988). The politics of state-directed privatisation: the case of France. *West European Politics*, **11** (4).

Baumont, S. (1991). Le régime présidentiel en question. *Cosmopolitiques*, **19**.

Bell, D.S. (2000). *Parties and Democracy in France. Parties Under Presidentialism*. Aldershot: Ashgate.

Bell, D.S. (2002). *French Politics Today*. Manchester: Manchester University Press.

Bell, D.S., Johnson, D. & Morris, P. (Eds) (1990). *Biographical Dictionary of French Political Leaders since 1870*. Hemel Hempstead: Harvester Wheatsheaf.

Bell, L. (2001). Interpreting collective action: methodology and ideology in the analysis of social movements. *Modern and Contemporary France*, **9** (2).

Belorgey, J.-M. (1991). *Le Parlement à refaire*. Paris: Gallimard.

Bénéton, P. & Touchard, J. (1970). Les interprétations de la crise de mai–juin 1968. *Revue française de science politique*, **20** (3).

Bensahel, L. (Ed) (1998). *L'Economie de la France face aux défis du 21ème siècle*. Grenoble: Presses Universitaires de Grenoble.

Berger, S. (1981). *Organising Interests in Western Europe*. Cambridge, MA: Harvard University Press.

Beriss, D. (1990). Scarves, schools and segregation: The foulard affair. *French Politics and Society*, **8** (1).

Bernard, P. (1992). La Fonction préfectorale au coeur de la mutation de notre société. *Revue Administrative*, **45** (2).

Berstein, S. (2002). *Le Chef de l'État*. Paris: Armand Colin.

Berstein, S. (1999). Nature et fonction des cultures politiques. In S. Berstein (Ed) (1999). *Les Cultures politiques en France*. Paris: Seuil.

Berstein, S., Rémond, R. & Sirinelli, J.-F. (Eds) (2003). *Les Années Giscard*. Paris: Fayard.

Berstein, S., Sirinelli, J.-F. & Rioux, J.-P. (Eds) (1994). La Culture politique en France depuis de Gaulle. *Vingtième siècle*, **44**.

Bevort, A. & Labbé, D. (1992). *La CFDT: organisation et audience depuis 1945*. Paris: Documentation Française.

Bézès, P. (2000). Les hauts fonctionnaires croient-ils à leurs mythes?. *Revue française de science politique*, **50** (2).

Biarez, S. (1989). *Le Pouvoir local*. Paris: Economica.

Bigaut, C. (Ed) (1993). *Le Président de la 5e République*. Paris: Documentation Française.

Birenbaum, G. (1992). *Le Front national en politique*. Paris: Balland.

Birnbaum, P. (1985). La fin de l'état? *Revue française de science politique*, **35** (6).

Birnbaum, P. (2003). *La France imaginée: déclin des rêves unitaires?* Paris: Gallimard.

Bloch-Lainé, A. (1999). Franco-German co-operation in foreign affairs, security and defence: a case study. In D. Webber (Ed) *The Franco-German Relationship in the European Union*. London: Routledge.

Bloch-Lainé, J.-M. & Moschetto, B. (1987). *La Politique économique de la France*. Paris: PUF.

Bocquet, D. (1996). La France et L'Allemagne. Un couple en panne d'idées. *Notes de la Fondation Saint-Simon*. February–March, 7–60.

Bodiguel, J.-L. (1990). Political and administrative traditions and the French senior civil service. *International Journal of Public Administration*, **13** (5).

Bodiguel, J.-L. & Quermonne, J.-L. (1983). *La Haute fonction publique*. Paris: Presses Universitaires de France.

Boussard, I. (1990). *Les Agriculteurs et la politique*. Paris: Economica.

Bouvet, L. (1998). La nouvelle crise de la conscience européenne: l'Europe politique entre nation et fédération. Regards français. In L. Bouvet *et al. France–Allemagne: le bond en avant*. Paris: Odile Jacob, 113–174.

Bouvet, L., Delors, J., Kluxen-Pyta, D., Lamers, K. & Rovan, J. (1998). *France–Allemagne: le bond en avant*. Paris: Odile Jacob.

Bréchon, P. (1999). *Les Partis politiques*. Paris: Montchrestien.

Bréchon, P. (2002) (Dir). *Les élections présidentielles en France: 40 ans d'histoire politique*. Paris: Documentation Francaise.

Bréchon, P., Laurent, A. & Perrineau, P. (Eds) (2000). *Les cultures politiques des Français*. Paris: Presses de Sciences Po.

Brender, A. (2002). *La France face à la mondialisation*. Paris: La Découverte.

Breuillard, M. & Cole, A. (2003). *L'École entre l'état et les collectivités locales en Angleterre et en France*. Paris: Harmattan.

Brubaker, R. (1992). *Citizenship and Nationhood in France and Germany*. Cambridge, MA: Harvard University Press.

Brunet, J.-P. (1996). *Histoire du parti communiste français: 1920–1996*. Paris: PUF.

Cameron, D.R. (1996). Exchange rate politics in France, 1981–1983: the regime-defining choices of the Mitterrand presidency. In A. Daley (Ed) *The Mitterrand Era. Policy Alternatives and Political Mobilization in France*. Basingstoke: Macmillan.

Camus, J.-Y. (1997). *Le Front national: histoire et analyses*. Paris: Laurens.

Capdeveille, J. (Ed) (1981). *France de gauche vote à droite*. Paris: Presses de la FNSP.

Carcassonne, G. (1986). Typologie des cabinets. *Pouvoirs*, **36**.

Carcassonne, G. (2000). Amendments to the French Constitution. One surprise after another. In R. Elgie (Ed) *The Changing French Political System*. London: Frank Cass.

Cautrès, B. & Dennis, B. (2002). Les Attitudes des Français à l'égard de l'union européenne: les logiques de refus. In P. Brechon, A. Laurent & P. Perrineau (Eds) *Les Cultures Politiques des Français*. Paris: Presses de Sciences Po.

Cerny, P. & Schain, M. (1985). *Socialism, the State and Public Policy in France*. London: Pinter.

Chagnollaud, D. (1996). *Le Gouvernement de la France sous la Ve République*. Paris: Fayard.

Charlot, J. (1970). *The Gaullist Phenomenon*. London: Allen & Unwin.

Charlot, J. (1983). *Les Gaullistes d'opposition*. Paris: Seuil.

Chaubrun, L. & Heriot, F. (1999). *Jean-Pierre Chevènement: biographie*. Paris: Editions du Cherche Midi.

Chenot, B. (Ed) (1985). *Le Conseil constitutionnel, 1958–85*. Paris: Economica.

Chenot, B. (1986). *Le Secrétariat général du gouvernement*. Paris: Economica.

Chevallier, J. (1996). La réforme de l'état et la conception française du service public. *Revue française d'administration publique*, **77**.

Cicchillo, R. (1990). The conseil constitutionnel and judicial review. *Tocqueville Review*, **12** (1).

Clark, D. (2000). Public service reform: a comparative West European perspective. *West European Politics*, **23** (3).

Clift, B. (2002). The political economy of the Jospin government. *Modern and Contemporary France*, **10** (3).

Clift, B. (2003). PS intra-party politics and party system change. In J. Evans (Ed) *The French Party System*. Manchester: Manchester University Press, 42–55.

Cohen, E. (1995). France: national champions in search of a mission. In J. Hayward (Ed) *Industrial Enterprise and European Integration*. Oxford: Oxford University Press.

Cohen, E. (1996). *La Tentation hexagonale. La Souveraineté à l'épreuve de la mondialisation*. Paris: Fayard.

Cohen, M. (1992). The French National Front and immigration: the appeal and the challenge. *Mediterranean Quarterly*, **3** (2).

Cohen, S. (1986). *La Monarchie nucleaire*. Paris: Hachette.

Cohen, S. (1989). *La Politique etrangère entre l'Elysée et Matignon. Politique etrangère*, **3** (89).

Cohendet, A.-M. (1993). *La Cohabitation*. Paris: PUF.

Cohen-Tangui, L. (1990). From one revolution to the next: the late rise of constitutionalism in France. *Tocqueville Review*, **12** (1).

Cole, A. (Ed) (1990). *French Political Parties in Transition*. Aldershot: Dartmouth.

Cole, A. (1993). The presidential party and the Fifth Republic. *West European Politics*, **16** (2).

Cole, A. (1995). *La France pour tous?* The French presidential election of 23 April and 7 May 1995. *Government and Opposition*, **30** (3).

Cole, A. (1997). *François Mitterrand: a Study in Political Leadership*. London: Routledge.

Cole, A. (1999). The *service public* under stress. *West European Politics*, **22** (4).

Cole, A. (2001a). *Franco-German Relations*. Harlow: Longman.

Cole, A. (2001b). National and partisan contexts of Europeanisation: the case of the French socialists. *Journal of Common Market Studies*, **39** (1).

Cole, A. (2002). A strange affair. The French presidential and parliamentary elections of 2002. *Government and Opposition*, **37** (3).

Cole, A. (Ed) (2002). The Jospin government, 1997–2002. Special issue of *Modern and Contemporary France*, **10** (3).

Cole, A. & Drake, H. (2000). The Europeanisation of French polity? Continuity, change and adaptation. *Journal of European Public Policy*, **7** (1).

Cole, A. & John, P. (2001). *Local Governance in England and France*. London: Routledge.

Cole, A. & Loughlin, J. (2003). Beyond the unitary state? Public opinion, political institutions and public policy in Brittany. *Regional Studies*, **37** (3).

Collard, S. (2002). The end of the French exception? Paper presented to the annual conference of the Association for the Study of Modern and Contemporary France, University of Portsmouth, September.

Collovald, A. (1999). *Jacques Chirac et le Gaullisme: biographe d'un héritier à histoires*. Paris: Belin.

Colombani, J.-M. (1999). *Le Résident de la République*. Paris: Stock.

Costa, J.-P. (1993). *Le Conseil d'état dans la société contemporaine*. Paris: Economica.

Courtier, P. (1994). *La Quatrième République*. Paris: PUF.

Courtois, S. & Lazar, M. (1995). *Histoire du parti communiste français*. Paris: PUF.

Crozier, M. (1963). *Le Phénomène bureaucratique*. Paris: Seuil.

Crozier, M. (1970). *La Société bloquée*. Paris: Seuil.

Crozier, M. (1974). *Où va l'administration française?* Paris: Editions de l'Organisation.

Crozier, M. (1992). La Décentralisation est-elle une réforme de l'état? *Pouvoirs locaux*, **12**.

Crozier, M. (1994). L'analyse des systèmes bureaucratiques. *Pensée Politique*, **2**.

Crozier, M. & Friedberg, E. (1977). *L'Acteur et le système*. Paris: Seuil.

Crozier, M. & Thoenig, J.-C. (1975). La Régulation des systèmes organisés complexes. *Revue française de sociologie*, **16** (1).

Culpepper, P. (1993). Organisational competition and the neo-corporatist fallacy in French agriculture. *West European Politics*, **16** (3).

Daley, A. (Ed) (1996). *The Mitterrand Era. Policy Alternatives and Political Mobilisation in France*. Basingstoke: Macmillan.

d'Arcy, F. & Rouban, L. (Eds) (1996). *De la Ve République à 1'Europe*. Paris: Presses de Sciences Po.

de Baecque, F. & Quermonne, J.-L. (1981). *Administration et politique sous la Ve République*. Paris: Presses de la FNSP.

Dedman, M.-J. (1996). *The Origins and Development of the European Union, 1945–95*. London: Routledge.

Dely, R. (1999). *Histoire secrète du front national*. Paris: Grasset.

Demaillie, L. (1993). L'évolution actuelle des méthodes de mobilisation et d'encadrement des enseignants. *Savoir*, **5** (1).

Dion, S. (1986). *La Politisation des mairies*. Paris: Economica.

Dirn, L. (1990). *La Société française en tendances*. Paris: PUF.

Drake, H. (2000). *Jacques Delors*. London: Routledge.

Drake, H. (2001). France on trial? The challenge of change and the French presidency of the European Union, July–December 2000. *Modern and Contemporary France*, **9** (4).

Drake, H. (2004). Perspectives on French relations with the European Union: an introduction. In H. Drake (Ed) *France and the European Union*. London: Routledge.

Drake, H. & Milner, S. (1999). Change and resistance to change: the political management of Europeanisation in France. *Modern and Contemporary France*, **7** (2).

Dreyfus, F. (1993). *Les institutions politiques et administratives de la France*. Paris: Economica.

Dreyfus, F. (1994). The control of governments. In P. Hall, J. Hayward & H. Machin (Eds) *Developments in French Politics*. Basingstoke: Macmillan.

Duchesne, S. (1997). *Citoyenneté à la Française*. Paris: Presses de Sciences Po.

Duhamel, A. (1990). *De Gaulle – Mitterrand: la marque et la trace*. Paris: Grasset.

Duhamel, A. (1999). *Une ambition française*. Paris: Plon.

Duhamel, E. & Forcade, O. (2000). *Histoire et vie politique en France depuis 1945*. Paris: Nathan.

Duhamel, O. (1993). *La Gauche et la cinquième République*. Paris: PUF.

Duhamel, O. & Parodi, J.-L. (Eds) (1988). *La Constitution de la cinquième République*. Paris: Presses de la FNSP.

Dumez, H. & Jeunemaitre, A. (1993). Les Privatisations en France, 1986–1992. In V. Wright (Ed) *Les Privatisations en Europe*. Paris: Actes Sud.

Dupoirier, E. (1998a). *Régions, la croisée des chemins*. Paris: Presses de Sciences Po.

Dupoirier, E. (1998b). L'offre identitaire des régions françaises et la construction des identités régionales. *Revue internationale de politique comparée*, **5** (1).

Dupuy, F. & Thoenig, J.-C. (1983). *Sociologie de l'administration française*. Paris: Armand Colin.

Dupuy, F. & Thoenig, J.-C. (1985). *L'Administration en Miéttes*. Paris: Fayard.

Duran, P. & Thoenig, J.-C. (1996). L'État et la gestion publique territoriale. *Revue française de science politique*, **45** (4).

Duverger, M. (1964). *Political Parties*. London: Methuen.

Duverger, M. (1977). *L'Échec au roi*. Paris: Albin Michel.

Duverger, M. (1986). *Les régimes semi-présidentiels*. Paris: PUF.

Duyvendak, J.W. (1995). *The Power of Politics: New Social Movements in France*. Boulder, CO: Westview.

Dyson, K. (1980). *The State Tradition in Western Europe*. Oxford: Martin Robertson.

Dyson, K. (1997). La France, l'union économique et monétaire et la construction européenne: renforcer l'exécutif, transformer l'état. *Politiques et management public*, **15** (3).

Dyson, K. (1999). EMU, political discourse and the Fifth French Republic: historical institutionalism, path dependency and 'craftsmen' of discourse. *Modern and Contemporary France*, **7** (2).

Dyson, K. & Featherstone, K. (1999). *The Road to Maastricht*. Oxford: Oxford University Press.

Eatwell, R. (Ed) (1996). *European Political Cultures*. London: Routledge.

École nationale d'administration (1992). *Les Corps de fonctionnaires recrutés par la voie d'ENA*. Paris: Documentation française.

Elgie, R. (1993). *The French Prime Minister*. Basingstoke: Macmillan.

Elgie, R. (Ed) (1999). *Semi-Presidentialism in Europe*. Oxford: Oxford University Press.

Elgie, R. (Ed) (2000). *The Changing French Political System*. London: Frank Cass.

Elgie, R. (2003). *Political Institutions in Contemporary France*. Oxford: Oxford University Press.

Elgie, R. & Griggs, S. (2000). *Debates in French Politics*. London: Routledge.

Epstein, P. (1997). The Uruguay round of GATT negotiations: limitations on government control of trade policy. *Modern and Contemporary France*, **5** (2).

Etienne, B. (1989). *La France et l'Islam*. Paris: Hachette.

Evans, J. (2002). Political corruption in France. In M. Bull & J. Newell (Eds) *Political Corruption in Contemporary Politics*. Basingstoke: Palgrave.

Evans, J. (Ed) (2003). *The French Party System*. Manchester: Manchester University Press.

Fabre, C. & Gallois, D. (1999). L'ouverture d'EDF à la concurrence divise la majorité plurielle. *Le Monde*, 15 January.

Fairbrass, J. (2002). Business Interests: Strategic Engagement with the EU Policy Process. PhD thesis, University of Essex.

Faucher, F. (1999). *Les habits verts de la politique*. Paris: Presses de Sciences Po.

Favereau, E. (1995). Ministères: les clandestins des cabinets. *Libération*, 11 October.

Favereau, F. (1993). *Bretagne contemporaine: langue, culture, identité*. Rennes: Editions Skol Breizh.

Favier, P. & Martin-Roland, M. (1990, 1991). *La Décennie Mitterrand. 1. Les ruptures 2. Les épreuves*. Paris: Seuil.

Feuillée-Kendal, P. (1998). La Réforme de la justice en France: un nouveau coup d'epée dans l'eau?. *Modern and Contemporary France*, **6** (1).

Flockton, C. & Kofman, E. (1989). *France*. London: Paul Chapman.

Fontaine, J. (1996). Public policy analysis in France: transformation and theory. *Journal of European Public Policy*, **3** (3).

Fourastié, J. (1980). *Les Trente glorieuses ou la révolution invisible de 1946–1975*. Paris: Fayard.

Fournier, J. (1987). *Le Travail gouvernemental*. Paris: Presses de la FNSP.

Foyer, J. (1992). Les Pouvoirs du Président de la République. *Revue des sciences morales et politiques*, **147** (3).

François, B. (1999). *Le régime politique de la Ve République*. Paris: La Découverte.

François, B. & Neveu, E. (Eds) (1999). *Espaces publics mosaïques*. Rennes: Presses Universitaires de Rennes.

François, E. (1998). Le Couple Franco-Allemand: exigence d'une ambition, d'imagination et de modestie. *Documents. Revue des questions Allemandes*, **53** (4).

Frears, J. (1981). *France in the Giscard Presidency*. London: Allen and Unwin.

Frears, J. (1990). *Parties and Voters in France.* London: Hurst.

Frears, J. (1991). The French parliament: loyal workhorse, poor watchdog. *West European Politics,* **14** (1).

Frears, J. & Morris, P. (1992). La Britannicité de la Ve République. *Espoir,* **85.**

Friedberg, E. (1974). Administration et entreprises. In M. Crozier (Ed) *Où va l'administration française?.* Paris: Edition de l'Organisation.

Friedberg, E. (1993). *Le Pouvoir et la règle.* Paris: Seuil.

Friend, J.W. (1998). *The Long Presidency. France in the Mitterrand Years, 1981–1995.* Boulder, CO: Westview.

Frognier, A.-P. (1998). Les Identités politiques territoriales. *Revue internationale de politique comparée,* **5** (1).

Furet, F., Juillard, J. & Rosanvallon, P. (1988). *La République du Centre. La fin de l'exception française.* Paris: Calmann-Levy.

Fysh, P. & Wolfreys, J. (1992). Le Pen, the National Front and the extreme right in France. *Parliamentary Affairs,* **45** (3).

Gaffney, J. (Ed) (1988). *France and Modernisation.* Aldershot: Gower.

Gaffney, J. (1989). *The Left and the Fifth Republic.* London: Macmillan.

Gaffney, J. (1991). Political think tanks in the UK and ministerial cabinets in France. *West European Politics,* **14** (1).

Gaffney, J. (Ed) (1996). *Political Parties in the European Union.* London: Routledge.

Gaffney, J. (Ed) (2003). *French Presidentialism and the Election of 2002.* Aldershot: Ashgate.

Gaffney, J. & Kolinsky, E. (Eds) (1991). *Political Culture in France and Germany.* London: Routledge.

Gaudin, J.-P. (1999). *Gouverner par contrat. L'Action publique en question.* Paris: Presses de Sciences Po.

Gavroy, J. (2002). Le projet de loi constitutionnelle relatif à l'organisation décentralisée de la République. *Regards sur l'actualité,* **286.**

Gildea, R. (1996). *France since 1945.* Oxford: Oxford University Press.

Girling, J. (1998). *France: political and social change.* London: Routledge.

Giscard d'Estaing, V. (1976). *La Démocratie française.* Paris: Fayard.

Godt, P. (Ed) (1989). *Policy Making in France.* London: Pinter.

Gordon, P. (1995). *France, Germany and the Western Alliance.* Boulder, CO: Westview.

Gordon, P. & Meunier, S. (2002). *The French Challenge: Adapting to Globalisation.* Washington: Brookings Institute Press.

Grémion, C. (1979). *Profession décideurs: pouvoirs des hauts fonctionnaires et réformes de l'état.* Paris: Gauthier-Villars.

Grémion, P. (1976). *Le Pouvoir peripherique: bureaucrates et notables dans le régime politique français.* Paris: Seuil.

Grossman, E. & Saurugger, S. (2004). Challenging French interest groups: the state, Europe and the international political system. *French Politics* (forthcoming).

Gueldry, M.R. (2001). *France and European Integration. Toward a Transnational Polity.* Westport: Praeger.

Guettier, C. (1995). *Le Président sous la cinquième République.* Paris: PUF.

Gugliemi, G.J. (1994). *Introduction au droit des services publics.* Paris: LGDJ.

Guilani, J.-D. (1991). *Marchands d'influence: les lobbies en France.* Paris: Seuil.

Guoyomarch, A., Hayward, J., Hall, P. & Machin, H. (2001). *Developments in French Politics 2.* Basingstoke: Palgrave.

Guoyomarch, A., Machin, H. & Ritchie, E. (Eds) (1996). *France in the European Union.* Basingstoke: Macmillan.

Guy-Peters, B. (1999). *The New Institutionalism.* London: Sage.

Hall, P. (1986). *Governing the Economy. The Politics of State Intervention in Britain and France.* Cambridge: Polity Press.

Hall, P. (1989). *The Political Power of Ideas: Keynesianism across Nations.* Princeton: Princeton University Press.

Hall, P. (1993). Policy paradigms, social learning and the state. *Comparative Politics*, **25**.

Hall, P. (2001). The evolution of economic policy-making. In A. Guoyomarch *et al. Developments in French Politics 2.* Basingstoke: Palgrave.

Hancke, B. (2001). Revisiting the French model. Coordination and restructuring in French industry in the 1980s. In P. Hall & D. Soskice (Eds) *Varieties of Capitalism: The Institutional Foundations of Competitiveness.* Oxford: Oxford University Press.

Hanley, D. (1999). France: living with instability. In D. Broughton & M. Donovan (Eds) *Changing Party Systems in Western Europe.* London: Pinter.

Hanley, D. (2002). *Party, Society, Government. Republican Democracy in France.* London: Berghahn.

Hanley, D.L. & Kerr, A.P. (1989). *May '68: Coming of Age.* Basingstoke: Macmillan.

Hanley, D.L., Kerr, A.P. & Waites, N.H. (1984). *Contemporary France: Politics and Society since 1945.* London: Routledge.

Hargreaves, A.G. (1995). *Immigration, 'Race' and Ethnicity in Contemporary France.* London: Routledge.

Harmsen, R. (1999). The Europeanisation of national administrations: a comparative study of France and the Netherlands. *Governance*, **12** (1).

Hayward, J. (1986). *The State and the Market Economy.* Brighton: Harvester Wheatsheaf.

Hayward, J. (Ed) (1993). *De Gaulle to Mitterrand: Presidential Power in France.* London: Hurst.

Hayward, J. (Ed) (1995). *Industrial Enterprise and European Integration.* Oxford: Oxford University Press.

Hayward, J. (1997). Changing partnerships: firms and the French state. *Modern and Contemporary France*, **5** (2).

Hayward, J. & Wright, V. (2002). *Governing from the Centre: Core Executive Coordination in France.* Oxford: Oxford University Press.

Hazareesingh, S. (1994). *Political Traditions in Modern France.* Oxford: Oxford University Press.

Hazareesingh, S. (Ed) (2002). *The Jacobin Legacy in Modern France: Essays in Honour of Vincent Wright*. Oxford: Oxford University Press.

Hecht, E. (1998). *Au coeur du RPR. Enquete sur le parti du Président*. Paris: Flammarion.

Helin, J.-P. (1992). Le Préfet, les élus et le juge. *Petites affiches*, **16** (151).

Hérard, A. & Maurin, A. (2000). *Institutions judiciaires*. Paris: Editions Sirey.

Hewlitt, N. (1998). *Modern French Politics*. Cambridge: Polity Press.

Hoare, R. (2000). Linguistic competence and regional identity in Brittany: attitudes and perceptions of identity. *Journal of Multilingual and Multicultural Development*, **21** (4).

Hoffmann, S. *et al.* (1965). *In Search of France*. New York: Harper Torchbooks.

Hoffmann, S. (1994). Les Français sont-ils gouvernables?. *Pouvoirs*, **68**.

Hollifield, J. (Ed) (1991). *Searching for the New France*. London: Routledge.

Howarth, D. (Ed) (2001). Public Administration in the UK and France. Special issue of *Public Policy and Administration*, **16** (4).

Howarth, D. (2001). *The French Road to European Monetary Union*. Palgrave: Basingstoke.

Howarth, D. (2002). The European policy of the Jospin Government: a new twist to old games. *Modern and Contemporary France*, **10** (3).

Howarth, D. & Varouxakis, G. (2003). *Contemporary France. An Introduction to French Politics and Society*. London: Edward Arnold.

Huber, J. (1996). *Rationalizing Parliament: legislative institutions and party politics in France*. Cambridge: Cambridge University Press.

Huchon, J.-P. (1993). *Jours tranquilles à Matignon*. Paris: Grasset.

Ignazi, P. & Ysmal, C. (1992). New and old extreme right parties: the French National Front and the Italian Movimento Sociale. *European Journal of Political Research*, **22** (1).

Im, T. (1993). *L'Administration de l'état face à la décentralisation: l'évolution du système d'action des préfectures*. Paris: Harmattan.

INSEE (2003). *Tableaux de l'économie française*. Paris: INSEE.

Institut français des sciences administratives (1987). *Le Secrétariat général du gouvernement*. Paris: Economica.

Isajiw, W. (1974). Definitions of ethnicity. *Ethnicity*, **1**.

Jackson, J. (2001). *France: the Dark Years, 1940–1944*. Oxford: Oxford University Press.

Jazouli, A. (1986). *L'Action collective des jeunes Maghrébins de France*. Paris: Harmattan.

Jobert, B. (1994). *Le Tournant neo-libéral en Europe*. Paris: Harmattan.

Jobert, B. & Muller, P. (1987). *L'État en action: politiques publiques et corporatisme*. Paris: PUF.

John, P. (1998). *Analysing Public Policy*. London: Pinter.

John, P. (2001). *Local Governance in Western Europe*. London: Sage.

Jones, G.W. (2003). *The Effects of the 1989–1997 Administrative Reforms on the Ministerial Field Services*. PhD thesis, Southampton Institute/Nottingham Trent University.

Jouve, B. & Léfèvre, C. (1999). De la gouvernance urbaine au gouvernement des villes? Permanence ou recomposition des cadres de l'action publique en Europe. *Revue française de science politique*, **49** (6).

Jullian, M. (1994). *La France à voix haute: le soldat et le normalien*. Paris: Fayard.

Kaltenbach, P. (1995). Sauver le bébé né en 1901. *Libération*, 24 July.

Kassim, H. (1997). French autonomy and the European Union. *Modern and Contemporary France*, **5** (2).

Kassim, H. & Menon, A. (1996). *The European Union and National Industrial Policy*. London: Routledge.

Keating, M. (1998). *The New Regionalism in Western Europe: Territorial restructuring and political change*. Cheltenham: Edward Elgar.

Keating, M. & Hainsworth, P. (1986). *Decentralisation and Change in Contemporary France*. Aldershot: Gower.

Keating, M., Loughlin, J. & Deschouwer, K. (2003). *The New Regionalism in Europe: A comparative study of eight regions*. London: Edward Elgar.

Keeler, J. (1987). *The Politics of Neo-corporatism in France*. Oxford: Oxford University Press.

Kelly, M. (2001). *French Culture and Society*. London: Edward Arnold.

Kergoat, J. (1997). *Histoire du parti socialiste français*. Paris: La Découverte.

Kessler, M.-C. (1986). *Les grands corps de l'état*. Paris: Presses de la FNSP.

Kimmel, A. (1991). *L'Assemblée nationale sous la cinquième République*. Paris: Presses de la FNSP.

Kiwan, N. (2003). *The Construction of Identity Amongst Young People of North African Origin in France: Discourses and Experiences*. PhD thesis, University of Bristol.

Kitschelt, H. (1997). European party systems: continuity and change. In M. Rhodes, P. Heywood & V. Wright (Eds) *Developments in West European Politics*. Macmillan: Basingstoke.

Knapp, A. (1996). *Le Gaullisme après de Gaulle*. Paris: Seuil.

Knapp, A. (2003). From the Gaullist movement to the President's Party. In Evans (Ed) *The French Party System*. Manchester: Manchester University Press.

Knapp, A. & Wright, V. (2001). *The Government and Politics of France*. London: Routledge.

Koza, M. & Thoenig, J.-C. (1995). Les écoles françaises et américaines de la théorie des organisations. *Revue française de gestion*, **1–2**.

Krause, J. (1994). The illusion of French exceptionalism in European security. *Contemporary French Civilisation*, **18** (2).

Kriegel, A. (1985). *Les Communistes français dans leur premier demi-siècle*. Paris: Seuil.

Kriegel, B. (1992). L' Idée républicaine. *Revue politique et parlementaire*, **94** (962).

Kuhn, R. (1995). *The Media in France*. London: Routledge.

Kuisel, R. (1979). *Capitalism and the State in Modern France*. Cambridge: Cambridge University Press.

Labbé, D. & Croisat, M. (1992). *La Fin des syndicats*. Paris: Harmattan.

Lacouture, J. (1965). *De Gaulle*. Paris: Seuil.

Lacouture, J. (1981). *Pierre Mendès-France*. Paris: Seuil.

Lacroix, B. & Lagroye, J. (Eds) (1992). *Le Président de la République: usages et génèses d'une institution*. Paris: Presses de la FNSP.

Ladrech, R. (1994). Europeanization of domestic politics and institutions: the case of France. *Journal of Common Market Studies*, **32** (1).

Ladrech, R. (2000). *Social Democracy and the Challenge of the European Union*. London: Lynne Reiner.

Ladrech, R. (2002). The Jospin government and European social-democracy. *Modern and Contemporary France*, **10** (3).

Lagroye, J., François, B. & Sawicki, F. (2002). *Sociologie politique*. Paris: Dalloz.

Lapeyronnie, D. (1992). *Les Immigrés en Europe*. Paris: Documentation Française.

Larkin, M. (1988). *France Since the Popular Front: Government and People, 1936–1986*. Oxford: Clarendon Press.

Le Bras, H. (1995). *Les Trois France*. Paris: Odile Jacob.

Le Bras, H. (2002). *Une autre France*. Paris: Odile Jacob.

Le Coadic, R. (1998). *L'Identité bretonne*. Rennes: Presses Universitaires de Rennes.

Le Galès, P. (1993). *Politique urbaine et developpement local*. Paris: Harmattan.

Le Galès, P. (1995). Du gouvernement local à la gouvernance urbaine. *Revue française de science politique*, **45** (1).

Le Galès, P. (2002). *European Cities*. Oxford: Oxford University Press.

Le Galès, P. & Lequesne, C. (Eds) (1998). *Regions in Europe*. London: Routledge.

Le Galès, P. & Mawson, J. (1994). *Management Innovations in Urban Policy: Lessons from France*. Luton: Local Government Management Board.

Le Galès, P. & Thatcher, M. (Eds) (1995). *Les Réseaux de politique publique, débats autour des 'policy networks'*. Paris: Harmattan.

Le Gloannec, A.-M. & Hassner, P. (1996). L'Allemagne et la France: deux cultures politiques?. *Esprit*, **5**.

Le Pourhiet, A. (1987). Les Emplois à la discrétion. *Pouvoirs*, **40**.

Lequesne, C. (1993). *Paris-Bruxelles*. Paris: Presses de la FNSP.

Lequesne, C. (1996). French central government and the European political system. In Y. Meny, P. Muller & J.-L. Quermonne (Eds) *Adjusting to Europe*. London: Routledge.

Les Echos (2002). L'Audit de la France. *Les Echos*, supplement to **18615**.

Levy, J. (1999). *Tocqueville's Revenge: State. Society and Economy in Contemporary France*. Cambridge, MA: Harvard University Press.

Levy, J. (2001). Territorial politics after decentralization. In A. Guoyomarch *et al. Developments in French Politics 2*. Basingstoke: Palgrave, 92–115.

Leyrit, C. (1997). *Les Partis politiques*. Paris: Editions Le Monde.

Limouzin, P. (2000). *La France et ses régions*. Paris: Armand Colin.

Lochak, D. & Chevallier, J. (1986). *La Haute administration et la politique*. Paris: PUF.

Long, M. (1981). *Les Services du premier ministre*. Aix-en-Provence: Presses Universitaires d'Aix.

Long, M. (1992). Le Conseil d'état et la fonction consultative: de la consultation à la décision. *Revue française de droit administratif*, **8** (5).

Long, M. (1995). Le Conseil d'état: rouage au coeur de l'administration et le juge administratif suprême. *Revue administrative*, **48** (283).

Lorrain, D. (1993). Après la décentralisation: l'action publique flexible. *Sociologie du travail*, **35** (3).

Lorwin, V. (1972). *The French Labor Movement*. Cambridge, MA: Harvard University Press.

Loughlin, J. (Ed) (2001). *Regional and Local Democracy in the European Union*. Oxford: Oxford University Press.

Loughlin, J. & Mazey, S. (Eds) (1995). *The End of the French Unitary State? Ten Years of Regionalization in France*. London: Frank Cass.

Lovecy, J. (2000). End of French exceptionalism? In R. Elgie (Ed) *The Changing French Political System*, 205–24. London: Frank Cass.

Mabileau, A. (1991). *Le système local en France*. Paris: Montchrestien.

Mabileau, A. (1997). Les Génies invisibles du local. Faux-semblants et dynamiques de la décentralisation. *Revue française de science politique*, **47** (3–4).

Machin, H. (1976). *The Prefect in the French Administration*. London: Croom Helm.

Machin, H. & Wright, V. (Eds) (1985). *Economic Policy and Policy-Making under the Mitterrand Presidency: 1981–84*. London: Pinter.

Maclean, M. (1995). Privatisation in France 1993–94: new departures, or a case of *plus ça change*. *West European Politics*, **18** (2).

Madelin, P. (1997). *Les Clans des Chiraquiens*. Paris: Seuil.

March, J. & Olsen, J. (1989). *Rediscovering Institutions*. New York: The Free Press.

Marcus, J. (1995). *The National Front and French Politics: The resistable rise of Jean-Marie Le Pen*. Basingstoke: Macmillan.

Massart, A. (1999). *L'Union pour la démocratie française: UDF*. Paris: Harmattan.

Massot, J. (1986). *La présidence de la République en France*. Paris: Documentation Française.

Massot, J. (1987). *L'Arbitre et le capitaine*. Paris: Flammarion.

Massot, J. (1997). Chef de l'état et chef du gouvernement: dyarchie et hiérarchie. *Notes et études documentaires*, **4983**.

Massot, J. & Fouquet, O. (1993). *Le Conseil d'état: juge de cassation*. Paris: Berger-Levrault.

Maus, D. (1996). *Le Parlement sous la cinquième République*. Paris: PUF.

Maus, D., Favoreu, L. & Parodi, J.-L. (Eds) (1992). *L'Ècriture de la constitution de 1958: actes du colloque du 30ème anniversaire*. Paris: Economica.

Mayer, N. (1999). *Ces français qui votent FN*. Paris: Flammarion.

Mayer, N. & Perrineau, P. (Eds) (1989). *Le Front national à découverte*. Paris: Presses de la FNSP.

Mazey, S. (1986). Public policy-making in France: the art of the possible. *West European Politics*, **9** (3).

Mazey, S. & Richardson, J. (Eds) (1993). *Lobbying in the European Community*. Oxford: Oxford University Press.

Mazzucelli, C. (1997). *France and Germany at Maastricht. Politics and Negotiations to Create the European Union*. New York: Garland.

McAna, M. (2003). *The Front National in Municipal Power in Toulon and Orange*. PhD thesis, University of Bradford.

McCarthy, P. (Ed) (1993). *France – Germany 1983–93: The Struggle to Co-operate*. Basingstoke: Macmillan.

McClean, M. (1997). Privatisation, dirigisme and the global economy; an end to French exceptionalism. *Modern and Contemporary France*, **5** (2).

McClean, M. & Milner, S. (Eds) (2001). France and Globalisation. Special issue of *Modern and Contemporary France*, **9** (3).

McMillan, J.F. (1996). France. In R. Eatwell (Ed) *European Political Cultures*. London: Routledge.

Mendras, H. (1996). *L'Europe des européens: sociologie de l'Europe occidentale*. Paris: Gallimard.

Mendras, H. (1989). *La Séconde Révolution française*. Paris: Gallimard.

Mendras, H. & Cole, A. (1991). *Social Change in Modern France*. Cambridge: Cambridge University Press.

Menon, A. (1994). Defence policy in the Fifth Republic: politics by any other means. *West European Politics*, **17** (4).

Menon, A. (1996). France and the IGC of 1996. *Journal of European Public Policy*, **6** (2).

Menon, A. (2000). *France, NATO and the Limits of Independence*. Basingstoke: Macmillan.

Mény, Y. (1992). *La Corruption de la République*. Paris: Fayard.

Mény, Y. & Thoenig, J.-C. (1989). *Politiques publiques*. Paris: PUF.

Mermet, G. (2002). *Francoscopie 2003*. Paris: Larousse.

Meyssan, T. (2000). *L'Énigme Pasqua*. Villeurbanne: Editions Golias.

Michel, H. (1998). Government or governance? The case of the French local political system. *West European Politics*, **21** (3).

Michelat, G. & Simon, M. (1977). *Classe, réligion et comportement politique*. Paris: Presses de la FNSP.

Milner, S. (2002). An ambiguous reform: the Jospin government and the 35-hour week laws. *Modern and Contemporary France*, **10** (3).

Mitra, S. (1988). The National Front in France: a single-issue movement? *West European Politics*, **11** (2).

Moravscik, A. (1991). Negotiating the single European Act: national interests and conventional statecraft in the European Community. *International Organization*, **45** (1).

Moreau-Defarges, P. (1994). *La France dans le monde au XXe siècle*. Paris: Hachette.

Moreau-Defarges, P. (2003). *Les institutions européennes*. Paris: Armand Colin.

Morris, P. (1994). *French Politics Today*. Manchester: Manchester University Press.

Mouriaux, R. & Bibès, G. (1990). *Les Syndicats européens à l'épreuve*. Paris: Presses de la FNSP.

Muller, P. (1992). Entre le local et l'Europe. La crise du modèle français des politiques publiques. *Revue française de science politique* **42** (1).

Muller, P. (1999). Gouvernance européenne et globalisation. *Revue internationale de politique comparée*, **6** (3).

Muller, P. (2000). L'analyse cognitive des politiques publiques: vers une sociologie politique de l'action publique. *Revue française de science politique*, **50** (2).

Muller, P. & Sorel, Y. (1998). *L'Analyse des politiques publiques*. Paris: Montchrestien.

Muron, L. (1994). *Pompidou: le Président oubliée*. Paris: Flammarion.

Nemery, J.C. (2003). *Intercommunalités*. Paris: Harmattan.

Neveu, E. (2002). *Sociologie des mouvements sociaux*. Paris: La Découverte.

Nicolaïeff, B. (2002). Expérience de l'expérimentation. *Regards sur l'actualité*, **286**.

Northcutt, W. (1992). *Mitterrand: a Political Biography*. New York: Holmes and Meier.

Oberdorff, H. (1998). *Les institutions administratives*. Paris: Armand Colin.

Offerlé, M. (1997). *Les Partis politiques*. Paris: PUF.

Offerlé, M. (1999). *Sociologie des groupes d'intérêt*. Paris: Montchrestien.

Padioleau, J.G. (1982). *L'État au concret*. Paris: PUF.

Padioleau, J.G. (1991). L'Action publique moderniste. *Politiques et management public*, **9** (3).

Palier, B. (2000). Defrosting the French welfare state. *West European Politics*, **23** (2).

Parsons, N. (2004). *Industrial Relations in France*. London: Continuum.

Paxton, R. (1972). *Vichy France: Old Guard and New Order*. New York: Columbia University Press.

Péan, P. (1994). *Une jeunesse française*. Paris: Fayard.

Pedersen, T. (1998). *Germany, France and the Integration of Europe: a Realist Interpretation*. London: Pinter.

Perrineau, P. (1997). *Le Symptome Le Pen*. Paris: Fayard.

Perrineau, P. (Ed) (2003). *Le désenchantement démocratique*. Paris: Editions de l'Aube.

Perrineau, P. & Ysmal, C. (Eds) (1998). *Le Vote surprise: les élections legislatives des 25 mai et 1 juin 1997*. Paris: Presses de Sciences Po.

Perrineau, P. & Ysmal, C. (2002). *Le vote de tous les refus. Les élections présidentielles et législatives de 2002*. Paris: Presses de Sciences Po.

Petersen, N. (1998). National strategies in the integration dilemma: an adaptation approach. *Journal of Common Market Studies*, **36** (1).

Picard, E. (1999). La Jurisprudence du conseil d'état et de l'Europe. In M. Long (Ed) *Le Conseil d'état de l'an VIII à nos jours*. Paris: Adam Brio.

Pierson, P. (1996). The path to European integration: a historical institutionalist analysis. *Comparative Political Studies*, **29** (2).

Pitts, J. (1981). Les Français et l'autorité. In J.-D. Reynaud & Y. Grafmeyer (Eds) *Français, qui êtes-vous?*. Paris: Documentation française.

Poignant, B. (1998). *Langues et cultures régionales. Rapport au premier ministre*. Paris: Documentation française.

Pontier, J.-M. (1998). *Les Contrats de plan entre l'état et les régions*. Paris: PUF.

Portelli, H. (1994). *La Ve République*. Paris: Grasset.

Portelli, H. (1998). *Le Parti socialiste*. Paris: Montchrestien.

Pouvoirs (2003). *Le Conseil constitutionnel*. Paris: Seuil.

Powell, W. & DiMaggio, P. (1991). *The New Institutionalism in Organisational Analysis*. Chicago: Chicago University Press.

Praedel, J. (1996). *Le Juge d'instruction*. Paris: Dalloz.

Py, R. (1985). *Le Secrétariat general du gouvernement*. Paris: Documentation française.

Quermonne, J.-L. & Chagnollaud, D. (1991). *Le gouvernement de la France sous la cinquième République*. Paris: Dalloz.

Quittkat, C. (2002). Les organisations professionnelles françaises: l'européanisation de l'intermédiation des intérêts. *Politique européenne*, **7**.

Racine, P. (1973). L'ENA et son evolution. *Revue administrative*, **26**.

Radaelli, C. (1997). How does Europeanization produce domestic policy change?. *Comparative Political Studies*, **30** (5).

Ravitch, N. (1990). *The Catholic Church and the French Nation, 1589–1989*. London: Routledge.

Raymond, G. (Ed) (1994). *France During the Socialist Years*. Aldershot: Dartmouth.

Raymond, G. (Ed) (1999). *Structures of Power in Modern France*. Basingstoke: Macmillan.

Reland, J. (1998). France. In J. Forder & A. Menon, *The European Union and National Macroeconomic Policy*. London: Routledge.

Rémond, R. (1982). *Les Droites en France*. Paris: Aubier.

Revue française de science politique (1990). *Naissance de la cinquième République*. Paris: Presses de la FNSP.

Revue politique et parlementaire (1992). Les Valeurs de la République. *Revue politique et parlementaire*, **94**.

Rideau, J. (1975). *La France et les communautés européennes*. Paris: LGDJ.

Ridley, F. (1970). *Revolutionary Syndicalism in France*. Cambridge: Cambridge University Press.

Rioux, J.-P. (1987). *The Fourth Republic 1944–1958*. Cambridge: Cambridge University Press.

Rondin, J. (1986). *Le Sacre des notables*. Paris: Fayard.

Robert, J. (1988). De l'indépendence des juges. *Revue du droit publique*, **1**.

Ross, G. (1997). Jospin so Far. *French Politics and Society*, **15** (3).

Ross, G., Hoffmann, S. & Malzacher, S. (1987). *The Mitterrand Experiment*. Oxford: Polity Press.

Rouban, L. (1994). *Le pouvoir anonyme. Les mutations de l'état à la française*. Paris: Presses de la FNSP.

Rouban, L. (1997). *La Fin des technocrates?* Paris: Presses de Sciences Po.

Rousellier, N. (1994). La Ligne de fuite: l'idée d'Europe dans la culture politique française. *Vingtième siècle*, **44**.

Roussel, E. (1984). *Georges Pompidou*. Paris: Lattès.

Ruane, J., Todd, J. & Mandeville, A. (2003). *Europe's Old States in the New World Order: The Politics of Transition in Britain, France and Spain*. Dublin: University of Dublin Press.

Sadran, P. (1992). *Le système administratif français*. Paris: Montchrestien.

Sadran, P. (2002). Le référendum local. *Regards sur l'actualité*, **286**.

Safran, W. (1999). *The French Polity*. Harlow: Longman.

Sainteny, G. (1997). *Les Verts*. Paris: PUF.

Sainteny, G. (2000). *L'Introuvable ecologisme français*? Paris: PUF.

Santamaria, Y. (1999). *Histoire du parti communiste français*. Paris: Editions de la découverte.

Sartori, G. (1976). *Parties and Party Systems*. Cambridge: Cambridge University Press.

Sauger, N. (2003). The UDF in the 1990s: the Break-Up of a Party Confederation. In J. Evans (Ed) *The French Party System*, 107–20. Manchester: Manchester University Press.

Saurugger, S. (Ed) (2003). *Les Modes de représentation dans l'union européenne*. Paris: Harmattan.

Sawicki, F. (1997). *Les Réseaux du parti socialiste: sociologie d'un milieu partisan*. Paris: Belin.

Schain, M. (1987). Racial politics in France: the National Front and the construction of political legitimacy. *West European Politics*, **10** (2).

Schild, J. (2000). Wählerverhalten und Parteienwettbewerb. In S. Ruß, J. Schild, J. Schmidt & I. Stephan (Eds) (2000) *Parteien in Frankreich. Kontinuität und Wandel in der V. Republik*. Opladen: Leske und Budrich, 57–76.

Schmidt, V. (1990). *Democratising France*. Cambridge: Cambridge University Press.

Schmidt, V. (1996). *From State to Market? The Transformation of French Business and Government*. Cambridge: Cambridge University Press.

Schmidt, V. (1997a). Running on empty; the end of dirigisme in French economic leadership. *Modern and Contemporary France*, **5** (2).

Schmidt, V. (1997b). Economic policy, political discourse, and democracy in France. *French Politics and Society*, **15** (2).

Schmitter, P. & Lehmbruch, G. (Eds) (1979). *Trends Toward Corporatism*. London: Sage.

Schnapper, D. (1994). *La Communauté des citoyens: sur l'idée moderne des nations*. Paris: Gallimard.

Schrameck, O. (2001). *Matignon Rive Gauche, 1997–2001*. Paris: Seuil.

Seurin, J.-L. (1986). *La Présidence de la République en France et aux États-Unis*. Paris: Economica.

Shennan, A. (1993). *De Gaulle*. London: Longman.

Shields, J. (1995). Le Pen, and the progression of the extreme-right in France. *French Politics and Society*, **13** (2).

Silverman, M. (1992). *Deconstructing the Nation: Immigration, Racism and Citizenship in Modern France*. London: Routledge.

Sirinelli, J.-F. (1992). *Histoire des droites en France*. Paris: Gallimard.

Smith, A. (1997). Studying multi-level governance. Examples from French translations of the structural funds. *Public Administration*, **75** (4).

Smith, A. (1999). Public policy-making in France. *Public Administration*, **77** (4).

Smith, A. (2001). Studying administrative reform in Britain and the UK. *Public Policy and Administration*, **16** (4).

Soutou, G.-H. (1999). La France et l'Allemagne vont-elles continuer à être le moteur de l'intégration européenne? *Géopolitique*, **65**.

Stevens, A. (1992, 1996, 2003). *The Government and Politics of France*. London: Palgrave.

Stirn, B. (1991). *Le Conseil d'état: son role, sa jurisprudence*. Paris: Hachette.

Stone, A. (1992). *The Birth of Judicial Politics in France: the Constitutional Council in Comparative Perspective*. Oxford: Oxford University Press.

Suleiman, E.N. (1974). *Politics, Power and Bureaucracy in France*. Princeton: Princeton University Press.

Suleiman, E.N. (1978). *Elites in French Society: the Politics of Survival*. Princeton: Princeton University Press.

Sweet-Stone, A. (2000). *Governing with Judges. Constitutional Politics in Europe*. Oxford: Oxford University Press.

Tacet, D. (1992). *Un monde sans paysans*. Paris: Hachette.

Thatcher, M. (1997). L'Impact de la communauté européenne sur la règlementation nationale: les services publiques en France et en Grande-Bretagne. *Politiques et management public*, **15** (3).

Thatcher, M. (1999). *The Politics of Telecommunications. National Institutions, Convergence, and Change in Britain and France*. Oxford: Oxford University Press.

Thoenig, J.-C. (1973). *L'Ère des technocrates*. Paris: Editions de l'Organisation.

Thoenig, J.-C. (1996). Les Grands corps. *Pouvoirs*, **79**.

Tiersky, R. (1974). *French Communism, 1920–72*. New York: Columbia University Press.

Tiersky, R. (1994). *France in the New Europe*. Boulder, CO: Westview.

Tilly, C. (1984). Les origines du répertoire de l'action collective contemporaine en France et en Grande-Bretagne. *Vingtième siècle*, **4**.

Todd, E. (1988). *La Nouvelle France*. Paris: Seuil.

Todd, E. (1995). Aux origines du malaise politique française. Les classes sociales et leur représentation. *Le Débat*, **83**.

Tombs, R. (1996). *France 1814–1914*. Longman: Harlow.

Tournier, V. (2000). Filiation et politique. La construction de l'identité et ses conséquences. In P. Bréchon, A. Laurent & P. Perrineau (Eds) (2000) *Les cultures politiques des français*. Paris: Presses de Sciences Po.

Védrine, H. (1996). *Les Mondes de François Mitterrand. À l'Elysée, 1981–1995*. Paris: Fayard.

Vesperini, J.-P. (1993). *L'Économie de la France sous la cinquième République*. Paris: Economica.

Villalba, B. & Vieillard-Coffre, S. (2003). The Greens: from idealism to pragmatism. In J. Evans *The French Party System*, 56–75, Manchester: Manchester University Press.

Vinen, R. (1996). *France, 1934–1970*. Basingstoke: Macmillan.

Viveret, P. (1977). *Pour une nouvelle culture politique*. Paris: Seuil.

Waters, S. (2003). *New Social Movements in France*. Basingstoke: Palgrave.

Webber, D. (Ed) (1999). *The Franco-German Relationship in the European Union*. London: Routledge.

Weber, E. (1979). *Peasants into Frenchmen: the Modernisation of Rural France*. London: Chatto & Windus.

Weil, P. (2001). The politics of immigration. In A. Guoyomarch *et al. Developments in French Politics 2*. Basingstoke: Palgrave.

Wieviorka, M. (Ed) (1997). *Une société fragmentée? Le multiculturalisme en debat*. Paris: La Découverte.

Williams, P.M. (1964). *Crisis and Compromise: Politics in the Fourth Republic*. London: Longman.

Williams, P.M. (1969). *The French Parliament, 1958–1967*. London: Allen and Unwin.

Williams, P.M. & Harrison, M. (1965). *De Gaulle's Republic*. London: Longman.

Wilson, F.L. (1987). *Interest Group Politics in France*. Cambridge: Cambridge University Press.

Winchester, H. (1993). *Contemporary France*. Harlow: Longman.

Withol de Wenden, K. (1999). *L'Immigration en Europe*. Paris: Documentation française.

Wolfreys, J. (2003). Beyond the mainstream; *la gauche de la gauche*. In J. Evans *The French Party System*. Manchester: Manchester University Press.

Worms, J.-P. (1966). Le Prefet et ses notables. *Sociologie du travail*, **8** (3).

Wright, V. (1974). Politics and administration under the French Fifth Republic. *Political Studies*, **22** (1).

Wright, V. (1994). Reshaping the state: the implications for public administration. *West European Politics*, **18** (2).

Wright, V. (1996). The national co-ordination of European policy-making: negotiating the quagmire. In J. Richardson (Ed) *European Union: Power and Policy-making*. London: Routledge.

Wright, V. (2000). The Fifth Republic: From the *Droit de l'état* to the *état de droit?* In R. Elgie (Ed) *The Changing French Political System*, 92–119. London: Frank Cass.

Ysmal, C. (1989). *Les Partis politiques sous la Vᵉ République*. Paris: Montchrestien.

Zarka, J.-C. (1994). *Le Président de la 5ᵉ République*. Paris: Ellipses.

Zeldin, T. (1983). *The French*. London: Collins.

Zysman, J. (1977). *Political Strategies for Industrial Order. State, Market and Industry in France*. Berkeley: University of California Press.

Appendices

Appendix 1 — Presidential elections in the Fifth Republic. First Ballot (% valid votes cast)

	65	69	74	81	88	95	02
Abstentions and spoilt ballots	16.11	22.81	16.54	20.22	18.62	24.46	30.05
Extreme left[1]	–	4.72	2.72	3.41	4.47	5.30	10.44
Communist[2]	–	21.52	–	15.35	6.76	8.64	3.37
Socialist[3]	–	5.07	–	25.85	34.09	23.30	16.18
United left [4]	31.72	–	43.25	–	–	–	–
Green[5]	–	–	1.32	3.88	3.78	3.32	5.25
Centre[6]	15.57	23.42	32.60	–	16.54	18.58	
UDF[7]	–	–		28.32			6.84
Gaullist[8]	44.65	43.95	15.11	18.00	19.94	20.84	19.88
Extreme right[9]	5.20	–	0.75	–	14.39	15.00	19.20
Other[10]	2.86	1.28	4.27	6.86	–	3.82	14.63

Code:

 1 Extreme left: Krivine (LCR) and Rocard (PSU) in 1969, Laguiller (LO) and Krivine in 1974; Laguiller and Bouchardeau (PSU) in 1981; Laguiller, Juquin (ex-PCF) and Boussel (MPPT) in 1988; Laguiller in 1995; Laguiller, Besancenot (LCR) and Gluckstein (PT) in 2002.

 2 Communist: Duclos in 1969, Marchais in 1981, Lajoinie in 1988, Hue in 1995 and 2002.

 3 Socialist: Defferre in 1969, Mitterrand in 1981 and 1988, Jospin in 1995 and 2002.

 4 United left: Mitterrand in 1965 (supported by SFIO, PCF, Radicals) and in 1974 (supported by PS, PCF and MRG).

 5 Green: Dumont in 1974, Lalonde in 1981, Waechter in 1988, Voynet in 1995, Mamère in 2002.

 6 Centre: Lecanuet in 1965, Poher in 1969, Giscard in 1974, Barre in 1988, Balladur in 1995.

 7 UDF behind Giscard d'Estaing in 1981. Divided in 1988 and 1995. Bayrou in 2002.

 8 Gaullist: de Gaulle in 1965, Pompidou in 1969, Chaban-Delmas in 1974, Chirac in 1981, 1988, 1995 and 2002. Balladur (1995) also a member of RPR, but classed under centre.

 9 Extreme right: Tixier-Vignancour in 1965, Le Pen in 1974, 1988 and 1995; Le Pen (16.86) and Megret (2.34) in 2002.

10 Mostly a rag-bag of no hopers, the main exceptions being: Royer (3.17 per cent) in 1974 (conservative); Crépeau (2.21 per cent) in 1981 (MRG); de Villiers (4.74 per cent) in 1995 (conservative), Chevènement (5.33 per cent), Madelin (3.91 per cent), and Taubira (2.32 per cent) in 2002.

Note:

For reasons of convenience, certain candidates have been attributed party families they might dispute. Rocard (PSU) and Bouchardeau (PSU) would certainly reject the extreme left etiquette; but both were supported by a radicalised left-wing electorate. Barre and Giscard (1974) were Orleanist conservatives, transformed into 'centrists' because of their opposition to Gaullist candidates. The UDF supported Barre and Balladur in 1988 and 1995 respectively, but neither considered themselves the 'UDF' candidate. Barre and Balladur were supported by most of UDF, especially CDS, and by some Gaullists. Balladur in 1995 was a member of the Gaullist RPR, but most of his support came from the non-Gaullist centre-right.

Source: Adapted from Interior Ministry figures for France including DOM-TOM.

Appendix 2 — Seven presidential election run-offs

Year	1965	1969	1974	1981	1988	1995	2002
De Gaulle	55.20						
Mitterrand	44.80		49.19	51.76	54.02		
Pompidou		57.6					
Poher		42.4					
Giscard d'Estaing			50.81	48.24			
Chirac					45.98	52.63	82.15
Jospin						47.37	
Le Pen							17.85

Appendix 3 — National Assembly elections, 1958–2002 (% of valid votes cast)

	1958	1962	1967	1968	1973	1978	1981	1986	1988	1993	1997	2002
Abstentions and spoilt ballots	24.78	33.33	20.73	21.40	20.42	18.37	30.12	24.9	35.3	34.4	34.99	37.88
Extreme left[1]		2.02	2.21	3.96	2.20	3.27	1.22	1.5	0.36	1.77	2.52	2.47
Communist (PCF)	18.89	21.87	22.51	20.02	21.41	20.61	16.13	9.7	11.32	9.18	9.98	4.82
Socialist[2]	15.48	12.43	18.90	16.54	20.82	24.95	39.52	31.6	37.55	20.29	27.65	25.20
Ecologists[3]						1.37	1.09		0.35	7.64	6.86	5.7
Other non-Communist left[4]	10.87	7.42										1.45
Non-Gaullist 'centre'[5]	11.09	7.88	17.35	12.41	16.67	UDF	UDF	UDF	UDF	UDF	UDF	UDF
Other right[6]	19.97	11.52	with centre	with centre	with centre	UDF	2.66	2.71	2.85	4.72	6.52	6.71
UDF+ allies						23.89	19.66	42.1 (with RPR)	18.49	19.08	14.34	4.86
Gaullists[7]	20.64	36.03	38.45	46.44	36.98	22.84	21.24	42.1 (with UDF)	19.18	20.39	15.59	33.3 (UMP)
Extreme right[8]	2.57	0.76	0.56	0.08	0.52	0.75	0.59	10.1	9.74	12.7	15.16	12.67

Code:

1 Includes PSU, LO, LCR and Trotskyite/Maoist groups.

2 Includes SFIO (1958, 1962), FGDS (1967, 1968), UGSD (1973), PS-MRG (1978, 1981, 1986, 1988, 1993), PS, PRS MDC (1997), PS, PRS (2002).

3 Includes all ecologists, principally *les verts* and GE (1993), *les verts*, GE, MEI and fringe groups (1997), *les verts* and fringe groups, (2002).

4 UFD, Radicals, UDSR (1958), Radicals (1962), Pôle Républicain, regionalists (2002).

5 Includes MRP (1958, 1962), CD, non-Gaullist radicals and *modérés* (1967), CD, PDM, non-Gaullist radicals and *modérés* (1968), Reformist movement and *modérés* (1973).

6 CNI and *modérés* in 1958 and 1962. Refers to *divers droite* clearly separate from UDF in subsequent elections.

7 Includes Gaullist allies, notably RI from 1962–73. Includes UMP in 2002.

8 Various extreme-right, 1958–69; FN + extreme-right 1973, 1978, 1981, 1986, 1988, 1993, 1997. FN, MNR and extreme-right, 2002.

Source: Adapted from Interior Ministry figures for France including DOM-TOM.

Index